THE HISTORY
OF
WORKING

From Earliest times to AD 1865

BY

Richard L. M. Byers

RICHARD BYERS
Bookseller & Publisher
Cockermouth

First published in 1998 by

Richard Byers
PO Box 25, Cockermouth, Cumbria. CA13 9GE

ISBN 0 9529812 2 X

British Library Cataloguing in Publication Data
A catalogue record for this book is available from the British Library

Text and Line drawings (unless mentioned)
© 1998 Richard Byers

Design & Typeset by Pages & Pages
Printed & Bound in Cumbria, Great Britain

Also available in this Series
Bradbury's History of Cockermouth
ISBN 0 9529812 0 3
Sugden's History of Arlecdon & Frizington
ISBN 0 9529812 1 1
History of Workington (1866-1955)
(In preparation) ISBN 0 9529812 5 4

*The publishers invite authors to submit any book ideas or
manuscripts, for this series of books
recording the history of Cumbria and Cumbrians.*

A S I glance through the pages of this book, it is difficult now after so many months to recall the extent of my efforts to produce this finished article. The long days and late late nights, tapping away at the keyboard. The hours of research, drawing, travelling and endless telephone calls, letters and faxes seeking out often elusive information.

All the time, I was conscious that no one had ever really written this history before, although I knew many others had started and never completed the task. I had been one of them, my first attempt began back in 1981. It was then hampered by having to type up my notes on an old portable typewriter, with a faded ribbon and a sticking letter e. But this time I had a marvellous magical and indispensable computer to help me sort, cut, paste and edit my work. This time I was going to succeed.

I also realised that much of the town's history that did exist in print, was so littered with obvious errors and mistakes. Much of it so badly researched or simply copied from earlier inaccurate accounts. Why is it some people seem to believe almost everything printed hundreds of years ago, must have been correct?

Although of course there may well be some sources of which I am unhappily ignorant of, I have attempted to verify almost all the facts and figures. If I haven't succeeded I've tried to tell you in the text. I've delved and plodded back through numerous archives of dusty papers, searching out what the history teachers call *"primary"* sources. If I feel anything is suspect, myth or legend, I hope I've made that clear. Despite this I am also very much aware that occasionally (but hopefully not too often) I too may have made a mistake.

I would like to add a very special thanks to Jo Byers, and gratefully acknowledge her assistance with research. Jo diligently also plodded through my text searching out the errors. This was no mean task, for at the last count there was in excess of 113,846 words to proof read (twice). On page 235 is a list of all those other people who willingly gave me so much support, help and assistance, perhaps I should have added a certain Bill Gates.

I hope you really enjoy this book.

Richard L. M. Byers.

READERS NOTES

The main text of this book is set in area **A** of the page layout (see right).   With further additional notes and references being provided in area **B**, to guide the reader through the work.   A reference number is used to link these notes to the appropriate point in text - eg. [3].

As many members of the influential **CURWEN** family share the same christian name, inorder that each can be properly identified, a reference is provided after each name - eg. **Henry [iii] Curwen**, refers to **Henry Curwen** (1661-1725). Chapter five contains further information on the family.

Some abbreviations have been used in the book, these are listed below:

C&WA&AS	- Cumberland and Westmorland Archaeological and Antiquarian Society.
C&WJR	- Cleator & Workington Junction Railway Co.
C&WR	- Cockermouth & Workington Railway.
H&WSRC	- Harrington & Workington Shipbuilding & Ropemaking Company.
LNWR	- London North Western Railway Company
OS	- Ordnance Survey.
WJR	- Whitehaven Junction Railway Company.

❧ CONTENTS ☙

CHAPTER ONE

BEFORE THE ROMANS

ALTHOUGH archaeological evidence has clearly been discovered to establish some very early settlements, elsewhere in surrounding districts of West Cumbria. Perhaps, the earliest known evidence of any human life, around the Derwent estuary, is the Bronze Age axes discovered in the town. [01] From these we can assume the existance of a basic and primitive settlement here, from around 1500 BC. Unfortunately, there is a distinct lack of anything further, until the arrival of the Romans, a millenium and a half later. Surely the existence of rich fishing and the odd outcrops of coal for fuel would have encouraged some early settlers to remain here, during this period.

Over the centuries, the Derwent estuary has undergone considerable and significant transformations. These have been the result of not just the natural action of the sea and the river at it's mouth, but also the effects of eighteenth and nineteenth century heavy industry. We know that the Derwent was once very much broader than now, and the sea level much higher. A study of today's coastline, points to the estuary being also certainly much further eastwards. To the north of the Derwent, at the Roman site of Burrow Walls, we can speculate that the sea once came upto the cliff, below this fort. Then, obviously the Oldside coastal strip, upto north of Siddick, simply did not exist.

To the south of the river, the area below St. Michael's church was then just the foreshore. Evidence of this is clear from the 1569 map of the town and harbour.[02] Here the parish church in its elevated position is the furthest building westward. The Marsh-side area, is also then interestingly marked *"the drye marche"*. Suggesting that the sea level may have only receded in the previous century or so. We can therefore assume that much of this area, from the church to the *"watch chapell"* [03] a little further south, was also below the high water mark, in Norman times. [04]

The north and south banks of the Derwent would then have been two distinct areas, separated by a deep fast flowing river almost half a mile wide. As there was no bridges or fords, anyone wishing to cross this wide expance of water would have had to use a small boat, such as a curragh . Alternatively, they could journey inland and attempt to cross at the river's narrowest point near Great Clifton, a round trip of almost six miles.

Obviously there is very little early evidence, in the form

"Over the centuries, the Derwent estuary has undergone considerable and significant transformations".

[01] See chapter ten for more details. ■
[02] The town plan dated 1569 is reproduced in chapter eight. ■
[03] The Watch chapel, see also generally referred to as How Michael or St. Michaels chapel, and was situated at Chapel Bank. ■
[04] Records of a series of tremendous gales which occurred at the end of January 1796, give us some indication of the estuary, before the sea receded. The severe conditions, with almost continuous rain and the flooded state of the Derwent, brought "unprecendented" high tides. The whole of the South Quay was submerged, as was Low Church Street, Griffin Street and the Cloffolks area, from the South Gut to Mill Field. Oldside was underwater, the road north to Maryport flooded and impassable, as the sea flowed over and engulfed Siddick Pond. This entire low lying area, covered by a wide expance of water, would now resemble the large estuary, likely to have existed perhaps a thousand years earlier.

5

of old maps or charts to plot these changes in our coast. In 1566, when Elizabeth I commissioned a report on *"all ports, creeks, and landing places in Cumberland"*. Apparently, an intelligence ship was sent to survey the coastline, *"plumbing and sounding all the way"*, up to Kirkcudbright. Although a written report was prepared, if a chart was also plotted it is now lost.

To view the whole estuary, our first real point of reference, must be Christopher Saxon's 1576 map of Cumberland. [01] Here the northern coastline is shown much further eastwards than the southern point. Although, in view of the scale of the map, it is not easy to accurately plot it's precise position. In Elizabethan times, we can surmise the shoreline to be still almost along the east side of (what is now) Siddick Pond, near again to Burrow Walls. Assuming of course, that these early mapmakers have shown the coastline at it's high water mark.

It might be difficult today to imagine the sea lashing this point, as it is now hundreds of metres from the Oldside coast. But as we will learn from chapter two, about a third of the Roman fort at Burrow walls, is presumed to have been lost to coastal erosion. Furthermore, we can speculate that the Curwen family may have abandoned the later Norman tower on the same site, for much the same reason. We know today, that the sea is certainly capable of such destructive action. The Cumbrian coastline having a very notable northwards drift. causing major erosion to the cliffs and foreshore.

When the sea began to recede, the foreshore and river banks became notably elevated with bars of sand and gravel. This aggradation over many centuries resulted in a significant re-shaping of the estuary. The Derwent, at it's mouth appears to have branched into at least two distinct channels or distributaries. It is supposed one took a line northwards, along the old coastline, past Burrow walls. Whilst the other followed much the same line as today's river. River sediment and silt began forming a delta or raised island, around Oldside. Gradual further tidal deposits added to this Oldside delta, enlarging and extending it northwards towards Siddick.

Eventually the course of the river, through Siddick pond became choked and impeded, as it's southern end silted up. So developing a natural basin, perhaps still open to the sea at Siddick, with the Oldside delta forming a protective breakwater. We know today how the existing river channel must be constantly dredged, so it remains open. Later the action of the Solway would have also closed off the northern end, to create Siddick pond, completely enclosed from the sea. Today, Ling beck from Seaton, now drains into the pond, maintaining it's level.

Anayalsis of the village place name, suggests further

"In Elizabethan times, we can surmise the shoreline to be along the east side of Siddick Pond, close to Burrow Walls."

[01] Christopher Saxon's map of Cumberland & Westmorland is dated 1576, and is believed to have been surveyed from around 1574. It was the first really accurate map of the county and was used extensively until at least the 1645-48 Civil War, many later maps are based on Saxons survey. ■

evidence to support this theory. Siddick is best defined as *"Sea-dyke or dike"*. Where a dike is *long ridge of earth* or an embankment. The first known historical reference to Siddick, in old documents and maps is around 1810, suggesting it's origin is fairly modern. The rows of terraced houses there, were not built until around 1880's. A 1792 plan of the harbour exists, which calls this area of the Oldside coastline, west of the Main Road (A596), *"part of Seagate"*. This place name *Sea-gate*, could well confirm an opening or *"means of entrance or exit"* to the sea, may well have once existed here.

Additionally, the existence of the area called Oyster Banks, just thirty or so metres north of Burrow walls, along the east side of Siddick pond, could support our assumption of this being the old coastline. Oysters attach themselves to rocks in river mouths and are found along shorelines, in shallow coastal areas. Interestingly in 1880, when William Dickinson recorded some early archaeological excavations at Burrow walls. He mentions quantities of oyster shells being uncovered in a old refuse tip, intermingled with ashes and bones of cattle. He thought this waste was from the twelfth century Norman keep, rather than the earlier Roman fort. But whoever consumed the oysters, and assuming they came from the nearby shore, it does tend to confirm the sea once came upto this point.

Industrialisation of Oldside; like Chapel Bank to the south of the river; has undoubtedly led to the foreshore being artifically elevated. In the period between 1845 and 1966, millions of cubic metres of waste was deposited along this coastal strip. Previously, it would have formed the northern section of a wide-sweeping sand and shingle estuarine bay. A once beautiful, very natural area with peeble and shingle raised beaches and long extensive sand dunes and grasslands. Early records point to Oldside, then being know as the *"Warrens"*, by virtue of rabbits who would have lived in these dunes.[01] I would suggest that it would have then been quite comparable to today's unspoilt Mowbray coastline, between Allonby and Silloth.

At the end of January 1796, when Cumbria was hit by tremendous gales and unprecendented high tides brought severe flooding. Contemporary accounts record nearly all the *"rabbits in the extensive warren"*, at Oldside were drowned. The rabbits were not just cultivated for food, their fur was once of considerable value. Hutchinson's 1797 *History of Cumberland*, describes at length how the rabbits were trapped.

Today, whilst passing along the A596, the Oldside area has now something of a deceptively natural-look. But thirty years ago, following the closure of St. Helens pit (1966) the scene was quite different. This whole area was a picture of

"Industrialisation of Oldside; like Chapel Bank to the south of the river; has undoubtedly led to the foreshore being artifically elevated".

[01] John Waite's simple but enlightening town plan, drawn around 1835, clearly calls the Oldside shoreline the *"Rabbit Warrens"*, adding the informative note *"Rabbits in thousands"*. This is not the earliest reference to the warrens, Thomas Denton (around 1688) describes a *"large rabbit-warren, worth around £20 a year."* ■

dereliction and degredation, dominated by the monsterous colliery spoil heap, towering to 55 metres height (180 feet) and comprising of 1.25 million cubic yards of tipped material. This tip is clearly visible in the photograph of Burrow Walls 1955 excavations on page 106.

This vast quantity of dumped material consisted principally of slag [01], spent moulding sand and flue dust from both the Oldside and West Cumberland Ironworks, just north of the dock. Together with shale and spoil from St. Helens Colliery, a little further north. In the latter years, this was also greatly added too by Workington Borough Council, using the site as a domestic refuse tip; and British Steel Corporation transporting further furnace waste, over the river from it's Workington Works.

The entire extent of all this tipped and dumped material, (technically referred to as overburden) is clearly detailed in a 1971 report, commissioned by the old Workington Borough Council. Nearly forty boreholes were sunk across the Oldside site, which revealed that over 75% of the area was covered at least to a depth of six metres (20ft) of waste. Containing a total volume of approximately five million cubic yards.

Three decades or so after the reclamation of Oldside, the vegetation has become established and now merely further disguises this virtally man-made landscape. But if you walk along the foreshore at low tide, one can still see the coastal face of the headlands, consists almost entirely of layer upon layer of dumped molten slag and furnace waste. The 1863 OS plan clearly shows Workington Haematite Ironworks (later Oldside works) then had at least three rail lines running to the shore. Here was deposited thousands of tons of molten slag into the sea, annually, for almost a century. So creating a man-made cliff face, in places over 15 metres high (50ft). The 1925 OS map, some sixty two years later, shows how these rail lines now extended much further westward, as the new coastline was constantly being created with every addition wagon of slag, poured down into the sea.

Exactly the same industrial tipping of ironworks waste has also lead to the creation of similar, yet taller man-made headlands, south of the Derwent along Chapel Bank. Although this only began when several ironworks, commenced here from the 1880's. A closer look at the oldest available plans and several geologists reports of the Clay Flatts area, suggests another branch of the Derwent may also have once ran through here. Alluvial clay found close to the surface, is evidence that water once flowed over this comparatively flat surface area, depositing sediment to form clay

This river may have isolating the hill where *How Micheal* once stood. Today, we may think of Clay Flatts covering

"Three decades or so after the reclamation of Oldside, the vegetation has become established and now merely further disguises this virtally man-made landscape".

[01] Slag is the waste from the iron furnaces which was discharged whilst still molten into the Slag tubs or bogies. On Oldside, these trucks generally ran along a rail track to the shoreline, where the slag was poured and later solidified.

[01] Writing in 1957, Alderman W.A *"Yankie"* Walker believed that that Dunbar's factory was a two-storey building just off Annie Pit Lane. The proprietor is thought to have lived on the upper floor, reached by an external staircase. The pottery appears to have made several pleasing items, including kneading bowls and preserving jugs. It is known to have been in existance from at least 1880, perhaps even earlier.

quite a large area, but previously it was the name simply given to just a small row of seven terraced cottages, situated around 50 metres south of Barnes Road. The name however, is obviously derived from the clay found here. Certainly, there are records of pottery clay being dug on a site, just north of the present road bridge to Derwent Howe, over the railway.

Once it was quite common for each town to have at least one pottery, and it is safe to assume that for many centuries, clay from here was also used to make domestic items. Originally of course the brown earthware clay, would have been used for very basic bowls and jugs. Unfortunately, the exact location of any early pottery buildings or kilns is something of a mystery. Nothing is mentioned on the 1863 OS plan. Towards the end of the ninteenth century, more sophisticated and finer items were known to have been manufactured at Dunbar's factory. [01]

❧ CHAPTER TWO ❧

ROMAN TIMES

A T the time of the Roman invasion of the British Isles around the year AD 43. West Cumbria formed part of what was to become Britannia Interior. William Hutchinson in his 1794 book - *History of Cumberland* wrote that when the Romans first arrived they found, *"the Brigantes possessed a very large tract of country on the west coast of Britain"*.

It was around AD 79, before our province was to be added to the Roman Empire. Petillus Cerialis [01] appears to have established supremacy over the Celtic tribe of the Brigantes, without serious struggle. By AD 122 with the start of construction of Hadrian's wall, Hutchinson felt it safe to assume that all the peoples living to the south of the wall, *"had submitted themselves to the Roman government"*. Roman history indicates a Brigante tribe called *Votadini*, may then have populated much of the Cumberland plain. Suggesting, they were quite docile and well-disposed towards their new rulers, readily accepting their laws and regulations. These Celtic people did not disappear they were just forced to conform.

It seems very likely that the Roman garrisons would have then also occupied some areas of West Cumbria. What is not quite as clear, is where and precisely when they began settling in our region. It is believed that Maryport may have had a Roman encampment from around AD 90, being almost continually occupied through the Hadrianic period to the late 4th century.

We have no real knowledge of the existence of a Pre-Roman settlement in the town. We should not totally dismiss the likelihood of a small Celtic encampment, then existing somewhere around the mouth of the Derwent. Unfortunately, it is most probable that later inhabitants, such as the Angles and Vikings merely occupied much the same site and simply built over any earlier buildings. Erasing for ever any evidence of these houses, which in any case would have been just basic timber and thatch structures.

At Burrow Walls, just to the north of the River Derwent (OS map ref NY003301), archaeological evidence has revealed the site of a Roman station or settlement. It is now thought to have been a fort, perhaps forming an important part of the Roman frontier defences. These once extended south along the Cumberland coastline, from the western

MAP OF ROMAN BRITAIN - giving guide to the territories around the end of the third century AD. ■

[01] Petillus Cerialis was a 1st century A.D. Roman general. who became governor of Britain in AD 71, where he is known to have defeated the Brigantes. ■

end of Hadrians wall. Although some evidence suggests that it may also have served as a secondary naval-base, for the anchorage of a Roman fleet.

This sea defence system of forts and smaller fortlets or mile-forts, is thought to have extended from Bowness in the north to at least Ravenglass in the south. Although it has yet to be really confirmed if they extended much further south, than the River Derwent. R.J.A Wilson in the 1997 book *Roman Maryport and its setting*, suggests that these coastal defences may have been initially constructed of timber, some being later rebuilt in stone. This may go some way to explain why there is no substantial evidence to locate any further watchtowers or fortlets, south of Risehow, near Maryport. Some believe that there should be at least two more of these lookout points, close to Workington. Generally, they were spaced about a mile apart, hence often being referred to as mile-fortlets. At least one further site is thought to have existed at St. Michael's Mount, near Chapel Bank.[01]

[01] St. Michael's Mount was certainly used as a lookout point in Tudor times, it is clearly shown on the 1569 map of the town, entitled simply as *"watch chapell"*. See chapter eight. ■

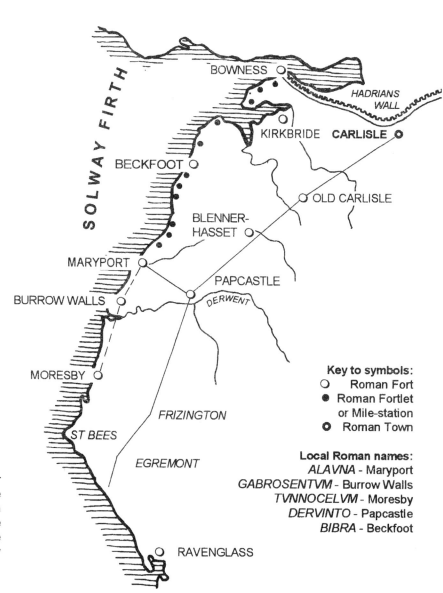

MAP OF ROMAN CUMBRIA
Showing the Forts and Fortlets or Mile-stations positioned down the coast, extending from the Western end of Hadrians Wall. These were sited to resist any invasion across the Solway Firth. The lines of the likely Roman roads are also indicated. ■

Key to symbols:
O   Roman Fort
●   Roman Fortlet or Mile-station
◉   Roman Town

Local Roman names:
ALAVNA - Maryport
GABROSENTVM - Burrow Walls
TVNNOCELVM - Moresby
DERVINTO - Papcastle
BIBRA - Beckfoot

Today, any chance of confirming this or discovering any further fortlets, either side of the Derwent estuary, has now disappeared. The last century of heavy industry has disturbed and changed the landscape along the coastline, both to the north and south of the Derwent forever.

Throughout the years many have speculated on actual purpose, formation and layout of these coastal forts. In the last forty years or so, some important archaeological evidence has given us a better understanding of what was an integral part of Emperor Hadrian's frontier defence system. Primarily it was to give an early warning of any raids across the Solway by the Picts or *Maetoe*. These often barbarous painted people, part the Caledonian tribes, [01] then occupied what we now know as Scotland. There is also a suggestion that the Hiberian people (from Ireland) would have then also attacked our coastline. Burrow Walls, like other Roman forts at Maryport and Moresby, may have been established to supply men to the individual mile-fortlets, located between each of these settlements. It is thought to have been capable of accommodating upto one thousand people. Soldiers may also have been garrisoned there, to be readily available should any raiders attempt a landing.

William Rollinson in his 1978 *History of Cumberland and Westmorland*, suggests that the Romans considered North Cumbria, to be little more than a *"military zone"*. An explanation perhaps for the absence of any major Roman domestic buildings, such as villas etc., so evident in southern England. However, the Romans are thought to have brought a level of civilisation to the native Brigantes.

Standing at Burrow Walls today looking out towards the Solway; although the nineteenth century railway embankment now obscures our view, the very notable extensive coastal views, are clearly apparent. It is quite intriguing to imagine a soldier, nearly two thousand years ago, standing here gazing seaward looking for any signs of invasion. One wonders what he thought of the glorious Solway sunsets or the wild and fierce storms which often lash our exposed coastline.

As we have learned from chapter one, it is also evident that the sea would have then been much closer to the site. It is likely that Burrow Walls then occupied a shoreside position. If Ravenglass was a Roman naval base, for Agricola's projected invasion of Ireland, as suggested by Robin Collingwood's writings. Then perhaps the mouth of the Derwent would also be used as an anchorage for the Roman naval fleet. If this was the case, the Northside fort may have been significantly more important than some previously believed. We may speculate it being its primary use, and not after all an integral part of the coastal defences. The absence of defi-

WHERE now I stand have warriors stood, in daring valour bold,
This was their camp, their dwelling place,
This was their firm stronghold.
But time has swept the face of things,
The strength of days of old.
Vainly the eye may scan the ground,
There's scarce a single trace,
To tell where once the Romans Camp'd, in all this lonely place;
Yet costly relics have been dug, from 'neath the dark earths face.

The Roman Camp by "EW" from *Cumberland Pacquet* 1837

[01] Contemporary accounts of the Roman Empire, usually referred to these tribes simply as the Caledonii. This has been forgotten by modern historians, who now generally call them the Picts (picti - painted people). However, it was AD297, before we appear to find the Caledonii, first being recorded as the Picts.

nite evidence of any major road to the fort, could certainly suggest it was almost self-sufficient. Although Richard Bellhouse in his analytical writings about our Roman coastal sites, suggests that changes in the geography of coastline may well explain the lack of physical evidence of other Roman towers or fortlets.

It is not easy today, for visitors to Burrow walls to associate these meagre and sombre remains with the Roman age. In fact, the type of wall construction has been identified as the ruins of a much later Norman castle or keep. It is thought to be the remains of a fortified Norman tower, built towards the end of the 12th century, by Orm (an ancient ancestor of the Curwen family). The Curwen records describe their Burrow Walls home as *"on the edge of a declivity sloping rapidly seawards"*. It is believed Patric de Culwen (who died around 1258) was responsible for moving the family residence, to the present defensively stronger Workington Hall site, on the opposite bank of the River Derwent. (see chapter nine)

Around 1880, William Dickinson of Thorncroft, [01] surveyed the remains and undertook a certain amount of excavation of the Burrow Walls site. Then an elderly man, certainly eighty years old, he clearly recalled sixty years earlier (1820) the walls being very much thicker, longer and higher. There were wall slits, very narrow on the outside and wider within, together with a good number of circular bolt holes. These he comments were for the *"purpose of dealing death to outside assailants and protecting the garrison inside"*. He also recorded that a small circular staircase, once existed built in the thickness of the walls. Unfortunately, earlier tenant farmers had *"robbed"* the stone from these dilapidated Norman remains for building walls etc. Despite this ignorant vandalism of *"skinning"* the facing stonework from the once thick walls, enough still remains to date the structure, to Norman times. There are rows of feathered or herring-bone stonework, bearing a *"great similarity"* to portions of existing walls at Egremont Castle. This suggests a similar date of construction, likely to be around 1175.

Dickinson also recorded excavations undertaken around the site. His finds included a number of what he believed to be carved Roman stones. Unfortunately, these all now appear lost. Also discovered were a number of bones and horns from large deer, cattle and other animals. Intermingled with these were oyster shells and ashes, as well as some unburied human skeletons. These he surmised were the *"bodies of enemies"*, who perhaps perished attacking the Norman stronghold.

The first recorded discovery of Roman remains on the Burrow Walls site was in 1852. Mr. Jackson, then the tenant

WILLIAM DICKINSON
(1799-1882)
He became a leading authority on Local History and customs, writing several books, some in dialect. He farmed most of his life around Arlecdon, but in his retirement moved to Workington and built Thorncroft house on Park End Road.

[01] William Dickinson was able to visit and survey the site, before the construction of the railway embankment. Opened in March 1887, it carried the Cleator and Workington Junction Railway, from Central Station upto Linefoot, via Seaton.

farmer at Seaton Mill Farm, was carrying out drainage work in the field surrounding the crumbling Norman building. It is thought that five stone Roman altars, some Roman coins and pottery, and also a quantity of hand millstones (for grinding corn etc.) were discovered. Most of the altars [01] were in a dilapidated state, but one was quite well preserved.

This stone, broken in several pieces and with some missing sections, was discovered in the foundations of the Norman keep. Where it appears to have simply been recycled as building material. Dickinson recorded it as having the inscription *"Lapidarium Seplentrionate"*, together with carvings of human figures. He believed one to be Hercules, and the other a figure of a woman. But Collingwood and Wright in their extensive 1965 book, *Roman Inscriptions of Britain*, provide a more complete, and slightly differing description, of what is believed to be the same altar. *"On the left side a goddess, probably Minerva, in stola stands on pedestal and holds a shaft in her right hand, and with her left hand rests her shield upon a globe. On the right side, part of Hercules on a pedestal holding a club at his right flank".*

A sketch of the front of the altar and its inscription is shown right. The fragmented lettering obviously differs from Dickinson's notes. Translated it appears to read *".....and for their children, Aurelius and Secundus..."* It could be that at least an additional three lines would have existed above the text on a now lost, upper part of the stone.

William Whellan's 1860 *History of Cumberland & Westmorland*, provides another slightly differing, but less detailed description which reads: *"It has upon one side what appears to be a priest in his vestments, with a rod or staff of office in his right hand, whilst in his left hand he holds what appears to be a small vessel for burning incense. On the reverse side is a female figure, also holding a staff in her right hand; she has something in her left hand, but it cannot be made out. Probably she is meant to represent Victory."* These slightly varying descriptions appear to refer to the same altar. But after a century and half it is difficult to explain the obvious differences, particularly regarding the inscriptions.

The present whereabouts of this one remaining Burrow Walls Roman altar are unclear. Originally it was simply being kept in Mr. Jackson's garden at Seaton Mill. But was later given to (or claimed by) the Earl of Lonsdale, the then landowner. It was then taken to Penrith and put on display at his Lowther Castle home. It was also known to have been exhibited at the 1859 Carlisle meeting of the *Royal Archaeological Society.*

Despite these apparent obvious Roman finds, many were still convinced that Burrow Walls, was not infact an

BURROW WALLS ROMAN ALTAR

Sketch of the Roman altar, found at Burrow Walls in 1852. This piece measured approx. 1040 x 508mm (41" x 20"), but may once have had a base and about three further lines of text on it's upper portion. Formerly, displayed at Lowther Castle, present whereabouts unknown.

[01] Roman altars were carved stones, designs and inscriptions varied, but usually dedicated to their native gods, such as Mars, Jupiter, Neptune, Hercules etc.

14

important Roman fort. With the building of the later Norman castle, much of the remains of the Roman structure had been robbed for building materials. Long before the eighteenth century, a great proportion of this had also vanished. Much more besides, had been lost under the plough. William Whellan (1860) was one who did believe it to be *"a Roman station of some importance"*. However for many years, some of the most eminent Roman historians and archaeologists overlooked and dismissed the site, as quite insignificant. John Horsley in his book, *Britannia Romana*, felt he *"could discover no appearance"* of a fort on the site. As late as 1928, Robin G. Collingwood also came to the same conclusion. Interestingly and a little critically, Richard Bellhouse in his 1955 report of the archaeological excavations commented that *"some facing-stones still remaining remind one forcibly of stone dikes and farm buildings, near Hadrian's Wall.......this alone should have prompted further site investigation"*.

Further archaeological investigation was only undertaken, after careful examination of the first aerial photographs of the site, taken in 1949. These photographs by Dr. J. K. St. Joseph [01], showed the clear outline of what appeared to be some form of ramparts or ditches. A distinctly visible, curved right angle corner appeared to exist, about 75 metres east of the existing Norman remains. This and subsequent archaeological digging finally proved that Burrow Walls was a major Roman station, covering around two and three-quarter acres.

Between 11-15th April 1955, the digging began on the site. It was carried out by Richard Bellhouse, Iain McIvor and Brian Blake. This small amateur group, undertook a well-planned and professional investigation., confirming for the first time the size of the fort. Brian Blake in his book - *The Solway Firth* describes how the fort was found to be 290 feet (88.4m) across the ramparts along its coastal axis, and perhaps 360 feet (109.7m) at right angles to the coast.

The latter dimension was only an estimate as the western portion of the fort appears to have disappeared due to erosion to the cliff face. The original length of the fort has since been speculated to be around 450 feet. The ramparts were also found to be protected by two outer ditches. The inner ditch containing some stone and timber remains. Bellhouse concluded that Burrow Walls is *"strictly comparable in shape and situation with Beckfoot and Moresby, a typical second century fort"*. [02]

Exactly when the Romans left Burrows Walls, is as unclear as the precise foundation of the site. Some suggest the fort was not actually occupied continuously, throughout the Roman period. Bellhouse speculates it could have been

[01] Dr J.K. St. Joseph was the Professor of Aerial Photographic Studies at Cambridge University. Over many years, he took many thousands of aerial photographs, of sites throughout the country. His work lead to the discovery or better understanding of many of our ancient monuments. ■
[02] There is a detailed report of the excavations, with photographs by Brian Blake, first published by the C&WA&AS. ■

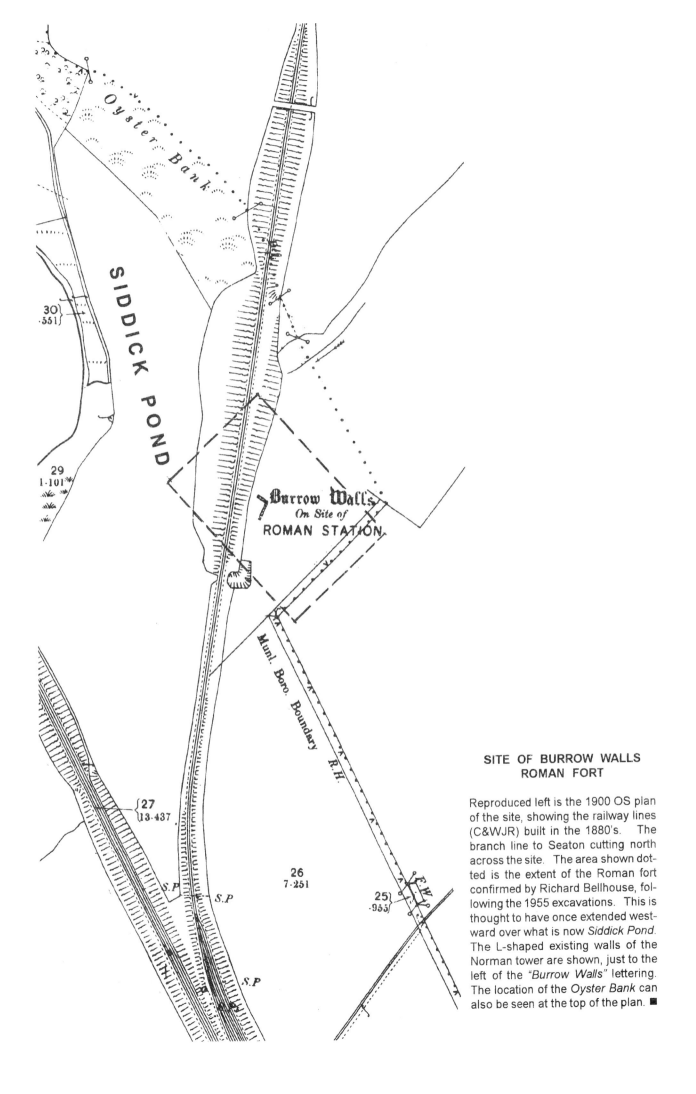

**SITE OF BURROW WALLS
ROMAN FORT**

Reproduced left is the 1900 OS plan of the site, showing the railway lines (C&WJR) built in the 1880's. The branch line to Seaton cutting north across the site. The area shown dotted is the extent of the Roman fort confirmed by Richard Bellhouse, following the 1955 excavations. This is thought to have once extended westward over what is now *Siddick Pond*. The L-shaped existing walls of the Norman tower are shown, just to the left of the *"Burrow Walls"* lettering. The location of the *Oyster Bank* can also be seen at the top of the plan. ∎

"Much of this pottery was identified as pieces of cooking pots of the Huntcliffe type, dated to the late fourth century".

abandoned around AD158, perhaps even dismantled. With some re-occupation occurring much later on a much smaller scale. He may have suggested this date as the Roman army was then retreating south from Scotland, and Hadrian's Wall was being dramatically refortified. However, we should not discount the likelihood of troops leaving the fort, much earlier around AD139. Then the Roman Army, lead by Emperor Antonius, was known to be pushing north through the Scottish Lowlands. Other forts in the Pennines, were being stripped of troops for this northern advance.

Evidence that the Roman's returned to Burrow Wall's was uncovered by Bellhouses' 1955 excavations. It revealed two later ditches, containing some Roman pottery fragments. Much of this pottery was identified as pieces of cooking pots of the Huntcliffe type, dated to the late fourth century. Re-occupation may have occurred around AD360-7, when the Picts (again aided by the Scots from Ireland) consistently and forcibly stormed south into the north of England, by both land and sea. So much so that Julian [01] was forced to send reinforcements to Britain. Eventually in AD369, Theodosius contained the invaders, and pushed them back to north of Hadrian's Wall. Major reinforcement and rebuilding of Roman defences, along both the north-east and west coastlines followed this period. Was Burrow Walls then reoccupied?

Did the lack of military threat or a change of strategy or plans, lead to Burrow walls being abandoned? Or was the fort only ever used as a naval base or anchorage? Perhaps it was abandoned only because of the coastal erosion. Maybe the loop of the Derwent subsequently become silted up and no longer accessible to ships. It may well have been a combination of several of these factors. By AD180, the Romans had added the province north of Hadrians wall, to their empire. Their frontier being pushed northwards, across from the Forth to the Clyde. This may have effectively reduced the need for the Cumberland coastal defences, and for much of Hadrians Wall itself.

At times, long before the full withdrawal of the Romans, troops were often moved away from the wall, leaving it vulnerable to attack. It is conceivable that this obvious shortage of personnel, may have lead to the demise of Burrow walls. With the Maryport and Moresby forts, each only five miles or so to the north and south respectively, was an additional fort here now unnecessary? But, over the next couple of centuries, we know that the wall was breached on at least three occasions as the *"barbarian"* picts, moved south and defeated the Roman troops. Records suggest one such major attack occurred in AD367. When the Picts and the Scots combined to attack, possibly by land and sea, sweep-

[01] Roman emperor Julian (361-363). Was the youngest son of Julius Constantius, who was half-brother to Constantine the Great. Created caesar in AD355, with government of Gaul, Spain, and Britain; ■

ing through the North of England, as far south as York. One other, not implausible theory is the fort was destroyed by attackers, and never rebuilt.

It is thought that the Romans called Burrow Walls - *GABROSENTUM*, although no clear evidence exists to really confirm this theory. Before the 1955 excavations firmly established Burrow Walls as an additional fort, Moresby was often referred to as being Gabrosentum. Moresby is now believed by most to have been Tunnocelum. Unfortunately, much of this is simple speculation. We do have two lists of the Roman site names, but cannot pinpoint their actual locations, but no Roman map exists to identify these sites. It maybe that when they were actually prepared, Burrow Walls was omitted from lists as it was no longer active, [01]

Today's name Burrow Walls is certainly much later, perhaps seventeenth or eighteenth century. No earlier historical references appear to exist. Thomas Denton in 1680, on his travels, mentions the building was then abandoned and left in decay, commenting *"the walls of the ruins of the mansion house are to be seen there at Seaton to this day"*. But he gives it no actual name, simply referring to it as the former home of the Curwens. Dickinson believed that the *Burrow* element of the name is *"undoubtedly a corruption"* of Burgh or Borough. Signifying a corporate place, town, large village or fortified place. Today some prefer to believe that the ruins generally obtain their present name from their once close proximity to the extensive rabbit warrens or burrows upon Oldside.

Efforts have been made to trace the whereabouts of the Roman coins found at Burrow Walls, with little success. An old photograph does exist at Workington Library of several coins thought to be from the site, but its provenance is doubtful and uncertain. Despite this, we do have records of at least two other Roman coins found in the area, which appear to confirm Roman activity spanning several centuries. The earliest coin was found at Siddick, in a sandpit, by W. Dawson in 1926. It was recorded as being a gold coin of Nero [02], which would suggest a date of at least AD 55. Unfortunately this coin has also been subsequently lost. If described correctly, it appears to confirm Roman activity, in the area around the time Cumberland was added to the Roman empire.

The other coin believed to be from the Severan period was thought to have been found in a garden in William Street. Quite close to the line of the suspected Roman road north to the Burrow Walls fort. The coin, in excellent condition, was said to be a Third Brass of Tetricus Senior. This would date it to around AD270. Unfortunately, its whereabouts today

"On a clear day, as I ride from Lilly Hall, towards the towne of Workington. I gaze in wonderment at how near the hills of Galloway and the (Isle of) Mann appear, a mere step across the sea."

This short note was scribbled in the journal of Thomas Falcon (Attorney) and written in 1826. I feel it vividly illustrates how the town has always been so much closer to the Isle of Man and Scotland, than to perhaps Keswick or Carlisle, overland. The easiest and most obvious invasion route, for not only the Picts, Scots, and later Norsemen. But also that used by the English troops, over many centuries, as they attempted to subdue the Kingdon of Strathclyde and the Scots. It's then not difficult to imagine why the Roman's needed to built their extensive coastal defences.

[01] Although the Roman historian Tacitus described Roman Britain (to AD85), in his biography of Agricola. The first geographical record, to include our region, was by Ptotemy, around AD120. Antoninus gives us a further list, three centuries later, around AD310. Numerous locations on both accounts are subject to speculation, and there accuracy is often questioned. Hutchinson in his *History of Cumberland* quite incorrectly suggests that Gabrosetum was infact Drumburgh Castle, not far from Bowness, on Hadrian's wall.
[02] Nero was born in AD 37, the last Roman emperor to be descended from Julius Caesar. He became emperor in 54, and is believed to have killed himself in Rome in AD 68.

are also unknown, it appears to have last been recorded as being purchased in 1877 by the Cockermouth antique dealer and bookseller, Henry T. Wake.

Throughout the country, as the Roman occupation increased, they laid down an elaborate network of well constructed and engineered roads. These linked together their forts, camps and settlements. Allowing both troops and goods to be moved rapidly between these points. During the 1955 excavations, Richard Bellhouse is believed to have discovered the trace of a Roman-age road leading north from Burrow Walls. With a kerb at its western side the road about 12 to 15 feet, was highly cambered and constructed from hard packed *"gravel and fines"*.

The 1956 *Ordnance Survey* map of Roman Britain shows a road from Maryport, passing through Workington, to Moresby. It is said to have connected the Roman station at Moresby with their Maryport settlement. William Whellan in 1860 understood *"It's course here would be along the Old Ford, over the Cloffolks, by Borough Walls Hill, where traces of a Roman Camp or station still exist; thence along by Siddick, or Sea Dyke, past Flimby, to Maryport."*
Bellhouse found no evidence of any road south from Burrow Walls, although his excavations were limited. Others appear to question the existance of this Roman road through the town.

There is little doubt that the Romans ships would have visited the mouth of the Derwent, and perhaps used it as a landing place. Their first visit may well have been when the Roman General Julius Agricola, while governor of Britain (between AD78-85), first circumnavigated the British Isles. In AD82, we also know Agricola (AD37-94) initially subdued the Caledonii (Picts) in Galloway, by a sea invasion from the Cumbrian Coast. But we have no accurate record of their exact departure point. We may assume that the estuary was used by their merchant vessels supplying the West Cumbrian forts and perhaps also by their massive warships or galleys, driven by sails and oars. Merchant ships may have also loaded locally available goods, such as coal, perhaps even iron-ore. But without any real evidence of an established Roman road structure, to the mouth of the Derwent, this may have been of lesser significance. The distribution of Roman objects found both in western Ireland and on the Isle of Man, does suggest some trading from West Cumbria, occurred during Roman times.

The Roman history of our coast, as elsewhere, is so much a question of interpretation and many times speculation. One historian has suggested that *"Stilico, a commander in the Roman state, made a wall for about four miles from hence (Workington) to the River Eln or Ellen, in all such*

ROMAN GALLEY OR SHIP

"There is little doubt that the Romans ships would have visited the mouth of the Derwent, and perhaps used it as a landing place".

places, as were convenient for landing". Yet nothing appears to have ever been discovered to confirm what must have clearly been such a large structure. Misleading fragments of local history like this, only serve to now cloud and obscure the true facts.

Unfortunately, nearly seventeen hundred years has passed since the Romans departed from the area. I have attempted to put into perspective the numerous finds and writings of the many historians and archaeologists. But, one hopes that other significant finds, will in future years uncover more evidence, so occupation of the region can be more clearly and positively defined.

❧ CHAPTER THREE❧

ANGLO-SAXON TIMES

FOR almost four centuries, Britain had been a province of the greatest empire, the world had ever known. Generally the Romans brought some degree of stability and civilisation to our area. Their retreat of AD410, resulted in a gradual disintegration throughout the country, and it became divided into a series of several small independent kingdoms. Our county was to became part of Strathclyde, which then stretched from the Clyde almost to Merseyside.[01]

Again, we can only surmise that some kind of Post-Roman settlement, once existed in the town. For their is no real evidence, probably for much the same reason as we have no knowledge of any earlier Pre-Roman encampments. It is likely that a small village may have developed, close to Burrow Walls, on either bank of the Derwent. Elsewhere similar small communities were to became established around Roman sites. If we consider the fort could at one time, accommodate around a thousand Roman troops. A local community may have sprung up to service the camp, many may also have been directly employed by the Romans.

As we believe that Burrow Walls was perhaps not continually occupied, it is also likely that any early settlement, near the fort, may have also been abandoned. It would certainly have been a prime target for any invading Picts and Scots, at times when the level of Roman soldiers, left it relatively unprotected. On several occasions it may have been overran, even burnt to the ground and destroyed, later to be reoccupied. The towns fortunes could well have been very closely linked to the occupation of Roman Fort at Burrow Walls.

William Whellan quite graphically believed that the Picts from Scotland and the Scots from Ireland (Hiberia) *"overran"* Cumbria, after the withdrawal of the Romans. But there a no real historical sources, so this may not be taken too literally. Any invasion or foray would not have been instant, it is likely to have been slow and gradual, taking perhaps several decades.

Today, one may initially imagine that any invasion would have generally occurred overland. However, it is far more likely that raiders came principally by sea. It would have been notably faster and more efficient, than moving of foot or by horseback. We have already established that the locally based Romans, had some trade links to Ireland and the

MAP OF BRITISH ISLES - giving a guide to the kingdoms between AD 600-900. ■

[01] This a general indication of north and south boundaries of Strathclyde. Obviously no authentic records exist, and should be viewed as a guide only. They were likely to have altered many times.

the Isle of Man. Furthermore, fifth to seventh century iron goods made from West Cumbrian iron ore, have been discovered on the Galloway coast, at such places as the Motte of Mark at Rockcliffe. If we travel to such places today, we make a trip of seventy miles or so by road. But across the Solway Firth, it is little more than eighteen miles by boat.

Until AD 605, as our area was somewhat isolated, deceptively long periods of peace may also have prevailed. That year the Angles of Bernicia, lead by King Aethelfrith (or Ethelfrith) defeated the Strathclyde Britons, at Degsastan.[01] This battle essentially gave Northumbrian Angles (or English) supremacy over their neighbours in Cumberland. Some historians differ by suggesting that the western side of Cumberland, then formed part of the British Kingdom of Rheged, And may not have been finally conquered by the Northumbrians till around AD 680.

The Angles and the other Germanic tribes, including the Saxons, Jutes and Fresians, [02] now began pushing westward, across Britain. Sullivan in his 1857 book *Cumberland & Westmorland - Ancient and Modern* tells us that the *"migratory tribes of Europe followed in the tracks of those who had gone before"* (the Romans). Not surprisingly, they would have eventually arrived at Workington, along the well engin-

[01] Degsastan is referred to by Bede, it is likely to be what we now call Dawstane Burn, at the head of Liddesdale.

[02] Around the fifth century the Angles, Saxons and Jutes began to migrate from their native Northern European homes. They used Frisia, now the Netherlands, as an intermediate habitation or a stepping stone, before their descendants moved on to Britain. All these tribes would have naturally mixed and this meant the Frisians are not generally recognised as independent, like the Angles, Saxons and also the Jutes.

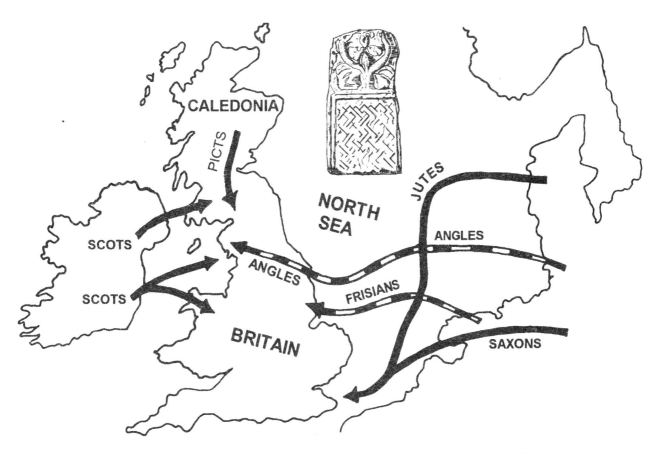

MAP SHOWING ROUTES TAKEN BY THE GERMANIC INVADERS

eered Roman roads which opened up much of West Cumbria. Rollinson believes colonisation also accelerated dramatically after the Battle of Chester in AD615, effectively split the Celtic tribes of Wales and Cumbria.

A basic analysis of the town's place name, gives us a link to the Angle tribe of the *Weorcgas*. Whose chief was likely to have been called *Weorc*. Generally, the *ton* (or tun) element of *Work-ing-ton* refers to the hedged in encampment or village, (farm or estate). Whilst *ing* (or in) is from the Old English suffix *ingas*, meaning tribe or people of. The first part of the place name being the tribal chief's name or a shortened version of the tribe name. Workington can therefore be translated as the hedged in encampment of the tribe of Weorc.[01] This personal name *Weorc* (also spelt Wirc or Wyrc) also occurs in place names in other Angle parts of England, such as Worksop, Worsall, Worsborough etc. However, it is almost certainly not the same person. We actually know very little about Weorc or his tribe the Weorcgas, who they were and where they originated.

He is not mentioned in any translation of the *Anglo-Saxon Chronicle*.[02] Cumberland (or Strathclyde as it was then called) receives no early mentions in these records. West Cumbria, like Galloway is quite devoid of Anglo-Saxon place names. With the exception of Workington, there are few others with the *"ington"* element. This could imply a sparsely populated area, almost vacant after the departure of the Romans. But Deirdre O'Sullivan contributing to the 1985 book *Scandinavians in Cumbria*, points out that *"absence of evidence is not evidence of absence"*. Such names may have been lost with the subsequent arrival of the Vikings or Norsemen, who renamed the settlements.

Exactly when the Weorcgas reached West Cumbria and settled here is also not known. Colonisation of Britain is believed to have occurred over several decades, the Germanic tribes spreading westward. As West Cumbria is quite remote, it is safe to assume their arrival here took some time. Peter Hunter Blair in his *"Introduction to Anglo-Saxon England"* suggests that Cumberland did not become occupied by the Anglo-Saxon people, until at least AD650.

Despite the obvious translation of the town's name, it is perhaps unwise to clearly define the people as simply Angles. By their arrival here, they may well have become a naturally mixed tribe of Angles, Saxons, Jutes or other Germanic groups. But it is no surprise that a settlement was established here, if we consider the relative safety of the Derwent estuary, with its anchorage and fishing and the obvious likelihood of odd outcrops of coal, for fuel.

As previously mentioned any Romano-Celtic community in the area, may well have been driven off by the Picts

[01] This is now the generally accepted definition of the place name. However, Leyland (or Leland) in 1533, thought the town derived its name from the River Wyre, which drains into the Solway at Harrington harbour, but has it's origins at near Ellerbeck, Hunday and Distington. Thomas Camden (1688) quotes Leyland but says the Wyre, *"falls into the Derwent at Clifton"*.
[02] The Anglo-Saxon Chronicle does not describe many events in the north-west of England. There are only the odd references to Cumberland or Cumbraland.

and Scots. However, it is likely that the town may have been later re-established by other Celts, driven westward by the invading Anglo-Saxons. Perhaps with some Northumbrian origins, this would go some way to explain similarities in sculptured stones, found at St. Michael's and in the North East. These may not be wholly explained on visiting Christian priests and missionaries. (see chapter six)

Two of the many archaeological finds at St. Michael's Church, not only contain a distinct Celtic influence; but also confirm the existance of this Anglo-Saxon settlement, dating from the eighth to ninth century. [01] The first find discovered after the 1887 fire at the church, was part of a grey sandstone cross-shaft (BC1) - see sketch right. It was found in the wall of the Curwen family burial vault, having been naively re-used as building material. The carving on the stone, although broken and quite weathered and worn, is characteristic of many other Anglo-Saxon Cumbrian designs. The upper portion has a elaborate deep carved, plant scroll with split leaves, similar to those found at Penrith, and St. Michael's Isel. Whilst the lower panel, is filled with a lightly cut, straight line interlacing pattern, again similar to the one at Penrith.

Rosemary Cramp of Durham University records that W.S. Calverley [02] compared this detail, with illustrations from the seventh century *Book of Kells*.[03] Indeed *"this piece reflects a shallow complex ornament which may be manuscript-derived"*. The carved stone lacks any obvious later Viking or Scandinavian influence, and should therefore be classified as Anglian. As well as going some way to confirm the existence of a pre-Viking, Anglo-Saxon settlement in the town, it also gives us some evidence of possible Irish or Northumbrian Christian missionary visits to the area.[04]

In 1926, the second stone was discovered by two local men, also underneath the church, again close to the Curwen vault. John Mason and Herbert Valentine found the *"cigar shaped"* stone (BC8) with what is believed to be an Anglo-Saxon inscription. The red sandstone fragment (only about 370mm long) had an almost square end, incised with border and some lettering. Like the other stone it was found built into the foundation walls, suggesting it predated the erection of the Norman Church on the same site. [05] The inscription (shown right) was quite worn and not easy to clearly decipher. It could read *OSI???ID*, but this is far from certain. Rosemary Cramp believes it to be a single personal name, although if male or female is impossible to tell. A similar stone has been found at the Jarrow monastic site, dating it as possibly 8th or 9th century. Further comment is difficult as the present whereabouts of this stone, is unknown. We must rely on it's 1926 description, and a single small photograph.

ABOVE - ANGLO-SAXON STONE BC1, one of only 29 fragments from 20 sites, discovered in Cumbria.

ABOVE - ANGLO-SAXON STONE BC8 (see text left) These and other stones found at St. Michael's Church are detailed in Bailey & Cramp's 1988 book - *Corpus of Anglo-Saxon Sculptured Stones*. The numbering system used by these authors, identifies the individual stones, and has also been adopted in this book. In addition each stone number is also prefixed by the initials BC. (eg. BC3 - refers to *Bailey & Cramp stone 3*). ∎

[01] & [02] See chapter six for further details of St. Michael's Church archaeological digs. Rev. W. S. Calverley and his study of the stones found on the site. ∎

[03] The Book of Kells was believed to have been created in Ireland and Northumbria. It's earliest history is still very much a matter of conjecture. However, this spectacular illuminated manuscript, lavishly illustrated with intricate shapes and patterns, dates from between the seventh and tenth centuries. ∎

[04] & [05] See chapter six for more details of Christianity in West Cumbria. Together with the early Norman church at St. Michaels. ∎

CHAPTER FOUR

VIKING TIMES

From around the start of the ninth century, the first Vikings were likely to have started to visit our coastline. Sir Frank Stenton in his Anglo-Saxon history tells us by the tenth century, *"it is generally accepted that much of Cumbria and Galloway"* had Norse settlers.[01] These Norwegian Vikings or Nordmanni, were supreme boat-builders and seamen who began pushing southward, from their colony in the Orkneys.

Unlike, the Anglo-Saxon tribes and the later Danish Vikings, who reached Cumbria by landing on the east coast and migrating overland. The Norse Vikings in their long boats, came southward around the Scottish coast, initially drawn by the wealth of the Irish monasteries. By 841, nearly half a century after their first attacks, they had firmly established and built a fortified Ireland base at Dublin. This was chosen strategically, for the intended invasion of the west of England.

We can only speculate on exactly when the Derwent estuary received its first Viking visit. We know the Isle of Man just twenty or so miles westward, was subjected to raids from the marauding Vikings, from 800 onwards. Later it was occupied and become a permanent Norse settlement. Geographically, it occupied a pivotal position, nearly equidistant from Ireland, Scotland, England and Wales. As we can often clearly see the Isle of Man, from our coast. Obviously West Cumbria, with its backdrop of the Lake mountains would be equally visible to the Norsemen from the summit of Snaefell. It is therefore highly likely that the Weorc's Anglo-Saxon settlement of Workington suffered Viking attacks, not much later than the Isle of Man. Whellan tells us that St Bees Abbey was *"entirely ruined"* by the Danes [02] on more than one occasion .

Their arrival makes a hauntingly evocative scene. The Viking long boats could land warriors and horses almost anywhere and everywhere, reaching the shallow waters of the Derwent estuary, that other boats could never navigate. Invasions were fast, versatile and predatory. One historic account graphically describes how *"the sea spewed forth such floods of foreigners....no harbour, no landing place, no stronghold might be found that was not submerged by waves of Vikings and pirates"*. It is very unlikely that our sparsely populated coastline could gather together any organised force of

[01] Sir Frank Stenton suggests that the boundary of Guthrims kingdom in 927, ran from Eamont to the Solway, following the line of the River Derwent. ■

[02] William Whellan like many early historians often refer to the Vikings generally as the Danes. But we now know that Britain, suffered attacks from two separate groups of Vikings, the Norwegians and the Danes. The Norwegians are accepted to have been responsible for invading the Cumbrian coastline, not the Danish Vikings. From 835, the Danish Vikings had began to plunder and later colonise, much of eastern England. Despite later crossing the Pennines and invading Carlisle, around 875. There appears no real evidence that they ever reached and settled in the Workington area.

local militia, to repel the Norsemen.

Modern day historians now highlight that the Vikings as not just the pagan savages that those writing the ancient Anglo-Saxon Chronicle would have us believe. Their restless voyages were something of a necessity as their homelands no longer produced enough to support them. Without a doubt, these fearless seafarers did viciously rape, loot and pillage, with bloodshed and death, but certainly not on every occasion.

In the period after AD 900, occurred the greatest influx of Norse settlers into West Cumbria. This followed the Irish driving the Norwegians from Dublin and western Ireland; and is generally accepted as when the Vikings began to colonize, the north west down as far as the Wirral peninsula in Cheshire. Although there were also several later influxes of former Irish and Manx Norwegians, notably around 980.

We can only speculate upon what happened when the Norwegian settlers first landed at Workington, and how they mixed with the existing Anglo-Saxon settlers. If they met

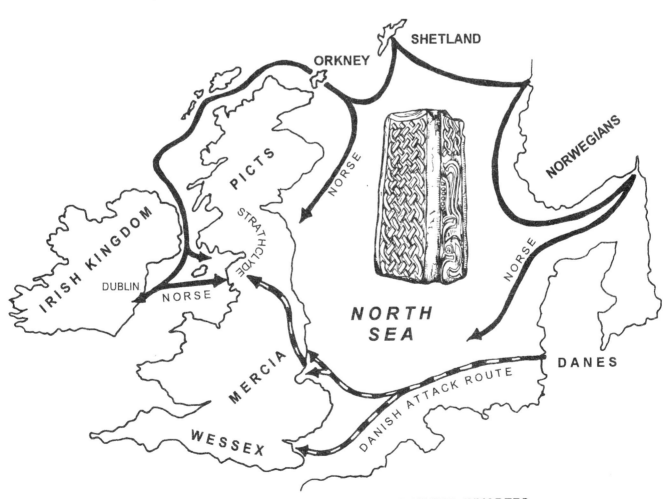

MAP SHOWING ROUTES TAKEN BY THE VIKING INVADERS

little resistance, they could have easily established settlements on the arable Solway plain. Attracted by the fertile, well drained coastal location, not unlike their Norwegian homeland. Without doubt some Viking men would have presumably inter-married with the native women. They would also have introduced some element of their wealth to the local economy. For they had money to buy land and farms, and any locally produced goods. Integration with the existing community is likely to have occurred with only minimal disruption.

After the 1994 fire at St. Michaels and the subsequent excavations, Viking graves have also been uncovered.[01] At least two Viking age belt buckles have been found, as well as distinctive fragments of possibly two Viking hogback gravestones. Examples of these decorative hogbacks, often with carved animal heads are quite rare. There are only fifteen or so known examples throughout Cumbria, the nearest being at Brigham.

Nick Higham contributing to the book *Scandinavians of Cumbria,* believes that such elaborate grave stones are *"most likely to represent a secular warrior aristocracy".* If two such stones exist at Workington, then it could be suggested that our Viking settlers, included an element of Norse nobility. Futhermore they apparently received Christian burials, suggesting they had abandoned their pagan beliefs. *Egil's Saga* implies that it was quite a common custom for the Vikings to accept a basic Christian baptism, as the price of alliance with their new neighbours.

It is at a site like St. Michaels, that one feels the history of Workington begins to take significant and formidable shape. Scholarly interest in the many decorated stones, now uncovered at the parish church, has proved a valuable source of information. Generally, the patterns can not simply be defined as solely Celtic, Anglo-Saxon or even Viking. All (except those mentioned in the previous chapter - the earlier BC1 & BC8) show a close affinity to established patterns from all three cultures. This could suggest West Cumbria's population had now become a complex racial mix of peoples from all these tribes. Although differing in race, language and custom, these designs now reflected an intermingling of all groups. Their native styles were now being fused together and developed into one quite distinctive *Celtic-Anglo-Scandanvinan* style.

At least two of the St. Michael's cross fragments have geometric patterns, which match almost precisely those found on the Isle of Man. The interlace stranded twist plaitwork on cross fragment (BC3) is identical to four known Manx examples. Simply confirming the influx of Norsemen into our area was likely to have been via that island.

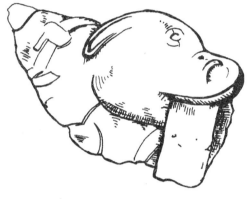

**VIKING HOGBACK
GRAVESTONE**

Part of what is suspected to be a Viking Hogback Gravestone, found at St. Michaels Church, after the 1994 fire. (see text right) ■

[01] This information has been obtained from the Carlisle City Archaeological Unit, who carried out the exploratory digs, within the church. It has yet to publish a formal report of their findings. It is anticipated that it will not be available until the year 2000.

This also positively dates this stone to between AD 950 and 1010. Furthermore and perhaps more significant, on the sides of this stone, is the quite distinctive *"foliate and tendril"* designs, typical of Mammen work. This again forms a important and historic link back to similar sculpured stones on the Isle of Man. Richard Bailey of Newcastle University, believes this stone is also almost unique, *"one of the few examples of Mammen art in England"*.

The designs on these stones are often dismissed as simple decoration. But it is thought by many that they were not just for pure ornamentation. There is a code to these patterns, a meaning or significance, perhaps Christian, maybe even political. No one has yet positively deciphered their message. Interestingly, some of the St. Michael's plaitwork was later to be adopted or influenced part of the Curwen heraldic coat of arms. [01] This could suggest some form of tribal (or family) identification, perhaps also conveying an element of status or prestige.

In the last century or so, at least ten good stone cross fragments (see page 29) have been recovered from St. Michael's. Each clearly indicating some distinct Viking influence in their carved patterns. We know that the Vikings were not stone carvers, no early stones are found in Scandinavia. But such sculpture was certainly a native traditional occupation of the local Anglo-Saxons and Celts. They must have initially been employed by the Norsemen, to undertake this work. Bailey implies that the presence of such a number of stones is clear *"evidence for the existance of a certain degree of local wealth"*. Furthermore, he adds that *"those patrons who commissioned monuments depicting the mythology, or the zoomorphic art of Scandinavia, must have been members of the new Viking aristocracy"*.

"There is a code to these patterns, a meaning or significance, perhaps Christian, may be even political. No one has yet positively deciphered their message".

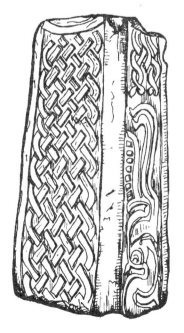

LEFT - Two views of the Viking stone (BC3) found at St. Michaels Church. Note it's flowing *"foliate and tendril"* designs on it's shorter sides, so typical of Mammen work. Overleaf is a possible reconstruction of this stone and another viking stone, BC6.

On its front face is the interlaced stranded plait-work, identical to Manx examples. Later this may well have been adopted or influenced the fret-work on the Curwen coat of Arms. Sketch of basic shield is also shown.

We can therefore conclude that before the Norman conquest, Workington had a small, but significant mixed race population. A quite peaceable, perhaps principally Christian community with a strong element of wealthy and influential Norsemen. It is likely they lived in a settlement of wattle and post houses, concentrated around the church site. This would have been a typical Viking location. Making use of the sea to protect them on one side, whilst probably being enclosed to the land, by a fairly rudimentary earthwork bank and ditch.

As well as existing on the once abundant herring and salmon fishing and no doubt some farming. They may have also traded from the Derwent estuary to Galloway, the Isle of Man and beyond. After all they arrived by sea and were experienced sailors. What commodities they exported is unclear, but like the Romans many centuries earlier, it may well have included coal, iron ore, iron objects, or other locally produced goods.

Sometime prior to 1904, a further Viking visiting card is believed to have discovered around the north bank of the River Derwent, A Viking sword in two pieces was said to have been found on a gravel ridge called *"Oyster tanks"*. Unfortunately, the discovery does not seem to be accurately recorded. Today, this exact location is not clear, it may well have been quite close to Burrow Walls. Perhaps it should have been recorded as *"Oyster Banks"*, the area just north of the Roman Fort. (see page 15) If so, then the Viking long boats may well have dropped anchor in Siddick Pond.

The sword is thought to have been later acquired by the Curwen family; and may be that once displayed at their Belle Isle home, during the early 1980s. Occasionally, this find appears to be often confused with a Viking burial site.

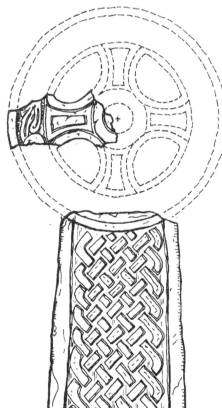

VIKING AGE CROSS FROM ST. MICHAEL'S CHURCH

Possible Viking-age cross, reconstruction from stones BC3 and BC6, found at St. Michaels Church. The latter stone was discovered by John Mason and Herbert Valentine in 1926, close to the Curwen family burial vault. Sadly, its whereabouts are now unknown, and we must rely on measurements taken in 1926.

Right is a sketch of BC6, based on the only surviving photograph of the stone, published in the C&WA&AS. ■

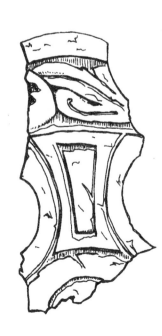

CHAPTER FIVE

THE CURWEN FAMILY
Lords of the Manor since Norman Times

IN Norman times, Workington lay in the remote area of the country which like the dark side of the moon was seldom seen. Around it's east side it was encircled by the then almost impassable Lakes mountains, to the west lay the waters of the Solway Firth. Nearly every historian tends to tell a different story, but it is generally accepted that much of Cumbria then lay unconquered on the Scottish side of the border. Our territory being little more than a very sparsely populated remote frontier district. For this reason, there is no mention of Workington in the Domesday Book of 1086. In reality it is questionable if William I ever knew much of it's existence, certainly he would not have grown any richer from taxing its meagre communities.

Around the start of the twelfth century, it is believed that Henry I divided Cumberland into five Baronies. The King generally granted these lands to Barons, who in return were required to do him political and military service. These Barons, in turn, subdivided their Baronies into several smaller Manors. Granting each Manor to the knights who pledged him their support. This was the basic form of Fuedalism which existed throughout Norman England. Workington was thought then to have been contained in the Barony first granted to William De Mechines, who resided at Egremont Castle.

The following pages contain biographical details of each Lord of the Manor of Workington, since Norman times until 1875. The earliest being the direct decendents of the influential Curwen family, who lived at Workington Hall. Below is a chronologically arranged list for easy reference.

Throughout this chapter and often elsewhere in this book, the works of *"J. F. Curwen"* are referred too. Generally, this information has been sourced from his substantial biography of his family - *"A History of the Ancient House of Curwen"*, published in 1928.

Ketel
Orm (b c.1070)
Gospatric de Wyrkington (died after 1179)
Thomas [i] de Wyrkington
Thomas [ii] de Wyrkington (d.c.1243)
Patric de Culwen (d c.1258)
Sir Gilbert [i] de Curwen (died after 1179)
Sir Thomas [i] de Curwen (d. c.1300)
John [i] de Curwen (d. c.1301)
Sir Gilbert [ii] de Curwen (d.1329)
Sir Gilbert [iii] de Curwen (c.1296-1370)
Sir Gilbert [iv] de Curwen (d.c.1403)
Sir William [i] de Curwen (d.c.1403)
Sir Christopher [i] de Curwen (c.1382-1453)
Sir Thomas [ii] de Curwen (c.1420-after 1473)
Sir Christopher [ii] de Curwen (d.1499)
Sir Thomas [iii] Curwen (c.1464-1522)

Sir Christopher [iii] Curwen (d c.1535)
Sir Thomas [iv] Curwen (c.1494-1543)
Sir Henry [i] Curwen (c.1534-1597)
Sir Nicholas [i] Curwen (1550-1604)
Sir Henry [ii] Curwen (d.1623)
Sir Patricius Curwen (1601-64)
Thomas [v] Curwen (1605-72)
Eldred [i] Curwen (d.1673)
Henry [iii] Curwen (1661-1725)
Henry [iv] Curwen (1680-1727)
Eldred [ii] Curwen (1692-1745)
Henry [v] Curwen (1728-1778)
Isabella Curwen (1765-1820)
John Christian Curwen (1756-1828)
Henry [vi] Curwen (1783-1860)
Edward Stanley Curwen (1810-75)

Ketel is believed to have been the second son of Elftred (or Eldred) and Adgitha. Very little is really known of his father, but J. F. Curwen surmises that *"he must have been a man of considerable position"*. His two eldest sons Gilbert de Furnesio (Furness) and Ketel becaming *"over-lords or mesne (or middle) lords"* of much of Cumberland, Westmorland and Furness. Around 1092, when English king William II (Rufus) moved north to claim the *"Lands of Carlisle"*, he is said to have made Ketel, the progenitor (or forefather) of Workington's Curwen family, over-lord of Cumbia. William Whelan in his 1860 *History of Cumberland*, suggested Ketel was also third baron of Kendal. He is known to have received the Manors of Workington, Salter, Kelton, and Stockhouse, by a grant of William de Meschines. Exactly when is not clear, but Ketel himself made a grant of the parish church of Workington, two carucates of land and a mill, to the monks of the Abbey of St. Mary's York sometime between 1092 and 1125. If it was the latter date, then Ketel must have then been well over seventy years old.

Although he held the Workington estates, J.F. Curwen is of the opinion that Ketel may have actually *"dwelt in the forified tower on the motte now known as Castle How, Kendal"*. He married Christina and had at least two sons, William (who died without issue) and Orm (see next entry).

"Orm may have been responsible for building the Norman castle at Burrow Walls, near Northside. (also referred to occasionally as *Seaton Castle*)"

Orm (born c1070) sometimes also spelt Orme, was the second son of Ketel and Christina. Thought to have inherited many of his father's estates in Cumberland & Westmorland, but also aquired the estates of Ceton (Seaton), Cambertone (Camerton), Flemingby (Flimby), Craiksothen (Greysouthen) as a marriage gift. His wife Gunilda, was the daughter of Gospatric (Earl of Northumbria) [01] and the sister of Walthof (Lord of Allerdale). They had at least four sons including Gospatric de Wyrkington (see next entry). It is interesting to note that Orm's father-in-law, Gospatric (d1074) was the nephew of Scottish King Duncan I, and also cousin to Malcolm III. Suggesting stronger links with the Scots, than with the Norman English. However, his grandmother was also the daughter of English king, Ethelred *"the Unready"*.

It has believed that Orm may have been responsible for building the Norman castle at Burrow Walls, near Northside. (also referred to occasionally as *Seaton Castle*) -see chapter nine. As will be later explained it is quite unclear whether or not Orm actually formally acquired full title to the Workington estates. However, during this period it is safe to assume he held some form of tenure to the lands.

[01] Around 1070, Gospatric is said to have been made Earl of Northumbria by William the Conquerour. It is suggested the English King did this to deter Gospatric and his forces moving south.

Gospatric de Wyrkington (died after 1179) son of Orm and Gunilda (daughter of Gospatric, Earl of Northumbria). It is wise to propose that Gospatric is the next known Lord of the Manor of Workington. As Rev. F.W. Ragg of the C&WA&AS, concluded he appears to have come into full title of the Workington & Lamplugh estates, from William de Lancaster (died c.1170) by a direct exchange of *"Mediliton in Lonsdale"* (Middleton). Although much earlier, he may have had tenure of the lands, but his heirs appear not to then have any *"rights of inheritance"*. [01] A copy of this deed of exchange (from c.1150) exists at Whitehaven Record Office. One condition of the exchange required Gospatric to do *"military"* service to the barony and castle of Egremont then also held by William de Lancaster.

J. F. Curwen suggests that Orm inherited *"his father's (Ketel) estates in Cumberland & Westmorland"*. But it is not clear if Workington actually included in with these properties. It may have passed to Ketel's brother Gilbert or directly onto his son, William.

Perhaps after Orm's marriage, if he moved to reside upon his *"wedding present"* of Seaton and Camerton etc. Then William de Lancaster may have granted him the Workington estate. Simply because he was so close on the opposite bank of the Derwent, and it may have been convenient to do so. Unfortunately, the terms of this tenure or lease are not recorded.

Because of the family connection, perhaps the arrangement may well have remained quite informal until Gospatric exchanged the lands. It is also possible, Workington was granted, leased or demised to Orm for the peroid of his life only. After his death, only then was it neccessary for his son to make alternative arrangements.

Gospatric is also recorded as confirming the grant of Ketel (his grandfather) of the church at Workington, and the mill and lands *"in the same township"*, to St Mary (at York) and St. Bega (St Bees). J.F. Curwen records that Gospatric was at the Court of English King Henry II, at Woodstock in 1157. The same year Scottish King Malcolm IV ceded or gave up Cumberland (and other northern counties) to the English King.

Around 1174, when William (King of Scots) invaded south to Appleby Castle, *"Gospatric the son of Horm"* is recorded as surrendering to him. At the time he was thought to be the *"constable"* or kings officer responsible for the castle, and it is said the *"old grey-headed Englishman......soon cried mercy"*. [02] However, J. F. Curwen (the family biographer) perhaps naturally, defends his actions by suggesting

THE King had very soon the castle of Appleby.
There were no people in it, but was quite unguarded.
Gospatric the son of Horm, an old grey-headed Englishman,
Was the constable. He soon cried mercy.

[01] It should be noted that William de Lancaster's father Gilbert, is thought to have been Ketel's brother. This would obviously make William de Lancaster, a first cousin of Orm (Gospatric's father).
[02] A contemporary account of Gospatric's apparent surrender at Appleby Castle, is recorded by a Frenchman Jordan Fantosme. He was a former Chancellor of Winchester. Although originally written in french, a Surtees Society translation by Francisque Michel exists, the few relevant lines are reproduced above.

that *"it would not be altogether the feebleness of old age"*. As explained previously, Gospatric was still quite closely related to many of the *"Scottish Kings and princes"*. It was far more likely that he would lean toward the Scots of Strathclyde, than to what some called a *"barbarian"* English King. In 1176, he was fined for *"his surrender"* the sum of *"500 marcs"*, thought then to equate to around £330.

He married Egelina (unknown family), and they had at least eight sons. These included Thomas [i], Orme (de Ireby), Adam (who became priest at Camerton), Robert (who was granted the Lamplugh estates before 1181, by Thomas, his brother).

Thomas [i] de Wyrkington (d.1200), son of Gospatric and Egelina. Inherited the Workington estates after the death of his father, sometime after 1179. He is also believed to have aquired the lands of the *"great lordship of Culwen"* (in Galloway) through his marriage to Amabilis, the daughter and heiress of Thomas de Culwen, (son of Uchtred, Lord of Galloway). The Culwen district of Kirkcudbrightshire, is now known as Colvend, and is about five miles south-east of Dalbeattie.

Thomas and Amabilis had three sons and one daughter. These included Patric de Culwen and Alan de Camerton. [01] Following Amabilis' death, Thomas de Wyrkington married Grace or Grecia, and they had a further four sons (Thomas [ii], Hugh, William and Gilbert). William was said to have been the rector of St. Michaels Church, Workington, from 1201-27.

Thomas [ii] de Wyrkington (d c.1243) son of Thomas [i] and Grace (family unknown) He inherited the Workington estates upon the death of his father. Married Joan, sister or daughter of Robert de Vipond. Thomas apparently produced no heir to suceed him, so after his death, the estate passed to his only daughter, also Joan. Despite marrying Robert de Haverington she died childless, and the Workington estates reverted back to her uncle Patric de Culwen, the half brother of her father Thomas [ii].

Patric de Culwen (d c.1258) son of Thomas [i] de Wyrkington and Amabilis, (the daughter and heiress of Thomas de Culwen, Lord of Galloway). He styled himself *"Patric de Culwen"* when he inherited the Galloway estates, after his father's death in 1200. He inherited the Workington estates, upon the death of Joan, daughter of Thomas [ii] de Wyrkington. (his brother) This obviously united together the estates of Galloway and Workington, although some mys-

"The Culwen district of Kirkcudbrightshire, is now known as Colvend, and is about five miles south-east of Dalbeattie".

[01] Around 1236, Patric de Culwen is said to have granted Camberton (Camerton) to his younger brother Alan. From here decended the *"de Camberton"* branch of the Curwen family. ■

tery surrounds how the family later came to be parted from or dispose of the Galloway lands. There is a reference to Robert de Bruce granting *"the lands of Culwen"* to Isabel, countess of Athol, and Alexander Bruce, his son. J. F. Curwen also noted that the lands, later passed from Alexander Bruce to the McDougall's under a charter of David II (1324-71). Through Patric's earlier adoption of the surname *"de Culwen"*, the use of the *"de Wyrkington"* surname of his father now seems to have been almost brought to an end. Only occassionally thereafter does it occur in a few later documents.

It was Patric who was believed to have moved the Curwen ancestral home from Burrow Walls, across the River Derwent to the present Workington Hall site. (see chapter nine) The earliest surviving example of the Curwen coat of arms dates from Patric. It was pressed into a wax seal, on an indenture of 1257 (see sketch right). Patric was to marry (at least once), but no mention of his wife's christian name can be found. The couple had three sons, Thomas (d c.1255), Gilbert [i] and Robert.

Seal of Patric de Culwen, taken from an original 1257 document. J.F. Curwen translates the inscription to *"By the Grace of God I am what I am"*. ■

Sir Gilbert [i] de Curwen (d c.1290) was son of Patric[i] and mother unknown. The Workington estates passed to Gilbert [i] after his father death, around 1258. The Curwen surname is now found spelt several ways; *Curewen, Corwenne, Corewen, Culewen* and *Culwen* in some documents. Gilbert also occasionally appears under the titles of either Gilbert de Culwen de Wyrkinton or just Gilbert de Wyrkinton. Appointed Governor of Carlisle Castle from 1278-83, by Edward I. But appeared to have later lost the King's favour. J. F. Curwen surmising that the family may still have *"retained strong leanings"* and ties on the Scottish side. Married (wife unknown) and had three sons Thomas [i], John [i], Gilbert [ii] and Patric (later of Drigg).

Sir Thomas [i] de Curwen (d. c.1300) was son of Gilbert [i] and mother unknown. Also shown as Thomas de Wyrkinton in the 1275 *"Pipe Rolls of Edward I"* as paying taxes relating to the Manors of *Wyrkinton* (Workington), Seaton and Thornthwaite. The Workington estates were granted to him by his father in 1268, around twenty years or so before his death. This could suggest the likelihood of him being in residence at Workington Hall from this time. Gilbert [i] must be assumed to have then lived elsewhere. Thomas [i] married Joan (d c.1314), former husband of John de Cansfield, before 1292. Thomas is thought to have died without issue, the estates then passing to his brother John [i].

John [i] **de Curwen** (d. c.1301) was son of Gilbert [i], and succeeed to the Workington estates following the death of his brother Thomas [i]. Thought to have fought at the famous *Battle of Falkirk* on 22 July 1298, where Edward I defeated the Scots under William *"Brave Heart"* Wallace. Said to have being captured there, by the Scots and imprisoned for around six months. Shortly after suspected of transferring his aligence and faith to Scotland. But returned to England around 1299, to claim he had taken the Scots side merely to *"save his life"*. As a result, claims were made for him to be stripped of his estates, but these were overturned by the King. John was Lord of the manor of Workington for only around twelve months before his death.

Sir Gilbert [ii] **de Curwen** (d1329) was the son of Gilbert [i] and succeeded to the estates, following the death of his brother John [i]. J. F. Curwen records how Gilbert, also fought at the *Battle of Falkirk* in July 1298. Perhaps alongside at least two of his brothers John (who was captured) and Patric. Gilbert and his forces, are thought to have arrived late onto the battlefield, *"just in the nick of time"*. The Curwen family tradition (not really supported by any clear cut evidence) points to Gilbert's arrival being the turning point of the battle. Edward I and his forces claiming a famous English victory. Gilbert in his euphoria, turned to the King and said *"Ah, where would you have been if I had not been there"*. Gilbert and later Curwen generations, adopted part of this perhaps boastful remark, as their family motto. *"SI JE N'ESTOY"* is often seen attached to the coats of arms, and simply translates to *"If I had not been there"*.

In 1309 Gilbert was appointed keeper of the Castle and Honour of Cockermouth Castle. In 1321, appointed with Andrew de Harcla, conservators of the peace in Westmorland, in 1321. Married Eda or Editha (d1352), of the *"de Harrington"* family around 1295. Believed to have had eleven children, eight sons and three daughters. These included Gilbert [iii] (see below) and John (1331-1348) who later aquired the Caton estates by marriage to Agnes de Caton.

Sir Gilbert [iii] **de Curwen** (c1296-1370) son of Gilbert [ii] and Editha. inherited the Workington estates upon the death of his father, around 1329. In 1314 was said to have fought with Andrew de Harcla's forces to repel a Scots invasion, near Stainmore. Tradition points to him, then as a youth of only around 18 years old, being embarrassingly *"unhorsed"* during the skirmish. May have also fought, against the Scots, when Carlisle was besieged for eleven days in July 1315. And the following year when they came and *"laid waste everything"* as far south as Furness.

ABOVE - Sketch of the full Curwen family coat of arms, based on that originally drawn by J.F. Curwen. The family motto *"SI JE N'ESTOY"* is often seen attached to their coats of arms, and simply translates to *"If I had not been there"*. ■

Again as with previous generations of the Curwen family, Gilbert was suspected of siding with the Scots. Afterall many of whom were his distant relations and the family may still have retained some lands in Galloway. As a result, in 1329 he risked having to forfeit lands in Shap and the Manor of Workington. However, Edward III granted him a pardon and his title to the manor was fully restored.

William Jackson in his 1892 *Papers and Pedigrees* tells us that on 26 August 1346, Gilbert received his knighthood on the battlefield at Crecy. Having fought alongside Edward III, as he attempted to seize the French throne, after the death of Charles IV.

Daniel Fleming in his 1671 *Description of Cumberland* says Gilbert [iii] *"built the chief tower at Workington, the stone was laid 8 May 1362"* (see chapter nine). This is believed to be the main pele tower at Workington Hall, remains of which can still be identified among the present ruins.

Thought to have been married twice, firstly to Avicia (family unknown). His second wife being Margaret (family also unknown). Had three sons Gilbert [iv], John and Thomas by this marriage.

Sir Gilbert [iv] de Curwen (d c1403) son of Gilbert [iii] and Margaret. Inherited the Workington estates after the death of his father in 1370. Became Knight of Shire of Cumberland in 1371, 1373, 1375, and 1381. Around 1379, received licence to fortify and crenellate his late fathers pele tower at Workington. (see chapter nine). Gilbert initially married Alice, daughter of Sir Hugh de Lowther. Producing perhaps four sons, William [i], John (who became Vicar of Bromfield), plus possibly Hugh and Giles (who are thought to have died in the plague of 1403). Gilbert also married Isabel, former wife of late Christopher de Moriceby, having a daughter Isabella. Gilbert is also thought to have died from the plague or *"great pestilence"* of 1403, which is thought to have spread throughout the north of England.

Sir William [i] de Curwen (d c1403) First son of Gilbert [iv] and Alice de Lowther. As he is thought to have died in the same 1403 plague, shortly after his father and brothers, he may only have held the Workington estates for a short period. In 1375 appointed *"Constable of Lochmaben Castle"*, a position J. F. Curwen records as then *"of considerable importance"*. Knight of Shire of Cumberland in 1379. Also appointed Sheriff of Cumberland in 1397. Before 1386, had married Eleana or Elena le Burn (d c.1395) coheiress of Sir Robert le Burn of Drumburgh Castle. Had two sons Christopher [I] and John (d.1441). In 1440, John was appointed the Governor of Porchester Castle.

ABOVE - Sketch of the Curwen & Le Burn coat of Arms, taken from a photograph of a carved timber panel, formerly in Workington Hall. It was thought to be one of three panels, which once hung in the passage, below the main entrance staircase, through to the Justices Hall. (see chapter nine) ∎

Sketch of Christopher [i] Curwen in typical fifteenth century armour. Taken from his effigy in St. Michaels Church. Where he lies beside his wife Elizabeth Huddleston. The full effigy is shown in chapter six. ∎

[01]   According to the Monuments Historiques, the French equivalent of our Royal Commission on the Historic Monuments. The Castle (or Chateau Fort) of Cany, formerly belonged to the Duke of Bauer (Barr). Unfortunately, very little now remains of this once vast fourteenth century fort. It was situated in the Caniel district of Cany-Barville (in Normandy) around 28 miles north east of Le Havre. Between 1978-86, excavations upon the site revealed it was once quite a large typical French castle, with several circular towers or turrets.

Sir Christopher [i] **de Curwen** (c1382-1453) was the first son of William [i] and Elena le Burn. Lord of the Manor of Workington from 1403 to 1450. Appointed Sheriff of Cumberland in 1417, 1424, 1428, 1434, 1438, and 1445. Represented the county in Parliament as Knight of the Shire of Cumberland in 1415, 1424-5, 1428, and 1431-2. Christopher is thought to have been the last family member to use the *"de Culwen"* surname, after 1428 he assumed the name *"de Curwen"*. J. F. Curwen believed that around 1404, Christopher built the first *Great Hall* at Workington Hall (with the vaulted cellars below). This adjoined the ancient pele tower, thought to have been built by his great grandfather, Gilbert [iii] in 1362.

Christopher is also known to have fought several times in France (for Henry V) from the summer of 1415, in what was known as the *"Hundred years' war"*. In 1428, as a reward for his good service, Henry VI granted him the *"Castle and land of Cany and Canyell"* in Gaux (Caux) France. From 1435, he appears to have leased this estate etc., to Thomas Clapham. When the English finally lost Normandy (in 1450) the castle was recaptured by the French. Copies of these leases are deposited in Whitehaven Record Office. [01]

In Oct 1429, called to arms to resist a further invasion by Scots. In 1442, Henry VI appointed him a commissioner to take the oaths of the Wardens of the West Marches, and to overseer the truce with Scottish King James II.

Married Elizabeth (d.c1468), daughter of Sir John Hudleston (of Millom), having two sons Thomas [ii] and William. J. F. Curwen records at length William's military experience in Gournay-en-Baux, in France.

Christopher died 17 July 1453, and was interred at Workington. In St. Michael's Church is a fine stone effigy of him and his wife, lying side by side. (see description on page ???) It is likely this was erected around 1470, perhaps by their grandson Christopher [ii] and his wife Anne Pennington, as it bears a Curwen coat of arms, impaled (or paired) with the Pennington arms. This date cannot accurately be determined, but it is suggested to be before Christopher [ii] married his second wife, Katherine Salkeld.

Sir Thomas [ii] **de Curwen** (c.1420-after 1473) son of Christopher [i] and Elizabeth Hudleston. Inherited the Workington estates after his father's death in 1453. Appointed a Justice of the Peace for Cumberland in Dec 1459, and commissioned to resist the rebellion of Richard (Duke of York) at the start of the *"War of the Roses"*. The extent of his involvment in this rebellion is vague, but Edward IV later *"granted honours"* to the family, in acknowledgement of Thomas' *"great and gratuitous service"* during the revolt. Appears to have married twice, his first wife being Alice (family unknown); his second wife being Anne, daughter of Robert Lowther. Known to have had at least ten children, five sons and five daughters. These included Christopher [ii], Gilbert (who inherited the Caton estates) and William (he became an attorney, also keeper of Carlisle Castle in 1471).

Sir Christopher [ii] **de Curwen** (d 1499) eldest son of Thomas [ii], his mother being either Alice or Anne (see above). Succeeded to the Workington estates, after his fathers death around 1473. Although it is suggested that he resided at Workington Hall from at least 1470 (perhaps much earlier) after his marriage to Anne Pennington (married c.1443) She was the daughter of John Pennington, and they had around ten children, six sons and four daughters. These included Thomas [iii], John (who became rector of Workington), William (who became rector of Distington) and Robert (whose grandson Hugh Curwen become chaplin to Henry VIII, strongly defended his second marriage to Anne Boleyn. Later Hugh who died in 1568, became Archbishop of Dublin and later Bishop of Oxford. His great-grandson Robert Bancroft was also Archbishop of Canterbury from 1604-10).

Christopher married for a second time to Katherine, widow of Thomas Salkeld. They are known to have had a daughter Isabella or Alice, who married Sir John Lamplugh. Katherine later claimed she had *"by him eight children"*, although J. F. Curwen felt he could not substantiate this.

BELOW - Sketch of Sir Christopher [i] Curwen in the *"knightly exercise of jousting"*. In 1417, he is known to have taken part in a great tournament on Carlisle Castle Green, with five other English knights, against an equal number of Scottish knights. ∎

Sir Thomas [iii] Curwen (c.1464-1522) was son of Christopher [ii] and Anne Pennington. Succeeded to the Workington estates after his fathers death in 1499. That same year he was accused along with his son Christopher, Thomas Curwen (*Black Tom of Camerton*) and others of killing Alexander Dykes (husband of Elizabeth Dykes). The circumstances of the alleged murder are not clear, but they all seem to have escaped punishment, by showing themselves *"meekly sorry for the death"*, and paying his widow *"four score"* pounds.

Thomas was later Sheriff of Cumberland in 1509 and 1517. He first married Anne, daughter of Sir John Hudleston (of Millom Castle). They had at least eight children, five sons and four daughters. These included Christopher [iii], Giles (of Poulton, from whom the North Lonsdale Curwen's are decended) and Lucy (who married Sir John Lowther in 1502). His second marriage was to Isabel, daughter of Sir Henry Percy. They had a daughter Jane (who married Sir William Musgrave)

Sir Christopher [iii] Curwen (d. c1535) was the son of Thomas [ii] and Anne Huddleston. Thought to have succeeded to Workington estates, upon the death of his father in 1522. However in 1524, both Christopher [iii] and his uncle William Curwen son of Christopher [ii], are sometimes mentioned in connection with the Manor of Workington. Christopher [iii] was Sheriff of Cumberland in 1525 and 1534. He married (around 1492) Margaret, daughter of Sir Roger Bellingham of Burishead. They had at least eight children, five sons and three daughters. These included Thomas [iv], Edmund (who became a monk at Calder Abbey) and Alice (who married Thomas Lamplugh of Dovenby)

Sir Thomas [iv] Curwen (c1494-1543) son of Christopher [iii] and Margaret Bellingham. Thought to have succeeded to the Workington estates upon his father's death around 1535. In 1526 and 1543, listed as one of the knights employed to defend English Marches, along the Scottish borders. His second wife's brother Sir Thomas Wharton, was then *Warden of the English West March*. Thomas also appointed Sheriff of Cumberland in 1537. J. F. Curwen attributes Thomas as re-building the *Great Hall* (56 x 22ft) over the fifteenth century vaulted cellars (still to be seen today). The original *Great Hall* being erected by Christopher [i] around 1404. (see chapter nine for full description of the Hall)

Edmund Sandford in his history of the county (written about 1676) believed Sir Thomas was an excellant archer *"at twelvescore marks"*. Around the dissolution of the monasteries (1536-40) he and his men are said to have *"shoote"* with Henry VIII. Legend has it that the King then gave Thomas

ABOVE - The impression from the silver seal of Sir Christopher [iii] Curwen. (based on a drawing by J.F. Curwen) It measured approx 40mm across, and would date from the late fifteenth century. Although J.F Curwen thought the sketch to be quite crude, he also felt it *"represents more or less faithfully the modelled impression of the Seal"*. ■

the lands and *"Abbie of Furness"*.   After his death, it is thought Furness Abbey passed to Thomas' sister Ellen, who married John Preston.

Thomas married at least twice, initially to Agnes, daughter of Sir Walter Strickland (whose grandmother was Anne Parr). William Jackson in his 1892 *Papers and Pedigrees*, suggests that by this marriage *"the royal blood of the Plantagenets came to the Curwen house"*, but J. F. Curwen casts some doubt on the suggestion. Thomas and Agnes are thought to have had two sons and two daughters. These included Henry [i] and William (from whom the Curwen's of Kendal are thought to have decended). Following Agnes' death, Thomas was married to Florens, widow of Thomas Foster (of Edderston) and sister of Thomas Wharton. They had two children, Thomas and Elizabeth. Thomas and his first wife Agnes are both thought to have been buried at St. Michael's Church, Workington.

Sir Henry [i] Curwen (c.1534-1597) was son of Thomas [iv] and Agnes Strickland. Inherited the Workington estates after his father's death in 1543. But as he was then *"not of age"*, Robert Turner, Sir Thomas Wharton, Walter Strickland and John Preston were appointed his guardians. In 1556, Henry was granted (upon a payment of £487) the Manor of Harrington, after it was forfeited to the crown on the execution of the Duke of Suffolk (father of Lady Jane Grey). [01]

He was Sheriff of Cumberland in 1561, 1570, 1580, 1589, 1590; and Knight of the Shire of Cumberland in 1554, 1555, 1556 and 1563.

It was Henry Curwen who was Lord of the Manor, at the time of Mary Queen of Scots famous visit to Workington (on 16 May 1568). However, some clear evidence exists which seems to suggest that Henry or his wife, were both then away in London, at the time. (see chapter eighteen)

In August 1570, Henry was included in the knights who went in pursuit of Scottish Reivers, in Galloway and Annandale. He is also said to have returned to Workington, with the iron gates of Carlaverock Castle. Afterwards these were believed to hang in the gatehouse entrance of the hall. J. F. Curwen comments that they remained there for *"some 300 years"*. Having visited Carlaverock and measured the likely openings which were then thought to have existed. It is difficult to find any that really correspond to the width of the arched opening at Workington Hall. It is sad to cast some doubt on such a legend, we would have dearily loved our measurements to match.

In 1580, Henry was appointed one of the commissioners for the survey of *"all the forts and castles upon"* the West Marches of the Borders; and to *"take a muster"* or list of all

ABOVE - signature of Mary Queen of Scots. Henry [i] Curwen was Lord of the Manor, at the time of her famous visit to Workington (on 16 May 1568). Whilst at the hall she wrote a letter to Elizabeth I, seeking her assistance. It is reproduced in full in chapter eighteen). ■

[01] It was Queen Mary I (1553-1558) and her husband Philip of Spain who made the grant of the Harrington estates to Henry Curwen. J. F. Curwen mentions that the original deed, dated 1 July 1556 - "bore splendid colour portraits of the grantors". Unfortunately he also notes (in 1899) that it was then "missing".   A fine white marble bust (or head) thought to be of Queen Mary was once on display in the main staircase area of Workington Hall.

men *"capable of bearing arms"*.

Around 1536, Henry purchased the estate of Sellow (Sella) Park at Calder Bridge from Thomas Fleming. J. F. Curwen believed this was formerly a *"deer-park"* belonging to Calder Abbey, and thought to have been granted to the Flemings, after Henry VIII's dissolution of the monasteries.

Like many of his ancestors, Henry married at least twice. His first marriage in 1548, was to Mary (daughter of Sir William Fairfax of Gilling Castle, Yorkshire). [01] They had four children, one son Nicholas [i] and three daughters. His second marriage was to Janet, daughter of Rev. Crosby of Camerton. They had seven children, three sons and four daughters. These included George, and Thomas (1590-1653) who later took over Sella Park estate. Sir Henry and his first wife are both thought to have been buried in the family vault of St. Michael's Workington.

Sir Nicholas [i] Curwen (1550-1604) born at Gilling Castle, son of Henry [i] and Mary Fairfax. Less than three months after Mary Queen of Scots famous stay at Workington (1568), Nicholas (then 18 and thought then to be a supporter of the Scottish Queen's cause) and six others were charged with causing a riot at Carlisle Cathedral. He appears to have escaped any punishment, likely by virtue of his father's prominent position.

Certainly by 1594, he is recorded in a letter as now being *"a gentleman loyal both to state and religion"* by Thomas Lord Scrope (then warden of English West Marches). Succeeded to the Workington estates following the death of his father in 1597. Appointed Sheriff for Cumberland in 1600 and 1601; and Knight of Shire of Cumberland in 1593. Knighted by James I at Lumley Castle in April 1603.

Prior to 1610, Nicholas rebuilt several parts of Workington Hall. J. F. Curwen commented that he *"transformed the old Border fortress into a Tudor mansion"*. (see chapter nine)

Sir Nicholas also married at least twice, his first wife was Anne (married c.1576), daughter of Sir Simon Musgrave of Hartley Castle. They had three children, two sons and one daughter, these included Henry [ii]. His second wife was Elizabeth (d.1611), daughter of Judge Thomas Carus of Halton (in Lancashire). They had three daughters, including Anne (1585-1606) who is buried in Lincoln Cathedral. His wife Lady Elizabeth Curwen, is thought to have given the site for Kirkby Lonsdale Free Grammar School (founded around 1591).

ABOVE - Sketch of the Curwen and Fairfax Coat of arms, just a small part of the large highly decorative carved overmantel in the Great Chamber at Gilling Castle, Yorkshire. The panel from the carving dated to around 1585, depicts the marriage of Henry [i] Curwen to Mary Fairfax, daughter of Sir William Fairfax. ◼

[01] A finely carved and painted sixteenth century Curwen and Fairfax coat of arms still exists along the lower edge of the timber overmantel of the fireplace, in the Great Chamber of Gilling Castle (now part of Ampleforth college). See sketch above. ◼

Sir Henry [ii] **Curwen** (d.1623) was the son of Nicholas [i] and Anne Musgrave. Succeeded to his father's Workington estates after his death in 1604. Married twice, his first wife was Catherine daughter of Sir John Dalton. They had two sons Patricius [i] and Thomas [v]. Around 1615 he was married again to Margaret, daughter of Thomas Buskill (or Bouskill) of Haversham. In 1626, Sir John Lowther claimed she was the former wife of Christopher Wright, one of the co-conspirator of the *"Gunpowder plot"*. In 1605, Wright along with Guy Fawkes and Robert Catesby had attempted to plant explosives under the Houses of Parliament. This appears never to have really been proven. William Whelan (in 1860) suggested that Henry's second wife's maiden name was actually *Wharton*.

Henry had nine children with Margaret, four sons and five daughters. These included Eldred [i], and Wilfred (1613-1661) who moved to live near Market Harborough and later had a grandson also called Henry (1691-1759), who married Mary daughter of Edward Spedding of Aikbank.

Sir Patricius Curwen (1601-64) son of Henry [ii] and Catherine Dalton. Succeeded to his father's Workington estates in 1623. Two years later, Charles I appointed him Knight of the Shire of Cumberland. Sir Patricius is recorded as pledging his allegiance to Charles I, desiring *"to present his service"* to the king's honour. J. F. Curwen comments that this was clear evidence that he followed *"the Royalist traditions of the family"*.

In 1637, appointed Sheriff of Cumberland, the same year Charles I introduced his *"Laudian"* or English style prayer book, to Scotland. The subsequent Presbyterian riots in Edinburgh and Scotland are well chronicled. From August 1638 Patricius was no doubt deeply involved, when plans were being prepared to transport hundreds of troops (by ship) to Workington (from Wales). They were urgently required to strengthen the borders from an expected Scottish revolt and invasion. In Feb 1639, Sir Nicholas Slanning may also have been greeted by Patricius, and entertained at the Hall, when he also arrived at Workington (by ship). With him he brought a further 60 of his *"best and old soldiers"* and 40 *"more besides"*, from Falmouth Fort in Cornwall. The *"West Country"* men brought with them sufficient *"victuals"* or supplies for two months, together with thirteen *"pieces of ordnance"* or artillery. Upon their arrival they joined nearly 600 Dragoons, already recruited and *"made ready"* from throughout Cumberland, Westmorland and Northumberland.

In July 1639, Sir Patricius (and Peter Senhouse) were later ordered to billet the soldiers at Isel, Sunderland Old

SIR PATRICIUS CURWEN
1601-1664

Sketch of Patricus Curwen based on an old oil painted wooden panel, which once hung in the Salon at Workington Hall. J. F. Curwen tells us the full painting shows Patricius in a slashed crimson doublet and truck hose, scarlet stockings, crimson garters and black shoes.

Park, Roseley and other adjoining places. They were still *"raised and ready"* in the spring of 1640. By the following August, the Scots did invade, but it was generally down the east coast towards Newcastle upon Tyne. Sir Patricius is then said to have raised another *"236 men, 160 muskets and 76 pikes"* just from the towns of the Allerdale Ward. It was estimated that the Scottish army would still then out number the English forces by around three to one. Charles I fearful of defeat being forced to buy them off.

During the Civil War, in the ensuing years Sir Patricius was involved in resisting the *Roundheads* in Cumberland. Not always successfully, for in Oct 1643, he is mentioned as re-treating from Millom; the day after Col. Huddleston's defeat. He was not at Carlisle Castle during it's long siege of 1644-5, but is said to have aided the Royalist garrison by sending foods and provisions. Unfortunately, it is not clear if he also fought with the *Cavaliers* at *Nantwich* (Jan 1644), *Marston Moor* (July 1644) or *Naseby* (June 1645).

After the King's execution, as a result of his staunch support for Charles I, Sir Patricius (along with many others) was ordered to pay a massive £2000 compensation to Parliament. We may well question his ability to pay such a sum, which today (1998) may equate to many millions of pounds. However, J. F. Curwen records that when he had married Isabella Selby in 1619, he may well have received a substantial dowry of £7000.

Around 1662, with Charles II now on the English throne, Sir Patricius was now actively involved in the persecution of the religious Nonconformists, particularly the Quakers. Records show he *"seized all the leading Quakers"* at Cockermouth (perhaps as many as sixty), nearly all were convicted under the penal laws. In a letter dated 24 Aug. 1663, to the Secretary of State, he stated *"The Quakers are now more quiet, and diligence will keep them in order"*.

At Houghton-le-Spring in 1619, Sir Patricius married Isabella (d.1666), daughter of Sir George Selby of Whitehouse, Durham. They had one child Henry, who died (at Amersham, Bucks) in 1636, aged just fourteen. Still today, on the chancel wall of St. Mary's Church, Amersham is a large highly decorative carved alabaster and black marble monument (by Edward Marshall) in remembrance of young Henry. J. F. Curwen describes it as *"quaint and almost grotesque"*. But Pevsner says it is a *"very beautiful hanging monument in the mannerist style...the upright figure in shroud with twisted stance"* resembling a Michelangelo figure.[01] Unfortunately, even if Henry had actually survived his father, he may not have inherited the Workington estates. For a clause in his grandfathers will, specified his uncle Thomas [v] should succeed Patricius.

"Around 1662, Sir Patricius Curwen *"seized all the leading Quakers"* at Cockermouth (perhaps as many as sixty), nearly all were convicted under the penal laws".

[01] A photograph of the monument appears in J. F. Curwen's History of the *Ancient House of Curwen*.

Sir Patricius (along with his wife) are thought to have been buried in the Curwen family vault *"upon the south side of the Parish church of Workington"* amongst their ancestors. His burial is the first member of the Curwen family recorded in the earliest surviving St Michael's parish register. On 12 April 1665, a grand state funeral for Sir Patricius took place in Workington, It is said to have cost a massive £680, an amazing sum for the time.

Thomas [v] Curwen (1605-72) son of Henry [ii] and Catherine Dalton. In 1664, succeeded to the Workington estates following the death of his brother Patricius. Even if Patricius had a surviving heir, Thomas would have still inherited the manor, by virtue of a clause in his father's will. Thought to have resided at Workington Hall, for much of the time his brother was away during the Civil War. He is also believed to have passionately defended Patricius' estates or *"goods from being sequestrated"*, because of his support for Charles I. (see previous entry) Around 1650, soon after he was made a Justice of the Peace, complaints were made again that he too had supported and fought with the *"Royalist"* enemy. No action appears to have been taken and he seems to have remained in office.

One explanation for the Curwens escaping any obvious punishment for supporting Charles I, is suggested in the writings of J. F. Curwen. His 1899 paper read to the C&WA&AS, describes some of the *"precious family heirlooms"*, then displayed at Workington Hall. He tells us of a *"silver snuff box given by Cromwell to his general, Fairfax on his marriage to Miss Curwen"*. It is said he came to Workington to sequester (or seize) the family estates, but instantly fell in love with Miss Curwen. He later sent back a favourable report and the family escaped with just the heavy fine previously mentioned. Unfortunately, J. F. Curwen does not seem to be able to clearly identify this *"Miss Curwen"* or the General Fairfax. [01] Further research by myself has also drawn a blank. Both Thomas [v] and Patricius (his brother) appear to have died without having any surviving children. Thomas is thought to have been unmarried, although he was once believed to have been betrothed to Dorothy Delavall, the niece of Lady Isabella (his brother's wife).

There is perhaps another quite plausible explanation for the Curwen family being in possession of this *"Fairfax snuff box"*. Between 1656-8, William Christian of Ronaldsway (the uncle of John Christian Curwen's great-grandfather) was appointed Governor of the Isle of Man, by Sir Thomas Fairfax. Perhaps the item entered the family around this time and it's true origins are now clouded in the previous legend, it is certainly much more romantic.

He tells us of a *"silver snuff box given by Cromwell to his general, Fairfax on his marriage to Miss Curwen"*.

[01] It has been extremely difficult to determine the true identity of both the Miss Curwen and the General Fairfax, referred to by J. F. Curwen. Some suggest it was Thomas Fairfax (1612-71) of Otley, Yorkshire. He was certainly Commander in Chief of the Parliamentary Forces, but there are numerous other Fairfaxes, not all of which can be so accurately traced. There seems to be no reference to a Fairfax-Curwen wedding around that time. ∎

Eldred [i] **Curwen** (d.1673) was the son of Henry [ii] and his second wife Margaret Buskill. Succeeded to the Workington estates in 1672, following the death of his half brother Thomas [v]. Sadly his period as Lord of the Manor of Workington was short lived as he died after just nine weeks at the Hall. Records suggest he had been a Captain in the Royalist armies. Previously he had lived at Rottington, and was buried at St. Bees Church. He married only once, to Catherine (d.1710), daughter of Michael Wharton of Beverley. They had four children, which included Henry [iii] and two who are believed to have died quite young.

Henry [iii] **Curwen** (1661-1725) the only surviving son of Eldred [i] and Catherine Wharton. Succeeded to the Workington, Harrington and Camerton estates, after the death of his father in 1673 (when around just 13 years old). In 1686, appointed Justice of Peace and later Sheriff for Shire of Cumberland in 1688 (by Catholic King James II).

Henry was also recorded as being a staunch Papist and ardent supporter of Roman Catholicism cause. At a time when it was in direct conflict with the now well established Anglican church. In December 1687, whilst still County Sheriff it was alleged he arranged for a ship laden with arms to be sent from Workington over to Ireland; where many of the population also supported James II's *"Catholic"* intents. When news of the ship's imminent departure reached Sir John Lowther (1655-1700). He and Andrew Huddleston with their tenants rode overnight the 40 miles or so to Workington. in order to seize the arms. Lowther later wrote of his journey as having *"infinite difficulties"*, the nights *"were at their longest"*; dark and the *"weather tempestuous"*; several horses were lost as they passed through *"places boggy"*, and extremely mountainous with rivers *"raised by disolving frost and snow"*. Some 500 muskets with bayonets, bandoliers, and cartridges were said to have been found, mostly hidden under a cargo of coal. Sir John reported *"All are in my custody.....and safe out of the hands of Papists"*. Henry was never charged, perhaps because there was no clear evidence linking him with the event.

From around 1689-96, He is thought to have disappeared abroad. Although some mystery surrounds the exact circumstances of his departure and his long absence. J. F. Curwen believed that Henry was a true *"Jacobite at heart"* and a fervent supporter of James II's Catholic causes. He states that *"along with his cousin Charles Pelham, he followed James into exile"*. Just months earlier in December 1688, James II had been forced to abdicate and to seek refuge in France. Here he hoped to persuade Louis XIV (the French King) to provide him with an army, to forcibly return and

In1687, it was alleged *Galloping Harry* arranged for a ship laden with arms to be sent from Workington over to Ireland. Hidden under a cargo of coal were some 500 muskets with bayonets, bandoliers, and cartridges.

create a Roman Catholic England.

Did Henry Curwen actually follow the King to France? If what J. F. Curwen tells us is correct, we can perhaps place him in France around this time. For Henry is thought to have acquired two of his famous stallions *"Curwen Bay Barb"* and *"Thoulouse Barb"*, from the sons of French King Louis XIV. Some have suggested Henry fought as a mercenary in the French armies, it was certainly common practise for Louis to recruit foreigners, including many Scots. It is also conceivable that he may have made a business of recruiting and supplying the French with high quality fighting men, obviously for a price. Certainly some evidence points to him amassing quite a fortune, during his absence. But he is unlikely to have received his fortune from former English king, it was accepted that James II had an *"empty treasury"*.

Although there appears to be no obvious evidence to confirm his collaboration with the French. Henry first disappeared as James II's war engulfed Ireland from 1689-91. Perhaps he did actively fight alongside the former King. We know that Louis XIV supported his cause, and his convoy of ships from France to Ireland, carried many English and Scottish Jacobite officers. Furthermore, many nationalities were also known to have fought on both sides during these conflicts. The long series of pitched battles and sieges were brought to a end with James II defeat at the Battle of the Boyne (July 1690), afterwards he fled again back to France.

If Henry Curwen was then an active and close sympathizer of James II, then perhaps he came in contact with the French court through this association. It is also likely Henry's fortune came from the extremely rich Louis XIV, not just for the supply of troops, but also from spying activities for the French king. The prized horses of Louis the *"Sun King"* may well have been received in recognition of services to the French Court. Romantic, but not totally inconceivable, Louis was renowned for bestowing often large bribes and gratuities on people from both his allies and his enemies. This way the powerful and very rich French king could assemble not just intelligence on his opponents, but sometimes find the true motives and plans of those he apparently supported.

As nothing was heard of Henry for many years, it was assumed he had died. In August 1696, Darcy Curwen of the Sella Park estates (the grandson of Henry [i] and son of Thomas) formally claimed the inheritance of Workington estate. But within less than a month of Darcy's claim being approved at the Carlisle Court, Henry made a surprise return to Workington. Ousting a disappointed Darcy from the estate and taking up residence again at the Hall.

After almost seven years, Henry made a surprise return to Workington. Ousting a disappointed Darcy from the estate and taking up residence again at the Hall.

Again Henry appears to have continued to openly display his Catholic beliefs, when they were now seemed to be scorned upon even more than before his departure. According to several entries in the diaries of Bishop Nicolson. Henry Curwen *"the papist"* was frequently *"surly and disrespectful"* to the Bishop. Between 1714-25, although not specifically named, he is also thought to have been one of 14 known Papists then living in Workington, listed in Bishop Gastrell's *Notitia*. [01]

During the Jacobite uprising of 1715, when suspected as a likely leader or supporter of the cause, he was also amongst those detained at Carlisle Castle. Although the actual term of his imprisonment cannot be determined, J. F. Curwen believed it could not be more than a few months. While detained, it is unlikely that he was badly treated, being not just a former Sheriff, but also an important landowner. Henry's *"house arrest"* may well have also secured the Curwen estates for the benefit of future generations. Many of those who took an active part in the rebellion, later found themselves *"condemned to death"* and their estates confiscated to the crown.

Henry is thought to have acquired the legendary *"Galloping Harry"* title, by virtue of his horse-racing and breeding activities. Today, all modern thorough-bred race horses are known to have as common ancestors, one or more of just three stallions, one of which is the famous *Godolphin Barb*. All were imported into Great Britain from the Middle East and North Africa, between 1689 and 1724. Henry Curwen's *Curwen Bay Barb* and *Thoulouse Barb* were without doubt a close relative of this *Godolphin Barb*. When mated with the strong English mares, they were legendary for producing offspring with both speed and endurance. Unfortunately the *British Stud* records were only began in 1791, so direct links cannot be fully determined. But many racehorses today are more than likely to have one of Henry Curwen's horses as their ancestors.

As *Galloping Harry* or Henry [iii] was to die without an heir, the Workington estates then passed to Henry [iv] Curwen, the eldest son of Darcy Curwen (of Sella Park). This Henry [iv] was the grandson of Thomas (1590-1653), a half brother of Nicholas [i]. Nicholas was Henry [iii]'s great grandfather.

After Darcy had attempted to seize the Workington estates, during Henry's absence. Relations between these two branches of the family, living just seventeen miles apart, became very strained and bitter. So much so that Henry bequeathed the remainder of his estates (which included both the manors Seaton and Camerton), to *"his well beloved kinsmen"* Sir Michael Wharton (of Beverley) and Charles Pelham (of Brocklesby, Lincs). J. F. Curwen comments that these

Henry [iii] Curwen acquired the legendary *"Galloping Harry"* title, by virtue of his horse-racing and breeding activities.

[01] For more information on Bishop Gastrell's *Notitia*, see the bibliography after chapter eighteen. ■

"ultimately fell into the hands of the great rival family of Lowther by purchase". As a result, future generations of the Curwens would now find themselves subjected to often acrimonious feuding with this other prominent local family.

J. F. Curwen recounts the famous ghost story of Workington Hall telling us: *"The story goes that when Galloping Harry was nigh unto death a French lady and her maid took him by the heels and pulled the old man down the stairs to a lower room, where they seated him in a high-backed chair. Telling the servants that their master was much better and was not to be disturbed, they immediately decamped with all the available jewellery and embarked in a small vessel from the harbour. Fifty years later an old woman appeared in Workington and reported that she had been the maid, that their vessel had been wrecked off the Scilly Islands, her mistress drowned and the valuables lost".*

Some speculate that *Galloping Harry's* death was arranged by members of his own family, perhaps the Sella Park branch, who are known to have fued with him. Whether he was murdered on not is a mystery yet to be solved. Henry died on 25 May 1725 and was buried at Workington.

Henry [iv] Curwen (1680-1727) was the eldest surviving son of Darcy (1643-1722) and Isabel Lawson, daughter of Sir Wilfred Lawson. He inherited the Workington, Winscales & Harrington estates in 1725, after the death of *Galloping Harry* or Henry [iii]. Sadly he only held and enjoyed the manor for just over two years. In July 1727, he died *"by a fall from his horse"* in London, being interred in the North west vault of St. Swithin's Church. He is recorded as being married, but his wife's identity is not clear; they are thought to have had at least one daughter, Mary.

Eldred [ii] Curwen (1692-1745) son of Darcy (1643-1722) and Isabella Lawson. Inherited the Workington estates in 1727, after the death of his brother Henry [iv]. In 1710, he was commissioned officer in *"ye excise"* (or customs officer), serving initially in Somersetshire. Appointed Sheriff of Cumberland in 1730. Following the death of his grandfather, Sir Wilfred Lawson, was elected MP for Cockermouth from 1734-41. Eldred married Julian Clenmore of Cornwall and they had at least seven children (some say maybe as many as seventeen), two sons and five daughters. These included Henry [v], Jane and Isabella (who married the Rector of St. Michael's, Rev W.Thomas Addison in 1749). Jane (1682-1762) married John Christian (1719-1767) in Sept 1745, and became the parents of John Christian (who later married his cousin Isabella Curwen and adopted the name John Christian Curwen). Eldred [ii] is thought to be buried at Workington.

Yet still that awful noise is heard
Which starts you from your bed,
That awful bumping down the stair
Of Henry's dying head.

ABOVE - signature of Eldred [ii] Curwen. ∎

HENRY [v] **CURWEN** 1728-1778

ISABELLA CURWEN 1765-1820

Based on the famous full length portrait by George Romney, reproduced in full on page 144. ■

Henry [v] **Curwen** (1728-1778) was the son of Eldred [ii] and Julian Clenmore. In 1745, succeeded to the Workington and Harrington estates after the death of his father. In 1753 was elected Sheriff of Cumberland, and between 1761-8 served as MP for the City of Carlisle. At the 1768 Parliamentary election for the County seat, Henry headed the poll and defeated his arch local rival Sir James Lowther (a Tory) by 161 votes. This was thought to have been the catalyst for years of often bitter and acrimonious feuding between the two families. The effects of which were clearly evident in the later affairs of Workington Harbour. (see chapter seven) and also St. Michael's Church (see chapter six)

J.F. Curwen states that Henry *"threw himself heart and soul into the development of the land and the prosperity of his people"*. He is benefited with opening up much of Workington's coalfield, including the installation of it's first really efficient steam engines. Furthermore he is thought to have build the *"Moorbanks"* waggonway (or railway) from Banklands to the harbourside; over which coal was efficiently transported for loading into ships (via hurries) on the quayside. Henry also built the first quay at Harrington, which developed into a thriving harbour.

He married Isabella, the only daughter of William Gale, a prominent Whitehaven merchant. They had two daughters, one of which died in infancy. The other Isabella, later married her first cousin John Christian, the son of Jane Curwen (also daughter of Eldred [ii], Isabella's aunt and her father's sister). Henry died 23 June 1778 and is known to be buried at St. Michael's Church, Workington.

Isabella Curwen (1765-1820) only surviving daughter of Henry [v] and Isabella Gale. J.F. Curwen tells us that upon the death of her father in 1778, the *"exceedingly long line of possessors of Workington, lasting over 650 years, was for the first time broken in its male decent"*. Isabella, then not even thirteen years old, found herself the heiress to here father's valuable estates.

As it would be many years until she could legally inherit her father's considerable fortune. Henry's executors maintained the estates, (including repairs to Workington Hall) and continued the day-to-day management of his extensive collieries and the harbours at both Workington and Harrington. Because of her fortune, the young heiress was certainly not without many proposals of marriage. Susan Hicks-Beach in her 1956 book *Yesterday's Behind Closed Doors*, lists at least six suitors including Lord Maitland and Lord Cranstoun. All appear to have been politely refused in favour of her first cousin John Christian (of Unerigg Hall, Maryport) the son of Jane Curwen her aunt. (see previous entry)

As Isabella was then only seventeen, the couple (forbidden by law to marry in England) essentially *"eloped"* over the border into Scotland. Being married in Edinburgh on Wednesday 9 October 1782. The event and general celebrations throughout the town being vividly recorded in the *Cumberland Pacquet*. As soon as the news arrived *"the bells were immediately set a ringing; next morning all the ships in the harbour displayed their colours; the bells rang at intervals throughout the day; the guns were fired, and in the evening every house in the town was illuminated"*.

She became an active and fervent supporter of her husband in his political career. So much so that in 1817, William Blamire (nephew of John Christian Curwen) [01] once suggested she herself would make an ideal Whig or *"blue"* member. [02] Highly flattered by the proposal, she wrote *"were it not for the trifling incumbance of my petticoats I think I might do very well, I could cover my expenses (for once at least) by the sale of my diamonds"*. Unfortunately, it was to be over a century later before the first woman MP was elected and women were to be given the right to vote.

Interestingly, in the famous portrait of Isabella, painted by George Romney (copy in Helena Thompson Museum) she is shown wearing a blue sash around her waist. She later confessed it was worn to show her allegiance to her husband's party. It has been suggested that Romney was asked to add the sash many years after the original portrait was first painted.

In the spring of 1781, Isabella is thought to have purchased *Long Holme* (an island on Lake Windermere). Although some accounts suggest it was purchased for her by her future husband, using her money. The island was later to be initially renamed *Bella Isle* after Isabella herself, later to be slightly corrupted to it's present name *Belle Isle*. Occasionally, their Windermere home was also referred to as *"Curwen's Island"*.

The house once described as *"a beautiful elysium"* [03] and the thirty eight acre island then cost just 1640 guineas (or £1722). Which seems quite a bargain as the previous owner is said to have spent around £6000 building the house and landscaping the gardens. Belle Isle is thought to be the first truly circular house, built anywhere in Britain. Designed by John Plaw and built around 1774, it is 55 feet (16.9m) diameter, and roofed in a dome. The only projecting section is the portico over the front entrance. (see sketch page 54).

In the Spring of 1783, shortly after their return from a honeymoon in Paris and other parts of Europe, John Christian Curwen began planning the enlargement of Harrington Harbour, first erected by Isabella's father. Her husband renamed the harbour *Bellaport*, again in honour of his new wife.

[01] Willaim Blamire (1790-1862) was the son of Jane Christian, sister of John Christian Curwen. Like his uncle he too was an ardent Whig, becoming the MP for Cumberland in 1831. He also shared his loved for agriculture, his chief interest being the breeding and rearing stock. Blamire frequently stayed at Workington Hall, and was a member of the *Workington Agricultural Society*. ∎

[02] The use of the colour blue was then associated with the Whig party (later the Liberals). Dr. Henry Lonsdale wrote in 1867, *"In Cumberland, the Whigs always hoisted blue banners, and the Tories yellow ones"*. Instead of the party name, the names Blues and Yellows were often more generally used, particularly in newspapers. Today of course blue is now associated with the Conservatives, (formerly the Tories) and once the principle opposition of the Whigs. Exactly when they adopted the blue flag cannot has not been determined. The Conservative Association have no clear records and neither do the Liberal Democrat History Group. ∎

[03] Description from the *Kendal Chronicle* of Aug 1819. An *"elysium"* is a place assigned to happy souls or a delightful place. ∎

Confirmation of the love and devotion between Isabella and her first cousin John Christian (later John Christian Curwen) is displayed in a letter from Christian Curwen to his agent Charles Udale, sent soon after his marriage. In it he wrote of his joy and said *"I am as happy as my fondest wishes could desire"*. (see next entry) His beloved Isabella died on 21 April 1820 and was buried at St. Michael's Church three days later.

John Christian Curwen (1756-1828) son of Jane Curwen, the daughter of Eldred [ii] and John Christian (1719-1767) of Unerigg and Milntown. Was only six when his mother passed away, and just eleven when his father died. [01] His uncle Henry [v] Curwen being appointed his legal guardian. Henry Lonsdale in his 1867 *Worthies of Cumberland*, suggests he may well have contributed greatly to his *"juvenile days"*, surmising that the young John Christian spent much of his youth at Workington Hall.

In Sept 1775 he first married Margaret, the daughter of John Taubman of Castletown, Isle of Man; they had one son also John. [02] Sadly his first wife was to die suddenly in Feb 1778, just a few months before his uncle Henry [v] Curwen. After Margaret's death John Christian spent much of his time travelling to Europe, making lengthy trips to France, Germany, Bohemia (Czechoslovakia) and Switzerland.

In October 1782, he married his first cousin Isabella Curwen (see previous entry) and later adopted the surname Curwen - previously being known as simply John Christian. Became Lord of the manor upon his marriage to the Curwen heiress. From around 1792, he became an active farmer and agricultural reformer, building his own experimental model farm at Schoose. (see chapter thirteen). He was also responsible for the last major alterations [03] and restyling of Workington Hall and it's grounds, between 1783-87. Appointing John Carr of York as his architect and Thomas White of Nottingham as his landscape gardener. (see chapter nine)

J.F. Curwen suggested that the young John Christian Curwen was educated at Eton and Cambridge. But Susan Hicks-Beach in her Christian family biography, states there was no trace of him in the Eton school records. Furthermore, she believed the heir to the Unerigg and Milntown estates actually *"rejected the suggestion of Cambridge"* and was first married at the age of just nineteen. Either way, his later life and writings certainly reveal he did receive a good standard of education.

He was High Sheriff of Cumberland in 1784, MP for Carlisle City for over thirty years (from 1786-1812 and 1816-1820). From April 1820, he was elected MP for Cumber-

JOHN CHRISTIAN CURWEN
1756-1828

[01] William Whellan (in 1860), Lonsdale (1867) and others appear to mistakenly record John Christian (father of John Christian Curwen) as dying in 1757, not 1767. ■

[02] John Christian (1776-1852), son of John Christian (Curwen) and Margaret Taubman became an attorney, and was later the Deemster (or judge) of the Isle of Man. He was also involved in a well-documented altercation with famous novelist Walter Scott, over how two of his ancestors were depicted in Scott's *Peveril of the Peak*. This appears to have been finally resolved with the help of poet William Wordsworth. He first met John Christian when they were both staying at Workington Hall, a few months before his son John married Jane Curwen. Wordsworth later wrote to his long-time friend Walter Scott, and subsequent editions of the novel, included a long Appendix (provided for him by John Christian) correcting the historical inaccuracies.

[03] It was of course only the *"last major"* works at the Hall, if we ignore Allerdale District Council's efforts to create the *"stable ruin"*, we see today.

land, holding the seat until his death on 10 December 1828. Believed to have been offered a peerage on at least two occasions (in 1801 and 1822) but declined the honour. In February 1815, received the freedom of the City of Edinburgh.

For almost all his political career in Parliament, his Whig party [01] were in opposition and certainly in the minority. This did not deter Christian Curwen from making many quite eloquent and prominent speeches. The Hansard parliamentary reports for this period, mention numerous debates in the Commons involving Christian Curwen. In May 1816, his extremely long and stirring speech in support of the Poor Laws, later occupied over eleven pages when printed in the report.

Anxious to graphically illustrate to the House of Commons the severe poverty and poor diet of his *"Cumbrian peasantry"*. Christian Curwen is said to have made a remarkable appearance in the House of Commons, wearing a woollen country suit of hodden grey, and heavy Cumberland clogs on his feet. Under one arm he carried a *"Brown Geordie"* (a leavened loaf of barley and rye bread, baked on the floor of the oven) and a hard Whillimoor cheese [02] under the other. With a huge *"gully"* knife he is said to have began cutting the hard black crust of the loaf producing a noise *"resembling the crushing of cinders"*. Dramatic perhaps, but his sensational actions are thought to have clinched the argument. One wonders how today's media would have covered such an event.

In 1809, he introduced a successful private member's Bill to the house in order to prevent bribery and corruption at Parliamentary elections. It became know as the *"Curwen Act"* and curbed the blatant sale of parliamentary seats to supporters. He was also responsible for promoting bills through Parliament for the Repel of the Salt Tax, Amending the Tithe Laws, and the Removal of Duty from Agricultural horses.

In the House of Commons on more than one occasion, Christian Curwen was prompted to defend the rights and independence of the *"House of Keys"*. The governing body of the Isle of Man, his ancestral family home. His well-argued and successful speeches earned him high praise and respect from the Manx residents. In November 1806, he had also established another agricultural society on the island, closely linked to his own *Workington Agricultural Society* (see chapter thirteen). Henry Lonsdale recorded in 1808, the grateful *"natives of the Isle of Man"* presented him with a *"fine silver vase, about two feet (60cm) in height, on a large inscribed salver, costing about 200 guineas (£210)"*.

J. F. Curwen tells us that in 1812, Christian Curwen first retired from Parliament *"because it was felt by his constituents that he urged forward agricultural questions in detri*

[01] The Whigs, were one of the two dominant political parties in Great Britain. from the 1680s to the 1830s. Led by a group of great landowning families, it drew its support mainly from the business classes and the Nonconformists. It advocated development of industry and commerce, a vigorous foreign policy, religious tolerance and parliamentary reform.

At the time Christian Curwen was an MP, the Whigs were in opposition. For seventy years (from 1760) the Tories retained balance of power in Great Britain. By a coalition with the Radicals, the Whigs later became known as the Liberal party. Traditionally in opposition to the Whigs, were the Tory party. The Tories later became known as the Conservatives from around 1836. ∎

[02] Whillimoor is an area close to the West Cumbrian village of Arlecdon. Rev. Edward Haigh Sugden in his 1897 history of the parish, described the hard cheese made from skimmed milk as *"not very appetising"*. Whilst William Dickinson, the local historian and poet wrote the following poem in 1862.

Fwok jibes aboot Whillimoor cheese,
An' mebby it's nea girt cracks;
But if you can't cut't wid a knife,
we can saw't through or hag't wid an axe.

ment to the interests of this manufacturing borough". At the time the country was gripped by the Napoleonic war. Vital and essential food imports were being blockaded by the French navy, as Bonaparte attempted to starve Britain into surrender. Christian Curwen strenuously believed to *"supply the sheer necessities of life"*, major improvements in British agriculture had to have priority. This draws into perspective his comments made just before the 1812 election, where he states *"Agriculture, I have uniformly contended, was the vital interest of the empire, manufactories, colonies and foreign commerce, its ornaments."*

These thoughts and reactions of his constituents shocked Christian Curwen. He felt betrayed, his past achievements on their behalf now apparently meaningless and so easily forgotten. With his enthusiasm and spirit so *"momentously"* destroyed, he like many other politicians (then and now) decided simply to retire. We know he sort some solace at his beloved Schoose Farm. For recorded in his 1812 annual *Workington Agricultural Society President's Report,* (between such mundane tasks as spreading manure and gathering potatoes) are his quite poignant thoughts of the 7th October.

"A bright day gave interest and animation to the scene.....What the result of twenty seven years of public life.....The calm and mildness of the day, the peaceful stillness of the surrounding scenery, formed a striking contrast to the bustle, riot and confusion, on which I so recently turned my back.....Fearlessly I must look forward.....Solaced by these reflections, I firmly resolved to bend the whole force of mind to the promotion of agricture.....My farm had hiterto formed but one important link in the chain of my occupations.....disengaged from all my public concerns, it remains my sole pursuit".

For the next four years, Christian Curwen appears to have concentrated on his farms and collieries, together with his other business interests in the town. But when the by-election of March 1816 was called, all had been forgotten and he was persuaded to stand again, being triumphantly re-elected. He was to retain the seat again, at the August 1818 general election serving till Parliament was dissolved in 1820, following the death of George III.

In March that same year, he was elected again as MP for Carlisle and also as MP for Cumberland, deciding to represent only the county seat. Less than a month later his wife Isabella sadly died (see previous entry). J. F. Curwen commented that a sombre Christian Curwen did *"hasten away from her graveside to re-enter Parliament as the unserving friend of both religious and civil liberty".*

On 10 May 1825, he made his final speech in Parliament, when he moved the Third Reading of the Roman Catholic Relief Bill. After prolonged debate and an ardent strug-

"With John Christian Curwen's enthusiasm and spirit so *"momentously"* destroyed, he like many other politicians (then and now) decided simply to retire".

gle, the bill to give people freedom and liberty to practice that religion, successfully passed through the House of Commons, only to be defeated in the Lords. Sadly the elderly Workington Squire was to die, just five months before the next Catholic emancipation bill finally became law in April 1829.

Many have strongly suggested that should the Whigs have been elected to form a government, during his time in Parliament. Then it is certainly likely that Christian Curwen may well have been given a prominent Cabinet position. Although Susan Hicks-Beech, whose grandfather Samuel Christian (1786-1852) was a cousin of Christian Curwen, wrote in her family biography; *"he was too original and independent to be the comfortable colleague beloved by Prime Ministers"*.

In 1808, Christian Curwen wrote a book entitled, *Hints on the Economy of Feeding stock and bettering the condition of the Poor*. In which he outlined much of what he had developed and achieved at Schoose. Together with some valuable details of the various Benefit Societies, [01] he had created many years earlier amongst Workington's working classes. Every fortnight around 3d (just over 1p) was deducted from his workers wage packet, and paid into a fund to aid *"the recovery of the sick, the support of the declining and the education of the young"*. To every ten pounds raised by these contributions, Christian Curwen personally added a further three pounds to the fund.

He then told how for over ten years, any member of these various societies who was unable to work (through sickness or disability) had each received five shillings weekly, until they were sufficiently recovered to return to work. In addition all doctor's fees, incurred by members were always paid direct from society funds. He also wrote how his plan so readily accepted by the *"labouring classes"* could and should be applied in every town, throughout the country. Essentially John Christian Curwen had then created in Workington, today's equivalent of the National Health Insurance. Although his Benefit Societies were active almost a 120 years before the national scheme would became effective.

J. F. Curwen also records how between 1795-1800, Christian Curwen planted around 815000 oak, ash, larch, beech, Scotch fir, elder and elm trees along the shoreline of Lake Windermere. Many of the acorns being brought by ship into Workington harbour. He is also thought to have been responsible for establishing the first sailing regattas on the lake. As a wedding present to Isabella, he purchased for Windermere, a *"elegant boat, ornamented in the most genteele manner, with awnings of oil-cloth, which will keep out the rain for 24 hours, and green silk curtains as a shelter from the sun"*.

"Essentially, John Christian Curwen had then created in Workington, today's equivalent of the National Health Insurance".

[01] Henry Lonsdale wrote *"Mr Curwen established the first Friendly Society as far back as 1783"*. From at least 1797, Workington had six active Benefit Societies, formed along Christian Curwen's guidelines. They were the Colliers, Sisterly, Honourable, Provisional, Schoose Farm and Friendly Societies. In 1808, he calculated that in total in excess of £735 was raised annually, yet the cost of maintaining the town's "sick and aged poor" was only around £600.

John Christian (Curwen) and Isabella had eight children (four sons and four daughters). These included Henry [vi], William (1789-1822) who was Rector of Harrington from 1817-23; and John Christian (1799-1840) who was the first curate of St. John's Church, Workington and later became Rector of Harrington from 1828-40.

Finally, Susan Hicks-Beach in her 1956 biography, paints an extremely sombre picture of an often *"moody and irritable"* elderly Christian Curwen. Alone after the death of his darling Isabella and almost retired from public life, he is said to have *"stalked about outdoors at Workington"*, in a shabby woollen suit. She quite ruthlessly suggests that his parliamentary labours had been *"well-nigh resultless"*, and his other enterprises *"just as ill-starred"*.

Surely not! granted Christian Curwen had lead a full and very active life, apparently spending much of his (and his wife's) fortunes on frequent and often lavish entertainment. But his many writings and energetic work clearly suggest he never really lost sight of helping and encouraging the less fortunate and poorer classes; particularly those who lived and worked for him in his beloved Workington. Today, everyone with a National Insurance number should remain eternally grateful and very proud of John Christian Curwen. For his Benefit Society structure alone is a sufficient and adequate legacy. Dr. Henry Lonsdale justifiably also placed him high amongst his *Worthies of Cumberland*. Christian Curwen died peacefully on 10 December 1828 and is believed to have been interred, with Isabella in the Curwen family vault below St. Michael's Parish Church.

Henry [vi] Curwen (1783-1860) the first son of Isabella Curwen and John Christian Curwen (see previous entries above). Appointed High Sheriff of Cumberland in 1834. He inherited the Workington estates upon the death of his father in 1828, when 35 years old. Previously, he is known to have lived quietly at the family's house upon Belle Isle, Windermere. Dorothy Wordsworth mentions in her letters that *"until the old man's death* (John Christian Curwen) *he had lived quite retired"*.

J. F. Curwen recounts a article from the *Kendal Chronicle* of Aug 1812, telling how Henry was visited there, by an elderly Dr. Samual Parr (1747-1825). Parr is described as the eminent *"English"* scholar, famous for his political and religious literature, and is said to have travelled extensively *"living with country gentlemen and clergymen, who flattered and feared him"* .[01] Exactly what effect Parr had on Henry is not recorded, they would appear to have certainly shared a strong interest in *"Whiggism"*. It is thought that one of his favourite pastimes was literary study, and a portrait once hung

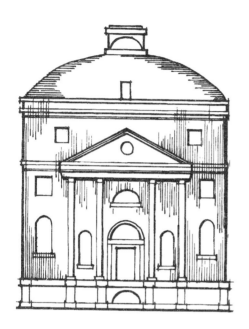

BELLE ISLE, WINDERMERE

Belle Isle remained in the Curwen family until the late 1980's. It was last occupied by Mr. and Mrs. Edward Curwen. In 1975, the house was opened up to the public for the first time. Edward Curwen acting as *"boatman"* transferring visitors back and forth to the island. Susan his wife, conducted the guided tours. I visited the house in August 1981 and particularly remember the high ceilings of the ground floor rooms. Here were also once displayed the *"Luck of Workington"* - the small agate cup and the elaborate gilt clock (said to have been given to the family by Mary Queen of Scots), together with a copy of George Romney's full length portrait of Isabella Curwen, the portrait of Mary Queen of Scots, and the Viking sword (said to have been found at Oystertanks - see page 28). Today the house is thought to belong to the Swinton Insurance Company, but is no longer open to the public. ∎

[01] Sydney Smith provided this description of Samuel Parr's travel habits in the Edinburgh Review (1802). His literary works, included strong evangelical sermons and political statements. In 1828, many of these and a mass of correspondence were published in eight volumes. ∎

in the Salon of Workington Hall, showing him with his books. He also met and dined with poet William Wordsworth, on several occasions both before and after the 1830 wedding of their children. (see below) Surprisingly, one would have thought that the two should have met much earlier, particularly as they had lived so very close to each other, in the heart of the Lake District. And we know from the Wordsworth letters that despite their clear political differences, they had been well acqainted with Henry's father, John Christian Curwen. But as Dorothy Wordsworth wrote in 1830, *"strange as it may appear we had never been in his company"*, until just months before the wedding.

In October 1804, Henry had also married his first cousin Jane (d.1853), daughter of Edward Stanley (merchant) of Whitehaven. Apparently, against the wishes of their families the couple eloped and were married at Gretna Green. Afterwards and for some time later they are also thought to have remained in Scotland.   They had at least eight children, five sons and three daughters. These included Edward Stanley (see next entry); Henry (1812-94) who was Rector of Workington from 1837-94; and Isabella (1806-1848) who married Rev. John Wordsworth, son of Poet Laureate, William Wordsworth.

Isabella's wedding took place at St. Michael's Church, Workington on 11 October, 1830. It was so eloquently described in several letters of the poet's famous sister Dorothy Wordsworth.   She tells how five carriages conveyed the families and guests from the hall to the church. *"The Wedding was a gay one if a large assemblage of affectionately attached relatives could make any wedding so.....All Workington was abroad making a lane for the carriages to drive through, some on house-tops, all windows crowded. The people shouted Hurra! Curwen for ever! and the two young brothers of the Bride outside her carriage kept off their hats, smiling and bowing all the way.....On their way from church they scattered silver among the people according to the family custom at Workington Hall.*

Guns were fired and ships in the harbour hoisted their flags......We all had a good cry - Fifty pepole sat down to Breakfast. Then departed the Bride and Bridegroom for Scotland". In addition her other letters described the bride as *"interesting in appearance rather than pretty or handsome; her manners and address are Lady-like, though perhaps at first even painfully shy; but that shyness soon wears off, though her modesty is always remarkable."*

William Wordsworth also affectionately mentioned the marriage of his eldest son in other correspondence. To novelist Sir Walter Scott he wrote of Isabella. *"We are quite charmed with her amiable disposition, her gentleness, her*

DOROTHY WORDSWORTH
1771-1855

Famous sister of Poet Laureate William Wordsworth, who wrote such a highly colourful account of the 1830 Workington wedding of Rev. John Wordsworth and Isabella Curwen, daughter of Henry [vi] Curwen. ■

delicacy, her modesty, her sound sense, and right notions - so that my son has a prospect before him as bright as any man can wish for." In other letters he described her as *"truely admirable, and her fortune such, as enables them to marry without im-prudence......The more we see of Miss Curwen the more are we pleased with her, and the higher are our hopes".*

Unfortunately, Isabella's health was not good and she was advised to spend at least the winter months abroad in a better climate. In 1843, she went to live in Rome taking with her the couple's children. Her husband John, despite his *"clerical"* duties stayed with them there for long periods of time. Sadly in December 1845, their youngest son Edward (Henry's grandson) when not quite five years old, died *"by an attack of fever".* The sad and melancholy *"tidings of his decease"* arrived from Italy, at the Wordsworth's Rydal Mount home on Christmas Eve. William Wordsworth later wrote *"the child lost was one of the noblest creatures both in mind and body I ever saw".* Soon afterwards he composed the 14 line sonnet entitled *Lines on the death of our Angelic Boy,* clearly portraying his grief at the loss of his grandson. Isabella herself died in 1848, and her father Henry [vi] died on 16 October 1860.

William Wordsworth's
Lines on the death of Angelic Boy

Why should we weep or mourn, Angelic boy,
For such thou wert ere from our sight removed,
Holy, and ever dutiful - beloved
From day to day with never-ceasing joy,
And hopes as dear as could the heart employ
In aught to earth pertaining ?   Death has proved
His might, his might and mercy, as beloved -
Not ignorant - that he only could destroy
The bodily frame. That beauty is laid low
To moulder in a far-off field of Rome;
But Heaven is now, blest Child, thy Spirt's home:
If this divine communion, which we know,
Is felt, thy Roman burial-place will be
Surely a sweet remembrancer of Thee.

WILLIAM WORDSWORTH
(1770-1850)

This is an early version of William Wordsworth's sonnet (composed in 1846) mourning the loss of his grandson Edward. The youngest son of Rev. John Wordsworth and Isabella Curwen, and also grandson of Henry [vi] Curwen. The copy above is taken from a original letter discovered amongst the Curwen papers, and is clearly written in Wordsworth's own hand. It is dated 1846, and was sent to Frances (wife of Edward Stanley Curwen), the sister-in-law of the child's mother. Lines 7, 8 & 12 differs slightly from that finally published in 1850. ■

Edward Stanley Curwen (1810-75) son of Henry [vi] and Jane Stanley. Inherited the Workington estates after the death of his father in 1860. Became a lieutenant in the 14th Light Dragons. He also was thought to have taken an active interest in the Curwen Coal mining business in the town. His initials can still be seen today, on the date stone of the western chimney at Jane Pit.

On 22 January 1833, he married Frances, daughter of Edward Jesse of Hampton Court. The poet William Wordsworth (father-in-law of Edward's eldest sister Isabella) wrote the couple a charming letter just a few weeks later. It began *"I cannot deny my self the pleasure of joining my own congratulations with those of your family and offering them to you upon this event. Your dear sister with whom I have the satisfaction of being so nearly connected speaks feelingly of her new sister and rejoices in the union"*.

They had at least eight children, five sons and three daughters. These included Henry Fraser (1834-1900); Alfred Francis (1835-1920) who became the Rector of Harrington between 1862-1920) and Edward Hassell (b.1847) who became Rector of Plumbland in 1875. Edward Stanley died at Cowes, on 1 April 1875.

As this volume of The History of Workington covers the period upto 1865. This completes the list of those principle members of the Curwen family who were Lords of the Manor of Workington. A further volume of this history is presently in preparation, covering the later period 1866-1955. Readers requiring additional Curwen family information, including that of those branches not directly relating to Workington. Are referred once again to John Flavel Curwen's *A History of the Ancient House of Curwen*, published in 1904 and 1928. This large book contains over 360 pages of his detailed notes, arranged chronologically wth detailed family trees. Unfortunately copies are now quite scarce and extremely sort after. Even reference copies at local libraries are rarely found. At Workington Public Library there is one, but it is *"kept in the safe"*, it is of course available on request.

John Flavel Curwen (1860-1932) was the son of Thomas Taylor Curwen. His father was the great-great-great-great grandson of Wilfred (1613-61), the son of Henry [ii] Curwen. He was to spent over two years researching almost every branch of his family which in 1904, extended to Austrialia and America. He was employed as an architect with a practise in Kendal, and also wrote numerous other books and articles relating to the history of the area. Being a well respected member of the C&WA&AS for forty years.

SOME OF THE CARVED STONES FOUND AT ST. MICHAELS CHURCH

CHRISTIANITY, CHURCHES & CHAPELS

THE arrival of Christianity in West Cumbria, is not easy to accurately chronicle or define. Christianity throughout Britain certainly existed during Roman times, and many of the Germanic fifth century invaders were already Christian. However the new faith in Romano-Celtic Britain, could hardly then be described as established and widespread. Even as late as AD600 although it was accepted that Britain was now largely Christian, there was also a visible resurgence of paganism. We know from the early biography of Pope Gregory (AD540-604) that the *Angli* from England were then still regarded as *"pagan"*.

Christianity when it arrived had all the attributes of Celtic paganism. It had ritual, legend and rites, with holy men to practise them. It had as it's central figure, a miracle worker and ancient beliefs. Furthermore, it offered a code for living and an afterlife. Because of this the Romanised-Celts of Cumbria seem to have embraced Christianity with relative ease.

The first British Christians were from the Celtic race, distant relations of the European Celts, who had began to settle in Britain from around 300BC. Locally, we know that the Brigantes had deep rooted Celtic beliefs. But it is also likely that through Roman occupation of West Cumbria, Christian Celts arrived from other areas. For instance, many non-Romans were conscripted into the Roman army, not just from throughout Britain, but from Gaul and beyond. These troops being generally sent to the frontiers of the Roman Empire, such as our region, thousands of miles from their homeland. This influx of other European Celtic cultures is clearly evident if we examine the Roman remains found at Maryport and elsewhere.

The Anglo-Saxon invaders gradually advanced, driving the Celtic Christians, *"further and further westward, into the hills of Cumberland, Wales, Cornwall and Devon, and beyond the seas to Ireland"*.

Charles Hole in his *Manual of English Church History*, tells us how the Anglo-Saxon invaders gradually advanced, driving the Celtic Christians, *"further and further westward, into the hills of Cumberland, Wales, Cornwall and Devon, and beyond the seas to Ireland"*. The term *"Celtic"* is usually applied in common to both the native churches of Britain and Ireland. It's form of worship was considered much simpler and less pretentious, than its Roman Church counterpart. This Celtic simplicity allowed the common people to relate more directly with teaching of the Gospel.

The early Christianity in West Cumbria, is undoubtedly from these Celtic origins.

It is generally accepted that Ireland was then the foremost centre of Christianity in Western Europe. From its monasteries, the Celtic Church sent out numerous missionaries and priests, to preach to and convert the pagan population. We know they travelled to the Scottish and Welsh coasts, and it is therefore quite certain they would have also visited the Cumbrian coast.

In addition the Celtic Church also became strongly rooted in Northumbria. Several histories chronicle the travels of the monks and priests, back and forth, between the North East and Ireland. We may speculate that they might often have sailed to and from the West Cumbrian coast, perhaps from the Derwent estuary. Stopping over on their journeys, to preach the gospel, to the local inhabitants. Frank Carruthers in his 1979 book *People of Cumbri* eloquently descrbed the Irish Sea as then *"more a highway than an obstacle or defence"*.

Perhaps one of the earliest to visit Workington, may well have been St. Ninian, the first great Scottish missionary. Charles Hole decribed Ninian as the *"Apostle of the Southern Picts"*. Around AD412-432, he founded Britain's first stone church, at Candida Casa (Whithorn) in Galloway. His work actually predating the establishment of the Roman church at Canterbury, by almost two centuries. It is quite conceivable that Ninian, who spent much of his life travelling and preaching Christianity to the Picts, did also visit West Cumbria. Whithorn being only a short distance across the Solway Firth. Add to this the simple observation that Ninian, is believed by many to have been born on the *"Cumberland shores of the Solway"* and this theory becomes a little more plausible.[01]

Like many other authors, Frank Carruthers expands on Ninian's life, and graphically speculates that he may have been the son of a Brigante chieftain. He then is vividly portrayed in many locations, throughout Cumbria, suggesting his likely wanderings and preachings. But Carruthers does not lose sight of fact that our only accounts of early Christianity are almost purely based on legend and tradition. However, he does conclude that *"Ninian's apostolate is the first distinct fact in the Christianization"* of our region, and as he is thought to come from a Christian family, *"the gospel had penetrated these parts"*, before his birth.

William Rollinson in his *History of Cumberland and Westmorland*, surmises on the legend of St. Patrick. also suggesting an early link to West Cumbria. Around AD389, when he was sixteen, Patrick was thought to have been

From its monasteries, the Church sent out numerous missionaries and priests, to preach to and convert the pagan population.

[01] Ninian's birthplace is first defined in his biography by Aelred of Hexham. It does not actually quote *"Cumberland"*, but appears to refer to the English side of Solway. We should be cautious of the fact that Aelred's writing were in the twelfth century, some seven hundred years after Ninian's death. How much is accurate or merely legend? ∎

captured by pirates and taken to Ireland and sold as a slave. These pirates are thought to have attacked Britain when the Romans left the Solway shores unprotected.[01] Rollinson like others implies that Patrick, may have actually been the son of a high-born Roman. Perhaps, being kidnapped from one of the coastal Roman forts, maybe even Burrow Walls.[02]

Many years later, Patrick escaped and trained as a monk at the famous French monastery of Lérins. He later returned to Ireland and established his first church. Like other Celtic missionaries, Patrick felt he must *"go into all the world"* and preach the *"gospel of Jesus"*. It is conceivable that he, (or other monks under his direction) are likely to have returned to the Cumbrian shores.

Later during the sixth century, St. Kentigren was known to have visited the area. He is also often referred to as St. Mungo, which simply means *"the beloved one"*. Rollinson describes St. Kentigren as Cumberland's *"County"* saint, referring to the number of Cumbrian churches, established in his name. Whilst he is more generally known as the *"Apostle of Strathclyde"*. It is said that Kentigren was the son of the Celtic Cumbrian prince, Owain. But his actual birthplace appears unclear, and is a puzzle and mystery yet to be solved.

He was made Bishop of Stathclyde (which then of course included Cumberland) when he was just 25 years old. Spending the next decade or so extending the Celtic Christian religion, throughout both southern Scotland and the north west of England (as we know it today). He is described as *"overturning images, building churches, defining parishes and ordaining clergy"*.

Frank Carruthers again in his *People called Cumbri*, sets out an almost plausible argument that Celtic Christianity, actually initially took root in Cumbria, before spreading to Ireland and beyond. Hinging his case on the fact that Ninan was Cumbrian born, and according to his biographers brought up in a Christian home. Furthermore, he is thought to have returned to work amongst his *"own people"*, late in the fourth century, before establishing Candida Casa.

In the seventh century, after the Celtic Church was re-established in Northumbria and Southern Scotland. We know from Bede that Cumbria was visited by St. Cuthbert. He made frequent visits, particularly to Carlisle as it lay in the old diocese of Lindisfarne. Bede says of Cuthbert *"He would resort most commonly to those places and preach in those hamlets lying far away in steep and craggy hills, which other people had dread to visit, and which from their poverty as well as upland rudeness teachers shunned to approach."*

ST. KENTIGERN or MUNGO

[01] The legend of St. Patrick, does not appear to actually specifically refer to the Solway, but mentions the Roman frontier down the west coast. Some other versions of this legend, often refer to his kidnapping from the Welsh coast. The date of the event is also suspect as so accounts give his capture as late as AD432. ■
[02] See chapter two, for more details of Burrow Walls. ■

62

VENERABLE BEDE
c.674-735

[01] Bede's Ecclesiastical History of English was completed around 731. It was originally written in Latin, but like other major religious works, it was later also translated into Anglo-Saxon. Apparently, in an attempt to revive the English Church, towards the end of the ninth century. ∎
[02] The bones of Bede, or what were considered such, were later moved to Durham Cathedral, with those of St. Cuthbert. ∎
[03] A curragh is a small boat, made of leather, stretched around a timber frame, usually driven by oars. Today, this type of boat is still used as a fishing boat in western Ireland. ∎
[04] This quote is from Symeon's *History of the Church of Durham*, translation of Symeonis - *Historia Dunelmensis Ecclesiae*. ∎

We should perhaps not discount the likelihood that the Venerable Bede (c.674-735) himself or one of his monks from Jarrow, would have also visited and preached in West Cumbria. We can cautiously link Workington to Bede's monastery at Jarrow, through the Anglo-Saxon stone (BC8) found at St. Michael's. (see sketch page 23) If its eighth century date iscorrect, it may be contemporary with Bede's time. As well as being a monk and presbyter (or elder) of Jarrow, Bede through his writings has provided us with a invaluable knowledge of English Ecclesiastical history.[01] One feels that it would be essential for him to have travelled throughout our region, to have assembled such a detailed account. After his death, Bede's tomb at Jarrow, also became the focus of many visiting monks and priests, hoping to revive *"holy memories of the past"*.[02]

Irish records also show that St. Adaman (679-704) sailed along the Solway coastline, on a *"mission to Saxonland"*. However, his exact route and any places where he may have stopped is unknown. It is suggested that he made the journey across the Irish sea, rowing in just a small leather curragh.[03]

St. Cuthbert died in 687, and was buried on Lindisfarne now known as Holy Island, off the Northumbrian coast. In West Cumbria we cannot escape from the presence of Cuthbert, either dead or alive. In 875, nearly two centuries after his death, and following many years of raids by the Vikings, Bishop Eardulf of Lindisfarne had no alternative but to evacuate Holy Island and seek safety elsewhere. Eardulf and his little band of fugitives, took with them the relics of St Cuthbert and other treasures of the monastery, including the Lindisfarne Gospels. Charles Hole (1910) referred to them as *"the Cuthbertines, a Church adrift, the sole representatives of Northumbrian Christianity"*.

For around seven years the small group moved from place to place throughout the North East and Cumbria. Their wanderings, being later chronicled at the beginning of the twelfth century by Symeon of Durham. By then the lives of the Celtic saints, particularly Cuthbert had become embellished with legend, myth and stories of miracles. We have no real accurate information of the route followed and how long they settled or spent at each point. Symeon [04] simply says they *"wandered throughout the whole district....like sheep flying before the face of wolves"*. At that time, obviously the north was overrun with the marauding Viking.

Battiscombe in his very studious 1956 book - *The Relics of St Cuthbert* sensibly comments that *"all that we can take for certain is that.......the wanderers got as far as west Cumberland.......to charter a ship and take the relics of St.*

Cuthbert and the rest of their treasures to Ireland". Obscurity again veils the journey, before their attempt to leave for Ireland from *"the mouth of the river which is called Dyrwenta"* (Derwent). It is thought that they had also settled for a while at Embleton and Lorton. Charles Hole comments that the group were *"distressed for provisions"*. Canon Rawnsley in *Round The Lake Country* suggests that they may have even sort refuge at the old Roman fort at Burrow Walls. But there is really no evidence to confirm this theory. However, it is not unreasonable to accept that where they rested the remains of St. Cuthbert, they would also preach Christianity to the settlers.

Interestingly one of the stone cross fragments, found at St. Michael's church, does suggest a further link to St. Cuthbert. The portion of sculptured stone BC4 (shown right) dated to around the tenth century, was found built into the wall of the old tower, after the July 1887 fire. Rev. W.S. Calverley (former Vicar of Aspatria) found an almost identical match to it's distinctive *"twist and ring"* pattern, in similar cross fragments at Chester-le-Street, in County Durham. St. Cuthberts remains were known to have been rested for many decades. William Slater Calverley (1847-1898) who devoted much of his life to recording existing Christian relics, throughout the county, positively assigns *the cross to the period of the Cuthbert pilgrimage"*.

When the attempt was made to take St. Cuthberts body across the Irish sea, from Workington. A violent storm erupted and the crossing had to be abandoned. It is said that the Lindisfarne gospels *"adorned with gold and precious stones"* were washed overboard and apparently lost. Accounts of this fierce storm, have themselves been subjected to a veneer of miracle and legend. Some understood it as a sign of the saint's displeasure. The *Rites of Durham* suggest *"that iij (three) waves of water was turned into bloode. The shippe was dreven back by tempest, and by the mightie powre of God"*. We can now only speculate how much of this is true. But we should remember that even those who recorded the event, were doing so many centuries after it actually happened. Canon Hardwick. D. Rawnsley comments that it may well have been a tidal wave, the result of some earthquake disturbance, which would send upward the red haematite ore that probably lies in the heavy mud beneath the Solway. I have not yet found a geologist who seems to be able to agree with the possibility of this explanation.

The miraculous recovery of the now famous Lindisfarne gospels is also quite mythical. Seemingly, St Cuthbert appeared in a dream to one of the party and told him where

Rev. W. S. CALVERLEY
1847-1898
"It is possible other fragments are hidden within the masonry of the old tower of St. Michaels"

ABOVE - Sketch of portion of stone cross (BC4) found at St. Michael's church, in July 1887. It was discovered built into the north side of arched eastern entrance, leading from the nave into the tower. Note the twist & ring design. ■

the manuscript could be found, undamaged by sea-water, *"three miles or more from the shore"* at Candida Casa (Whithorn) in Galloway. Early history is littered with such myth and legend, without any real accurate confirmation or evidence. We may well dismiss the loss and later recovery of the Lindisfarne gospels in the Solway Firth, as just simply implausible.

Nevertheless, Miller in his 1923 book *The Lindisfarne Gospels* says that there are *"undoubted water-stains on some of the leaves"* of these Gospels, and gives a list of the pages. Did this world famous masterpiece of manuscript painting (now displayed at the new British Library) really receive a baptism in the Solway? It presumably must have been exceptionally well wrapped and protected. Rawnsley suggested in 1909, we should take a microscope and we may see adhering to the leaves some salt crystals.

Unfortunately, even this Saint Cuthbert episode of Workington's history, is no longer well remembered. At one time, every pupil who attended the old Workington Grammar school would easily recall the opening line of the school song. *"Where Cuthbert's body sort the sea"*. The first verse of the song, composed by Hardwick D. Rawnsley is reproduced bottom left.

The Abbess St. Bega (Begha or Bec), believed to have once been an Irish princess, has perhaps the strongest and most plausible link to Christianity in the town. Legend has it that she sailed from Ireland, and was shipwrecked on the Solway coast off St. Bees. She founded a small nunnery there and the village appears to have derived its name from the saint. Again, there are several contradictory accounts of exactly when her nunnery was founded, and much of her life is also shrouded in myth and legend. Edmund Sandford thought the nunnery dated from 650, whilst others; including John Todd, who wrote a short history of the village, believe it was established much later, maybe 900.

The Christian Church modelled its structure on that of the Roman Empire. Throughout Europe, the dioceses mirrored the administrative divisions of Diocletian. [01] Bishops being based in the chief cities of each area. With the decline of the Roman Empire, and their subsequent withdrawal. The Church and its Bishops now seem to have emerged to oversee daily life, and in doing so amassed vast estates and influence. Workington was originally in the old ecclesiastical Diocese (or See) of York, forming part of the Arch deaconry of Richmond. This ancient diocese was created in the seventh century. It's first archbishop being appointed in AD625, when Northumbria was divided into two bishoprics. At this time however, West Cumbria would not have formed part of this diocese, as it

CANON H. D. RAWNSLEY

*Where Cuthbert's body
          sought the sea
And Scottish Mary sought the land,
As glad as Derwent flowing free
We boys and girls are hand in hand,
All vowed to seek from early youth
The Sea of Knowledge, Land of Truth.*

The first verse of the old Workington Grammar School song.

[01] Diocletian became the Roman emperor in AD284. ■

was still in the kingdom of Strathclyde.

We can surmise that our region was not joined into the York diocese, until a century or so after the Norman conquest (1066). It certainly become part of York, after William De Meschines (Lord of Egremont) founded St. Bees Priory, around 1120. For around five years later, St. Bees records show the *"church of Workington"* being granted to St. Mary's Benedictine monastery at York. St. Bees Priory was colonised by the monks of St. Mary's, and administered from York. It was to become the chief monastic presence in West Cumberland and a focal point for the Christian religion in West Cumberland.

It is impossible to determine if there was an earlier connection to the York Diocese, as their records only survive from around 1079. In the previous four centuries or so, who oversaw and cared for the pastoral needs of the town, is unclear and apparently unrecorded. However, we should not discount earlier connections with St. Bees. Daniel Hay comments that the creation of St. Bees Priory was *"a development rather than an innovation"*. Despite being attacked and ranksacked by the Vikings, on several occasions, the nunnery of St. Bega may well have survived and still been active. A church certainly still existed then at St. Bees. One interesting stone depicting St. Michael fighting the dragon (see sketch right), thought to date from the eighth or ninth century is still displayed at St. Bees today. Could this link the Abbey at St. Bees to caring for a church at Workington, in the period before the Priory was established?

In the year 1541, after the dissolution of the monastries by Henry VIII, he created a new See (or Diocese) of Chester. Including much of West Cumberland in this new diocese. The first clear reference to when Workington was formally transferred appears in a 1545 grant of the *"Rectory & Church of Workington"* to Robert Brokisby. Although a certain amount of uncertainty surrounds the period of transition from the See of York to Chester.

Within the Diocese of Chester, Workington formed part of its Deanery of Copeland. The boundary between the Diocese of Chester and Carlisle then followed the line of the River Derwent, until it almost reached Workington. Where it strangely turned northwards, to include the township of Seaton and the parish of Camerton in the Chester diocese. This slight deviation of the boundary is unusual, as the river would generally have formed a recognised natural physical border. Some have suggested that the inclusion of parts of Seaton and Camerton was a simple mistake by the King's cartographer or map-maker. It is suggested that he assumed that Seaton, actually referred

ABOVE - Sketch of the carved stone of *St. Michael fighting the Dragon*, which can still be seen at St. Bees Church. It is thought to perhaps date from the eighth century, and may survive from the original nunnery. Suggesting a strong link with the parish of Workington and St. Bega. St. Michaels Church, Arlecdon, has similar links to St. Bees, through this and other stones. ■

ABOVE - Coat of Arms of the Diocese of Chester. Workington became part of this diocese, soon after it was created by Henry VIII in 1541. ■

ST. MICHAEL

from a wall painting in St. Michaels
Church, Arlecdon.

[01] Saint Michael was one of the
seven archangels, presumed to be
the principal or leader of angels and
guardian angel of Israel. Interestingly, he is the patron saint of sailors,
which has an obvious link to maritime Workington. Whilst also being
known as the patron saint of soldiers,
horses and horsemen. In art he often appears holding a shield, scales
or a banner and flourishing a sword
against a dragon.
[02] Anglo-Saxon churches were built
by the chief landowner, for the convenience of his family and his people, and usually regarded as his property. Later, it was standard practice
to "grant" or transfer the church to a
particular monastery. By attaching
gifts of lands and buildings, (like the
"mill" in Workington's case) you also
provided an income for the church.
Funds that would pay for an incum-
bent, so the spiritual welfare of the
local people could be maintained. ■
[03] A "carucate" is thought to have
been approx 60 acres, being the area
of land, one man could plough (or be
tilled) in one year (using a single
plough, drawn by eight oxen).■
[04] Whilst granting the church to
William, the Abbot retained half the
income from the "tithe of fish" for his
abbey. ■

to the ancient *"Nunnery of Seaton"*, near Bootle. Know-
ing this was to be included in the new Chester diocese, he
simply altered the boundary accordingly. In 1847, a new
Act of Parliament, transferred the area south of the Derwent, (which included Workington) to the Diocese of Carlisle.

ST. MICHAEL'S PARISH CHURCH

ST. Michael's Church has always been regarded as the
town's Parish Church, and as far as we can determine
it is the site of the first church in the town. It's dedication
to St. Michael [01] alone, could indicate Christianity did
flourish here in these very early times. Bede mentions a
burial place near Hexham, being dedicated to the saint,
late in the seventh century. William G. Collingwood suggests that this may be the reason why many of the twenty
seven ancient churches in this diocese, are dedicated to
him. Furthermore, Richard Bailey of Newcastle University shows there is a strong link between our Anglo-Saxon
ecclesiastical sculptures and those at Hexham. Also giving some credence to the likelihood that much of the town's
early Christian teaching, came via the Celtic Church of
Northumbria. Perhaps through the visits or influence of
St. Cuthbert and his followers; we do know Cuthbert was
made Bishop of Hexham in 684.

Some believe that the dedication of the church to St.
Michael did not occurr until the twelfth century. Unfortunately, the earliest documentary reference to a church in
the town, dated around 1125, does not actually show any
specific name or dedication. In the St. Bees Priory records,
we find Ketel, son of Eldred made the following grant to
the monks of St. Mary's Church, York [02] - *"...the Church
of Wirkington and two carucates [03] of land and a mill in the
same town."* Furthermore prior to 1201, when Robert,
Abbot of St. Mary's York, appointed William, one of the
churches earliest incumbents, again it was simply referred
to only as *"the church of Workington"*. [04] The parish
church was only one of numerous Cumbrian churches (or
benefactions) granted to the monks of York and St.Bees,
by whom Bulmer (1901) calls the *"many pious Normans"*.

As previously mentioned in chapter three, the earliest stone sculptures (BC1 & BC8) found at St. Michaels
seem to confirm this beyond much doubt; an earlier Anglo-
Saxon church in Workington perhaps as early as the eighth
century. But Ketel's grant is perhaps the first evidence of
the establishment of the Parish of Workington. Charles
Hole in his *Manual of English Church History*, considered that the parochial system, with its parish church, rec

tor-incumbant, patron, glebe and tithes etc., had began to develop as early as 800. But the first legal establishment of the parish church, (in England) was not until AD970.

Over the last century or so, a clearer understanding of the early history of St. Michael's and the town generallly, has only really unfolded due to the archeological finds. Had the major fires of 1887 and 1994, not seriously ravaged and destroyed much of the church. It's important history could have remained hidden forever.

After the second fire at St. Michaels in September 1994, the Carlisle City Council Archaeological Unit began further excavations. This work, carried out under the guidance of archeologist Paul Flynn, was to last nearly two years. As mentioned previously, the formal report of this most recent dig, have yet to be published. However, the initial findings and conclusions do not only seem to confirm the Anglo-Saxon date. But perhaps suggest another earlier church may have existed, not far from the present site. Around four hundred skeletons were discovered, beneath the floor of the present church, having been excavated in places upto 2 metres depth. Many of these burials were found lying south to west, rather than the customary east to west orientation. Suggesting they relate not to today's church, but to an earlier church a little to the east.

Interestingly these people may well have witnessed the visit to the area of the Lindisfarne community, with the relics of St. Cuthbert, as they attempted their crossing to Ireland. One can perhaps imagine Bishop Eardulph, around 878, preaching the Gospel to the Weorc townspeople. But was it in a small timber church, or in the open, on the hill overlooking the sea, where St. Michael's now stands?

Accurate testing of some skeletons is planned, perhaps at Bradford University. It should diagnostically provide not just their age and sex, but could also highlight nutrition, diet, any diseases and injuries. Carbon 14 testing could give a broad indication of the period our skeletons lived, but may only be accurate to within a few centuries.[01] However, just an indication of life expectancy, Infant mortality etc., can only add further detail to our picture of pre-Norman Workington.

In order to expand on the theory of a much earlier nearby church, further exploratory excavations in the garden of the adjoining Old Rectory, were undertaken. In several places, at a depth of around two metres, some remains of stonework or foundations were unearthed. But, it is not yet possible to determine the type of building, they represented. In the same trenches, several pieces of

St. CUTHBERT (d.c.687)

[01] It is unlikely that this Carbon 14 dating, will be performed for each body, due to the considerable cost involved. Only some of what is believed to be the oldest remains will probably be selected. ∎

pottery were also found. This appears to date from the Medieval period, suggesting the structural remains well pre-dated the twelfth century. Paul Flynn has speculated that St. Michaels may itself have once been the site of a monastery. If confirmed it could change our understanding of ancient religious sites in West Cumbria, a thousand years ago.

In very early times, before the significant geographical changes to the Derwent estuary, outlined in chapter one. St. Michaels in its elevated position, was once the most westward building in the town. In Anglo-Saxon times the high tide may well have lapped up to the level of what is now Church Street, entirely covering the Marsh area, to the west of the church.

Looking closely at the church today, we can see the remains of the square solid Norman tower. (see photograph on page 102) Then it was much lower, two thirds it's present height, with the narrow loophole windows. This section is likely to date from before the fourteenth century. It was certainly a strategically placed tower and must have also acted as a look-out point for any Scottish invaders. Perhaps the church bell being rang to signal an alarm to the townspeople. The design of this tower, like many others throughout West Cumbria, is *"fortress like"*, resembling a small pele tower. Implying that for many years it may have also acted as a *"sanctuary from attack"*. It may well have had thick doors hung on the inside of the round arch, into the nave. Suggesting that it could be made secure in times of attack. Then there was no west door, this is a much later addition, perhaps eighteenth century.

Some mystery also surrounds what is believed to be the earliest illustration of the parish church. This small sketch appears on the 1569 manuscript plan of the town. The relevant section is enlarged and shown left. It seems to suggest the Elizabethan church once had a central castellated tower, with buildings either side. However, archaeologist Paul Flynn has commented that he has found no evidence to suggest this layout. Pondering on this depiction and after discussions with Peter Barker at the British Library. It can be concluded that map-makers then often attempted to provide a simple birds-eye view of a building, along it's longest elevation. At this scale, it would be unwise to rely on it as an accurate representation of the church. It is likely that another building did exist close-by, but its exact orientation and position, cannot really be determined from what is essentially just a sketch map.

The first accurate plan of the church dates from the latter half of the eighteenth century. The existing square

ABOVE - the small thumbnail sketch of St. Michaels Church from the 1569 town plan. (see text right) ■

Norman tower is clearly shown, with an adjoining nave and chancel. When this church was erected is not recorded. However, we can surmise that at least the chancel (perhaps also the nave) may have been re-built around 1543. For in Sir Thomas [iv] Curwen's will, he states *"my body to be buried within the new chantry of my Parish Church of Workington"*. Here he may well be referring to the chantry as the small Curwen family chapel shown on plan below. A chantry can often refer to a private chapel, endowed to support a priest to chant mass daily for ones deceased. Certainly at that time the family are believed to have held the *Rectory & Tithes* of the Parish, one condition of which was to maintain the chancel of St. Michaels.

Around half a century later in the will of Henry[i] Curwen (dated 7 October 1595) we find another reference to the rebuilding of *"the chantry"*. Here Henry makes allowance for his son Nicholas to *"cause the chantry to be rebuilded and builded with one lean-to roof covered with lead, with two glass windows of four lights"*. Into these windows he asked that stained glass be installed depicting the coat of arms of his parents, himself and the families of his two wives, together with those of his children and their marriages. [01]

[01] Henry [i] Curwen's will specified the stained glass was to show "the Curwen arms joined with the arms of Strickland, and also the Curwen arms joined with the Fairfax arms of Gilling, also the Curwen arms joined with the Musgrave, and also the Curwen arms joined with the Carus arms, and also the Musgraves with the Curwen arms, and also the Bellingham arms with the Curwen arms and likewise the Fairfax arms of Steton with the Curwen arms".

S! - SPIRAL STAIRCASE TO LOFT ABOVE
S2 - STAIRCASE TO GALLERY IN NAVE
F - NORMAN FONT   NA - NORMAN ARCH
OTHER GALLERIES NOT SHOWN - See pages 70

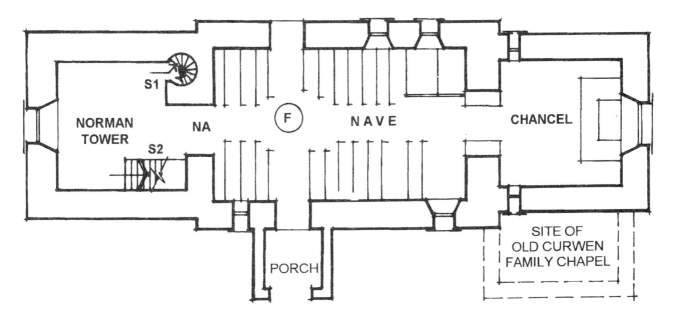

BASIC PLAN OF SMALL NORMAN CHURCH AT ST. MICHAELS

As Workington's population began to increase, this small parish church began to become overcrowded. So much so that additional lofts or galleries were added within its nave and chancel to accommodate larger congregations. The earliest was a public or free loft for servants and children. It was situated above the west end of the nave, and reached by a straight flight of steps rising from within the tower, along it's south wall. It is possible this may have been a permanent feature of the old church, included when it had last been rebuilt or altered. But this is unclear, it was certainly referred to as *"ye old gallery"* when permission was sort to add a further loft in 1707.

Here we find the Bishop of York granting a licence (or faculty) for a new gallery along the north side of the nave. It was reached by a external straight flight of steps, around the mid point of (and at right angle to) the north wall of the nave. Without doubt any churchgoers using these pews must have felt a little detached from the service, as they would certainly not see the altar.

Sometime after, it appears a further gallery of twenty one pews, was also added above the *"old gallery"* at the west end of the nave. This I find almost unbelievable, but records suggest it is correct. It too was also reached by another external flight of stairs through the west corner of the nave. We now have pews on three levels facing the chancel, headroom there must have been extremely tight. The upper level was lit by just two small roof lights.

Furthermore there was also thought to be two other smaller and narrower galleries along the north and south walls of the chancel. Reached again from another external straight flight of steps, at right angles to it's north wall. The south loft or gallery opposite was reached by a narrow walkway or bridge across the cancel and almost above the altar, just a few feet below.

Ivy Benn [01] noted in her excellent research of the church, comments how it *"must have presented a rather asymmetrical exterior appearance"* particularly along its north wall, *"with three outside staircases"*. Internally, this very cramped church with it's numerous galleries, many at different levels would have been very claustrophobic and a disaster aesthetically. The act of taking communion must also have created quite a scene and disturbance to the order of the service. The congregation in the galleries would descend by the outside staircases, then re-enter the church by its side door, and proceed to the altar down the narrow central aisle. Then of course, to return to there seats by the same route. In the winter months, with the wind and rain lashing the church, those in the galleries must have dreaded this journey. Whilst those seated on the

---

"The act of taking communion must have created quite a scene and disturbance to the order of the service".

---

[01] Ivy Benn now retired, taught English at Workington Grammar School (now Stainburn School) from 1969-83. She was also head of Victoria School when it was a secondary girls school between 1964-7. A former member of the *Cumbria Religious History Society*, she diligently researched the history of St. Micheal's in the mid 1980s. In February 1987, much of her work was published by the society in their Bulletin XIV. ■

ground floor would be chilled by blasts of cold air, whistling through the open doors.

For how long this particular arrangement continued is unclear, certainly a new larger church may have been built, if sufficient funds could be raised amongst the congregation, and a majority agreed. Unfortunately up until 1725, it was unlikely that they could then rely upon any further support from the wealthy Curwen family. For the present *"patron of the livings"* and Lord of the Manor was Henry [iii] Curwen (or *Galloping Harry*) an ardent Roman Catholic and believed staunch supporter of the Jacobite cause. (see chapter five) It was not until locally born William Thomas Addison was appointed Rector in 1753, that the impetus for a new church grew. Ivy Benn suggests this was perhaps the *"first task"* in his new ministry.

Unfortunately matters did not progress rapidly, it was February 1762 before everyone appeared to agree to re-building the nave and chancel of St. Michaels. In the Vestry minute book [01] we find the existing cramped church described as *"indecent and incommodious, too little so some people stay at home on the Lords day, for want of a seat"*. A committee was formed to progress the work, [02] with around eighty parishioners signing a resolution to re-build the church.

The description of the proposed work was quite informative. It involved demolishing the porch, nave, galleries, chancel etc., whilst retaining only the Norman tower or steeple. The chancel was to be extended around 12 feet (3.6m) eastwards into the churchyard. With the access to the Curwen vault or *"burial place"* being built over as the nave was to be greatly widened. Two new upper galleries of pews were to be added along the north and south sides of the nave, supported on pillars, built off the foundations of the old Norman nave walls.

Having finally agreed to the work, the next step was to secure permission to commence rebuilding the church and raise the necessary funds. All did not go well, money was subscribed, but the neighbouring townships of Stainburn, Windscales, Great and Little Clifton (all contained in the Workington parish) submitted lengthy objections to a faculty being granted. Even Sir James Lowther known as *"Wicked Jimmy, the Bad Earl"* and a bitter political and business rival of Henry Curwen lodged almost identical objections. The legal arguments continued for almost another three years, before the matter finally reached the consistory (or ecclesiastical) court. Permission was granted in the spring of 1766, but Sir. James Lowther immediately lodged an appeal. After a further legal examination the judgement was reversed and went against St. Michaels. The principle

"The existing cramped church was indecent and incommodious, too little so some people stay at home on the Lords day, for want of a seat".

[01] The earliest surviving St. Michael's Vestry minute books appears to date from Feb 1762. Unfortunately, some gaps exist as the records of some later meetings are missing or lost. ■
[02] The 1762 St. Michael's committee included Henry [v] Curwen, William T. Addison (rector), Thomas Brough, John Steel, William Watts, Robert Steel, John Hodgson, John Falcon and Henry Fawcett.■

point of objection being the allocation of the pews in the church and the rules of their ownership.

The parishioners appear to have resolved this problem through their local vestry meetings, as a second faculty application was submitted in May 1767. Again objections from Sir James Lowther and others were defiantly submitted, and a further consistory court heard much of the same evidence as before, together with it's lengthy litigation and legal argument. St, Michaels finally received it's licence to re-build it's church on 5 April 1769.

Unfortunately building work could still not be commenced as not surprisingly a further appeal was submitted. Ivy Benn noted Lowther's third appeal was again *"repeating much of the original citation"*. Stubborn revenge seems to have been the primary motive of the very wealthy and influential Sir James. On top of the bitter struggle between these two prominent local families, he is thought to have been deeply hurt and offended when Henry Curwen's Whig party had gallantly defeated him at the Carlisle Parliamentary elections of April 1768. J. F. Curwen noted that he later become known as *"Brave Henry Curwen"*, by virtue of his opposition to the tyrant Lowther.

This time the appeals were to be dismissed and by the beginning of April 1770, St. Michael's did receive it's faculty. Within two years the new spacious Georgian church had been completed. The cost was said to be around £2700. Externally, it was a relatively plain structure without any major architectural pretensions. It's proportions were much the same as the existing church today, still standing roofless awaiting renovation after the 1994 fire.

"He later become known as *"Brave Henry Curwen"*, by virtue of his opposition to the tyrant Sir James Lowther".

ST. MICHAELS CHURCH
The Georgian church, destroyed by the fire of 1887. So remarkably identical in many respects, particularly internally, to St. James church at Whitehaven. ■

The Norman tower had been retained and increased in height. Along the new side walls of the nave were two rows of nine typically semi-circular headed Georgian windows, surrounded by plain stone bands. Whilst the east end of the chancel was square externally, inside it had a rounded aspe end. A tall semi-circular headed arch, almost the full width of the chancel, separated it from the nave. The external walls were initially stone faced, but by 1796 they were all roughcast, probably because of a penertrating dampness problem through the solid stone walls. Soon after in 1797, William Hutchinson described it as a *"handsome structure"*.

Continuing he tells us *"the inside of the church is neatly finished, and the altar is ornamented with a painting of our Saviour taken down from a cross"*. Along the north and side walls of the nave were wide upper galleries of pews, each side supported off a row of six quite plain painted *"Tuscan style"* columns, which then continued as unfluted *"Ionic"* ones, upto its high flat ceiling. The internal plasterwork and joinery had much typically eighteenth century neoclassical detailing. Few old illustrations or photographs survive to show how the interior of this church, looked before the 1887 fire. Those that do bare a quite amazing resemblance to the present interior of St James' Church, Whitehaven. [01] In 1967, Nikolaus Pevsner so eloquently wrote of St James'. *"The thrill of this church is the interior, the finest Georgian Church interior in the county"*.

As was quite common a large timber panelled, two storey pulpit (perhaps four metres high) dominated the chancel, so much so that it would have obscured much of the altar. Then of course preaching to the congregation was of prime importance at services. Behind the altar was a wide pointed gothic arched window of *"three lights, the upper part of which is filled with stained glass."* [02] As previously mentioned this church was eventually to suffer the same fate as the present building, being almost completely destroyed by fire on Monday morning of the 17 January 1887. Although St. Michael's was re-built almost immediately and dedicated again in April 1890. We may reflect on Pevsner's description of St James' Whitehaven, so remarkably identical in many respects to St. Michaels then, and ponder what we have really lost.

Also destroyed in this fire was the *"fine old carved"* pew of the Curwen family. This once occupied the north east corner of the nave of the old Norman church, and was retained when the church was enlarged. Carved delicately upon the pew, was the Curwen coat of arms; Samuel Jefferson (writing in 1842) says *"in one place impaling on a*

"The thrill of this church is the interior, the finest Georgian Church interior in the county".
Nikolaus Pevsner (1967)

[01] Inside St. James' (built 1752-3) there is a very similar high chancel arch, although it is a little wider and flatter than that which once existed at St. Michaels. The flat ceiling and arrangement of the side galleries appear identical, particularly the column supports and the fine joinery detailing to front of the gallery and pilasters. Externally, other features of St. James would also remind us of the old Georgian church at St. Michaels. See sketch opposite. ■
[02] This description appears in William Whellan's *History of Cumberland*, published in 1860. ■

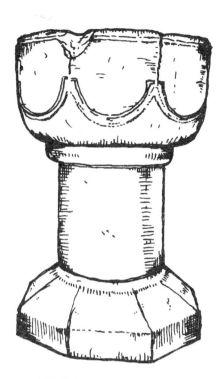

**ST. MICHAEL'S CHURCH
SANDSTONE BAPTISMAL FONT**

[01]   The existing belfry at St. Michaels is thought to have been added around 1770, when the church was re-built. It is now reached by a steep timber staircase from the room immediately above the west entrance to the church.   This room likely to have formed part of the original ancient Norman tower, is reached by a narrow stone spiral staircase (of thirty three treads) rising clockwise in the north east corner of the tower.   Today, there are now eight bells at the parish church (pitch F sharp) two more than Carlisle Cathedral. ∎

fess two lions' heads between three St. Andrew's crosses".   He also noted that in 1809, *"a handsome brass gilt chandelier"* was bequeathed by John Kay to St. Michael's Church. It once hung above the middle aisle of the church, apparently lost in the fire.

In November 1774, a decision was made by the vestry meeting to replace the existing bells, and purchase by subscription a new peal, together with a clock. The details and antiquity of those obsolete bells is unknown. But we do know that a peal of six new bells were cast in 1775, by *Pack & Chapman* at their Whitechapel foundry. Today in the belfry of the tower, despite the two disastrous fires, the original eighteenth century oak bell frame still supports the bells. (see photograph page 102) Unfortunately, the bells themselves have all been later recast and technically are not original. Each does however, bear a date of when they were returned to the foundry. [01]

The clockface on the west side of the tower is thought to have originally had just one hour hand, and would strike each hour *"upon the tenor bell"*, the largest of the peal. It escaped without damage during the 1887 fire and newspaper reports suggest it kept on chiming the hour, as the fire brigade frantically fought the flames engulfing the rest of the church.

Perhaps the oldest item of antiquity at St. Michaels, besides the stone fragments previously mentioned, is the octagonal sandstone baptismal font. Today, it is found under the main tower, but originally stood centrally in the aisle of the old Norman church. It basically resembles a plain squat or short medieval column, with its capital forming the basin.   Pevsner dates it as being probably from 1335 to 1530, the Perpendicular period of English gothic architecture. Others are a little more precise suggesting it to be early fourteenth century. (see sketch left)

This exterior of this upper basin section of the font is octagonal. The lower edges of it's vertical panel sides are decorated with a plain concave semi-circular flute, just above their taper into a plain circular shaft or column below. An almost true roll moulding occurs at the top of the shaft below the basin section. The font has a octahedral plain base or socle, as wide as the basin above. Its edges gently taper up at an angle, into the shaft.

In addition to the font, St. Michael's also has a fine altar tomb, with the effigies of Sir Christopher [i] Curwen and his wife Elizabeth Huddleston. Lying upon the tomb (around 2.2 metres long) is Sir Christopher in a typical fifteenth century knight's armour, beside his wife. It must date from around 1470, and it has been suggested that it was erected by his grandson Christopher [ii] And his wife Anne

Pennington. (see page 37)

Before 1770, when the church was quite small itoriginally stood under the tower, after it was enlarged the effigy was relocated in the north east corner of the nave. Here it was severely damaged in the 1994 fire, so much so that current rector Canon Terance Sampson described it as being *"transferred almost to rubble"*. But following painstaking restoration it will be returned to the church when eventually fully renovated and rebuilt. [01]

Hutchinson in his 1797 *History of Cumberland* recorded that the *"Living"* or benefice (income) of the Rector, was one of the best in the county. It was then said to be around £100 per annum. Within the church adjacent to the arched opening into the tower, are three plaques listing the former Rectors of St. Michaels. This almost complete list dating from 1150, was prepared by Thomas Iredale [02] following extensive research. He gifted the tablets to the church and they were erected under a faculty, approved in Nov. 1908. Each plaque is headed with a *"cinquefoil"* decorated pointed head, very similar to those on the side of the altar tomb of Sir Christopher [i] Curwen (see sketch below). The panels also bear the coat of arms of the York, Chester and Carlisle Diocese.

[01] The restoration of the effigy was carried out by an expert conservator in York, at a cost of around £13500.

[02] Thomas Iredale (1834-1913) was the son of brewer John Iredale who moved to the High Brewery in 1839. He originally started work as a bank clerk with the *Cumberland Union Bank*, but later joined his father and brothers in the Brewery business. He was elected one of the first members of the County Council. As well as a member of the Local Board, and Workington's Mayor in 1890-1. He died in September 1913 and is buried in Harrington Road cemetery.

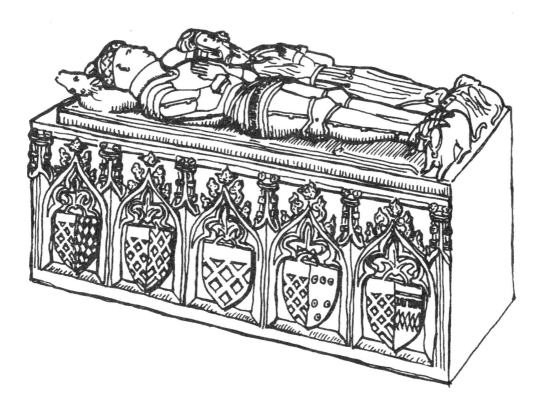

The altar tomb, with the effigies of Sir Christopher [i] Curwen and his wife Elizabeth. Along it's west side are five niches, with *cinquefoil* decorated heads, each bearing a carved coat of arms on a shield. These arms represent the marriages of Christopher's parents; his own marriage to Elizabeth Huddleston; together with those of his son Thomas [ii] and that of his grandson, Christopher [ii]. The central shield depicts just the Curwen arms. An inscription along it's top edge is thought to read *"Orate pro animabz xtoferi Curwen militis et Elizabethr uxoris ejus"*. (see also page 36) ■

The early Rectors of
ST. MICHAELS CHURCH

Walter (1150), Thomas (1184), William (1201-27), Roger de Seleby (1247-58), Eudric de Wyspayns (1303), John de Cokermuth (1315), William de Aykheved (1330-41), Richard de Askeby (1365), John Blaunchard (1375), William de Tanfeld (1379), William de Egremund (1387-1401), Alan Humbreston (1429), Robert Stiel (1430), Roger Crakenthorp (1430), Laurence Roche (1463), William Eure (1463), John Lancastre (1473), Thomas Markham (1473), John Curwen (1525), Edmund Whalley (1534), Robert Turner (c1543), Christopher Share (1557), Edward Heide (1557-64), John Harison (1564), Gregory Scott (1575), Laurence Shuttleworth (1577-95), George Lamplugh (1595-1634), Lancelot Lowther (1634), Christopher Matteson (1662), John Bolton (1679), Robert Loxam or Loxham (1724), John Stanley (1726-53), William Thomas Addison (1753-91), Edward Christian - later took surname Hare (1792-1803), Peter How (1803-31), Edward Stanley (1831-34), John Wordsworth (1834-37), Henry Curwen (1837-95). ∎

Thomas Iredale's list of Rectors is reproduced left, together with an additional name discovered by chance, nearly a century after his research. Robert Turner is mentioned in the will of Sir Thomas [iv] Curwen, dated 1 Nov. 1543. Where it states to *"my servant Robert Turner, priest, all his fees and other commodities which he hath now"*. Rev. Turner was also appointed an executor and guardian to Thomas' son Henry [i]. Obviously this was an extremely turbulent time in English Church history, some precise details may have been left unrecorded or been subsequently lost. I have already touched on the problem, and Iredale himself recognised the problems with this *"difficult period before the foundation of the see of Chester"*, and left obvious gaps in his list. He hoped that *"more names may be discovered"*, perhaps Rev. Turner should now be added.

Rev. John Wordsworth (1803-75)

The eldest son of Poet Laureate William Wordsworth, was Rector of St. Michael's Church between 1834-37. He was also married to Isabella, eldest daughter of Henry [vi] Curwen. (see page 55). William Wordsworth often stayed with his son at the Rectory. During a visit in Sept 1834, he wrote of bathing in the sea *"with a hope principally of strengthening"* his eyes. He explained that each winter, for the last thirty years he had suffered from *"inflammations"*. Now his vision was *"so weak as to make reading and writing, unless for a very little at a time, injurious to them"*. For several days, the elderly Wordsworth (then 63 years old) would take a swim each morning *"between seven and eight"*. Unfortunately, it is not recorded if this *"seabathing"* treatment was beneficial or successful. ∎

Parish Registers of St.Michael's

Some Baptisms and Burials are recorded from 1664. However, more complete registers (including Marriages) begin in 1670 and appear to run continuously upto the present day. Today these early registers have been deposited at the Whitehaven Record Office. They are available to view on microfilm, with the deposited copies also available if required.
A list from the Marriage register (covering the period 1670-183) was also published in 1910 by Phillimore & Co., in volume 2 of their *Cumberland Parish Registers*. The IGI for Workington covers the period 1670-1855 and is available at local public libraries. The majority of gravestones in St. Michael's cemetery have been removed, just a few remain. A list of the original 838 stones inscriptions is at Whitehaven Record Office.∎

HOW MICHAEL CHAPEL

AROUND five centuries ago, despite the early existance of St. Michaels Church, Workington also had at least one other place of worship. The chapel once stood on the summit of the cliff, overlooking the Solway, about 45 metres above the shoreline, Situated about 700 metres south of the old Isabella pit, it is shown on the earlier OS maps. Although exactly, when it was built and for whom is not clear, some tradition points it being a chantry chapel but its founder is not known. Richard Bellhouse believed that a Roman watch-tower may have existed on the site, as part of their coastal defences . What appears certain, is the chapel existed before Elizabeth I came to the throne in 1558. For seventeen years later, when she granted to Percival Gunson and John Sonky, - *"three acres of land know as Chappell Flatts in Wirkington, and one chapel there with an acre of land."*

The land was then already commonly known as *"Chappell Flatts"*. In addition to this reference we also have the earlier additional information in the will of John Curwen [01] the former Rector of Workington, who died in 1530. He bequeathed to the *"church of Workington one silver cup with covering in part gilt, also to the chapel of St. Michael 6s 8d [33p]"*. This seems to confirm that How Michael was then in use as a chapel.

On the 1569 town plan, the building is simply referred to as *"watch chapel"* and clearly also shows St. Michaels parish church. At this time it is unlikely that the town needed an additional place of worship. For we know that Workington consisted of around just 30 households, which would equate to just a few hundred inhabitants. Although, it is also possible that it then may have served as a Roman Catholic chapel. Created after Henry VIII denied the papal authority and dissolved the monasteries.

By 1770, the building was possibly no longer used as a chapel. Pennant mentioned having noticed the old building, and calls it *Holme Chapel*. He describes it then as a small watch tower, adding that some believed it was built to mark the motions of the Scots in their naval roads. But adds it is more likely to have been an Elizabethan chapel.

In 1777, Nicholson & Burn referred to the hill where the chapel once stood as *Workington Hill*. They tell us that from the fifteenth century warning beacons had been lit upon the mound. These beacons were fired across the county, primarily to warn of possible invasion by the Scots and to call the local men to arms. Many times throughout the centuries, there are references to beacons being made ready and lit here. In May 1568, shortly after the famous arrival of Mary Queen of Scots in Workington, the beacon warned that the Scots may attempt to recapture their fugitive Queen. The 1640 *English State Papers* record that *"on firing of the beacons"* local men must *"repair with all speed to Carlisle, with seven days provisions. Every soldier must bring, besides his arms, a spade, shovel of pickaxe"*.

Certainly by 1860, the old chapel building was then almost derelict, as William Whellan refers to the structure as *"an ancient roofless building, generally known as the Old Chapel"* He describes the masonry of the almost square

"What appears certain, is *How Michael* chapel existed before Elizabeth I came to the throne in 1558".

[01] John Curwen (d. 1530) appears to have been appointed *Rector of Workington* around 1524. He was the son of Sir Christopher [ii] de Curwen and Anne Pennington. (see page 37) John may not have remained the rector of St. Michaels until his death, as there is a further entry in his will, referring to Sir Richard Richardson *"my parish priest"*, to whom he bequeathed his *"black cassock"*. ■

two-storey building as rude or crude. Adding *"the ground floor is arched; and a narrow winding staircase, sufficient only for the passage of one person, leads to the upper floor. The windows were narrow loopholes except for two on the land side, which are larger dimensions, but destitute of all ornamention"*.

Whilst Sergeant C. Hall in his sometimes blunt (and often also amusing) 1883 *Inductive History of Workington* says *"If the building was used in former times as a chapel, the congregation must have been an exceedingly small one and the services held there of the briefest description, for I imagine that twenty persons would be unable to stay inside for twenty consecutive minutes, without suffocation"*.

"The Chapel Bank area obviously derives it's name from being adjacent to the site of the old chapel".

For centuries, because of it's prominent cliff-top position, it was used by mariners as a land mark and was commonly called How Michael. William Whellan told how it was *"kept regularly whitewashed"* to guide the ships along the Solway coast. Christopher Saxon's 1576 county map, clearly shows the building as *St. Michael's Chapel*, at the mouth of *Derwentfote haven*. It was also sometimes referred to as *St. Michaels Mount*. The Chapel Bank area obviously derives it's name from being adjacent to the site of the old chapel.

Shortly after Whellan's 1860 comments, the building was repaired and renovated to be used by the 4th Cumberland (Workington) Artillery Volunteer Corps. One of hundred's of local defence units formed throughout the country. When it was believed that the French were planning an invasion of the British Isles. Cannon balls and gunpowder were then stored within the old chapel, to supply two 32 *"pounders"* cannons then placed in a nearby mud fort. It was then said that *"no vessel can pass the Isle of Man without being espied"*.

Earlier the same year, How Michael had also served as a triangulation point, for the government surveyors preparing the first large scale Ordnance survey plan. They erected a *"crows nest"* upon the tower inorder to map out the town. At the time it was common to see the *"red coats"* of the Ordnance Corp busily measuring properties throughout the town.

[01] Some comparisons may be drawn to St. Michael's Mount in Cornwall or even perhaps Mont St. Michel situated off the French coast. But it would appear that Workington's *"St. Michael's Mount"* has only been occasionally called this, for the last two centuries or so. However, is it just something of a coincidence that these once basically similar sites were all dedicated to St. Michael. Perhaps not, St. Michael is often referred to as the patron Saint of high places. ∎

Tradition also suggests that the sea may have once flowed all around the mound where the old chapel once stood. It is said that it was possibly connected at only low tide by a causeway to the mainland.[01] It is known that a band of alluvial clay exists close to the surface. Between where How Michael stood and the town, in the area now known as Clay Flatts. This suggests that water must have once flowed over this area, inorder to form this band of clay. Although very difficult to imagine today, if we consider the changes in the physical geography of the coast line and estuary outlined in chapter one, it is really not so inconceivable.

Although the building has now disappeared forever under hundreds of tons of slag waste from the nearby steel works, John A. Byers (the authors father) remembers the building being used by the Home Guard during the 1939-45 war. It again served as a look out point, and for sentry duties.

ST. JOHN'S CHURCH

ST. John's Church, at the corner of Washington Street and Guard Street, was built between 1821-3. It was erected by the Commissioners for Building Churches in thanksgiving for victory at the Battle of Waterloo and the end of the Napoleonic war. The commission, also often called the *Church Building Society*, was founded in 1818 and was funded by £1 million from the Government.[01] This large new church, despite it's size, was then referred to as St. John's Chapel, within the parish of St. Michael's.

In 1835, the parish of Workington was ecclesiastically divided into two districts, (but not two separate parishes) one was assigned to the mother-church St. Michael's, the other to St. John's. It was 1856 before the Church, became a separate and distinct parish.[02] St. John's parish also including the township of Windscales and part of Stainburn. The population in 1851 of the St. John's area of the parish was then around 3000.

It was John Christian Curwen and George Henry Law (then Bishop of Chester) who asked the commissioners to provide a new church for the town. St. Michael's Church with only 500 seats was now considered far too small, for the town's ever increasing population.[03]

After the grant was approved on 24 July 1820, Christian Curwen gifted the site, and work began in November 1821. It is thought the site was actually chosen by a ballot or vote amongst the people who would use the new church. At least two other sites were also proposed, one of which was thought to be where the old St. John's Vicarage was eventually built, on Park End Road, whilst the other location is unclear. The actual site is simply defined in John Christian Curwen's *Deed of Gift* (dated 1 October 1821) as *"a plot of land known as Longcroft"*.

The distinctive warm yellow sandstone, very similar to Workington Hall, was hewn at the Schoose and Hunday quarries. Much of the construction work is thought to have been undertaken by Paul Nixon, a builder from Car-

[01] The 1818 *"New Churches Act"* allocated funds to build new churches, in industrial areas, where an increase in population had meant the spiritual needs of the people, were no longer being met. ■
[02] St. John's Chapel (not Church) is often mentioned in the early St. Michael's Vestry (or church council) minutes. ■
[03] St. John's was initially designed to hold 1600 people, despite the original grant from the commissioners specifying it to be *"capable of containing 2000 persons"*. The pews in the gallery were *"let to the benefit of the minister"*, whilst all the seats on the ground floor were free, *"for the use of the poor"*. This latter arrangement was an essential clause in the 1818 New Churches Act.
The letting of pews was then an essential element of funding a church and its activities. After someone died, generally the pew was valued along with their estate. Often being sold off at auction along with their house, furniture etc. ■

St. Johns Church is *"lamentable proof of modern degeneracy in church-building.....miserable and unecclesiastical"*.

Samuel Jefferson (1842)

lisle. For an 1822 agreement to supply the stone for the new church exists, between Nixon and Christian Curwen who owned both the quarries. Interestingly, despite referring to the stone colour as grey, it tells us that the stone for all the *"Plinths, Quoins, window dressings and Door cases, Ashlars, Shafts of Pilasters, Columns or Window sills, steps and landings"* was to cost one shilling (5p) a cubic foot; measured after each stone has been wrought or shaped and also included delivery to the site. The construction work took around two years, the church being finally consecrated on 27 November 1823. [01]

John Martin in his concise history of St. Johns (published in 1973 for it's sesqui-centenary or 150 year anniversary), quotes at length the consecration and dedication service. Whilst also providing a description of the new church, taken from a contemporary local newspaper report. He states the church has *"a handsome portico of the Roman Doric order, after the architecture of Vetruvius. The roof was only partly slated with slabs of stone at it's front end, the rear being of uncovered wood boards. There was also a wooden steeple which housed a bell weighing 7 cwt (356.4kg)"*. This almost temporary roof covering soon caused problems, for the 1826 St. Michael's Church Vestry minutes show reports of water leaking through the roof.

Many accounts of the town's history seem to repeatedly refer to St. John's as something of an architectural failure. Although many simply appear to copy almost word for word, the comments of the earlier historians. Perhaps the first to record his views, was Samuel Jefferson in his *History and Antiquities of Allerdale Ward, Above Derwent*, published less than twenty years after the church was built. He believed it to be *"lamentable proof of modern degeneracy in church-building"*. Adding that its masonry was *"miserable"*, and its style was *"unecclesiastical"*.

We may sympathize with Jefferson views, if we look closer at the history of the building. Originally the church was built with just the small wooden tower, this being blown off in the January gales of 1839. Today's more substantial stone tower was only added between 1844-46, around four years after he completed his book. It is quite likely that when Jefferson visited the church, it may not even have had a tower.[02] No doubt this would have greatly contributed to this scathing criticism. Despite its well proportion facade, without any tower to break-up its large roof slopes, its overall appearance may well have been considered very plain and truly uninspiring.

One of the many who later quoted Jefferson's views was Thomas Bulmer in his 1901 Trade Directory, adding that *"this pretty accurately describes what most people who have any pretensions to speak on the subject would say".*

I now question Bulmer's comments, after the addition of it's new square stone tower topped with its cupola, surely the church had instantly gained much more balance, stature and a credible *"church-like"* appearance. As the building is externally, much the same as it was then, anyone who truly takes time to pause and look at St. John's, should surely appreciate its architectural merits.

The initial church cost £10000, which is often described as *"an immense sum for that period"*. In 1846, when Henry [vi] Curwen (Christian Curwen's son) added the new tower, it cost a further £1700. By comparison, the Methodist church (now still standing in South William Street), when re-built nearly seventy years after St. Johns, cost a total of just £5000.

The architect for St. Johns was Thomas Hardwick. [01] Who in 1795, had rebuilt St. Paul's Church, in London's Covent Garden. The *"mighty Tuscan portico"* of St. John's (as described in Nikolaus Pevsner's 1967 guide) is an enlarged copy of that at St. Paul's. [02] Being originally designed by Inigo Jones (1573-1652), the once surveyor-general to Charles I. Despite it's early criticism, St. John's is now listed in the top three of the best surviving examples of British *"Classical"* churches designed by Thomas Hardwick.

Internally, St. John's with it's very high flat ceiling, and lit by ten tall side windows has always been bright and airy. However, when the church was first erected the layout was quite different from today. The altar was still in it's present position at the west end, [03] but it had no large gilded canopy or baldachino. The side galleries are very much the same, still supported on the two rows of the original thin fluted cast iron columns.

The area in front of the altar was dominated by a very large *"three-decker"* pulpit, placed immediately in front of the altar rails. Former curate Rev. David Woods [04] observed that it must have then obscured *"the holy table from much of the congregation"*. The pulpit, made from plain dark panelled wood, had the clerk's desk at ground level. Above and behind which was a reading desk, reached by it's own flight of steps. At the upper level was a tall pulpit, again with it's own stairs. Because of it's prominence Woods believes that the church was first designed *"primarily for the ministry of the word"*. The clerk's desk was thought to have been abolished in 1878, by 1882 the pulpit had been reduced in height, to just two levels.

Behind the altar was a large tall, carved dark oak reredos or ornamental screen. It was decorated with festoons of flowers and cherub's heads, and was painted with

[01] At the time Thomas Hardwick (1752-1829) was commissioned to design St. Johns, he was in partnership with his son Philip Hardwick (1792-1870). Philip is believed to have greatly assisted his elderly father in much of this work, being mentioned several times in records and correspondence. He also went on to design the famous monumental Doric gateway to London's Euston Station, built between 1836-40 (and sadly demolished in 1962). ∎

[02] St. Paul's, Covent Garden (built in 1631) is the earliest surviving classical church, in England. It's portico, with columns and pediments, is modelled on the sixteenth century Italian churches, which themselves are based on Roman Tuscan temples. Even then, this church and its style of architecture did not escape criticism. Shortly after it was erected it was described as the *"handsomest barn in Europe"*.

Between 1788-9, Thomas Hardwick had also carried out extensive re-building works at this church, including re-casing its exterior. When it had to be re-built after the 1795 fire, he is thought to have adhered very closely to Inigo Jones' original designs. ∎

[03] Some of the more elderly members of the St. John's congregation may still remember that the altar was once at the east end of the church, under the tower. It was moved here in 1904, but the whole church was reversed again to it's original position by late 1931. ∎

[04] In 1966, Rev. David Woods, a former curate at St. Johns, wrote a well-researched and detailed history of the church. This was published in a small 16 page booklet. ∎

the Lord's Prayer, the Ten Commandments, and Apostle's Creed. John Christian Curwen gifted the first organ in 1826, It was rebuilt in 1904, when the church was altered.

The oldest ornament to be found in the church is the Royal Coat of Arms, which can be seen on the East Gallery above the font. Although quite deceptive, it is actually a piece of well executed wool cross-stitch, said to be by Misses May and Christian How (the sisters of Rev. Peter How). For 37 years, Peter How (1759-1831) was Rector of St. Michaels, and also the first Vicar of St. Johns. Woods records it as having been presented to the church in 1828. However, it appears to bear the later date of 1845, and just the name *"C. How"*, which more than likely refers to Christian How.

As St. Johns was initially a chapel, administered from St. Michaels, it was 1856 before it had it's own Vicar. Previous to then it had been cared for by a perpetual curate attached to the mother church. Rev. John C. Curwen (1799-1840) the fourth son of John Christian Curwen, was appointed the first curate of the chapel, at its consecration. Rev. Curwen later became Rector of Harrington in 1828. A list of the early incumbents of St. John's (upto 1871) is shown below. In 1863, a vicarage for the rector of St. John's, was built on Park End Road, opposite the top of Elizabeth Street.

List of early Incumbents of St. John's Church

John C. Curwen (1823-28),
John Simpson (1828-31),
Peter Von Essen (1831-40),
William Jackson (1840-56),
John Irving (1856-61),
John Thomas (1861-62),
James Pearson (1862-71).

Parish Registers of St. John's Church.

Baptisms are recorded from January 1824. Although between May 1824 and Nov 1835, there appears to be a gap in the records. Some may then have been recorded in St. Michael's registers. Whilst the Marriage and Burial registers, appear complete and date from around December 1835. Today these early registers have also been deposited at the Whitehaven Record Office. ■

The Graveyard at St. John's Church

The Graveyard extended in 1850s, today contains around 180 stones many now broken and decayed. Like St. Michael's other stones have also been removed for easy maintenance. A basic (but incomplete) transcript of some stone inscriptions is also available at Whitehaven Record Office. A Parish Magazine appears to have began in October 1889. ■

ROMAN CATHOLICISM
OUR LADY & ST. MICHAEL'S CHURCH

FROM around the Reformation, despite the Curwen family's patronage and support for the Parish Church and its Church of England teachings; many successive Lords of the Manor appear to have adhered to the Roman Catholic faith. They had there own chapel at the Hall and at times their own chaplain.

Some confusion exists as to who was the last eighteenth century Roman Catholic Curwen. Certainly there is little dispute that Henry [iii] Curwen, who died in 1725 was an devout *"papist"*. Whilst others record his successor Henry [iv] Curwen, who died just two years later, as the last of the line. Either way it has been described as calamitous for the Catholics of the town, when Eldred [ii] Curwen eventually succeeded to the estates, as he was a practising Anglican. Almost immediately they lost not just their only place of worship in the town, but perhaps also their resident priest. Whilst the size of Workington's Catholic congregation was never great, it soon was dwindled to just a couple of households. Bishop Gastrell's *Notitia* written between 1714-25 had recorded that there were then around fourteen Catholic residents in the town. By the Bishop of Chester's 1779 parish survey just one Roman Catholic family was listed. Their only local spiritual support coming from the Benedictine mission at Whitehaven.[01]

It was many decades later before another Catholic chapel was again established in Workington. John Christian Curwen anxious for hard-working labourers for his collieries and farms, had induced quite a number of Irish families to move to the town.[02] Irish workers were also well known for their cheapness in wage terms. But, many of those who arrived to take up his offer of employment, were naturally Catholics. In October 1810, Fr. Clement Rishton was sent from St. Laurence's monastery, Ampleforth, to take charge of a new mission in the town.

Fr. Rishton, aided and supported by Christian Curwen, was initially allowed to say mass in the colliery school at Chapel Bank. As the congregation increased a larger room in the Assembly Rooms was later used in Portland Square. By 1814 a new chapel, (about 18m in length by 9m wide) had been erected on the present Banklands church site.[03] Here we find the first dedication of a Catholic church in the town to St. Michael the Archangel. A small school room was also added quite soon after, adjoining this new chapel. Later also a presbytery or priest's house was built. The congregation was now said to be several hundred. Of the town's population, at least one person in twenty could now be considered Catholic.

Whellan in 1860, provides us with a very brief description of this first Banklands chapel, saying simply *"It is beautifully fitted up, and will seat about five hundred persons"*. In 1814, his work almost completed Fr. Rishton returned to Ampleforth, to be replaced by Fr. Stephen Barber, the new priest.

As Workington's Parish church now followed the Anglican or Church of England teachings, the Catholic members of the Curwen family, are said to have attended mass in the chapel at Workington Hall.

[01] The Benedictine (or "Bens") mission at Whitehaven was established in 1706. ■

[02] Between 1809-12 it is estimated that John Christian Curwen brought nearly five hundred migrant workers into the town to work in his pits alone. The 1861 census revealed 1589 non-indigenous workers in the town, nearly 24% of the population. A great proportion of which were of Irish decent.

[03] This site owned by John Christian Curwen, was let to the Catholic Church on a 999 year lease at an annual rent of £5. Every year when received by the family, it is said to have always been *"gracefully"* returned to the church, as a donation. ■

Almost immediately the town was gripped by days of sometimes serious violent and vicious riots and disorder. There had in recent months been a large influx of apparently hard-working Catholic Irishmen into the area; and a strong feeling of jealousy appears to have developed amongst the Protestant working-class townspeople. This envy and animosity seems to have been fuelled by both their religious differences, and a nervousness that these Irish workers would threaten their employment.

Few contemporary details exist of this rioting. However, a long account was published by the *"Maryport Locomotive"*, a local newspaper. Much of the following information has been drawn from this article, supplemented by information which has since surfaced in correspondence and other newspapers.

As Easter 1814 approached, there had been a gradual increase in clashes and incidents between the two groups. Many brawls occurring in or around the various pubs and beer houses. The most serious incident happened just before midnight on Sunday 13 April, in Elizabeth Street. John Murphy an Irishman and tailor in the town was seen in an intense scuffle with three or four other unidentified men. During the fight Murphy appeared to draw a musket, which some say was fired during the struggle.

No one appeared to be injured, but soon after Murphy was discovered dead in the street. He had a deep cut on his temple, evidently from being struck with a axe or *"sharp iron instrument"*. The *Cumberland Pacquet* graphically reported how *"his skull having been fractured in the most shocking way"*. This news spread rapidly and greatly shocked the town. But despite the offer of a fifty pounds reward, the perpetrators seem never to have been discovered.

Through the following months, the indifferences and turmoil smouldered on. Then James Grenan, a collier and protestant Orangeman, [01] returned from Ireland with a copy of the *"Orange Lodge Warrant"*. This famous document publicly denouncing the Catholic Creed, was distributed throughout the town. As the Catholic people [02] gradually learnt of its existence, the serious division between the communities became almost intolerable.

On the evening of the second Saturday in September, both groups clashed in the Butter Market, Washington Street and Franklin Street. [03] But as the *Maryport Locomotive* reported *"Nothing occurred, however, beyond a desultory running fight, and a few broken heads"*. In the same streets, the following evening the scene was quite different, the crowds were very much larger, some carrying sticks and the few skirmishes become increasingly vicious. John Christian Curwen, then 58 and described as

"The town was gripped by days of sometimes serious violent and vicious riots and disorder".

[01] The Orangemen (members of the Orange Lodge, Order or Society) were formed in 1795, by Protestants in county Armagh, Ireland. Their aim to work for the continuation of British rule and Protestant supremacy in Ireland. The Orangemen were, however, charged with anti-Roman Catholic bigotry and were forced to suspend their activities in 1836. ■

[02] Locally the Irish population, who were principally referred to as *"Trashers"* or *"Croppies"*, because many of them then worked on John Christian Curwen's farms. ■

[03] The Butter Market was located in what is now referred to as Market Place (between Wilson Street and Nook Street). Franklin Street was the name of a street which once connected the Market place to Washington Street. ■

the *"Old Squire"*, rode over from Workington Hall and fear-lessly *"through the throng"*. As he called for them all to retire to their homes, he was apparently loudly heckled by the anti-Catholics. Resolutely he repeated his demands, hoping that events would not escalate, until he could muster the militia, from Whitehaven.

The crowds did eventually begin to disperse, the Irish apparently almost immediately, Christian Curwen eventually persuading the others to also follow. However early the next morning, a group of several hundreds marched through the streets again, preceded by the sound of the drum and fife. The group was thought to have been lead by a methodist minister and his brother in law, each with a broad bright drawn sword. Although the *Maryport Locomotive* report did not name these leaders, it did hint at their identity by giving them the initials H.C. and J.S. For twenty four hours this motley group, many of whom were armed *"with swords, muskets, pikes and treenails"*, [01] moved menacingly from one Irish house to another. Ransacking each in search of anti-Protestant documents and propaganda.

Many Irishmen and their families quickly fled from the town, some hiding for days in quarries and fields. A few even took refuge at Workington Hall, some foolishly even attempted to fight off the crowd. But worst was to come, rumours surfaced that Christian Curwen had smuggled over an additional 500 Irishmen. Some believed they lay in wait, hidden in the stooks of a corn field (on Harrington Road) close to the Catholic chapel. Armed and ready to take possession of the town.

It is said truth is stranger than fiction, but what happened next is quite amazing, if true. The protestant crowd now surrounded the field, ready to attack. Each and every stook was violently hacked through and destroyed, but not one Irishman was found dead or alive. Aggravated further by being foolishly deceived, they desecrated and attacked the nearby Roman Catholic chapel and its school room. Windows were smashed and the furniture destroyed, their brutality not satisfied until they had desecrated the altar, the crucifixes and other sacred relics.

By Wednesday morning, after over three days of mob unrest, the local militia (or local volunteer band of part-time soldiers) finally arrived from Whitehaven. They set up their guard room in the Hall's stable yard, (where the Magistrates court now stands). Despite further isolated incidents, an uneasy peace was generally restored quite quickly, A troop of the 3rd Kings Own Dragoons, [02] under the command of Captain Bower, later replacing the militia. Light infantry such as these soldiers were often

".......a group of several hundreds marched through the streets, preceded by the sound of the drum and fife......armed with swords, muskets and pikes".

[01] A treenail was a long wooden pin, used for fasterning planks of a wooden ship to the timber frame. ■

[02] John Martin recorded that the 3rd King's Own Regiment of Dragoons, finally re-linguished their duties as peace keepers, leaving the town on the morning of 25 June 1815. Their orders were to reinforce the troops fighting at Waterloo. Although it is doubtful if they saw action, for twenty-three days later Wellington had finally defeated Napoleon. The 3rd King's Own Dragoons are now amalgamated into the Queen's Own Hussars. ■

Abbot Vincent Cuthbert Clifton
(1818-91)
Ordained in 1843, he was the priest at Our Lady & St. Michael's R.C Church, from 1844 until his death in 1891. He died on 5 Dec1891 and is buried in Banklands cemetery. ■

Priests of Our Lady & St. Michael R.C. Church (to 1891)
Clement Rishton (1810-14), Stephen Barber (1814), Bede Rigsby (1814-16), Clement Rishton (1819-20), Adrian Towers (1820-22), Ignatius Abram (1822-30), Anselm Glassbrook (1831-38), Francis Ker-shaw (1838-41), Ignatius Sutton (1841-42), Michael Ginnovan (1843-44) Cuthbert Clifton (1844-91).   William Whellan in 1860 provides much the same list as above, but many have a different, more traditional christian names. One not listed above was Francis Williams (1844). ■

Registers of Our Lady & St. Michael R.C. Church
The baptism and marriage registers appear to begin around Oct 1810, although few are recorded between Nov 1816 and Sept 1819 (some are thought to have then been performed at Whitehaven during this period). The baptisms are then recorded upto present day. Whilst marriages are recorded from 1856 to present day. The register of burials cover the period of 1855 to present day. These registers can be examined upon application to The Priory, Banklands. ■

The Graveyard
Today there remains just 35 decaying gravestones in the Banklands cemetery. Like other graveyards in the town, many stones have been cleared inorder to make maintenance easier. There appear to be no recorded list of inscriptions. ■

used during similar disorder, as there was then simply no established police force. They remained in the town for almost nine months. Becoming almost a permanent presence, whilst the inhabitants reconciled their religious differences. As well as patrolling the streets, soldiers were almost constantly on guard at the Catholic chapel and school room.

Exactly if the principle perpetrators of these tragic scenes, were ever brought to justice, is not clear. Today, correspondence available in the Lowther papers, names the prominent shipbuilder Kelsick Wood, as leading the protestant group, *"armed with a musket"*. He is also said to have given some of the mob, *"both money and drink"*. John Christian Curwen was said to have threatened him with eviction from his shipyard. But he appears to have escaped any real punishment. After all the commotion, only few are known to have been arrested and charged with disorder offences.

No doubt this shameful blot on the town's history and the general feeling of unrest, again dramatically affected the size of the Catholic congregation. For when Fr. Bede Rigsby left in September 1816, the town was once more without a priest for almost three years. It is unclear who officiated at services, they may even have ceased for a time. During this period, only eleven baptisms are recorded at the chapel, the majority of others seem to have been performed at Whitehaven.

In Sept 1819, Fr. Clement Rishton who had previously helped establish the new church, returned to the town. His task much as before was once more to consolidate the Catholic community. For the next twenty years or so, six more priests followed each staying on average four years.

Appointed in 1844, Abbot Vincent Cuthbert Clifton was the next parish priest. Despite recording that on his arrival he found *"the chapel in a shocking condition, a wretched school with about a dozen children in it; the house badly furnished and scarcely fit for habitation"*. He stayed at Workington for almost half a century, making an outstanding contribution to Catholicism in the town. Among his many achievements was the building of the present church, opened 21 Sept 1876. Together with establishing St. Michael's convent for the Sisters of Charity of St. Paul. The nuns not only staffed and taught in the school, but also cared for the church and visited the poor and sick throughout the parish.

WESLEYAN METHODIST CHURCH.

THE Wesleyan Methodists, often referred to as simply the Wesleyans, are named after their founders John & Charles Wesley. From 1749-88, John Wesley was a frequent visitor to West Cumberland, preaching at White-haven (then one of the largest ports in the British Isles) some 26 times, from 1749-88. His journals tell us that he made his trips on horseback, usually travelling by way of and stopping off in Cockermouth. He is also thought to have visited Workington on at least two occasions.

He first sermon in the town was delivered on Sunday afternoon of 16 April 1761, at the Assembly Rooms in Portland Square. Preaching the doctrines of Christian perfection and personal salvation through faith, John Wesley had quickly won an enthusiastic following among the working classes. However, one record of this visit questions if *"the greater proportion"* of the congregation actually *"understood anything"*.

Although Wesleyan Methodism dates its birth from 24 May 1738, the actual date of the establishment of its first church in the town, is not quite clear. Whellan writing in 1860, thought Rev. Jonathan Brown formed the first congregation around 1767. When they would assemble for worship in the Hall stables, on Bridge Street. Others suggest that an early place of worship was in a building (perhaps a private house) in Ritson Street, off Nook Street.

In 1772, when Wesley is thought to have returned again to the town. He later disappointingly wrote in a letter to John Mason, *"scarce anyone came to hear....I am afraid there is no more place for us at Workington"*. For almost twenty years the very small congregation appear to have struggled on and continued to worship in the Ritson Street building. But gradually the methodist preaching seemed to gain increased popularity. As Dr. John Burgess[01] observed Methodism was rather akin to Quakerism in it's *"strict moral attitudes, a reaction to the immorality and crudeness prevalent"* at the time. But people generally trusted the Methodists and found their services truly inspirational to their thoughts, both from the preachings and prayers, and through communal singing of uplifting hymns.

On Sunday 15 April 1792, their first chapel was opened in Tiffen Lane. [02] This *"beautiful new"* building described as almost *"square and barn-like"* was situated at the Brow Top end of Tiffin Lane, on it's east side. A closer look at the north west corner of the Opera House, reveals the remains of the old chapel structure. Often Tiffin Lane is also referred to as Methodists Lane. [03]

"The world is my Parish and Methodism is the friend of all and the enemy of none"
John Wesley (1703-1791)

[01] Dr. John Burgess *wrote "The Achievements of Cumbrian Methodism"*, in 1982. He has also carried out enormous amount of research into the religious history of the county. Although most of this work has not been widely published. Copies of his manuscripts are deposited in Local Studies sections of most Cumbrian libraries. ■

[02] A report from the *Cumberland Pacquet* records - At the first service in the new 1792 chapel an *"excellent sermon"* was preached by a Mr. Brown. (perhaps Rev. Jonathan Brown) Based on John XIV. v2 *"In my father's house are many mansions"*. ■

[03] The 1851 census reveals there was then 25 adults and 15 children living in a dozen cottages in this narrow thoroughfare. Many of these dwellings ran along the east side of the lane now occupied by the Opera House. ■

In June 1810, when the first Sunday School commenced it had an attendance of almost 450 children. This provides an indication of the size of the adult Wesleyan congregation. Then it must have numbered many hundreds. As the town's entire population was less than 5800, upto around 15% may be assumed to be have been methodist.

In 1840, a new Church was built on the South William Street site, now occupied by the present Trinity Methodist Church. It was opened by Rev. J. Beaumont on Christmas Day. It was a elegant georgian building, set back from the street, a sketch of which appears below.

The principle partners in one of the town's prominent employers Messrs. Guy & Harrison, were then also both very prominent methodists. Jonathan Guy, Jonathan Harrison together with their families were for many years the major subscribers when funds were required to improve the church. In 1855, one such fund was raised amongst the congregation to pay for the installation of an organ in the church. It cost a little over £110, and was installed in the arched end of the church, above the altar.

The early church records, including the minute books of the church trustees are now thought lost, so not many of its other active members are now known. Rev. John Talbot is recorded as the first superintendent of the new 1840 church. Whilst Joseph Dunn (1807-49) is known to have been one of the trustees at the time this church was built. He sadly died in August 1849 from the cholera outbreak, which was then prevalent in the town.

BELOW - sketch of the Georgian style, Wesleyan Methodist Church, which once stood on the site of to-day's Trinity Methodists Church. Built in 1840, it was destroyed by a fire on 6 April 1887. ■

At the time this new church was constructed, sufficient funds were simply not available to build a new Sunday School on the same site. The old Tiffin Lane chapel was then converted into a Sunday School and remained in use for a further forty years. Internally, it was partitioned down it's centre, inorder to divide the girls from the boys. The Sunday School students being marched in procession, along Finkle Street, between the two buildings. In 1883 the present Sunday School rooms were built at the rear of the new Church, both now were accommodated on the same site.

Unfortunately the original South William Street church was destroyed by a tragic fire on the Saturday evening of 6 April, 1889. For the second time in just over two years the town had lost another major church building. The Methodist church, not even fifty years old, had like St. Michaels, been totally reduced to ashes. The present church (now called the Trinity Methodist church) was rebuilt on the same site and opened on 9 Oct 1890.

"For the second time in just over two years, the town had lost another major church building, through a tragic fire".

Ministers of Weslyan Methodist Church
Between 1769-1840 the ministers of the church were part of the Whitehaven circuit. From 1840-54 a separate Workington circuit, was formed out of Whitehaven, but the names of the ministers are not easily determined. The two groups were reunited again between 1854-66, but afterwards split again. Some of the known ministers at Workington are John Talbot (1854), Matthew Salt (1854), Jonathan Barrowclough (1857), Joseph R. Cleminson (1857) and George Hobson (1866). ■

Baptism Registers

Baptism registers for the Workington Circuit of the Wesleyan Methodist Church exist from 1841-1992, and are deposited at Whitehaven Record Office. Pew rent books are also available for 1827-1916. ■

PRIMITIVE METHODIST CHURCH

AROUND 1810, the Methodist Church split into several separate Methodist denominations, each maintaining its own version of the Wesleyan tradition. One such group were the Primitive Methodists. The Workington congregation was founded in 1823, and three years later they built their own church on a site in the upper part of John Street. This church which cost £930, and held a congregation of 500 people, 260 pews being free to the poor.

Little further is known of the first church, as it was replaced by an entirely new structure in 1882. This Gothic style building with a school-room in it's basement, is the one many older readers will recall. Later it was demolished by Workington Borough Council, to make way for the first stage of St. John's Shopping Precinct. In 1965, as the Primitive Methodist Church had closed, the congregation merged once more with the Wesleyans, to jointly use the South William Street church. After much debate the new group was named Trinity Methodist Church.

Baptism Register of Primitive Methodist Church

Baptism Registers dating from 1884 to1965 and is deposited at Whitehaven Record Office. ■

PRESBYTERIAN CHURCH

THE old Presbyterian church (now the Workington Christian Fellowship) still stands in Sanderson Street (almost opposite the Midland Bank and presently surrounded on three sides by car parks). Although clearly part of the Presbyterian Church of England, due to it's origins it was often referred to as the *Scotch Church* or *High Meeting House*.

Whellan in his 1860 history recorded that the congregation was first formed around 1742. The inscription on the gravestone of it's first minister, Rev. Mr. William Thompson, seems to confirm this. It once stood in St. Michael's churchyard and recorded how he *"formed a Society of Protestant Dissenters in Workington, collected funds, and built a Meeting and dwelling House"*. He was 73 years old when he died on 24 March 1782, being *"Forty years as their Pastor"*.

The existing church building was entirely rebuilt around 1888. It stands on the same site as two early chapels, one built around 1858, replacing a first chapel (built in 1750) and a manse on the same site. This 1858 church cost only around £700, being designed by local architect Charles Eaglesfield, in the *"Early English"* Gothic style. Internally the church held 400 people, of which 10% of the pews were then free for the use of the poor. The roof was supported by exposed stained timber roof trusses.

PASTORS OF PRESBYTERIAN CHURCH (upto 1859)

The following list may not be complete (dates are only shown where known) - Rev. Messrs. Thompson (1742-82), John Selkirk (1782-1829), Turner (1829), Nicholson (1842), Turbit, William Gordon (1851), Alexander Douglas, David McLeod. ■

REGISTERS OF PRESBYTERIAN CHURCH

At Whitehaven Record Office, the Baptism registers exist for the following periods 1745-1827, 1865-71, 1889-1979. The Marriages are recorded for 1838-82 and 1889-99, with some additional entries for church members married elsewhere. Burials (in Harrington Road Cemetery) are listed for 1879-1882. There is also Communicants lists for 1860-64 & 1868-1980. ■

INDEPENDENT CONGREGATIONAL CHURCH

THE church we now refer to as the United Reform Church also situated on South William Street, (virtually opposite the Methodist Church) was originally called the *Independent Chapel* or *Low Meeting House*. The present gothic style building was not erected till 1884. The Sunday School to the rear has a 1887 datestone above it's entrance. These replaced a much older buildings thought to have been erected before 1786, and later much remodelled and enlarged in 1855. The cost of these 1855 alterations, which included the enlargement of the burial ground and provision of a new organ were around £408. The congregation which had always essentially managed it's own affairs, was received into the County Congregational Association in 1843.

The original chapel or meeting house was initially thought to have been endowed by Lady Glenorchy. [01] Whellan (in 1860) believed that in 1786, Lady Glenorchy had *"on her way to Scotland, stopped at Workington, where she purchased the ground for the erection of the chapel, and saw the work commenced before she left"*.

However, he appears only partially correct, the minutes of the early chapel reveal that Lady Glenorchy did visit the town in June 1786, returning from her mother's in London. Here she discovered a small congregation in the recently built small chapel, burdened by large debts. She greatly sympathised with the Presbyterian persuasions of the group, and cleared their debts of around £250, owed to Peter McCan (a mercer or dealer in silks, linen or cotton cloth). Thereby becoming the owner of the meeting house and its adjoining graveyard. [02]

The Workington chapel was the last of many, to be endowed by Lady Glenorchy, for she died less than a month later on 17 July 1786. One of her last tasks was to appoint preacher, Rev. Henry Muschet, who had previously been at her Carlisle *"Glenorochy"* chapel. Muschet was to remain at Workington till 1787, records infer him departing under something of a cloud, after the church accounts were inspected.

Rev. John Selkirk is thought to have then taken over from Muschet. Although a plaque on the north wall of the present church, extols the virtues of Rev. Samuel Peel (1765-1848) recording him as the second minister. Serving as pastor of the chapel for 56 years, until his death at the age of 83. This would suggest that Peel didn't take over as minister until 1792, someone therefore must have been appointed to supersede Mushet, perhaps Selkirk. This may also be the same Rev. John Selkirk (1750-1829) who was pastor at the town's Sanderson Street Presbyterian Church (from around 1782). It is quite possible for him to have preached at both chapels. Presbyterian worship has always allowed for considerable flexibility in forms and practices, and their teachings were very much alike.

REGISTERS OF INDEPENDENT CONGREGATIONAL CHURCH

Deposited at Whitehaven Record Office, the Baptism Registers cover the periods 1787-1847, 1853-86, and 1907-24; Marriages - 1856-84 and 1908-18; Burials - 1789-1846, 1864-1940 and 1856-1904; Elders are listed for 1787-1836; and Church members for 1802-1904, 1897-1910 and 1900. The church yard (which faces onto Vulcan's Lane) is said to date from before 1786. Today it contains only around thirty stones. The last burial is thought to have be performed by Rev. David Wiseman, in autumn 1966. ■

[01] Lady Glenorchy was Williema Maxwell (1741-86). She was born in Kirkbean, in Kirkcudbright, daughter of a very wealthy doctor. She married into the titled Campbell family of Glenorchy in 1764. Despite meeting John Wesley several times, her religious views were aligned more to the Calvinistic Protestant dissenters of Scottish Presbyterian convictions. With her inherited fortunes, she endowed several such independent chapels throughout the country, including one in Annettwell Street, Carlisle. ■

[02] A record of the payment of the debt, and the purchase of the *"New Chapel & Burying ground adjoining"* exists dated 19 June 1786. The deed being drawn up by Jeroni Thompson, attorney of Workington. ■

CHAPTER SEVEN

PORT, HARBOUR & SHIPPING

*"The Harbour of Working-
ton is an ancient public port or
harbour, formed by a creek or gut
of the River Derwent."*

PERHAPS the first historical reference to any ship based at Workington occurs in the 1299-1300 accounts of Edward I. It tells us that the ship *"Mariote"* was hired to carry supplies to the Kings forces, then fighting the Scots in Galloway. Written in Latin it states - *"Alexo de Werkenton, magro navis que vocatur le Mariote de Werkenton, et 6 sociis nautis, pro vadiis suis, per idem tempus £1.8.0."* This roughly translates to *"Alexander of Workington, master of the ship - Mariote of Workington and his six associated seamen"* receive £1.8s.0d. (now £1.40) for an unknown hire period. In the same accounts, locally there was only one other ship requisitioned along the West Cumberland coast, being from Whitehaven. [01]

There are very few further references to Workington as a harbour, until the sixteenth century. Around 1535, John Leland, [02] then the Kings Antiquary, visited the town and described it as *"wher as shyppes cum to, wher ys a pretty fysher town, cawlid Wyrkenton, and ther is the chif house of Sir Thomas Curwyn"*.

A further account exists from the *English State Papers*, dated April 1566. Henry Lord Scrope, John Aglionby and George Lamplugh were commissioned by Queen Elizabeth, to report on *"all ports, creeks, and landing places in Cumberland; also of the towns and inhabitants, what ships, boats, and other vessels belong to them, with regard to the transporting of corn, victuals, and other unlawful merchandise out of the realm, as also for the receiving the like hither, brought by way of piracy, or in any other unlawful manner."*

Initially, one might suppose that the need for such a survey was related solely to combat the likelihood of smuggling, along the Cumberland coast. But it is far more conceivable that this information was being assembled, to identify landing places for Her Majesty's troops. The English-Scottish frontier was being plagued by the perpetual hostilities of Border Reivers. Henry Lord Scrope was infact the Warden of the English West March. [03] A governing officer appointed to maintain law and order, along the western end of the border on the English side.

George MacDonald Fraser in his book of the Border Reivers *The Steel Bonnets*, points out that the border country was divided into six separate administrative areas or zones, *"three on the Scottish side and three on the English"*.

[01] J. Topham transcribed these details from the original manuscript in 1787. The translation is attributed to Dr. Brian Moffat, being published in the fourth volume of the Unicorn journal (see bibliography). ■
[02] John Leland or Leyland (c1506-1552) was the King's Antiquary, who visited the town around 1533, whilst on a journey throughout England. ■
[03] Henry Scrope (1534-1592) was the ninth Lord Scrope of Bolton. He was Warden of the English West March in 1563-92, becoming a prominent Border official. His son Thomas was to succeed him as Warden. ■

Cumberland was in the English West March, while Galloway came into the Scottish West March. At the eastern end of the English-Scottish border, around Berwick, there was the Scottish East March and the English East March, which were north and south of the borderline respectively. In between we had the Scottish Middle March and the English Middle March.

Their concise three page, report listed Bowstead Hill creek, Skinburness, Ellnesfoot (Maryport), Workington, Parton, Whitehaven, Ravenglass and Powsfoot creek. The Workington entry is interesting in so much as it provides an indication both of the size of the town in the sixteenth century, as well as its early fishing industry.

It reads: *"Workington creek, having a town; - Deputies John and William Curwen, Henry Hewetson and Thomas Scale; 30 households of the inheritance of Henry Curwen, but he has never given licence for the loading or unloading of vessels. There are three vessels here called pickerdes, of seven or eight tons, belonging to John Day, John Sybson and Leonard Hodgeson; their trade is to go to Chester and Liverpool with herrings, and they bring back salt. The mariners are hired fishermen."*

It seems that of the few other fishing boats, berthed at the *"havens or creeks"* between Workington and Ravenglass, all were concerned with fishing for herrings. Catches were then usually taken south and landed at Chester or Liverpool. When the vessels returned they brought back salt or occasionally iron or wines. The report concluded that no other ships frequented these small ports.

Herrings, which included the pilchard (the young of which is the common sardine), and the shad, were once economically the most important group of fish caught in the Solway. Once quite abundant, they would swim near the surface of the water in huge schools, feeding on plankton. It was often said that there was so many that you could almost *"walk on them"*. By 1850, the situation was obviously quite different as newspaper reports frequently state how unproductive herring fishing had become. Today, herring catches off the West Cumbrian coast are almost nonexistent, although some are still landed on the Isle of Man.

Besides fresh, salted or pickled herring, these fish were often also smoked until it hardened, as well as being kippered. The 1569 town plan shows *"the fyish houses"* close to the mouth of the Derwent, and a *"salt pan"* a little further south along the shoreline. This evidence seems to suggest that the herring catches could have been processed here, before being taken south. However, exactly what method was used to preserve them be

It was often said that there was so many herrings in the Solway, you could almost *"walk on them"*.

it smoked, salted, or both is not recorded.

Following on from his 1566 report, Lord Scrope in a later letter to Lord Burghley, dated April 1572, comments how *"ships of great burden may arrive at Ravenglass, Whitehaven, Workington and Elnefoot, where a ship of 60 or 90 tons may come in on the spring tide"*. Apparently, an intelligence ship had been sent to inspect the coastline, *"plumbing and sounding all the way"*, up to Kirkcudbright. There is little doubt that on this occasion his survey was now primarily for military purposes.

The earliest surviving plan of the mouth of the Derwent is likely to be the 1569 plan. [01] It highlights an area of land then owned by Henry [i] Curwen, and required by the Keswick based *Company of Mines Royal,* [02] for a wharf or quay. This German mining company had been formed in 1564, and granted permission by Elizabeth I *"to seek out and mine gold, silver and copper"*, throughout the North of England. They had began their operations at Keswick in April 1565, bringing with them around fifty German miners. At the time German mining methods were considered the most advanced throughout Europe.

Henry Curwen initially requested 20 marks (£13-6s-8d) per annum, for the land situated on the south side of the Derwent. This was considered quite an excessive sum and Simon Musgrave (of Eden Hall) was later asked by both the Secretary of State, to intercede on behalf of the company and persuade Henry to reduce the asking price. Following some negotiations, Musgrave [03] succeeded in obtaining a much more acceptable annual rent of just £5. It was during these negotiations and subsequent trading between the German miners and the Curwen family, that the Augsberg clock reputed to have been given to the family by Mary Queen of Scots, may well have been given as a gift, or even used as a bargaining tool. (see chapter eighteen)

Whether or not, the Keswick mining company eventually built its wharf on the site is unclear. Around a century later, it is recorded that no wharf existed actually at the harbour. It is more than likely that goods were then simply landed on the shore, or river banks. W.G. Collingwood in his 1912 book *Elizabethan Keswick*, suggests that Workington was not actually used to export the copper, mined at Dalehead and Goldscope in the Newlands valley. This copper, inspite of the added expense and greater distance, was usually transported overland east to Newcastle. Perhaps as from there it was a much shorter sea route to London and the continent. With or without a wharf structure, Workington was certainly used by the

[01] This plan, again from the English State papers, shows the piece of ground, together with a plan of the river and town adjacent. It is to be found in the Public Record office at Kew. (see chapter seven) ■

[02] The agreement forming the *Company of Miners Royal* was between Queen Elizabeth I, Thomas Thurland, Master of Savoy, and Daniel Hechstetter (the agent for Haug, Langnauer and Company, from Augsberg in German Bavaria). Daniel Hechstetter is said to have died in 1581 and is buried at Crosthwaite Church, Keswick. ■

[03] Simon Musgrave was then the former father-in-law of Nicholas [i] Curwen, Henry's eldest son. He had married Anne Musgrave, around 1576. However, she appears to have died before 1586, as Nicholas then married Elizabeth Carus. The choice of Simon Musgrave, as mediator, must have been quite significant as he was the grandfather of Nicholas' eldest son, also Henry. ■

German miners, for the landing of goods and supplies brought by sea from London, before being taken upto Keswick.

It is likely that this proposed wharf was probably intended for importing timber and fuel (perhaps peat) from Ireland. The company is known to have had concerns, that there was then a shortage of suitable fuel locally, to smelt their ore. If only they had then known about the millions of tons of coal, lying undiscovered beneath West Cumberland. Henry Curwen is recorded as sending small quantities of *"sea or stone coal"*, by horseback upto Keswick, for the mining company. This may not have been available in sufficient quantities or it's quality may have been inferior.

The 1569 plan is quite significant to the town's history, as it also tells us a great deal about the Elizabethan town and port. Principally, the note which states, *"the harborye for bote at this present"*. Clearly indicates boats were then being moored and unloaded, on the south side of the South Gut. Perhaps this is where Mary Queen of Scots stepped ashore, when she arrived in the town around a year earlier. (see chapter eighteen)

A 1682 *Exchequer Return* provides the next description of the port. It indicates that there were still *"no wharves or quays"* and goods were simply transferred on and off the river bank. This return also confirms that the south side of the south gut, was still the only recognised landing place. It states *"...that open place at Workington, a creek under the collection of Whitehaven, from the house of late Jno. Miller, near the church, 500 yards down the River Derwent, on the south side thereof."*

From the beginning of the eighteenth century, there was a notable increase in local coal production. Much of which was now exported from Workington to Ireland. In the intervening years since the 1682 report, a small quay must then have now been constructed on the south side of the South Gut. Gradually, coal was beginning to replace fishing as the major trade of the port.

In 1722, there was great concern at the general condition of the harbour. Which is then described as *"of late fallen into decay"* and *"of want of proper fund raising"*. Here we appear to find the first formal agreement to create a group of harbour trustees. From charging a tonnage duty or fee, to be paid by each vessel, they intended not only to repair and maintain the harbour, but also improve it's facilities.

With the introduction of the Harbour trustees, we have the first accurate accounts of the level of trade. In the year ending 1727 - 187 ships visited the port, although

The 1569 plan is quite significant to the town's history, as it also tells us a great deal about the Elizabethan town and port.

there was only 36 different vessels, making two or more return trips (30 of which were registered at Workington). By 1730 - 208 ships sailed from the port, principally with coal to Ireland, the majority returning *"in ballast"*. [01] These first trustees included Henry Curwen (Lord of the Manor of Workington), John Porter (proprietor of Banklands Colliery), John Robertson (who held other Workington colliery leases), Robert Grear and James Gorton (both of Camerton Colliery) and Thomas Bacon (who had pits at Harrington). These being some of the *"proprietors, owners and farmers of coals or coal mines, adjacent to the town"*. In addition there was also the *"owners, mariners and commanders of ships trading from the existing harbour"*. A list of many of the trustees, who served from 1722-1802, is included on page 119. Although not complete it adds greatly to our knowledge of the people who used the eighteenth century port.

Another small quay also now existed, on the north (or Oldside) bank of the estuary, which too was adopted by new trustees. Later plans show this was for exporting coal brought across from Seaton and Clifton. It appears to have been erected initially at the expense of the coal owners or lessees of Camerton colliery. Probably James Gorton of Rubbing House [02] and Robert Grear of Kirkby Stephen. In September 1732, despite both being members of the first trustees, they had to complain about the *"ruinous condition"* of their quay. Reminding the other trustees that they had also agreed several years earlier, to *"further continue"* this north pier *"towards the sea"*. Soon after both the repair work and improvement works were undertaken.

The trustees also permitted ballast to be unloaded on the north side of the South Gut.[03] In the area later to become known as the Merchant's Quay. Ballast was also then being laid on the Crossfitts and Priestgate Marsh areas, then rented by the trustees from the Rector of Workington.[04] After the creation of the trustees, the improvement to the general condition of the harbour was far from instantaneous. Most probably because they were restricted by a lack of working capital to pay for such works. In 1726, we find the harbour *" so choked and barred by the beach which is thrown up by the violence of the sea, and the alteration of the River Derwent, and the disorderly discharge of ballast"*. The trustees being urged to take steps as it was likely to *"prejudice trade"* and *"improverish the inhabitants of Workington"*.

At this time the course of the River Derwent through it's estuary was quite different from today. The river originally looped in a curve along the South Quay. Merchants

[01] The term *"in ballast"* refers to a ship carrying mainly a heavy waste material, such as stone or gravel. It is loaded into ships, when they were to carry little or no cargo, to increase their stability in the water. Before loading a new cargo, the ballast was disguarded on the quayside, and later reused or utilised as building materials. ■
[02] Rubbing House was originally on the Oldside bank of the Derwent. It is shown on the 1863 OS plan. The area of land, between the main road (A595) and Burrow Walls, was also once known as Rubbing House Farm.
[03] Very occasionally, the harbour records show some ships, also leaving the port *"in ballast"*, but these were certainly in the minority. ■
[04] See plan of harbour, opposite for more details. ■

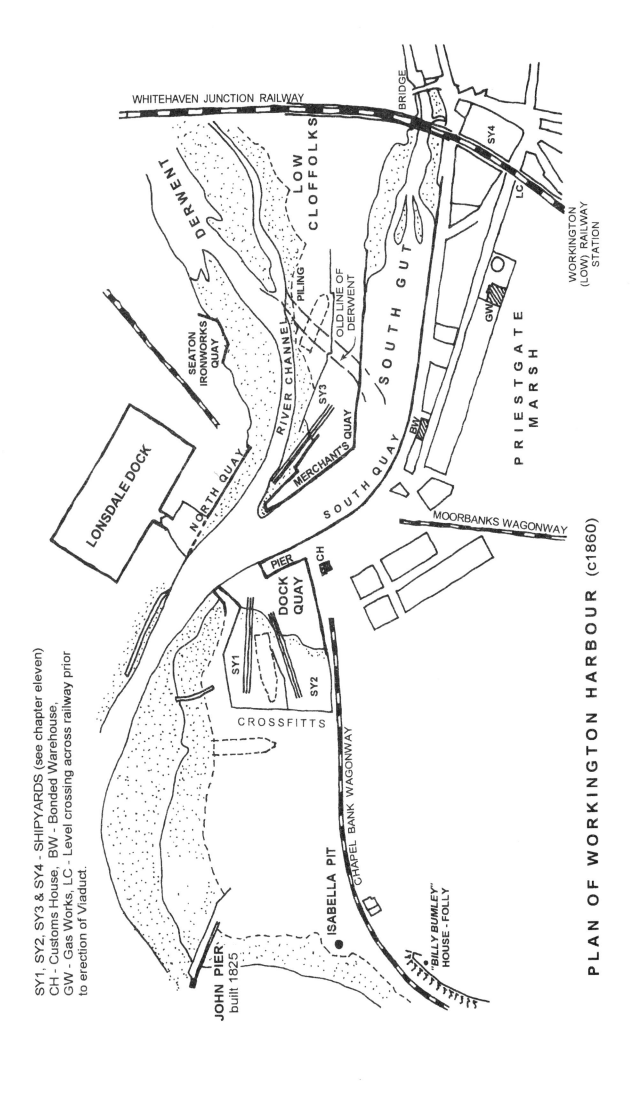

SY1, SY2, SY3 & SY4 - SHIPYARDS (see chapter eleven)
CH - Customs House, BW - Bonded Warehouse,
GW - Gas Works, LC - Level crossing across railway prior
to erection of Viaduct.

PLAN OF WORKINGTON HARBOUR (c1860)

WHITEHAVEN JUNCTION RAILWAY

DERWENT

LOW CLOFFOLKS

BRIDGE

SY4

LC

WORKINGTON (LOW) RAILWAY STATION

SEATON IRONWORKS QUAY

PILING

OLD LINE OF DERWENT

RIVER CHANNEL

SY3

MERCHANT'S QUAY

SOUTH GUT

GW

PRIESTGATE MARSH

LONSDALE DOCK

NORTH QUAY

SOUTH QUAY

BW

MOORBANKS WAGONWAY

PIER

DOCK QUAY

CH

SY1

SY2

CROSSFITTS

CHAPEL BANK WAGONWAY

ISABELLA PIT

"BILLY BUMLEY" HOUSE - FOLLY

JOHN PIER
built 1825

.....the North Quay was used principally to ship coal mined to the north of the Derwent, from Seaton and Clifton.

ABOVE - sketch of the front and reverse sides of a Curwen Colliery Token (from the author's collection). It measures 1.03 inches (26mm) diameter, and is made of copper based metal. It is thought to date from the eighteenth century and was used for the payment of coal transported by horse and cart, from the Curwen pits to the quayside. (see text on opposite page) Another identical example exists in the British Museum Montague Guest collection. ■

Quay as we know it today, was just a sand bank or island, likely to be almost underwater at high tide. Ships, returning for another cargo of coal, now began to deposit their ballast on this area. The eventual aim was to divert the course of the river away from the South Gut, to it's more westward present day line. But in reality the ballast was constantly shifted by the action of tides, and began silting up the approaches to the South Quay.

Robert J. Walker in his well-researched history of the *Port of Workington*, describes how *"a series of wooden stakes were driven into the mouth of the old course, with wicker baskets full of stones deposited in between"*. With this man-made help, the south bank of the Derwent was both reinforced and diverted. This gave added protection to the South Quay and formed a much more sheltered harbour. It was 1765, before the first wharf was build here to form Merchants Quay. Between 1785-7, it was extended by a further 150 feet (45.7m).

In 1764, the North Quay on the Oldside bank of the Derwent, was also extended with *"a very large addition"*. A *"strong wall"* being built and back filled with ballast and gravel. Today, if we look down, as we cross the railway bridge between Merchant's Quay and Oldside, we can still identify almost 150 feet (45m) of this original wall. It surrounds the south east corner of the Prince of Wales Dock. Inset into its face are around twenty steps down from the quayside, now well worn by the feet of innumerable mariners.

Then the North Quay was still used principally to ship coal mined to the north of the Derwent, from Seaton and Clifton. But adjoining it's east corner, as the river bends slightly, was another smaller wharf used by Seaton Ironworks. (see chapter twelve) We know from the harbour records that limestone for the Barepot works, was discharged here from as early as 1791.

Today, we can see that the South Quay extends from west of the old *"swing"* (railway) bridge to the viaduct road bridge, close to St. Michaels Church. But originally it was very much shorter, the first wharf being at it's seaward end. Here were four coal hurries, said to have been erected before 1763 by Henry [v] Curwen. These wooden bridge-like structures, projected over the side of the quay, to allow wagons of coal to be emptied directly into the ships below. They are clearly visible on William H. Barlett's 1837 steel engraving of the harbour, reproduced on page 101. The one nearest the sea was built first and called the *"Low Hurry"*, and that closest to the town the *"High Hurry"*.

Around 1770, Pennant in his description of the port

port records that - *"On each bank near the mouth are piers, where the ships lie; and the coals are conveyed into then from frames occasionally dropping into them from the railroads."* Whilst Matthew Patten (b.1807), who became an apprentice mariner at just 13 years old, records that *"one by one over the mouth of the shoot, the bottom of the wagon was dropped and the coal fell into the ship"*.

Over the years as the size of ships greatly increased, these original hurries, were found to be now too low. Many times it was just impossible to load coal into the vessels, particularly at high spring tides. As a short term measure the hurries were raised in March 1800, but eventually they all had to be replaced with taller structures.

Much of the coal from the town's pits, now arrived at the quayside along two wagonways or railways. One looped around the shoreline from Lady pit; whilst the other much longer track, came down from Banklands and Moorbanks pits. The rails of these trackways were typically of oak and around 4½ inches (115mm) square, pinned to close set sleepers laid on a ballast bed. [01] Generally these wooden railways were also laid on an incline from the pitheads, so gravity aided the motion of the loaded wagons to the harbourside. Where this was not possible the trucks (often also called chauldrons) were horse drawn. As the wagons approached the quayside the tracks led directly up onto the hurries, so they could be easily and quickly emptied.

Without a doubt this railway system, would have greatly decreased loading time and the turn round of ships. Before their construction, coal would have been carried from the pit to the quayside by packhorse, and later horse and cart. Now the port became much more efficient and productive. Furthermore, it had the advantage of reducing the wear and tear, to the towns badly made-up roads. Although on the south side of the harbour, these wagonways were quite deliberately built and controlled by the Curwen family. For a fixed annual rent and they also allowed other coal proprietors to bring their coal down to the harbour, along the tracks.[02] There were also several similar hurries erected along the North Quay.

Small metal tokens (or coins), about the size of an ten pence piece, exist which appear to relate to the transportation of coal to the harbour. Some tokens had the name *"CUR-WEN"* on one side, with the family coat of arms on the reverse. (see sketch opposite) Others are known to have had the initials *"EC"*, believed to have been issued by Eldred Curwen (1692-1745). Harbour accounts record that they were made from a variety of metals, some were brass, copper or even lead. There is no real contem-

[01] The earliest wooden wagonway was thought to have been erected around 1603, at Wollaton in Nottingham. By 1660 Tyneside had around nine, gradually it was quite common for every respectable colliery to acquire one. Oak was used for these early trackways because iron was then quite a scarce and a very expensive material. The design and working of these early trackways played a crucial role in establishing the fundamentals of later steam railways.

Under heavy traffic the wooden rails of the wagonways needed replacement almost every year. The Curwen accounts reveal that in 1806, the Lady Pit wagonway oak rails cost *"8d a yard"* (or 3½p per metre). ■

[02] The hurries on the South quay were also used almost exclusively for the shipment of coal, from the Curwen pits. Except between 1771-8, the Banklands Colliery leasee (see chapter ten) was also allowed to load coal at this quay, afterwards the tenant was also given the privilege. For the privilege the Curwen's received a annual rental. ■

porary evidence to confirm the exact purpose of these coins. However it is suggested that they related to when coal was brought to the harbour by horse and cart, probably before the construction of the wagonways, and later the railways.

Each time a load of coal arrived at the quayside, one of these tokens (or tallies) may have been given to the carrier, and kept by them until the end of the shift, day or week; when they were redeemed for their payment or wage. Between 1765-69, there are several entries in Henry [v] Curwen's accounts for *"tokens delivered at Workington, for coals shipped"*. They clearly show that around £70 worth of these tokens were encashed each week, although it is difficult to deduce their actual value. The issue of similar mining or colliery tokens was quite common particularly throughout West Cumberland. In Whitehaven, some Lowther family tokens exist dated as early as 1679. Although their sizes and styles differed greatly, their designs do seem to confirm the transportation of coal was of major importance to their issue.

This theory regarding the use of these tokens is made more plausible, when Henry Curwen appears to have withdrawn his tokens around May 1769, almost about the same time as his new wagonways would have come into operation.[01] By then it is estimated that there was many thousands of pounds worth of these coins, in circulation around the town. As elsewhere, these tokens may have actually developed into a form of unofficial currency. Particularly as there was a general shortage of official small copper coinage, until late into the eighteenth century.[02]

With the exception of the period 1782-1804, many of the early minute books of the Harbour Trustees now appear lost. Those that do exist provide an indication of their constant struggle against the bank of sand and gravel building up across the mouth to the South Gut. Many times they attempted to deepen the channel, to *"make the harbour capable of receiving vessels of a larger draught of water"*. William Hutchinson in his 1794 *History of Cumberland* records that the town's chief imports were then *"timber, bar-iron and flax"*. The timber was more than likely for the shipbuilding industry, the bar-iron for Seaton Ironworks, and the flax for linen or sail-cloth.

Between 1784 and 1798, the South Quay was extended many times, gradually upwards towards the town. Whilst also rebuilding the older sections, which were described as now being in a *"ruinous condition"*. In September 1788, ninety yards was added to *"breast wall on the south side of the South Gut"* by local mason's John Barton

[01] There is no evidence to suggest the system did not continue for those pits, isolated from the wag-onways. Despite an apparent lack of further later entries in the Curwen accounts, we do know of the existence of local tokens with the initials *"JCC"*. This appears to refer to John Christian Curwen. These one inch (25mm) diameter brass tokens were quite plain, with the raised initials within a raised border on one side only. The reverse side being blank. If not used for the town's pits, they may well have been used at Curwen's Harrington Colliery. ■
[02] Occasionally, employees were also thought to have been paid in such tokens, rather than currency. They were exchangeable for goods at shops (sometimes also ran or controlled by their employers). But there appears little evidence that this practice was widespread in Workington. The system often led to many abuses and was made illegal by the *"Truck Acts"*, the first of which was passed in 1831.

(continued on page 107)

Workington Ropery & Saw Mill.

TOP - William H. Bartlett's 1837 engraving of Workington Harbour. Note the coal hurries on the South quay.

MIDDLE - Fisher's Ropery, also known as the Workington Ropery & Saw Mill. The building at the rear then stretched from Fisher Street, following almost the line of Gordon Street, for several hundred yards, down Corporation Road.

RIGHT - Finkle Street, almost where the Appletree now stands, was once very much narrower than today. The street was widened at the beginning of January 1894.

Old Finkle Street, Workington

ABOVE LEFT - The tower of St. Michael's Church, much of the structure of it's lower two sections are thought to date from Norman times. Formerly, the clockface on the west side had just one hour hand, and would strike each hour "upon the tenor bell", the largest of the peal. The present clock is famous for its timber clockface; built around 1894 by Joseph Harding, who had his joinery workshop in Bell Street. When the clockface was ready to install, it was wheeled on its edge to the church. **ABOVE RIGHT** - In 1775, a new peal of six bells were cast for St. Michaels by Pack & Chapman, at their Whitechapel foundry. Today in the belfry of the tower, despite the two disastrous fires, the original eighteenth century oak bell frame is still to be seen. Although the bells themselves have all since been recast. Now there are eight (pitch F sharp), two more than Carlisle Cathedral.

ABOVE LEFT - St. Michael's Rectory, sections of which are thought to date back to Elizabethan Times. Although recent archaeological evidence suggests that there was a building on this site many centuries earlier, perhaps of monastic origin. **ABOVE RIGHT** - The Anglo-Saxon and Viking stones displayed in the west porch of St. Michael's Church. (see chapters 3,4 and 6 for full descriptions). The stones sit on an unusual base, which Nikolaus Pevsner describes as part of a "huge Norman two-scallop capital". He surmises that "It must be late 11th century or early twelfth....where did it come from".

RIGHT - St. John's School (demolished in the late 1960s) occupied part of the site of today's St. John's Shopping Precinct; on the east side of John Street, which then extended through to Pow Street. Opened in 1860, it originally had separate classrooms for Boys, Girls and Infants; and children of all ages were taught. When it closed it accommodated just Junior and Infant pupils, who transferred to the newly build Ashfield Schools.

ABOVE LEFT - A group of St. John's pupils with their teacher, at the rear of the building, which had a cobbled school yard. **ABOVE RIGHT** - View of one of the classrooms at St. Johns, quite different from the modern classroom of today.

St. Johns Church, Workington.
Pub⁴ by J. Mordy, Workington.

BOTTOM LEFT - St. John's Church on Washington Street, consecrated in November 1823. This illustration is a steel engraving, published by J. Mordy around 1850. It is not quite a true depiction of the church, as the tower is actually positioned centrally over the ridge of the roof. (see chapter 6)

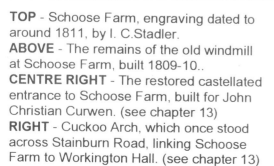

TOP - Schoose Farm, engraving dated to around 1811, by I. C.Stadler.
ABOVE - The remains of the old windmill at Schoose Farm, built 1809-10..
CENTRE RIGHT - The restored castellated entrance to Schoose Farm, built for John Christian Curwen. (see chapter 13)
RIGHT - Cuckoo Arch, which once stood across Stainburn Road, linking Schoose Farm to Workington Hall. (see chapter 13)

TOP LEFT - Men digging coal on waste ground in the town, during the 1912 Coal Strike. (see chapter 10)

TOP RIGHT - In the foreground is the Dock Quay built by John Christian Curwen in 1794.

LEFT - The railway bridge over the river Derwent carrying the Whitehaven Junction Railway, opened in 1846. Called locally "Ha'penny Billy's Bridge". (see chapter 16)

BOTTOM LEFT - Seaton Iron-works at Barepot, around 1850.

BOTTOM RIGHT - The "pear shaped" Bessemer convertor, removed from the British Steel Workington Works in 1974. (see chapter 12)

ABOVE - The folly which once stood on the foreshore close to John Pier. Generally referred to locally as "Billy Bumley house". Although it had no actual doors or windows and was used simply for the navigation of boats into the estuary. Note the Iron-works at Oldside in the distance.

LEFT & BELOW - The 1955 excavations at Burrow Walls, carried out under the direction of Richard Bell-house. Which finally proved the existance of a Roman Fort here. (see chapter 2)

and William Longcake. The specification clearly details that the foundation *"or bottom"* course of stones, had to be not less than a massive *"3 feet by 12 inches thick"* (900 x 300mm). The builders were then paid 10s-2d (51p) per cubic or solid yard of wall. [01] Three generations of Barton family continued to repair and extend the harbour walls for many years. John was followed by his son Joseph, and he appears to have later employed his son when *Joseph Barton & Son*, are recorded as repairing the walls again in 1810.

Prior to 1725, with the exception of the Crossfitts, Priestgate and foreshore area, [02] the Curwen family had owned all the land where the harbour stood, to both sides of the River Derwent. But following the death of Henry [iii] Curwen, problems arose when the Manor of Seaton (which then included the North Quay) was bequeathed to Charles Pelham.[03] Effectively, now splitting the ownership of the harbour, in half, down the centre of the side of the river. As it had previously been customary for the Curwens (as landowners) to receive *"one shilling"* (5p) anchorage duty, from each vessel using the port. Pelham, as the new landowner of the north bank, was strictly speaking entitled now to receive his share of anchorage duty, for those ships berthed at his North Quay.

Although occassional disputes developed between these two landowners over harbour matters. Generally, these were resolved without major difficulty. The real problems for the port only arose after the Manor of Seaton was later purchased by the Lowther family of Whitehaven. Following Henry [v] Curwen's 1768 election defeat of Sir. James Lowther, a long acrimonious dispute between these two local families soon developed. This bitter rivalry, often spilling over into the commercial life of Workington harbour. Sir James Lowther [04] who also worked the coal pits at Seaton, collected not just the anchorage duty from ships, moored at the North Quay. But also insisted on now claiming a tonnage duty of vessels loaded on his side. In the past this tonnage duty had been received by the harbour trustees to cover the cost of repairs to the quays etc. He employed his own collector and received both till around April 1782.

By often adopting shady and manipulative tactics, Sir James was brandished a tyrant. Despite his wealth and power, bolstered by his father-in-law becoming Prime Minister, he quarrelled constantly and bitterly with many people, including much of his own family. One cannot read Hugh Owen's account of Sir James life, without being aware that nearly every paragraph is peppered with detrimental adjectives describing his life and reputation.

[01] Interestingly, the 1788 harbour accounts show that John Barton received £421-18s-4d (£421.92), for rebuilding 830 yds of the South Quay (beneath the Low Hurry). Equating this to current (1998) building prices, one would now expect to pay an astonishing £2100 for a similar cubic yard of harbour wall. Over two centuries later, the total cost of Barton's work if undertaken today, would be over £1.74 million. (figures courtesy of Laing Stonemasonry, Carlisle) ■
[02] The Crossfitts, Priestgate and foreshore were then owned by St. Michaels Church. ■
[03] Because of *"the old feud"* with the Sella Park branch of the Curwen family. Henry [iii] Curwen alienated them, by leaving his Seaton estates to Charles Pelham of Brocklesby, Lincolnshire, his cousin once removed. (see also page 45) ■
[04] Sir. James Lowther (1736-1802) was the fourth child and eldest surviving son of Robert Lowther and Katherine Pennington. Hugh Owen in his family biography refers to him as *"Wicked Jimmy, the Bad Earl"*. Amongst the fortune he inherited, was the Whitehaven estates, in April 1756. He was elected to Parliament in 1754, and was thought by then to be one of the richest men in Britain. ■

His next move was to stake a claim to ownership of the Merchants Quay, inorder that he could also collect the revenue for ships berthing there.   He based his case on the fact that the boundary between the Manors of Workington and Seaton ran along the centre line of the River Derwent.   Refering back to the old course of the river, before ballast had been laid down to form the land upon which the wharf was now built.   He strongly believed Merchant's Quay was effectively also on his land.

Furthermore, he threatened to restore the old course of the river, by removing the breakwater to the north side of the Merchant's Quay.   Robert Walker commented that *"had the Derwent reverted to it's original course, it would certainly have swept away the structures of the South Quay"*, so ruining the harbour.   It should be remembered that the old tidal dock to the seaward side of the South Quay, was yet to be built.   Ships could only then be loaded either side of the South Gut, and on the North Quay.

Was Lowther attempting to just manipulate more control over the harbour, and increase his share of the profits.   Or was it a real vindictive attempt to totally ruin and destroy the Curwens.   After 1782, he closed the Lowther pits to the north of the Derwent, and it was perhaps no longer in his interest to maintain a harbour at Workington.   It would appear that both families were then exporting vast quantities of coal to Ireland.   If the port was forced into a decline, how could the Curwens continue to export the coal produced in the town's pits.   At that time there was no railways, to move it elsewhere.   The Lowthers would then have acquired a virtual monopoly of the Irish coal trade.

In 1777, after the trustees submitted a Bill to Parliament for the improvement of the harbour and its management.   Sir James Lowther immediately opposed the improvements and appointed the prominent engineer John Smeaton [01] to examine their proposals.   In two reports Smeaton outlined what he believed were several serious design errors in the plans.   If the new stone pier was built projecting westward, from the end of the existing North Quay.   Then *"the Great Seas that affect the harbour"* would upon striking the framework, range along Lowther's North quay in a most *"violent manner"*; so disturbing ships berthed there to unload coals at the hurries.

John Smeaton also proposed that if a new longer pier be constructed, following much the same line as today's breakwater around the entrance to *Prince of Wales* dock. Then there would be a *"very considerable improvement to the stillness of the waters"*.   Many more vessels could also be moored in quite relative safety along the internal face

Was Lowther attempting to just manipulate more control over the harbour, and increase his share of the profits. Or was it a real vindictive attempt to totally ruin and destroy the Curwens.

[01] John Smeaton (1724-1792) was the prominent engineer famed for his original design and construction methods used to build the Eddystone Lighthouse (1756). He had worked on many other harbours including St. Ives, Ramsgate and numerous Scottish ports.   He was also a founder member of the Institute of Civil Engineers. ■

of this new pier. It is said the trustees were quite impressed with the revisions, particularly the enlargement of the facilities. They too thought the harbour *"ought to be enlarged as well as repaired"*. Unfortunately, with Smeaton's scheme likely to cost in excess of £14500, it was to be quite prohibitive. Interestingly, it was almost a century and a half later, before the pier suggested by Smeaton was too be built. The 1777 Bill was later to be abandoned.

In 1794, work was began on building the Dock Quay, to the western end of the South Quay, paid for almost entirely by John Christian Curwen.[01] It was constructed on Glebe or Rectory land previously called Crossfitts. Which was exchanged for other Curwen land, under an agreement with the Bishop of Chester.[02] Completed in August 1798, this new quay, although called *"Dock"*, was not strictly a dock, as it was tidal and had no gates. More accurately it was a tidal basin, opening onto the south side of the Derwent, and protected by a wharf across part of its entrance. With it's completion, there were now eighty-eight mooring points along the south quay, and around the new dock.

Today, we can still see the remains of the Dock Quay basin, to the west of the old swing bridge. (see photographs on page 105) It is now used principally by pleasure craft, and only the odd small trawler still moors at what remains of the main pier or wharf. In 1967, the south and shorter west dock walls were torn down, to provide better access for public use. Much of the remaining western side of the dock, formerly accommodated two *"patent"* slipways, for the adjacent shipbuilding yards. Now, there remains a simple short slipway for the Vanguard Sailing Club.

Prior to the Dock Quay, there was a single smaller wharf and pier here, projecting from the south bank into the estuary. Records suggest that it was erected around 1737, alongside Priestgate Marsh or Mire, and called the Glebe Quay. Although some later accounts also refer to the Dock Quay as the Glebe Quay; perhaps because it was built on the former Glebe or Church land and replaced the original structure.

From the old Glebe Quay, those who used it had the *"liberty or privilege of laying ballast on the marsh, near or adjoining it"*. This effectively began to raise and consolidate the Crossfitts and Priestgate Marsh area, which would later be built upon, forming the Marsh and Quay. [03] From around 1781, the Rector of St. Michaels Church received three guineas (£3.15) a year, for allowing ballast to be deposited here.

In 1809, the Church exchanged much of this land

"Ninety-seven vessels of different burdens, some even of two hundred and fifty tons, belong to the port of Workington."

Thomas Pennant 1801

[01] It would appear that Christian Curwen initially lent the funds to the Harbour Trustees, to build the Dock Quay. He was to be repaid in instalments, with interest, from future anchorage duty. By 1815, he had been repaid virtually nothing, and accounts indicated he wasn't likely too, in the foreseeable future. Harbour revenues had infact dropped by almost a third since 1800.

[02] This agreement did not formally convey full title of the Dock Quay land, to Christian Curwen. But in 1809, by virtue of a clause in the Workington Inclosure Act, the Rector of Workington exchanged nineteen acres of Glebe land with Christian Curwen. This included the dock itself and much of the adjoining land. The parish of Workington was formerly in the Chester Diocese - see page 65-66. ■

[03] By comparing the first edition of the OS map (dated 1863), with the second edition (1898); we find that much of Priestgate Marsh is first shown as simply a open area, but the later plan shows it built over. Rows of terrace houses had been erected to form Berry Street, Southey Street, South Marsh Street, Lawrence Street and Marsh side. Whilst the Marshside Ironworks, the Workington Bridge and Boiler works, Quayside Ironworks and the Haverlock Road foundry, occupied the ground between Stanley Street and Marsh side. ■

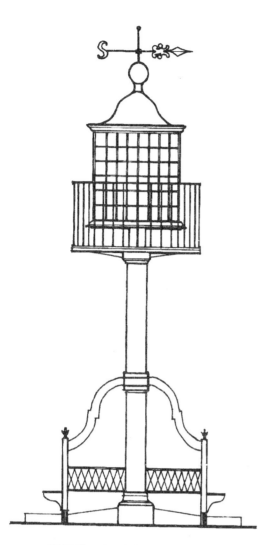

ABOVE - sketch based on an initial design for the hexagonal light-house, at the end of John Pier. The actual cast iron structure was higher, and had a staircase upto the circular "crowsnest". (see text opposite) ■

[01] Henry Street was named after Henry Curwen. Whilst Swinburn Street is likely to be in honour of William Swinburn, Curwen's agent, who died in 1825. ■
[02] The English ton (20cwt) is the equivalent of 1016 kg. ■
[03] The method of charging tonnage duty "by the wagon" was fast and efficient. Eliminating the need to weigh the coal at either the pithead or the harbourside. Each wagon initially then being a standard size of three English tons (60cwt). However from around 1835, the standard wagons load was reduced to 2.4 English tons (48cwt). ■
[04] The 1798 Harbour "Articles of Agreement" were for a period of seven years. ■

with the Curwens, under the *Workington Enclosure Act*. For a further thirty years, ballast continued to be laid over this area. Then Henry [vi] Curwen began to sell off plots of this reclaimed land. The first group houses, along Henry Street, Swinburn Street [01] and Harbour place were completed shortly afterwards. Until around 1830, at least two arched openings still existed under the South Quay, allowing the tide to flow back and forth across the Marsh.

In 1976, an Allerdale District Council report concluded that much of the residential property of the Marsh and Quay, was now sub-standard and in a poor state of repair. The area had become *"a classic case of blight"* and *"uncertainty"*, principally brought about by planning decisions made over a decade earlier. The direct cause of this decay, stemming from the old Workington Borough Council's decision not to grant householders improvement grants after March 1965. Large scale clearance of rows of terraced houses followed, entire streets disappeared, to be replaced with industrial sites. There were then 233 homes in the area, with 637 residents. The average length of time each resident had lived on the Marsh was over 38 years. By the early 1980's, almost the entire community had moved out and been re-housed, despite over two-thirds of residents wanting to stay.

In the closing years of the eighteenth century, confidence in the success of the harbour was heightened. The new Dock Quay had opened, essentially safe-guarding at least part of the harbour from Lowther's destructive threats. Furthermore in 1798, John Christian Curwen began opening up his Chapel Bank pits (see chapter ten). Contemporary harbour records tell us that they *"promise almost inexhaustible supplies of the stable commodity of exportation"*.

Between 1801-05, an average of 45000 wagons of coal produced from the towns pits, were shipped out of the harbour annually. For each wagon loaded, which then contained three English tons, [02] ships were charged a tonnage duty of 6d (2½p). Each day, an average of two vessels left the harbour carrying a cargo of coal, equivalent to 64 wagons (192 tons). Between 1806-10, the annual average coal exports had dropped to around 32500 wagons. Whilst for each of the five years ending 1815 they averaged 26600 wagons.[03]

In January 1803, John Christian Curwen ceased to act as a harbour trustee and his formal agreement with the Harbour trustees lapsed two years later.[04] Although it may have continued informally, for almost a further ten years. At this point Christian Curwen took over the exclusive day to day management of the port, effectively disbanding the trustees. His motives for this action appear vague, but it is suggested that he saw little likelihood of ever receiving repayment of the funds he had advanced to the trustees. He may have merely been safeguarding his family's business interests.

As early as 1800, when Christian Curwen was owed around £3267, attempts had been made to put the borrowings on a more formal footing. Then the harbour trustees agreed to pay five per cent annual interest on the balance outstanding, previously no interest had been levied. However, harbour profits, either under the management of the trustees or Curwen were never great. Little or nothing appears to have ever been repaid. Despite Christian Curwen's action he appears to have maintained some degree of support from the former trustees. Many were shipowners who relied on transporting the huge volumes of coal, produced at his pits. Others were shipbuilders who rented their shipyards from Curwen.

Between 1824-25, John Pier, a breakwater [01] was built out into the sea on the southern edge of the Derwent estuary. It was located to the south of the present long concrete breakwater,[02] although it projected not nearly as far. It was demolished and disappeared when this area of the coastline was landscaped, after the closure of the Steel works. A stroll along this pier, to its substantial square stone platform end, was once a favourite Sunday afternoon walk. Here there was also a quite unusual hexagonal lighthouse fixed high above the pier end, on a single iron post. Around the light was a circular, observation walkway, resembling a *"crows nest"* reached by a steep iron staircase. (see sketch left) Although called a *"pier"* no vessels were actually moored or loaded there. Originally access to the pier by foot, was only through the Peile & Co. shipbuilding yard. (see chapter eleven)

It was built to further protect the harbour entrance and prevent gravel and shale being deposited in the river channel. The funds for its construction being raised partly by public subscription and the remaer from John Christian Curwen. Both were to be repaid from the harbour dues, and receive 5 per cent interest.

Accounts published by Christian Curwen show that the breakwater (including its parapet walls) contained over 157000 cubic feet of masonry, being about 26 feet (7.9m) high. The total cost was £7000, his contribution was nearly £3000. The prospects of anyone ever receiving full repayment were once again quite slim. The harbour accounts then showed an annual income of around only £1500, with expenditure often exceeding income by several hundred pounds.

[01] William Whellan (1860) tells us that when there is eight feet (2.4m) of water in the harbour, *"a red ball is hoisted upon a pole on St. John's Pier, and at night a light is exhibited upon the pierhead, which answers a like purpose."* Whellan mistakenly recorded the pier as *"St. John's"*, elsewhere it is almost always called *"John Pier"*. It is thought to have been simply named after John Christian Curwen.
From around 1817, the harbour navigation lights were lit by gas, previously candles and oil had been used. Vessels were now required to pay a new *"Lights"* duty of one old penny (½p) per ton, for maintaining the lights, as well as paying their anchorage duty. Previously, the Lights charge was just one (old) half penny, giving the Harbour trustees, a revenue of around £15.00 per month. ■
[02] Around 1869, it was becoming obvious that John's Pier, as a breakwater was now almost ineffective. Over the years the shoreline had gradually built up either side of the pier, and now threatened the channel into the harbour. Initially it was proposed to simply extend the existing pier, but eventually it was decided to build the new present breakwater. ■

"The river is navigable for ships of four hundred tons burden. There are now an hundred and sixty vessels belonging to this port, on average about an hundred and thirty tons each; and every ship of an hundred tons costs £1500, and so in proportion. The chief trade in export is in coals for Ireland, but some are taken here for the east country service. The imports are timber and shipbuilding materials."

William Hutchinson (1794)

[01] Sir John Rennie had also been consulted by Whitehaven Harbour Trustees in 1823 and again in 1832, regarding the design and problems with the harbour silting up. He was famed for his scientific knowledge and sound practical skill, being the son of John Rennie (1761-1821). His father, also an engineer, had been responsible for erecting the breakwater at Plymouth, East India Docks and Holyhead Harbour. ■

The rivalry and dispute between the Curwen and Lowther families and the former harbour trustees, rumbled on for years. Lord Lonsdale appeared to show continued disapproval of the Curwen's sole management of the port. He still strenuously claimed ownership of both the North and Merchants Quays, and insisted that the Curwen's carry out no further repairs, improvements or alteration there. An indication of his continued distrust and contempt is displayed in a 1822 letter from Lonsdale's agent to the port's Customs officer. He points out that should Curwen attempt to repair the Merchant's Quay, the matter would be *"too serious"* for the agent alone to deal with. *"His lordships particular direction"* must be obtained, especially *"where such a man as Mr. Curwen is concerned"*. As the Curwens would have received no financial reward for such repairs, it is assumed that it involved essential maintance to safe guard the rest of the harbour.

By 1834, an Act of Parliament was proposed which would essentially reform the harbour trustees, and give them back the day to day management of the port. The South Gut was again to be deepened, to allow larger vessels better access to the harbour. Even, Lord Lonsdale agreed to co-operate, providing his *"rights and privileges are given due attention"*. Sir John Rennie [01] was appointed the engineer to advise on the scheme and he first visited the port in May 1835. Unfortunately, the preparation of any Bill for submission to Parliament is not a speedy process. It was June 1838, before any draft documents were available. In the meantime, the Chapel Bank Colliery had been lost, and Henry Curwen was now quite dissatisfied with the fall in harbour trade and profits. Curwen subsequently withdrew his support as he did not feel *"the immediate prospect for trade is such as to make it desirable"*. Lonsdale surprisingly, but sensibly agreed with Curwens views, and the project was suspended.

But the town's shipowners, under the chairmanship of Michael Falcon, were resolute and determined to push on with the Act. But obviously the bill was unlikely to succeed without Henry Curwen's support. He was the principle landowner and the family were still owed a vast amount, principally for the erection of John Pier. When further negotiations broke down, they began to refuse to pay their harbour dues. Interestingly, only on the Curwen owned South Quay, and not on Lonsdale's North or Merchants Quays. It seemed they were anxious not to alienate Lonsdale, whose support may be relied on, should Curwen change his mind.

This unpleasant position appears to have continued for many months, Lonsdale's agent even attempting to arbitrate matters. Finally, the shipowners agreed to resume the payment of Curwens duty, if he would agree a comprimise on the clauses of a new Bill. No doubt, Henry Curwen was then much happier with the situation, as coal production had now resumed at Buddle pit. (see chapter ten) Surprisingly, the Earl of Lonsdale himself only proposed minor alterations to the draft Bill, when he first viewed it in the autumn of 1839. John Waite, the port's customs officer, recording that *"matters went on more smoothly than was anticipated"*. The Act *"for regulating and preserving the harbour at Workington"* finally received Royal Assent in 1840. It basically appointed a new Board of Trustees to manage the harbour (which included both sides of the Derwent), agree duties and tonnage rates, cleanse, scar and deepen the south gut. Yearly rentals were paid thereafter to the Curwen family.

The next major development at the harbour was the construction of Lonsdale Dock, on the North Quay. This occupied part of the site of today's Prince of Wales Dock. Work began in December 1860, several months before being formally sanctioned by Parliament. Generally there was little resistance to the proposals, an amicable agreement was easily reached with the Harbour Trustees. [01] The town's bankers, merchants, shipowners and shopkeepers all petitioned in support of the bill. Initially a rail connection was laid to the Whitehaven Junction Railway and the site cleared. Following receipt of full approval, 600 men were engaged in the construction of the new dock.

Named after William Lord Lonsdale, the new dock measured 600 feet (184m) length by 300 ft (92m) breath. Technically, this was the town's first real dock. Being shut off from the sea by movable gates, so retaining the water level inside at low tide. It's entrance, did not face westward, like the present Prince of Wales Dock, but was to the south into the channel of the Derwent, almost opposite the Dock Quay.

The walls of the new wet-dock, were 28 feet (8.6m) high above the dock bottom, stone faced and topped with massive 4ft (1.2m) granite edge blocks (each 18ins or 0.45m deep). Below these walls, the entire perimeter of the dock was also surrounded by cast-iron sheet piling, extending a further 10.5ft (3.2m) below the dock bottom. The gates (40ft or 12m wide) maintained a water level in the dock of 18ft (5.5m), following a 16ft (4.9m) high tide. Unfortunately, the entrance channel in the estuary had to be later deepened, so larger vessels could be accommodated. Within a few years of being opened Lonsdale Dock was found also to be too small to efficiently handle the increased trade from the newly opened ironworks.

In 1856, there were twenty eight collieries throughout Cumberland producing around 913900 tons of coal, 118239 tons, or about 13%, was shipped from Workington, whilst 211347 tons or 23% was sent from Whitehaven.

Workington and Maryport Steam Navigation Company

In the early part of 1820, this new company began to run a twice weekly *"steam boat"*; between Maryport, Workington and Liverpool. The service was generally unprofitable, particularly in the early years, as it then only sailed in the summer months. It would usually berth at the North Quay, and for several years, the Earl of Lonsdale allowed the vessel to dock, without claiming an anchorage duty. Although this arrangement ceased when the company became better established.

[01] Lord Lonsdale's plans for his new tidal dock on the North Quay, were laid before the Workington Harbour Trustees in October 1860. After much debate it was resolved to accept the proposals, but appoint a parliamentary agent to protect there interests. They had hoped that a new dock could have been built on the Marsh, and had asked engineers to report on this proposal. Unfortunately, there findings were *"less than favourable"*, and these plans were axed. ∎

"In 1798, Workington had 7000 inhabitants and about 150 ships of between 50 and 300 tons burden".

In 1791 the trustees agreed to built a house and office for their piermaster, at the low end of the South Quay, near the end of the old waggonway. The property cost the trustees £210, which was again lent to them by John Christian Curwen.[01] The piermaster's duties were to oversee the running, repair and improvement works to the harbour. As well as to collect the duty from each vessel, on behalf of the trustees. Robert Jackson is thought to have been one of the earliest piermasters, employed around 1735. Whilst John Smith (d.1790) is shown in the 1763 trustees records. He was succeeded by John Walker (till 1816), Thomas Moore (till 1819), with Edward Smith (son of the above John Smith) being then appointed.

From at least 1682, although the port was under the general supervision of the Customs Officer at Whitehaven.[02] Although, there must have been some presence of an Excise man or Customs Officer in the town. Perhaps the duties were then carried out by a riding officer, who would generally patrol our area of the coastline on horseback. Smuggling around the Solway Firth was then a considerable problem. Often heavily taxed goods like tobacco, spirits, tea, silk and even salt were discreetly hidden amongst the traditional cargoes of coal, iron ore or ballast. A significant amount of this smuggling was well organised and involved the crews of not just collier vessels, but also the fishing boats. Officers who challenged vessels and searched their holds were in constant danger of being violently attacked by crews. In December 1780, at Workington, Customs officer Joseph Wilson was shot by a musket from a Scottish ship engaged in smuggling . The port did not have it's own Customs boat until 1730, when a seized fishing boat was adapted.

By 1750 a full-time Customs Office existed in the town, inorder that vessels could be properly checked and duties received on goods imported into the harbour. Before 1772, a small single storey watch house was built close to the shipbuilding yard and on the site of the Dock Quay.[03] In 1796, this was demolished and moved further westward, when John Christian Curwen started work on the new Dock Quay. The Commissioners of Customs, then leased the building from the Curwens, for an annual rent of five guineas (£5.25). It is often shown on old harbour plans as the "King's Watch House".

These buildings on the shoreline were as the name suggests, simply small covered surveillance posts. But around 1825, a new Customs House was built on the South Quay, close to the east side of the Dock Quay. [04] Prior to this, a property had been rented in the town, to accommodate the Customs House. Anthony Peat was listed as the

[01] It appears that the Curwen family retained ownership of the premises, possibly because they owned the land and may never have been repaid by the trustees. After the 1840 Harbour Act, the "harbour house and office" was rented to the new trustees for £18 per annum. ■

[02] Whitehaven was appointed "a customs port" in 1685, being responsible for the entire coastline from Maryport in the north, to Ravenglass in the south. ■

[03] A twenty one year lease exists, dated October 1772 from Rev W.T. Addison (Rector) to Joseph Burrow (Collector of Customs), for the King's Watch House at Workington. ■

[04] This Customs House on the quay, was demolished in 1967. ■

as the collector in 1811. John Waite was principle coast officer for HM Customs and Excise from 1831-40. also R.V. Innes (upto 1860) and R.H.D. Mahon (from 1860).

An 1850 Act of Parliament, redefined the *"Port of Workington"*, essentially creating a Custom office, no longer supervised by Whitehaven. The content of the bill is interesting, as it not only details the area or zone covered by Workington's Customs officers, but also details the length of the South and Merchant's Quays. South Quay is shown as 570 yards (521m) length, and Merchant's Quay 420yds (384m). The North Quay and the Dock Quay (although then referred to as the New Quay) are also mentioned but no dimensions are shown. Whilst the officers had jurisdiction over the coastline, from Lowca beck, near Moresby to Canker Beck, in the north. The limits also stretched three miles out to sea, from the low water mark.

By February 1858, the West Cumberland Coast also got it's first regular force of Coast Guards. Still visible today on the South Quay, is the old Bonded Warehouse, built in 1823. It is no longer used by Customs and Excise, and is occupied by Swan Bearings.

Around the time of the well-chronicled and daring dawn raid of John Paul Jones at nearby Whitehaven, on Thursday 23 April 1778. A small semi-circular fort was quickly built close to where Isabella pit was later sunk. Constructed from just basic materials, it was armed with cannons, to provide some degree of protection to the harbour entrance. A report in the *Cumberland Pacquet* suggests it soon saw action. On the following Saturday around midnight, *"a boat full of men"* is said to have attempted to enter the harbour. It was just three days since the landing at Whitehaven, when an unidentified cutter was seen *"stood between the perches"*, on the north side of the estuary. Fortunately, when the guards threatened to fire their cannons, the vessel turned and steered away. [01]

Britain was then at war with both America and it's French allies. Before arriving in the Solway, John Paul Jones who commanded the American Navy's 18-gun sloop *Ranger*, had been ordered to generally *"harass British Shipping"*. His attack on Whitehaven was soon followed by a stubborn and spectacular duel with the 20-gun British sloop *Drake*, off Belfast Lough. After a battle of more than an hour Jones succeeded in capturing the *Drake*. He proceeded to tow his crippled prize to Brest in France, there her 200 prisoners were exchanged for Americans held in Britain. At least three of the sailors aboard the *Drake* were from Workington. They were William Davis, Thomas Morgan and John Kay and each was listed amongst the wounded.

"In 1814, of the 698 shipments of coal that left Workington for Ireland, 286 unloaded at Belfast and 267 at Dublin".

Michael Flinn
History of the British Coal Industry

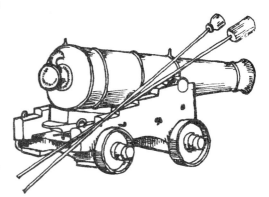

[09] A constant round-the-clock watch was kept from the fort for many months after. Robert J. Walker in his unpublished history of the port believed the almost *"temporary"* fort was finally to be demolished in the early nineteenth century. Probably when John Christian Curwen began sinking the Isabella pit in 1808. ∎

All three are also recorded as being forced to enlist in the navy, by the notorious *"press-gang"*. Able-bodied men of all ages and professions were then often seized whilst simply walking in the street or enjoying a drink in a public house. Snatched without warning they were dragged away from their homes and families, to endure many dreadful months aboard a *"man of war"*. They had little choice, if they complained they were flogged, if they deserted often they would never return. Interestingly, this quite rare information strongly suggests that press-gangs were once active within Workington itself. One wonders how many more locals were also *"impressed"* into naval duty, against their will.

Throughout the centuries, perhaps Workington's most unusual export was hundreds of notorious Border Reivers and their families, deported to Ireland at the beginning of the seventeenth century. Following the death of the elderly Queen Elizabeth I, the last of the Tudors, in March 1603. James Stuart, the only son of Mary Queen of Scots, and the present king of Scotland, had also ascended to the English throne. England and Scotland were now to be governed by the same monarch. Within weeks, the new king set himself the principle task of effecting a complete union between both kingdoms.

His proclamation of 19 May 1603, makes special reference to the need to repress the *"slaughters, spoils, robberies, and other enormities, which were so frequent and common upon the Borders of these realms"*. The accustomed reivers from both countries were now referred to as *"enemies to peace, justice and quietness"*. Those who persisted with *"robberies, bloodshed or other disorder"*, would no longer be tolerated and incur the most severest of punishment.

It is perhaps easy to assume that the Borderland quarrels would now have been brought to an end. Afterall, they could no longer play one side off against the other, when ruled by the same king. But as MacDonald Fraser comments in his book *The Steel Bonnets*, whole communities had for many decades become dependant on this *"plunder and organised banditry"*. Even the threat of the gallows or being transported to exile, could not deter the hard-core habitual offenders. Many resisted this new rule of law through sheer necessity and the need to support their families. But the new king was determined to purge the Borders of the remaining reivers, who would not conform. Many fugitives were relentlessly now pursued, Macdonald Fraser records 32 as being hung, and 15 more banished or exiled, within the first year of James' reign.

Workington was later to feature in the further eradi

cation of rebellious Reivers. The Derwent estuary being chosen as the departure point, for those being deported(or transplanted) in Ireland. [01] In December 1603, James I had also commanded the complete removal of the entire clan (or families) of Grahams (then called Grames or Graymes) from their lands in the Esk, Leven and Sark areas of Southern Scotland.[02] Because of their crimes, King James ruthlessly considered them no longer fit or proper *"persons to live"* in the country. Their lands were to be confiscated and taken away, to *"be inhabited by others of good and honest conversation."*

In little over a year, the bulk of the Grahams had been rounded up, and their homes burnt to the ground. But for the lack of sufficient funds, those Grahams in custody would have been immediately deported.   However as an alternative, many were simply conscripted into the British Army, and billeted near Oxford and in Cornwall. But almost all were later to desert and return home as fugitives.

During the early months of 1606, despite a degree of peace returning to the borders, those who had escaped and nearly anyone called Graham, was now considered an *"open outlaws"*. The Commissioners for the Borders, who had replaced the Wardens of the *"Marches"* [03] made extensive and concerted efforts to hunt and apprehend the escapees. Most of which were then detained in the gaol at Carlisle Castle.   Transportation to Ireland, was now the only apparent option to rid the Borders of this once infamous and notorious Border clan.

On 12 September 1606, those that had been recaptured, together with women, children and even some servants of the Graham families were herded, many on foot, south to Workington. They took with them around forty five horses and many possessions, described then as "much household stuff", carried in carts.   This large group was guarded on their journey, by a troop of horsemen, under the command of John Musgrave of Plumbton.

Initially around fifty families of the *"most notorious"* Grahams had been selected. But the *Irish State Papers* seem to list only around 33 families, made up of 91 adults, 28 of which were women, together with around 32 children (under 14 years old). Anything like this quantity must have created quite a stirring scene among the town's population, which itself then must have numbered less than two hundred. Their stay in Workington was quite short, for the following day (a Saturday) they were taken by several boats to six ships, anchored off the Derwent estuary. Then there was no actual harbour, wharf or quay, usually goods were simply transferred on and off the river bank.

[01] Sir Wilfred Lawson (of Isel), one of the commissioners for the Borders, wrote in July 1606 - Workington or Ravenglass would *"afford the most ready passage to Ireland"*. ▪
[02] The English State papers (Dec 1603) contains a list of 99 Grames or Grahams (and their families) *"fit to be transplanted"*. George MacDonald Fraser in his 1971 book *The Steel Bonnets*, suggests that the Border gentry who supported the disposition of the Grahams, had something of a ulterior motive. The Esk district was the most fertile land in the Borders, and when vacant the *"pickings would be rich"*. ▪
[03] The six *"Marches"* of the Borders effectively disappeared following the above proclamations of James I. They were replaced with the *"Commissioners of the Borders"*, which included Sir Wilfred Lawson of Isel, and the Bishop of Carlisle. ▪

Their journey to Ireland took less than three days, as they arrived safely in Dublin on Tuesday morning. One hundred and fourteen Grahams were then deported, the remaining ten or so were held back to be sent the following spring. All of these were thought to be women, either pregnant or with very young infants. An interesting, (but rather difficult to read) account of the cost of the transportation is contained in the *Pennington Muncaster Castle* papers. Each of the six ships [01] contained around twenty people, and the Grahams took with them their horses and possessions. Food for the voyage cost £48.12s.6d (£48.63p), including hay for the horses, which equates to around 29p a head.

The same day they embarked on their voyage the Commissioners wrote to the Earl of Salisbury, commenting that *"all the notorious offenders whose manner terrified all peaceable men, are gone away"*. The site of their relocation in Ireland chosen was the almost bleak wastelands of Roscommon, one of its central counties. Even after their journey across the Irish Sea to Dublin, they would still have at least an eighty mile journey overland, before they reached their new home. Each family did not arrive penniless in Roscommon, for they had been promised around £20 per household, to maintain themselves until their new *"land shall yield profit"*. [02]

Just over four hundred pounds to fiance the resettlement was raised by a special collection or voluntary tax, from among the people of Cumberland and Westmorland. Nicholson & Burn in their 1777 *History of Westmorland & Cumberland* listed each of the contributors. Sir Henry Curwen of Workington, is shown as providing two pounds. Macdonald Fraser comments that to raise such an amount was *"a testimony to the general desire to get rid of the Grahams"*.

Further Grahams were round up, including many of those who had avoided the first deportation. On 24 April 1607, another 23 families were also transported from Workington. Followed by 15 further households on 11 September, the same year. In total seventy one families, perhaps as many as 270 Grahams, had now been deported to Ireland, in an effort to purge the Borders of Reiver menace. But just how successful was this banishment?

[01] Hutchinson says in the Workington chapter of his 1794 History of Cumberland - *"from whence a number of unreclaimable moss-troopers were shipped for their voluntary banishment, in which few, and those very small barks (barques) were employed"*. ■

[02] This was the compensation promised to the Grahams, in July 1606, when they were first told or their transportation (or transplanting). In return they had agreed to co-operate and bring with them their "friends and fugitives". But in reality they received much less, on average around £9 per household, and much of this apparently went in payment to Sir Ralph Sidley, the Roscommon landowner, who deducted the cost of their new farms. Nicholson & Burn (1777) list in detail how much of the money was actually distributed among the *Grames*, and in most cases it was less than a couple of pounds. ■

119

TRUSTEES OF WORKINGTON HARBOUR

As many of the minutes of the harbour trustees meetings, appear not to have survived. This list has been compiled from a variety of documents and sources, and should therefore not be regarded as full and conclusive. Where not shown, the Lord of the manor and the Rector of Workington, should also be included. Occasionally, we find the trade of a trustee is shown, and has been included below.

(1722) Henry Curwen, John Robertson, Robert Grear, James Gorton, Thomas Bacon, John Nelson, John Kendall, Robert Steele (snr), Henry Steele, Anthony Walker, Simond Muncaster, Thomas Brough, Henry Birkett (jnr), Joseph Paiteson, John Porter.

(1725) Robert Steele (jnr), Henry Walker, and William Jackson, had replaced - Simond Muncaster, Henry Birkett (jnr) and Joseph Paiteson respectively.

(1733) Eldred Curwen, Richard Cooke, John Porter, Edmund Gibson, Richard Watts, Robert Steele (jnr), Henry Steel and Thomas Brough (both mariners), Joseph Harrison (joiner)

(1773) Edward Stanley, John Ellwood (both merchants), John Falcon (shipcarpenter), Henry Fawcett (gent), John Hodgson (ropemaker), Thomas Brough (gent), Michael Falcon (mariner), William Watts and William Stevens (both gents), Henry Gaitskell, John Parkin and Joseph Parkin (both merchants), Joseph Hird (mariner).

(1782) Peter Brown, Peter Taylor, Wm. Thomas Addison (Rector), Thomas Brough, John Hodgson, William Thompson, John Ellwood, Wm Dickinson (for Anthony Bacon - who was the proprietor of Banklands Colliery), Richard Bell (for John Cookson - Clifton Colliery) and William Watts, John Whiteside, John Falcon, Michael Falcon

(1784) John Christian, Wm. Thomas Addison (Rector), John Hodgson jnr., Maitland Falcon, Michael Falcon, Peter Brown, John Ellwood, William Watts, John Whiteside, Thomas Brough. (also William Thompson - resigned)

(1793) Matthew Russell, John Marshall and Joseph Westray, replaced - Wm. T. Addison (d.1791), John whiteside and Peter Brown (also deceased)

(1794) John Christian Curwen, Rev. Edward Christian, Rev. Peter How, Michael Falcon, Henry Bowman, Robert Jackson, John Hodgson, Wilton Wood, Joseph Westray, Matthew Russell, John Barns, William Dickinson (surgeon), Benjamin Thompson (Attorney), John Whiteside, John Wilson, William Dickinson, John Fearon, Musgrave Ellwood, Richard Bower, Joseph Dixon.

(1802) John Christian Curwen, John Whiteside, Richard Bowes, Peter How, Michael Falcon, John Thompson, Robert Jackson, Benjamin Thompson, Jonathan Fawcett.

"Workington possesses a safe and capacious harbour, with a breakwater and extensive quays, which are, however, capable of much further improvement. The Merchants' Quay and the South Quay are built on the opposite banks of a wide branch of the Derwent, called the South Gut, which, with the mill-race, separates the town from the large meadow or common called Cloffolks, about 1800 yards long and 200 broad. The depth of water, at spring tides, is from fifteen to eighteen feet, and at neap tides from eight to ten feet. Vessels can sail into the harbour with a southerly, westerly, or north-north-east wind. When there are eight feet of water in the harbour a red ball is hoisted upon a pole on St. John's Pier, and at night a light is exhibited upon the pierhead, which answers a like purpose, and can be seen in clear weather at about three leagues from any point seaward. On each of the inner piers are two smaller lights to guide ships into the harbour."
William Whellan (1860)

CHAPTER EIGHT

THE EARLY TOWN

CUMBERLAND or more importantly Workington, unfortunately does not appear in the *Domesday Book* of 1086. The northern most boundary of this famous survey being along a line from just above Millom, eastwards across to Cleveland. As previously mentioned our district was then still very much a part of Scotland.

Perhaps the first recorded description of the manor of Workington dates from 1330. It is contained in the details of the estate of Sir Gilbert [ii] Curwen. Basically listing a *"chief manor house, a water mill for grinding corn; 60 acres of land, 12 acres of meadow, 24 bovates of land (then rented) and 14 cottars then holding 14 cottages"*. Workington would have then been little more than a very small village, it's inhabitants surviving on farming and some fishing.

We can surmise that at this time Sir Gilbert lived in a predominantly timber and thatch manor house, upon the site of the present Workington Hall. St. Michael's Church would have also existed overlooking the Derwent estuary. Then there was no harbour or wharf, and just a few further houses which grouped around and between these two ancient buildings, just over half a mile apart.

Our next real point of reference is the 1569 plan shown right. This is assumed to be the earliest surviving plan of the town, produced within a year after the visit of Mary Queen of Scots. Again Workington Hall and St. Michael's Church are the most prominent properties. The road linking the two appears to follow the line of (what we know today as) Brow Top and Ladies Walk. There was only around a further thirty or so other properties, the majority grouped around the Hall. Here too is a suggestion of a *"square"* or open space, perhaps located close to the present Portland Square area. The population would surely then have been no more than a few hundred people and again Workington could not really yet be properly described as a town.

In October 1573, however, it was awarded a market charter by Queen Elizabeth I. In addition Henry [i] Curwen then Lord of the Manor was also granted authority to hold two fairs annually, upon Ascension and St. Luke's Day. [01] Although Samuel Jefferson in 1842, tells us these fairs had *"fallen into disuse"*. Until the 1730's, the town's market was located at Crosshill, in the area close to the top of today's Guard Street, held (as today) on a Wednesday and Saturday.

A *Queen Mary* coin dated 1554, likely to be a *groat,* was found recently by a Workington women in her garden. (exact location never revealed). It was identified by Mr T. H. Dalzell of William Street, a local *"numismatist"* or coin expert, and is thought to bear the inscription *"Veritas temporis filia"*. A groat, was a ancient coin equal to around 4d (1½p), once often mistaken for a shilling.

Cumberland Pacquet (Oct 1862)

[01] Ascension Day is officially forty days after Easter. whilst St. Lukes Day is October 18th. ∎

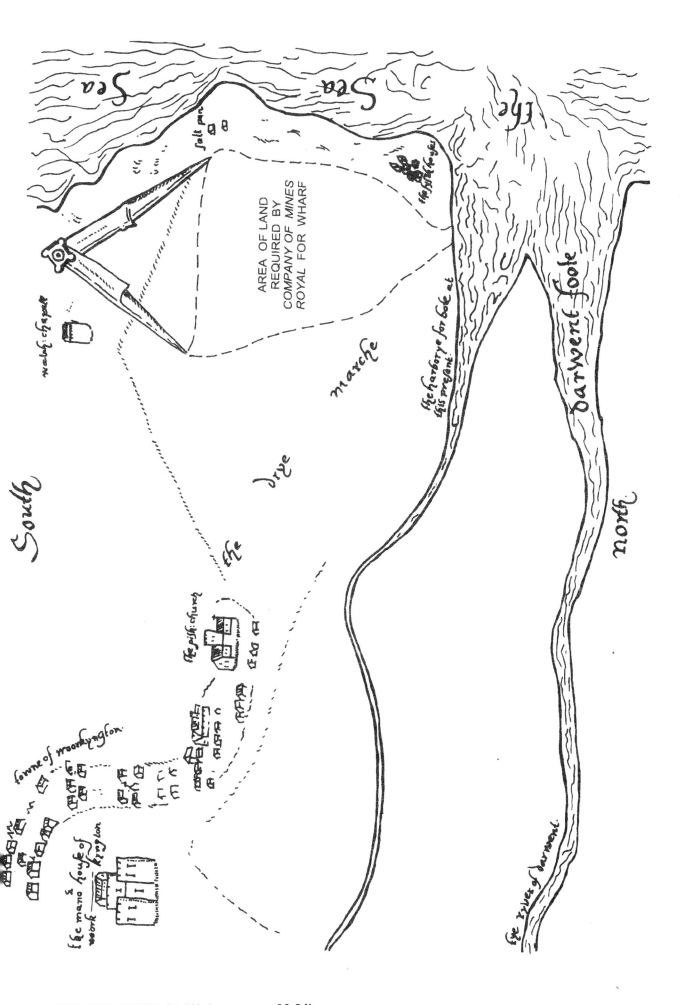

THE 1569 TOWN PLAN (see pages 93-94)

The existence of any market in the town earlier than the sixteenth century is not clear. We know that in 1292, Thomas [i] Curwen claimed the right to hold a weekly market at Seaton, and a three-day fair around *"St. Peter ad Vincula"* day. For the Crown solicitor's later twice summoned him to the Assizes at York to question his valid licence. Thomas in evidence, told how *"he and his ancestors"* had held the markets *"from times beyond memory of man"*. Later he produced the family charter and his claim was allowed. [01]

At Cross Hill there are two stone crosses built into the front walls of two adjoining houses. One of these, has over the years been the subject of much debate and speculation. It appears to bear the inscription *"WH 1103"*, but the date is more generally believed to actually read 1703, perhaps the year the property was erected. William Whellan (1860) and others have suggested that *"the cross may have originally been the finial from the gable of an old chapel, that once stood nearby, built during the reign of King Richard I"*. But it is truly doubtful that such a chapel ever existed. If the 1103 date is to be believed it cannot relate really to the reign of Richard I, which was 1189-99.

Tradition also states that in olden times when a corpse was being brought to the town for interment, it was set down here for a short time, while a homily or portion of the burial service was read. The remains of this stone cross may have formed the upper part of a larger freestanding cross to make the spot. But it could quite conceivably have also been a ancient boundary cross, like *Crosslacon* at Frizington or *Crossfield* at Cleator Moor. Although it does not appear to relate to parish boundaries as we know them today. Another possibility is that it was at the *"cross roads"* or junction of The Guards, The Row and General Street (now Guard Street, Park End Road and King Street) with the road to Whitehaven. Finally, if the earliest market was held on this spot it may have been simply a part of an old market cross, marking the spot. The other cross on the adjacent house, bearing the inscription *"Rebuilt 1881"* is presumably just a copy of this earlier original cross.

Around 1676, Edmund Sandford provided just a few lines to describe the town, saying it then was *"a very fair large village"*. From the end of the seventeenth century, the town began to show substantial growth. Considerable coal production now brought a gradual influx of workers and their families to the town. The first permanent wharf was built at the harbour, principally to handle increased coal exports.

By 1770, Pennant now estimated Workington's population to around 4500. Nine years later, the survey of the parish by the Bishop of Chester, states the town had around 600 houses and 700 families.[02] Pennant also confirmed

[01] Interestingly, the same summons states that the Curwen family also then had a "cucking-stool and a pillory" in their Seaton manor. Both allowed minor criminals to be secured, so they could be jeered at and pelted by their neighbours. No doubt a similar form of punishment may also have existed in their Workington manor.
After 1889, Workington Borough Council became responsible for the market, after they purchased the rights from Henry Frazer Curwen. ■
[02] The 1779 survey of the Workington parish is contained in Bishop Porteus' *Notitia*. Notitia (or Notabilia) simply referring to *"things worthy of notice"*. Also recorded were the number of families of other religions. (see chapter six). ■

firmed that the town layout was still very much the same as two hundred years earlier. He wrote *"the town extends from the castle to the sea; it consists of two clusters, one, the more ancient, near the castle, the other nearer the church and pier"*.

This is confirmed when we look at the first accurately drawn town map, prepared around twenty years later. Commissioned by John Christian Curwen [01] and surveyed in 1793. There was now quite a number of houses north of Priestgate (later Church Street), in the area directly west of where *Allerdale House* now stands. These included Brewery Street and Griffin Street. Brow Top was still the main thoroughfare linking the lower part of the town to the upper area around the Hall. Although some development had now began along Pow Street and Finkle Street (then referred to as *"Back of Town"* and later often found spelt *"Fincal"*).

On the south side of Finkle Street, to the east of where the Appletree now stands, was then a row of about eight small white-washed cottages.. The front of these houses then projected well into the street, making the roadway very much narrower than today. These were knocked down and the street widened at the beginning of Jan 1894. A report from the West Cumberland Times of this demolition work, recorded that a date stone of *"1728 had been found with the coat of arms of the Curwens"*. [02] (see also page 101)

Near the main gates to the Hall, stood just Bridge Street and Udale Street. There was no Washington Street or any other roads south of Pow Street. The main street up into the Old Market place followed the line of Wilson Street. Being then called General Street and running from the bottom of Ramsey Brow,[03] all the way upto Crosshill. This area was also previously called Uppergate and followed the line of today's King Street. Curwen Street, Christian Street and Cavendish Street all had now been laid out from Ramsey Brow, into Portland Square. In 1750, a street named Moot Hall Lane is known to have existed in Uppergate. Although it's exact location cannot be determined, it does confirm the existence of a meeting place for the eighteenth century town. It may have become obsolete after the opening of the Assembly Rooms in Portland Square.

Hutchinson in his 1797 *History of Cumberland* appears to refer to Portland Square when he says *"a new square in the upper town, consisting of twenty neat houses"* was built in *"the last twenty years"*. These appear to have replaced the much older properties in this area. The task of re-building this area, may have been began by Henry [v] Curwen, then almost certainly completed by his son-in-law John Christian Curwen. The name *"Portland"* is thought to have been adopted in honour of the Duke of Portland, [04] the prominent political leader and fellow Whig member of Parliament.

[01]   This map was later sent to Francis Jollie, the Carlisle printer, for inclusion in the soon to be published *'Hutchinson's History of Cumberland'.,* published from 1794-97. ▪

[02]   If this date is correct then it suggests these cottages in Finkle Street were built for Eldred [ii] Curwen. (see page 45) ▪

[03]   In the 1851 census *"Ramsey Brow"* is referred to as *"Turnpike Side"*. No doubt because it lay on the Cockermouth to Workington Turnpike road, and ran alongside Portland Square, its Census Enumeration District. ▪

[04] William Bentinck (1738-1809) was the third Duke of Portland. He like Christian Curwen was a member of the Whig party, but much more prominent, holding office under Lord Rockingham in 1765 and 1782. Appointed nominal Prime Minister of the famous coalition Government in 1783. He was also an ardent opponent of Sir James Lowther, whose family were then of course bitter local rivals of the Curwens. ▪

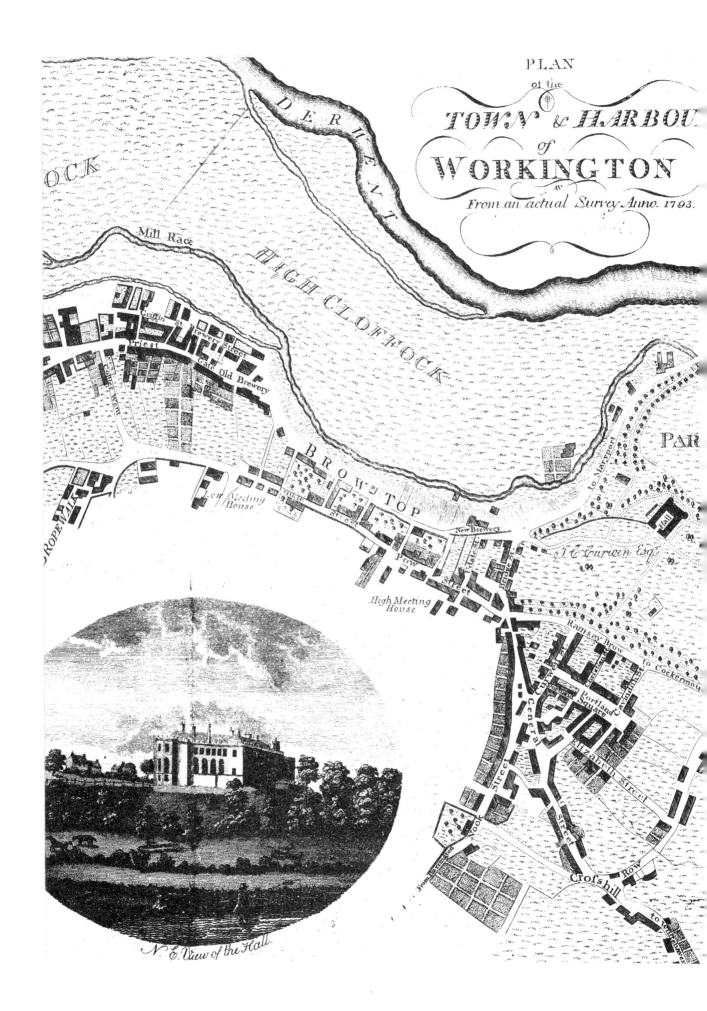

PLAN
of the
TOWN & HARBOUR
of
WORKINGTON
From an actual Survey. Anno. 1793.

DERWENT

HIGH CLOFFOCK

Mill Race

OCK

Griffin St.
Brewery Street
Priest
Gate Old Brewery

BROW TOP

ROPE WALK

Low Meeting House

Street

New Brewery

Pow

Street

High Meeting House

Hall

J. C. Curwen Esq.

PAR

to Maryport

Ramsay Brow

to Cockermou

Cavendish St.

Portland Square

Elizabeth Street

General

Street

Nook

Street

Crofshill Row

to Whitehaven

N. E. View of the Hall.

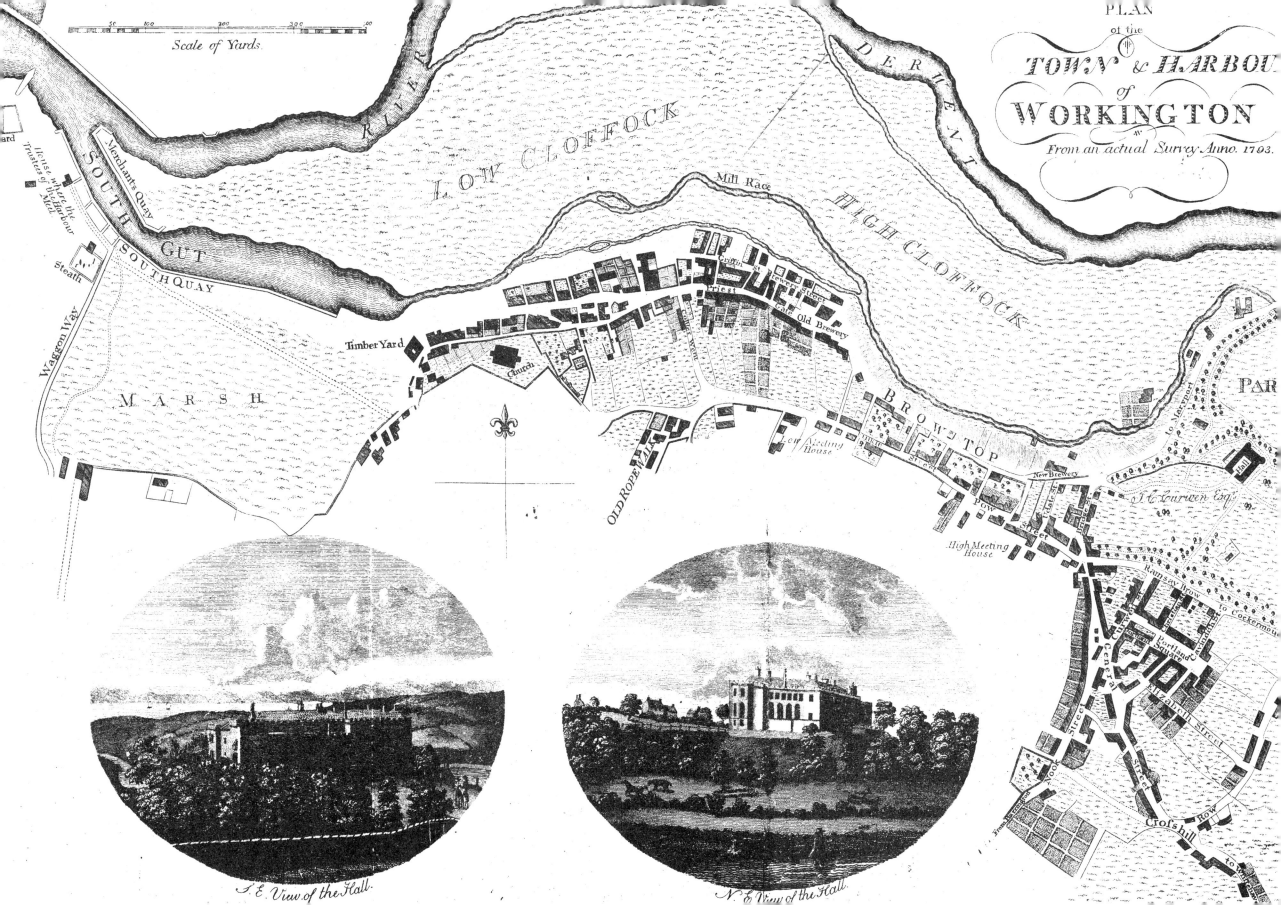

Scale of Yards.

PLAN
of the
TOWN & HARBOUR
of
WORKINGTON
From an actual Survey Anno. 1793.

RIVER DERWENT

LOW CLOFFOCK

HIGH CLOFFOCK

Mill Race

SOUTH QUAY

SOUTH GUT

Merchant's Quay

House where the Trustees of the Harbour Meet

Steath

Waggon Way

MARSH

Timber Yard

Church

OLD ROPE WALK

Griffin St.

Brewery Street

Priest Gate

Old Brewery

Low Meeting House

BROW TOP

New Brewery

High Meeting House

J. Curwen Esq.

PARK

to Harport

to Cockermouth

Ramsay Brow

Portland Square

Elizabeth Street

General Street

Crofshill Row

to Whitehaven

S.E. View of the Hall.

N.E. View of the Hall.

firmed that the town layout was still very much the same as two hundred years earlier. He wrote *"the town extends from the castle to the sea; it consists of two clusters, one, the more ancient, near the castle, the other nearer the church and pier"*.

This is confirmed when we look at the first accurately drawn town map, prepared around twenty years later. Commissioned by John Christian Curwen [01] and surveyed in 1793. There was now quite a number of houses north of Priestgate (later Church Street), in the area directly west of where *Allerdale House* now stands. These included Brewery Street and Griffin Street. Brow Top was still the main thoroughfare linking the lower part of the town to the upper area around the Hall. Although some development had now began along Pow Street and Finkle Street (then referred to as *"Back of Town"* and later often found spelt *"Fincal"*).

On the south side of Finkle Street, to the east of where the Appletree now stands, was then a row of about eight small white-washed cottages.. The front of these houses then projected well into the street, making the roadway very much narrower than today. These were knocked down and the street widened at the beginning of Jan 1894. A report from the West Cumberland Times of this demolition work, recorded that a date stone of *"1728 had been found with the coat of arms of the Curwens"*. [02] (see also page 101)

Near the main gates to the Hall, stood just Bridge Street and Udale Street. There was no Washington Street or any other roads south of Pow Street. The main street up into the Old Market place followed the line of Wilson Street. Being then called General Street and running from the bottom of Ramsey Brow,[03] all the way upto Crosshill. This area was also previously called Uppergate and followed the line of today's King Street. Curwen Street, Christian Street and Cavendish Street all had now been laid out from Ramsey Brow, into Portland Square. In 1750, a street named Moot Hall Lane is known to have existed in Uppergate. Although it's exact location cannot be determined, it does confirm the existence of a meeting place for the eighteenth century town. It may have become obsolete after the opening of the Assembly Rooms in Portland Square.

Hutchinson in his 1797 *History of Cumberland* appears to refer to Portland Square when he says *"a new square in the upper town, consisting of twenty neat houses"* was built in *"the last twenty years"*. These appear to have replaced the much older properties in this area. The task of re-building this area, may have been began by Henry [v] Curwen, then almost certainly completed by his son-in-law John Christian Curwen. The name *"Portland"* is thought to have been adopted in honour of the Duke of Portland, [04] the prominent political leader and fellow Whig member of Parliament.

[01]   This map was later sent to Francis Jollie, the Carlisle printer, for inclusion in the soon to be published *'Hutchinson's History of Cumberland'.*, published from 1794-97. ◼

[02]   If this date is correct then it suggests these cottages in Finkle Street were built for Eldred [ii] Curwen. (see page 45) ◼

[03]   In the 1851 census *"Ramsey Brow"* is referred to as *"Turnpike Side"*. No doubt because it lay on the Cockermouth to Workington Turnpike road, and ran alongside Portland Square, its Census Enumeration District. ◼

[04] William Bentinck (1738-1809) was the third Duke of Portland. He like Christian Curwen was a member of the Whig party, but much more prominent, holding office under Lord Rockingham in 1765 and 1782. Appointed nominal Prime Minister of the famous coalition Government in 1783. He was also an ardent opponent of Sir James Lowther, whose family were then of course bitter local rivals of the Curwens. ◼

PLAN
of the
TOWN & HARBOUR
of
WORKINGTON
From an actual Survey Anno. 1793.

At the top of Portland Square, in it's south east corner, facing north were the Assembly Rooms. It is thought they were first built in the late1780's, at the expense of John Christian Curwen. Here the townspeople once met for public meetings, lectures, plays, dinners and balls etc. Originally, it was then quite small, being described by Hutchinson (1797) as *"neat...and well attended during the winter season"*. By 1810 it was extended and remodelled into what Bulmer described as quite *"a large and roomy place"*, capable of holding over 900 people. Then it basically became L-shaped in plan, the large room at it's rear extending west up Elizabeth Street. Part of the building was also used for a schoolroom both during the week and also on Sundays. By the end of the nineteenth century, it was also to serve as a drill hall. Now (1998) only the front section onto Portland Square remains, on its facade is a neat smooth cement panel bearing the date *"1810"*. The modern flats, fronting onto the north side of Elizabeth street, now occupy the site of the rear of the building.

Today, if you walk through the Portland Square area, it is not difficult to imagine this cobbled square, bustling with activity in Georgian times. Obviously it would then have been devoid of the mature trees and the grey marble obelisk, [01] not erected till after 1877. But in this area of the town lived the wealthy sea captains, attorneys and surgeons. Nikolaus Pevsner [02] described it as the one place that *"can really be perambulated.....The square itself is delightful, long and narrow, cobbled.....not at all like England"*. It was then the centre for much of the commercial activity in the town. Now it lies almost slumbering, yet still very impressive, but for being unnaturally filled with too many bright modern motor cars. Once it was visited daily by the horse drawn mail coach, which called at the Green Dragon.

Crosshill appears still to be quite prominent, although the market had now moved down to the area between Nook Street and Curwen Street. Here was a corn market and Hutchinson (1797) records that *"at no great distance"* is the butchers market. In the butchers market, every trader had a separate apartment or stall, *"in front of which the occupiers name is put up"*. The 1851 town census reveals that this area later became known as *"Old Market Place"*. In 1828, much of the market had been moved again into the lower end of Portland Square. The Old Market Place then remained in use as a Butter Market, it was still called this in the 1851 census.

Around May 1860, a new covered market hall was completed. [03] It's main entrance was from the south side of Portland Street, with another leading from Market Place, down a narrow lane. L-shaped in plan, the market was built on the site of an old slaughter house. It contained about twenty

[01] The grey marble monument in Portland Square is in memory of Anthony Peat (1820-77) former surgeon (or doctor) in the town. ■

[02] This description by Nikolaus Pevsner, appears in the Cumberland & Westmorland volume of his famous *Buildings of England* series, first published in 1967. These essentially sightseer's guides have grown into an amazing architectural archive of nearly every town in England. ■

[03] It was built by a private Limited company, its first directors being W. Elliot, G. Armstrong, D.L. Hodgson, W. Ferguson, T. Bowman, Joseph Fawcett and J. G. Howe. The company issued 250 shares at £5 each, to finance the new market. ■

two fixed stalls and the upper part of the roof being almost fully glazed. Although sufficently large enough when first erected. Workington's population was to almost double, within the next twenty years. [01] By 1883, another market was urgently needed in the lower part of the town. This was accommodated on Falcon Place (or Hagg Hill), close to St. Michael's Church.

Shortly after it's erection, the Portland Street Covered Market was also used as a drill hall for the 7th Cumberland (Workington) Volunteer Rifle Corps. At this time, one of hundred's of local defence units formed throughout the country. When it was feared the French may be planning to invade. This unit with around 66 members, also had a rifle range to the west of Burrow Walls, with it's targets upon the Oyster Bank close to the edge of Siddick Pond. As well as being used for general shooting practice, this rifle range was also used for competitions arranged with other local rifle corps. Each unit had a team of five members, firing five rounds at targets placed at 200, 300, 400 and 500 yard distances. Peter Iredale, a local J.P. and partner in Workington Brewery, was then their sergeant major.

This was certainly not the first time local Volunteer forces had been raised to defend the country. In the summer of 1803, when the war with Napoleon had recommenced following just over a year of uneasy peace. Henry Addington, then Prime minister, mobilised almost the entire country for defensive action. There were nine local battalions of around 55-60 people each, raised from the towns of Workington, Harrington and Maryport. Each was led by a Captain and had a Lieutenant, Ensign, three Sergeants, three Corporals and a Drummer. The local Captains were Michael Falcon, Wilton Wood, John Fawcett, Thomas Cragg, Maitland Falcon, David Fletcher, William Swinburn, Joseph Hetherington and Benjamin Thompson.

In Sept 1803, a *Manual for the Volunteer Corps of Infantry* was issued to each unit. The book contained details of drill to be practised, and guidelines on what may be expected. It contained the following introduction *"In a country such as Britain, much intersected with inclosures and covered in many parts with extensive woods. It is necessary that all corps of infantry should become acquainted with the mode of warfare generally practised by the light troops"*. A similar little book, principally for the use of the Carlisle based Cumberland Rangers, was also printed by Frank Jollie in 1803; and will more than likely also have been used locally.

A detailed list of these local Volunteers still exists in their *"Muster Roll"*, now deposited at Whitehaven Record Office. The regiment which was generally drilled and exercised weekly, was commanded by John Christian Curwen.

Workington's Population

1801 - 5716
1811 - 5807
1821 - 6424
1831 - 6415
1841 - 6045
1851 - 6280
1861 -10765
1871 -13789

Based on the first reliable figures extracted from the census returns, taken every decade from 1801-71. During this seventy year period Workington's population was to gradually increase by 241%. More than doubling in the last two decades. This rate of growth was under half that of Newcastle and Liverpool, for the same period. ■

[01] The census figures for Workington record that in 1861 there was a population of 10765, by 1881 it had reached 20823. The full census figures for 1801-71 are shown above. ■

As a mark of their respect his officers, N.C.O's and privates later presented him with a beautiful, finely engraved sword. This once hung on the wall at one end of the Salon, in Workington Hall.

Above Cross Hill along the road to Whitehaven was Townhead, now called High Street. Although there was then very little development here, only the odd buildings dotted along either side of the road. At Thomas Close, near Low Ellerbeck, (now situated off the top of High street) was the parish poorhouse or workhouse. Opened around 1792, Hutchinson in his *History of Cumberland* mentions the *"spacious"* workhouse costing about £1600. He comments that it is calculated to hold around 150 persons, though the *"number now received there does not exceed twenty"*.

It's principle purpose was *"for employing, lodging and maintaining the poor of the township"*. The Vestry minutes record how a committee of prominent townspeople was formed to build the workhouse for the parish. [01] John Christian Curwen agreed to lease the land at *"a reasonable rent for ever"*, and is also shown as lending much of the money required to complete the project.

When the workhouse closed, the building was later used by Messrs. Guy and Harrison for their straw hat factory. In 1888 it was purchased by the Workington Board of Health, for conversion to a fever hospital. Later as well as accommodating tuberculosis patients, some geriatrics were also moved there from Workington Infirmary. It was closed in December 1965, and later demolished.

Unlike nearby Georgian Whitehaven which is well planned and with its gracefully laid out streets. Nearly all of Workington was then to develop without any real blueprint or master-plan. One exception of course, being the attractive Portland Square, and some of its adjoining streets. William Hutchinson in his 1797 *History of Cumberland* observed this when he recorded the town had *"not been laid out upon a plan of elegance, or for pleasure, but merely for the advantage of those concerned in trade"*. He also tells us that *"the town cannot boast many elegant buildings, or the streets of being well paved"* but does record *"many are wealthy, and in general the people are affable and open-hearted"*.

At this time, many of the houses in the town would then have had simple thatched roofs, made from straw or reeds. Even as late as 1812, *"thatch"* was still prepared at Schoose Farm, for sale as a roofing material. Slate was only then used on better quality properties. Although extensively quarried at many places around Buttermere. It was then quite expensive as it could only be brought to the town in small horse drawn carts. On older properties this local slate can be identified by it's dark green colour. The dark bluish slate

"The town has been built without reference to regularity of design; it is a long, narrow, straggling place, extending about a mile in length".
Samuel Jefferson 1842.

[01] The first Parish Poorhouse or Workhouse committee was appointed in December 1791. As well as raising the required funds and managing the building works, they also became responsible for *"directing and regulating the management"*.
The committee included Rev. W.T. Addison (rector), William Watts, John Steele, John Thompson, John Rumney, Thomas Martindale, Henry Bowman (all listed as gents), John Hudson (whitesmith) and John Kay (mercer). ■

so extensively seen throughout the town on later Victorian houses, was quarried in Wales. Large quantities being shipped into the town's harbour by vessels, returning for cargos of coal.

The next obvious printed map of the town is the first edition of the larger scale Ordnance Survey plan, not published until 1863. But an earlier hand drawn map exists prepared around 1835, by John Waite (then town's Customs officer). [01] It may not be the best example of draughtsmanship, but his additional notes have provided some valuable information, not found elsewhere.

Although the earlier 1793 plan names around fifteen streets. John Waite's plan, forty years later, names just seven. Conscious of the lack of street names he added the following note - *"you will observe that the names of only a few streets are mentioned, the reason is that the natives themselves don't know their names, this may appear strange but is a fact!!!"*. It appears that those other less established street names, which appeared on the 1793 plan were not then generally adopted by the residents, until many years later.

It is not impossible to conceive that in a small town nearly everyone would know virtually everyone else. Street names were then simply not really a necessity. This is quite evident when we examine old legal documents such as property title deeds. Often we find few street names, then properties were only described as being located next to that occupied by such and such on one side, and someone else on the otherside. Clearly more accurate property addresses only became necessary with the need to properly assess rates, the arrival of the first full census of 1841, and to a lesser extent with introduction of the uniform penny post.

John Waite's plan also shows Washington Street had now been laid out. Together with the east end of what was later to become Jane Street. It also indicates a new street now linked the Market place with Washington Street. Today we often refer to this street as Upper Jane Street, technically it is just an extension of Jane Street. Around 1814, some records suggest it was also once called Franklin Street. Waite map also shows that Collier Went was then called William Street. It is thought that it was named after William Curwen (1789-1822), a son of John Christian and Isabella Curwen.

The practise of naming the town's streets with the christian names of Curwen family members was then quite common. Henry Street on the Marsh was one of the first, named after Henry [vi] Curwen, the son of John Christian and Isabella. Other streets were named after the agents of the family, but this time their surnames were used. One of the first was Udale Street, named after the much respected Charles Udale. He first served as the agent for John Chris-

[01] John Waite (c1780-1840), a Scotsman from Berwick on Tweed, was the principle Coast officer for the HM.Customs and Excise at Workington, between 1831-40. The hand drawn town plan mentioned is not reproduced in this book, but much of it's information has been included as appropriate in several other chapters. The original is deposited in Whitehaven Record Office.

129

tian, before his marriage to Isabella Curwen. Then afterwards continued to be employed by the Curwen family. Swinburn Street was also named after their steward William Swinburn.

As with Portland Square, some of the other town's streets were also named after Christian Curwen's political allies. Cavendish Street, linking the top of Portland Square with Ramsey Brow, is thought to have aquired its name from Lord John Cavendish.[01] Whilst the now quite insignificant Fox Lane, is thought to be named after another equally famous and distinguished statesman, Charles James Fox. [02]

Around thirty years, after John Waite drew his small town plan, the large scale Ordnance Survey map was published. This was the first really accurate survey, and the later subsequent editions clearly show how the town had grown in the last 120 years or so. The Workington of the 1860's was still virtually confined to the southern edge of the Cloffolks, stretching along the bank of the Derwent and around the Hall. There was still almost no development south of Pow Street and Finkle Street. But they did now continue down to Hagg Hill (or Falcon Place), as South William Street and Fisher Street had now been laid out. Although there was then a few new buildings here, much of the land to either side of these streets was still just open fields.

Just west of the Wesleyan Methodist Church (see chapter six) was Tuscan Villa, the home of John Guy and his family. [03] Built in 1843, it was described by Mannix & Whellan as a *"neat Gothic residence"*. It was set well back from the roadside, a large formal garden with a central fountain, separated the fine house from South William Street. Around 1830, Guy was believed to have patented an improved method of making fine natural straw hats and bonnets, then such a popular fashion accessory. (see sketches above) Initially, the hats were made from an Italian wheat straw, imported from Leghorn (or Livorno) in Tuscany, hence the name of his home. But later Dunstable straw, more easily grown in this country, became an acceptable and very much cheaper alternative.

In partnership with Jonathan Harrison, they first established a factory in Christian Street. But were also believed to have had another factory in Halstead in Essex. Later they moved to premises at 4 Wilson Street. Employing several hundred people cultivating, plaiting and sewing the fine textured bonnets, with wide curved brims. After John Guy retired (around 1845) the business was continued by his son John Harrison Guy, who lived above the business premises in Wilson Street.

John Waite's 1835 town plan, also noted that there was a *"Leghorn Hat Manufactory"* west of the present Park End

[01] At the same time as John Christian Curwen was serving as MP for Carlisle. Lord John Cavendish, like the Duke of Portland, was one of the most prominent members of the Whig party. He was twice appointed one of the *"lords of the treasury"*, under Lord Rockingham in 1765 and 1782. A post with similar duties to that of today's *"Chancellor of the Exchequer"*.
[02] Fox Lane may now appear to link just Portland square to Elizabeth Street, but on earlier town maps it is shown as running from the square down to King Street. Charles James Fox (1749-1806), was Secretary of State under Rockingham's government, and later Foreign Secretary in 1782-3 and 1806. Both the above men, Portland and others must have made quite an impression on Christian Curwen when he first entered parliament in 1786. Then his Whig party was in opposition to the Tories, but these men had all held prominent posts in the last Whig government of 1782-3. ■
[03] John Guy, born in Maryport in 1790, was an active Wesleyan methodist, frequently providing accommodation at Tuscan Villa for their visiting ministers. ■

Road, close to Stainburn School (formerly the Grammar School) playing fields. Exactly who ran this establishment has yet to be determined It may have been Joseph Walker (b.1790), the watchmaker and ironmonger of Bridge Street. Mannix & Whellan recorded in their 1847 *Directory* that he was then also involved in *"the growth and manufacture of tuscan straw, and is perhaps the only person at present in England engaged in this branch"*. Certainly by the middle decades of the nineteenth century this industry had reached it's peak, before suffering a rapid decline.

Another very obvious new structure on this 1863 OS plan was *Fisher's Ropery*, also known as the *Workington Ropery & Saw Mill*. (see page 101) This very long thin building stretched from the Fisher Street, and followed the line of the west side of Corporation Road, for several hundred yards. It was known to have been built on the site of where an *"Old Ropewalk"* [01] had once stood, but who established it is a mystery. The Proprietor, Mr Fisher died around 1860 and the works were taken over by a Whitehaven company.

Stout strong ropes of all sizes and lengths, were then in almost constant demand, primarily for the rigging of ships and the hauling of coal up the pit shafts. All ropes were then commonly made of hemp fibres, the yarn was first spun to form strands, which were then twisted around each other to form the rope. This unusually extremely long building allowed similar long ropes to be manufactured in one piece without any joints or splicing, making them much stronger. Supplies of hemp used in the roperies were generally imported into the harbour.

There was then also another ropery in the town. Situated close to Priestgate Marsh, on the south side of the street that later became known as the Marsh Side. It must have existed before 1793, as it appears on the town plan. David Fletcher ran the business up until November 1856, when it was purchased by William Briggs & Co. Their first advertisement in the *Cumberland Pacquet*, tells how they made ropes of every description, including *"standing and running rigging, bolt rope, cables, hawsers, and flat rope for mining purposes"*.

Just to the east of Fishers' Ropery, standing alone in it's own wooded gardens, was an elegant house called *Shrub Hill*. Later it was also called *Field House* and became the Town Hall, after it was purchased by Workington Borough Council. *Shrub Hill*, later the home of the Hodgson family, was then reached by a narrow road called *Lowsa Lane*, which ran from South William Street, following the line of what we know today as Park Lane.

Then of course there was also no Oxford Street, just open fields and the remains of the abandoned pitheads and

[01] The Old Ropewalk is shown on the 1793 town plan (see page 124). The history surrounding who operated the business here is not quite clear. John Hodgson, once a partner in the Chapel Banks colliery, is thought to have had his ropery here between 1770-1813. We can surmise it must have existed much earlier, as it had then aquired the *"Old"* element in it's name. There was also a further smaller ropeworks behind St. John's Church, It occupied the site of what we know today as Roper Street, hence it's name. ■

spoil heaps of Elizabeth, John and Hope pits. The 1851 census shows the fields around John Pit Hill, behind St. John's Church were then being farmed by Henry Steele. The only two roads between here south to Annie Pit Lane, were Vulcans Lane and what we now refer to as Harrington Road, both were little more than tracks cutting across fields and meadows. St. Michael's School also stood almost alone on what was then called Cooke Lane (later renamed Station Road). Cooke Lane only then ran from Belle Isle Street upto Hagg Hill.

The layout of Washington Street and the upper part of the town was then very similar to today, although Carlton Road and much of Park End Road had yet to be built upon. The north end of John Street (which disappeared when St. John's Precinct was built) had been laid out, with St. John's School occupying its east side and the Primitive Methodist church opposite. This street is thought to have been named after John Christian Curwen. The 1851 census reveals only around a dozen houses then in this street. John Waite had recorded only a very short section of Jane Street extended across Washington Street. Now much of this area had been built upon, but the street still only extended 50 metres or so westward. Jane Street is believed to have aquired it's name from Jane Stanley who married Henry [vi] Curwen in 1804.

Guard Street (formerly referred to as just the Guards) now ran down to the corner of Washington Street. Whilst Nook Street is then shown as extending across the junction to also occupy the upper end of what we now call Harrington Road. Again there was then little development south and west of Guard Street and High Street, only the Gas Works (on Harrington Road), St. Michael's R.C. Church and School. Today's sprawling modern housing estates of Moorclose, Salterbeck and Westfield, obtain their names from isolated farms that once existed there.

CHAPTER NINE

WORKINGTON HALL

PRIOR to the construction of Workington Hall, we be
lieve that the Curwen family and their ancestors, lived
in the Norman castle at Burrow Walls; upon the same site
once occupied by the Romans. (see chapter two) Occasionally, Burrow Walls has also been called *Seaton Castle*, originally of course it did lie in the Manor of Seaton.

J. F. Curwen in his *History of the Ancient House
of Curwen*, states that Patric de Culwen was responsible
for moving the family home across the Derwent to the
present Workington Hall site. It is suggested this occurred around 1250, although the exact date is not very
clear. The first Hall may have been built predominately
from timber, with a thatched roof. It is thought that Patric, like other generations of Curwen's did not permanently
reside at Workington. Certainly the family still held lands
in Galloway and elsewhere. It is more probable that Thomas [i] de Curwen (Patric's grandson) became its first permanent resident, around 1268.

Exactly why the Curwens moved from the Burrow
Walls site is unclear. Brian Blake speculates that it may
have been an *"adulterine"* (or unlicensed) Castle. Perhaps, the coastal erosion lead to the abandonment of the
old pele tower. Or was it simply because it was a defensively stronger site. Around 1610, John Denton in his
Account of Cumberland, mentions the Curwen's former
home as then abandoned and left in decay, commenting
*"the walls of the ruins of the mansion house are yet to be seen
there at Seaton to this day"*. Nicholson & Burn in 1777,
refer to Burrow Walls as *"an old ruinous tower, standing
nakedly at the west of the town"*. Perhaps, it's demise
was due to an attack from the Scots, many centuries earlier.

Throughout this early period, Cumberland like other
English border counties, was almost consistently subjected
to forays from the Scottish forces. Despite the Tweed-
Solway borderline being properly established in 1237; and
Alexander II, King of Scots apparently giving up all claims
to the North of England. Perpetual distrust and feuding
became something of a way of life. Then and for centuries, the locals along both sides of the border essentially
lived under constant threat, surviving in something of a
war zone. In addition to clashes between the English and

"Locally, Workington Hall is
often referred to as *Curwen Hall*
or *Curwen Castle*. By virtue of
the Curwen family who built the
original pele tower, and lived there
for almost eight hundred years".

Scots forces, they also had to endure the often vicious forays of the Border Reivers, so synonymous for marauding attacks, theft, arson, kidnap and murder.

We know the Scots invaded Cumbria in October 1297, when Edward I was leading his army to fight the French in Flanders. And countless other large and small raids and attacks occurred in the next half century. In 1316 they are said to have *"laid waste everything"* as far south as Furness. Whilst William Rollinson writes that in Sept 1322, *"on into Allerdale and Copeland the raiders swept, burning and pillaging in a whirlwind of destruction"*. Without doubt the Scots did reach Workington, travelling overland or as earlier invaders had done, by sea across the Solway Firth. The existence of the substantial fortified tower of St. Michael's Church, overlooking the Derwent estuary, tends to confirm this theory.

Although we have no record of specific attacks on Workington or the Hall. Some suggest it was almost completely destroyed on at least two occasions. It is known that two of Thomas [i] de Curwen's brothers, fought at the Battle of Falkirk, alongside Edward I when he defeated William Wallace's Scottish forces. Surely, this alone could have perhaps warranted reprisal attacks on their homes and estates.

According to Daniel Fleming in his *Description of Cumberland*, it was Gilbert [iii] de Curwen who *"built the chief tower at Workington, the stone was laid 8 May 1362"*. Today, we can still identify much of the remains of this substantial rectangular pele tower, among the present ruins of the south east corner of the Hall. The basic design of a fourteenth century pele tower was fairly standard through the north of the country. Workington's measures 13 metres long by 10m wide, the same length as the neighbouring pele at Isel (near Cockermouth), but around 2 metres wider.

How long it took to construct the new tower is unclear, but a *"licence to crenellate"* was formally granted by Richard II in 1379. Around this time the likelihood of further hostile attacks must have been quite high as the wardens of the English Marches were instructed *"to see that all Castles and Fortalices within three or four leagues of the frontier are fortified, repaired suitably manned and provisioned"*.

Initially, this peel tower probably stood alone within an outer courtyard surrounded by a high wall or fence. Within this courtyard were probably other smaller and less important timber and thatch outbuildings. What is referred to as the barbican (or fortified entrance), being added sometime later. Perhaps, when the next range of other

"Today, we can still identify much of the remains of this substantial rectangular pele tower, among the present ruins of the south east corner of the Hall".

buildings were added to the north. Then there may have been another entrance into the tower, at first floor level from above the vaulted cellar or store, still to be seen today. On the east wall of the pele tower, at this level, is the remains of a narrow doorway, with a sloping roof above.

It was the beginning of the fifteenth century, when the adjoining three vaulted cellars were added. Above which was thought to be the Great Hall (or Alua). J.F. Curwen described this as a *"noble apartment, with an internal measurement of 56 feet* (17.25m) *by 22 ft* (6.8m)*"*. This Alua is likely to have had a *"high pitched and massive oaken timber roof"*. At the same time the ancient kitchen block was also added to the north east adjoining corner.

Around 1538, with the increased refinements of the sixteenth century, Thomas [iv] Curwen is attributed to have re-built this Great hall, (situated over the vaulted cellars). Comparisons have been made to the similar great halls at Naworth and Wharton. [01]   Next to them Workington would have possessed by far the largest hall of any other fortified tower in Cumberland and Westmorland. Perhaps, confirming the Curwens as one of the most prominent and important families in these border counties. Adjoining this room and above the vaulted kitchen at it's north end, were the rooms or chambers once occupied by Mary Queen of Scots.[02]

It is now difficult to imagine these actual rooms, through which this famous house guest would have strolled. As all we see today, are the remains of the much later eighteenth century structure. One exception being the large fireplace opening, now visible in what was later known as the Salon. This was actually part of the Great Hall at this time.

The hall would also have stood in a large courtyard, now about the same size as the outside walls of today's ruin. It is likely to have been enclosed by a high curtain wall, with the existing gatehouse in it's present position. Then the gatehouse was much narrower, the rooms either side being much later additions. There is still evidence of several narrow loophole windows around this area. Allowing the entrance to be defended from within, by archers with their bows and arrows. In the late eighteenth century, an extra storey was added to the existing gatehouse we see today. In addition the two semi-circular topped windows were also added.

If we look at the 1569 Town plan (see page 121) we find a small sketch apparently depicting the hall. It appears to show the main pele tower, with probably the Great Hall above. The two towers in the foreground could be part of a wall surround the courtyard. Whilst some doubt

ABOVE - the small thumbnail sketch of Workington Hall from the 1569 town plan. How accurately it depicts the Elizabethan Hall is open to conjecture. (see text right) ■

[01] Naworth and Wharton Great halls were build by Thomas Dacre and Thomas Wharton respectively. Both were important and prominent Warden's of the English West Marches. As such they were obliged to entertain important guests. ■
[02] Mary Queen of Scots slept at the Hall on Sunday, 16 May 1568. (see chapter eighteen) ■

is cast over the St. Michael's Church sketch on the same plan. According to Peter Barber of the British Library, important houses and other significant buildings on similar maps were generally *"clearly depicted by the cartographer"*. But can we rely on a manuscript illustration of this size and scale, as being an accurate depiction of building.

Around the start of the seventeenth century, J. F. Curwen believed Nicholas [i] Curwen *"transformed the old Border fortress into a Tudor mansion"*. He added the narrow south wing, which included the chapel. Together with a similar wing opposite, which would appear now to totally enclose the courtyard with buildings. Still visible today particularly along the south side of the courtyard, are windows (with their stone mullions) and door surrounds, these clearly date this part of the hall to this period.

Today within Workington's Helena Thompson Museum is a rather worn and damaged carved stone shield bearing the remains of a Curwen family coat of arms. It once hung above the retainers entrance, [01] and represented Sir Patricius Curwen. Once the date 1665 could be clearly seen along its bottom edge. It was removed and stored by Workington Borough Council, when the Hall was vandalised in the 1960s. It has since suffered some further damage whilst in their safe keeping, as the last two numerals of its date are now lost. Clearly visible in it's lower left hand corner are the figures *"16"*, but in the opposite corner, the surface is now quite badly chipped. [02]

In 1671, Daniel Fleming provides the next recorded description of the hall. He describes it as *"built as a collegeway in the form of a quadrangle"*. Whilst around seventeen years later Thomas Denton [03] describes the hall as *"very commodiously seated both for pleasure and plenty......Workington Hall stands on the top of the River Bank, at the east end of the town, within less than a mile of the sea......the River Bank, near the hall is covered with a thick wood"* also to the north and east sides it is *"beautified with large gardens, orchyards and long walks (shaded with firr trees on the south) which are.......with all sorts of good fruit, herbs, plants &c"*.

Exactly which Curwen family member was responsible for planting these apparently now quite mature grounds is not recorded. We can surmise it was perhaps Thomas [v] Curwen, who is known to have lived at the hall, from long before 1664 until his death in 1672. A century later John Christian Curwen was to greatly re-landscape nearly all the estate. Between 1783-86, he commissioned the then quite prominent gardeners, Thomas White & Son from Retford, Nottinghamshire to replant much of the grounds of both the Hall and Belle Isle

[01] This coat of arms can be seen in the centre photograph on page 141, above the retainers entrance. ■

[02] Samuel Jefferson (in 1842) and J.F. Curwen (1899) both mention this stone shield and refer to it's 1665 date. It is also mentioned in the old Workington Borough Council files, and some 1965 photographs clearly still show the full date. Sadly this damage must have therefore occurred in this period before it came to be displayed at the museum. It is thought to have been stored in the outbuildings of the nearby Hall nurseries, now (1998) where *"The Greenhouse"* stands.

[03] Thomas Denton was Lord of the manor of Warnell Hall, Sebergham. A former barrister-at-law and recorder of Carlisle. He was commissioned to compile the *"perambulation"* by Sir John Lowther of Lowther. It has not been established if he was related to the John Denton, who wrote a similar earlier account around 1607. However, R.S. Ferguson of the C&WA&AS comments that the latter work *"follows very much the plan of his predecessor John Denton, but being much fuller in detail"*. Both the original manuscripts are still in the Lowther papers at Carlisle Record Office.

Many later histories such as Lyson's *Magna Britannia* and Hutchinson's *History of Cumberland*, refer to these Denton manuscripts; and they form a backbone for much of the county's early history. Although they are often to be mistakenly quoted as just one work.

Having examined both original manuscripts, I have arrived at the conclusion that they had obviously been prepared around the dates indicated, maybe even a little earlier. In the context of Workington's history, John Denton indicates Nicolas [i] Curwen living at the Hall; which he did do to 1604. Whilst, Thomas Denton's later work, obviously mentions Henry [iii] Curwen's habitation of the Hall; which was until 1725. ■

at Windermere. Although not entirely clear from the Curwen accounts, it is thought the cost of White's work, at both sites, was in excess of £2355. During the summer of 1794, John Sander of Keswick, is also known to have carried out further planting in the hall grounds.

Sometime shortly before his death in 1778, we know Henry [v] Curwen carried out some further extensive alterations to the hall. It is recorded that he died before the work was fully completed, leaving certain re-built areas to be later roofed over by his executors. Unfortunately, it is not exactly clear which areas were affected. One suspects that it may have included the north west corner of the hall, containing the main kitchen. Here are two built-up almost square windows, either side of the top of the existing large semi-circular window. The appearance of the stone surrounds of these former windows, suggest they could well be dated to that period.

It is thought John Christian Curwen later added the larger window to this kitchen; together with the identical one in the former chapel, at the opposite end of the front elevation. It is quite likely that this chapel window replaced a narrower one, with a pointed arched head (perhaps once containing stained glass). This work formed only one small aspect of the major re-building and internal alterations carried out by Christian Curwen.

"John Christian Curwen appointed York architect John Carr (1723-1807) to convert the hall into a stylish Georgian mansion".

This work began shortly after his 1782 marriage to Isabella, daughter of Henry [v] Curwen. After returning from their honeymoon, the newly weds went straight to live at Unerigg Hall (now Ewanrigg) near Maryport. They remained there till around August 1788 while the work to Workington Hall was completed. Christian Curwen appointed York architect John Carr (1723-1807) to convert the hall into a stylish Georgian mansion. Carr had began work as a stonemason, before becoming one of the most prominent northern architects. Largely self-taught, he became one of the most competent and successful of Georgian architects. He was a contemporary of the famous Scottish architect Robert Adam, working with him on many projects, including Harewood House, York County Assizes and Newark Town Hall. His practice was based on the patronage of the Northern gentry, and country houses like Workington Hall, formed the bulk of his work.

In the latter quarter of the eighteenth century, architecture, decoration and furniture generally reflected a fine neoclassical style, made popular by Adam. Carr imitated, adapted and made use of much of this detailing within his restyled interior of Workington Hall. Rooms were enriched with fine Greek and Roman ornament. This appeared on cornices, friezes, panel mouldings, skirtings, door and window surrounds. Chimney pieces were of marble and doors of mahogany and rooms were designed with aspidal or recessed ends often formed a screen of classical columns.

This was clearly evident in rooms such as the Dining Room, Salon, Library and the adjoining staircases. Here were once elaborate ceilings with decorative cornices and ribs, incorporating finely detailed dentils and corbels. Each room had carefully proportioned recesses behind an entablature, supported on rows of corinthian columns. These columns constructed from timber, resembled marble; and were just part of the hall's once magnificent joinery work. Few details remain to tell us much about the craftsmen who actually carried out this work. The Curwen accounts certainly show Ellwood & Co., shipbuilders in the town, supplying *"men and timber"* for the Workington Hall improvements. But an account from February 1784, for just under £90, does not clearly show the extent of their work. There is also some suggestion that the fine plasterwork was carried out by craftsmen from Italy, although very little further is known.

John Carr is also thought to have added the new main entrance, reached across the courtyard directly opposite the gatehouse. It incorporated an elegant double staircase, rising in two flights, either side of the wide entrance doors, to a balcony above. From this landing a door entered the Salon, or one could overlook the front doors below. Centrally from this entrance level, six wide steps also dropped to the ancient vaulted cellars below. Within the adjoining semi-circular tower, a further graceful cantilevered curved staircase swept upto the suites of bedrooms above. Both these staircases had delicate cast iron balustrades and stone steps, with finely cut moulded nosings. Other aspects of Carr's work are detailed later in this chapter.

One important feature of the eighteenth century hall, often forgotten and overlooked was it's superb collection of fine period furniture. In the summer of 1788, as the main structural work was almost complete, Christian Curwen asked Gillow & Company of Lancaster to supply an almost complete range of new furniture and other furnishings. Obviously having extensively restyled the hall in such a magnificent way, this was essential inorder to properly complete the task.

His choice of Gillows, without doubt then one of the most prominent cabinet makers and upholsterers in the country, was not altogether a surprise. For we know they had already largely furnished many other distin-

"John Carr was one of the greatest eighteenth century architects working in the provinces"
John H. Haugham
(County Architect) 1951

guished country houses designed by John Carr. Their craftsmen were exceptionally skilled and their furniture produced during this period was of remarkable quality. Furthermore, they had already made several pieces of furniture for both Belle Isle and Unerigg Hall.

We know from the company's meticulous records (still in existence today) that George Gillow (1766-1822) visited the hall and listed the Curwen's requirements on 5 July 1788. After which the firm prepared many elaborate sketches, some tinted in watercolour, of the various pieces of furniture. Many of these still also exist along with the original Gillow estimate books. The relevant Curwen entries contain not just their materials and labour calculations, but further neat working drawings of most pieces.[01] The Workington Hall order was dispatched by ship, from Lancaster in two cargoes. They arrived in October 1788 and March 1789. Although the second shipment should have been received in early January, it was delayed by adverse weather.

Some of the most significant and notable Gillow pieces were those made specifically for the entrance hall areas and dining room. (see photographs on pages 142-3). Included were a set of fourteen chairs, a sideboard-table, a pair of pier (or side) tables, and a pair of pedestals and urns. In May 1948, these pieces, together with two elegant upholstered window sofas, were sold (as one lot) by auctioneers Christie, Manson & Woods (now Christies) for £3675. They later crossed the Atlantic and were eventually aquired by the United States Government. It is thought they may have once been used within the White House, in Washington. Today (1998), this much travelled furniture, which once stood in Workington Hall, has returned again to Europe, now it graces the State Dining Room of the American Embassy in Vienna, Austria.

All these chairs had square tapering legs, and a finely moulded *"Hepplewhite style"* shield-shaped backs, carved with the Prince of Wales' plumes. From the Gillow papers we know they charged the equivalent of just £2.82 for each chair, and this included the leather upholstery. The sideboard-table had six similar square tapering legs, and a bowed centre section. It's narrow front panel or frieze and legs being carved with pendant and scrolled foliage. Gillows charged the Curwens only £18.90 for this sideboard, which also included a brass rail (or gallery) attached across the back. [02]

The pier or side tables were semi-circular, to stand against a wall. Their were veneered with an inlaid central fan design, whilst the fronts and legs had similar carving

(continued on page 145)

[01] Gillow & Company's extensive records are now on deposit in the archives of Westminster City Libraries. [02] The two brass rails at the back of the sideboard-table, were intended to stand silver dishes and plates against. Supported centrally on the upper rail were two candle holders on branches. Sheraton in his *Cabinetmaker's and Upholsterer's Drawing Book* wrote that these *"when lighted gave a very brilliant effect to the silverware"*. ■

TOP LEFT - The Salon at Workington Hall, With it's full-sized billiard table, and walls lined with large paintings. **ABOVE** - Later view of the Salon (when empty), looking through the open door into the Library.

LEFT - Sketch of the finely detailed white marble Corinthian fireplace, which was positioned between the two central windows of the Salon; and can just be seen on the left of the photograph above. Some believe it was brought from an Italian Palace by John Christian Curwen. **ABOVE -** A rather sad photograph of the same fireplace in 1964, showing it now vandalised and damaged beyond repair.

ABOVE - Workington Hall (c1920) from the south-west, before it was allowed to crumble and decay. In the foreground is the octagonal vinery and glasshouses which ran almost the full length of the side elevation. You can compare it's appearance to that of today - see photograph on opposite page.

ABOVE LEFT - Fine piece of old coloured stained glass, depicting the coat of arms of Patricius Curwen (1601-64). In heraldic terms, it has fifteen quarterings impaling a quartered coat of Selby. The crest is a horned unicorn's head erazed argent. The supporters are to the left - Dexter, a maiden proper, with golden hair girdled round the loins; to the right - Sinister, a horned unicorn argent. SI IE N' ESTOY is the family motto, and translates to "If I had not been there". The glass is dated 1634 and was once displayed in the Salon at Workington Hall.

The white marble bust of John Christian Curwen which once stood in the Salon of Workington Hall. Now in a private collection in Essex.

The lower room of the original fourteenth century pele tower at Workington Hall. It is the oldest remaining part of the building, and now generally referred to as the Justice's or Judge's Hall. It's rough rubble walls are over 2.1m (7ft) thick, and originally it is thought to have had a stone vaulted ceiling, traces of which are still visible today. The staircase leading up from the right is a later addition, but remains of the original stone spiral staircases can also still be seen today.

ABOVE - View of Workington Hall today, a roofless ruin.

View from the courtyard, through the main entrance of Workington Hall, towards the doorway into one of the four vaulted basement rooms. Over the door opening is the stone Curwen family Coat of Arms, now displayed in Helena Thompson Museum. Note the balustrades of the landing level at the top of the picture, from here there was a wide door opening into the Salon.

View of staircase and gallery or landing above main entrance. The balustrades were of finely detailed cast iron. Overhead was a semi-circular vaulted plaster ceiling, with it's ribs enriched with floral decoration; remains of which can be seen on the far wall. The central doorway on the landing led into the Salon, whilst the other door lead through to an elaborate semi-circular staircase upto the second floor.

ABOVE - Dining Room of Workington Hall, added by architect John Carr in the late eighteenth century. The primary feature of this room was its highly decorative "Adam style" plasterwork; particularly its cornice, with fine dentils and corbels. He was also responsible for detailing some of the hall's once magnificent joinery work, including the Corinthian columns of this room. The fine carved white marble fireplace was flanked either side by columns of Blue John Derbyshire Spar. By May 1965, virtually all this priceless work had been lost forever.

ABOVE - The sideboard-table seen in background of the Dining Room photograph, made for Workington Hall, by Gillow of Lancaster in 1788. It has six similar square tapering legs, and a bowed centre section. It's narrow front panel and legs being carved with pendant and scrolled foilage. (shown in detail - **RIGHT**) Gillows charged only the equivalent of £18.90 for this sideboard. It is now in the State Dining Room of the American Embassy in Vienna, Austria.

ABOVE - The Library of Workington Hall (also added by John Carr) was almost elliptical in plan. Here again was another beautiful carved white marble mantel piece and fire surround, very similar to that in the Dining Room. This 1964 photograph shows much of the fine plasterwork was then still apparently intact.

LEFT - One of the pedestals and urns, which once stood either side of the side-board-table, in the Dining Room of Workington Hall. They were not purely for decoration, one is lined with tin and has racks to be used as a plate warmer; the other has three inside drawers, one of which is probably intended to hold wine bottles. The vase-shaped urns have flame finials, and carved vertical flutes. in 1788, both pedestals and urns cost the Curwens just £26.25, from Gillows of Lancaster. Now also in the State Dining Room of the American Embassy in Vienna.

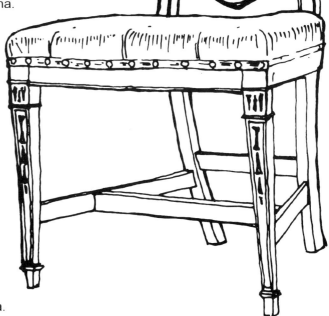

RIGHT - Sketch of the dining chairs made for Workington Hall in 1788. Each has square tapering legs, and a finely moulded "Hepplewhite style" shield-shaped back, carved with the Prince of Wales' plumes. From the Gillow papers we know they charged the Curwen's the equivalent of just £2.82 for each chair, and that included the green leather upholstery. Now also in the State Dining Room of the American Embassy in Vienna.

to that of the sideboard. Gillows supplied the pair for the equivalent of a mere £9.20. The pedestals and urns, were intended to stand on either side of the sideboard-table. They were not purely for decoration, one of the pedestals was lined with tin and had racks to be used as a plate warmer; whilst the other had three drawers, one of which was lined in copper and probably intended to hold pots or wine bottles. The urns were vase-shape with flame finials, and had carved vertical flutes. Each urn had a small brass tap projecting from it's plinth, and held water *"for the use of the butler"*. Both these pedestals and urns cost the Curwens just £26.25.

Gillows originally also made four window sofas for the hall, two of which were also later sold by Christies. All had elegant scrolled end arms, and were *"stuffed with curled hair into canvas"*, before being upholstered. The Curwen's were to pay only £4.95 for each of these sofas All the furniture was originally covered in the *"best green Morocco leather"*, and made from solid mahogany. John Christian Curwen was to pay a little less than £104, for all the above furniture now in Vienna. This was just over a tenth of the full value of his original 1788 order from Gillows, the final cost being £939. Although this could be considered a colossal amount for time, it did also include many other items of furniture, such as a full sized billiard table; together with the supply and installation of furnishings such as curtains, cornices, mattresses, pillows, blankets, cushions, roller blinds and floorcloths. The scale of Christian Curwen's huge order was then far larger than anything Gillows had previously undertaken.

There once hung upon the walls of the hall many superb portraits and paintings. Amongst those in the Salon, were two very fine full length portraits, painted by George Romney. [01] The most famous of these depicts Isabella, wife of John Christian Curwen, with their house at Belle Isle in the background. (see photograph opposite) The other was of her husband, in a blue coat with buff breaches and riding boots, his hat and whip in his left hand. Standing alongside his horse. Hilda Gamlin in her book *George Romney and his Art*, comments that it shows *"an attitude suggestive of true dignity and high breeding"*. [02] It has been said that the famous artist Thomas Gainsborough may actually have painted in Christian Curwen's horse, although the actual reason for this is unclear.

Both Isabella and John Christian are recorded as sitting for these portraits between September 1782 and January 1783. We do know that Christian Curwen also purchased two other Romney paintings in 1782. These were a pair illustrating two parts of William Hayley's poem *The*

[01] George Romney (1734-1802) was born in Dalton in Furness. Following an apprenticeship under Kendal painter, Christopher Steele, he went on to became a famous and fashionable portrait painter and rival to Joshua Reynolds and Thomas Gainsborough. Perhaps his best work is the dancing *"Levenson Gower Children"*, presently on display at Kendal's Abbott Hall. He also painted the Duke of Portland, John Wesley and Rev. Doctor Samuel Parr. ■
[02] In March 1961, The Curwen family sold both Romney's paintings of Isabella (size 96 x 59 inches) and John Christian Curwen (96 x 59 inches), at auctioneers Christie, Manson & Woods Ltd (now Christies International). The hammer price, (including commission) was £6825 and £1470 respectively. Today (1998) both are in private collections, John Christian is still in this country, but Isabella is now in the United States. See opposite page for photographs of both paintings. ■

[01] J. F. Curwen recorded that one of these pictures depicted Serena in the *"Boat of Apathy"*. Whilst the other shows her reading a book by candlelight, under the *"Spell of Romance"*. William Hayley (1745-1820) was an intimate friend of George Romney, writing a biography of the artist in 1809. His poem *"Triumphs of Temper"*, was first published in 1781. The present whereabouts of these paintings is unknown. *"Boat of Apathy"* was sold by the family at Christies in March 1961, for £787. ■

[02] Today (1998) the Romney painting of Lady Hamilton, entitled *"The Spinstress"* hangs in the Music room of Kenwood House. An ideal setting as this room is still decorated in the late eighteenth century Adam style, once so visible at it's former home within Workington Hall. The *"Dancing Baccante"* is believed now to be in a private collection abroad, being last sold by auction in New York, on 10 October 1991. ■

Triumphs of Temper. [01]   In 1899, J.F. Curwen noted both these paintings were then also hanging in the Salon.   In 1788, we know from Romney's biography that, Christian Curwen also purchased *"The Spinstress"*; depicting the infamous Lady Emma Hamilton, for 150 guineas (£157.50); together with a painting entitled *"The Dancing Bacchante"* in 1791.   Where these two were hung in the Hall does not appear to be recorded. [02]

There was at least a dozen further pictures around the walls of the vast Salon, one of which was the portrait of Henry [vi], son of John Christian Curwen.   J. F. Curwen tells us that there was a further full-length and life-size oil painting on wooden panels. It depicred Sir Patricius Curwen (d.1664), wearing *"a slashed crimson doublet and trunk hose, scarlet stockings crimson garters and black shoes"*. The sketch on page 41, is based on this picture, however its present whereabouts are unknown.

On following pages are sketch plans and reconstructions of Workington Hall. Included also are addition notes to guide the reader through this once magnificent place.

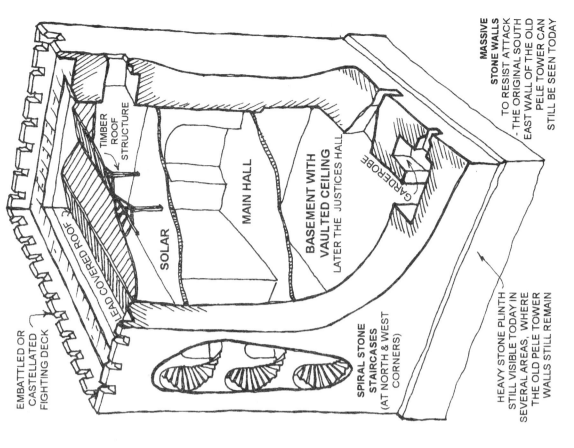

TIMBER ROOF STRUCTURE

SOLAR

MAIN HALL

BASEMENT WITH VAULTED CEILING
LATER THE JUSTICES HALL

GARDEROBE

LEAD COVERED ROOF

EMBATTLED OR CASTELLATED FIGHTING DECK

SPIRAL STONE STAIRCASES
(AT NORTH & WEST CORNERS)

MASSIVE STONE WALLS
TO RESIST ATTACK
- THE ORIGINAL SOUTH EAST WALL OF THE OLD PELE TOWER CAN STILL BE SEEN TODAY

HEAVY STONE PLINTH STILL VISIBLE TODAY IN SEVERAL AREAS, WHERE THE OLD PELE TOWER WALLS STILL REMAIN

THE OLD PELE TOWER AT WORKINGTON HALL

John Flavel Curwen in his 1928 *History of the House of Curwen*, tells us that around the start of the 13th century, Patric de Culwen (later spelt Curwen) moved his family tower or hall from Burrow Walls, to *"a stronger site on the opposite bank of the Derwent"*. There is little doubt that Patric chose the same hill, now occupied by the present remains of Workington Hall.

Defensively it was the most suitable location available. Standing there today, one can still imagine the clear panoramic views, now mostly obscured by the large mature trees, many only planted in the 1780's. To the north the elevated site had an unrestricted view to the Derwent estuary below. This is likely to have been the most probable invasion route. Eastward is the almost vertical sloping bank, dropping rapidly down to the Mill field and the wide valley below.

At this time, King John was on the English throne, and the borders had yet again lapsed into a state of unrest. Primarily in consequence of both sides claiming sovereignty over the northern counties. The county was also being subjected to frequent Border Reiver raids and attacks. Many organised to simply plunder and ravage, if not totally destroy every homestead of value and importance. Workington must have been overrun several times, perhaps Burrow Walls was ransacked, even almost burnt to the ground. Was this why Patric sought out somewhere else to built his new home?.

Daniel Fleming in his 1671 *Description of Cumberland* recorded that *"Sir Gilbert Curwen Knight"* who *"built the chief tower at Workington, the stone was laid 8th May, 1362"*. Gilbert was the great grandson of Patric Curwen, who had built the first house on the site. Fortified pele towers, like that at Workington, sprung up all along the English - Scottish Border. These towers were built for defence, strength and fire-resisting capabilities, with massive thick stone walls; pierced only with small apertures or loopholes.

The pele tower on the Workington Hall site was rectangular in plan, being 13m in length by 10m wide externally. It's massive rough rubble walls were all over 2.1m thick, in places upto 2.9m. Evidence of which can still be seen, at least upto first floor level. It's location is shaded on the plan on page 150.

Although we can no longer be sure, the tower may have had perhaps three floors, with a flat roof or fighting deck above, surrounded in a castellated parapet wall. On the ground floor was a vaulted basement. Originally, this would have been used to stockpile food and other supplies, for both winter use and in the time of a siege. Later it was also used by the Lord of the manor, to administer justice, before the creation of police courts. Hence its name today being the *"Justices"* or *"Judges Court"*. There was even a lavatory or garderobe in the south corner.

Above the basement, was likely to be the Main Hall of the tower. We can still see the fireplace opening on the north east wall. The top floor was occupied by the Solar, the Lord of the Manors room. Here would also be his sleeping quarters, likely to be partitioned off by an oak screen. The roof of the solar was likely to have been covered in sheet lead; and all floors would have been reached by narrow spiral stone staircases, built into the thickness of the massive walls, at it's north and west corners.

WORKINGTON HALL AS IT WOULD HAVE LOOKED AROUND THE END OF THE EIGHTEENTH CENTURY.

Above is a reconstruction of how Workington Hall may have looked around 1800. This was after the last major re-building work was undertaken, under the guidance of York architect John Carr.

John Carr is described as one of the greatest architects working outside London, being responsible for several large mansion houses, throughout the northern counties. Much of his work was in the style of his famous contemporary Robert Adam. He was co-architect with Adam on many projects, including Harewood House, York County Assizes and Newark Town Hall.

When John Christian Curwen undertook to complete the earlier improvement works, started by Henry Curwen and left uncompleted by his death. He commissioned John Carr around 1783 to transform the hall into a stylish Georgian mansion house. Exactly how much was spent on the work is not clear. However, Christian Curwen's personal accounts show a expenditure for building work at the hall, of at least £7758 between 1783-6. In addition he paid his extremely fashionable architect, fifty guineas (£52.50) for each site visit and return journey from York.

A - Main gateway into the courtyard. Although the lower two floors of the gate house, date from the fifteenth century, the dressed stonework around the semi-circular arched main entrance, is not original. It is likely to have been rebuilt when the front facade of the hall was re-modelled by John Carr, around 1783-6. The moulded arch stones to the courtyard side, are thought to be original and those on the front facade would have been similar.

B - The north west corner of the front of the hall, was also greatly re-styled by Carr. He added the splayed projecting section, which accommodated the main kitchen. Although slightly larger than it's earlier opposite corner of the front elevation, (accommodating the chapel) at C, it does supply a degree of balance and symmetry to the facade.

C - John Carr also added the new larger semi-circular headed window to the chapel, to match the new window installed in the kitchen, installed in the north west corner (see B above).

D - Originally the gatehouse had only two floors, an additional upper room was also added by John Carr.

E - Carr also almost completely rebuilt the north wing, adding the two rows of large sliding sash windows, virtually equally along the elevation. Each opening surrounded by a stone band. The only section of the north wing retained by Carr, was the ground floor cellar to the north east corner, over which he built the dining room. (marked F)

G - Large chimney from Main Kitchen ranges below.

H - Kitchen yard, now almost totally disappeared. It contained several outbuildings, including a laundry. It was demolished around September 1958.

J - North east corner of stone terrace, along west wing.

K - Location of Salon, with suites of bedrooms above on the second floor. It is built over the Barbican and the three vaulted cellars, in an area once occupied by the Aula or Great Hall. This was a large single room, measuring externally around 17 m length by 6.7m wide, with a steep pitched, massive oak timbered roof.

L - Curved stone wall, resembling a tower, enclosing the elegant semi-circular staircase, added by Carr. (see plan on page 152)

M - Location of ancient Pele Tower, the oldest part of the hall. Unfortunately, the only remaining original walls, are those at ground floor level, surrounding the Justices Hall; and the single wall between the Library and Drawing room, at first floor level. The thickness of these rubble walls is over 2.1m, in places upto 2.9m. The remaining upper walls of the Pele tower were considerably thinned during Carr's restyling; in some places they were demolished and rebuilt much narrower. Perhaps the reason for this was they were structurally unstable, or he wished to utilise the vast quantity of stone to rebuild other sections of the hall.

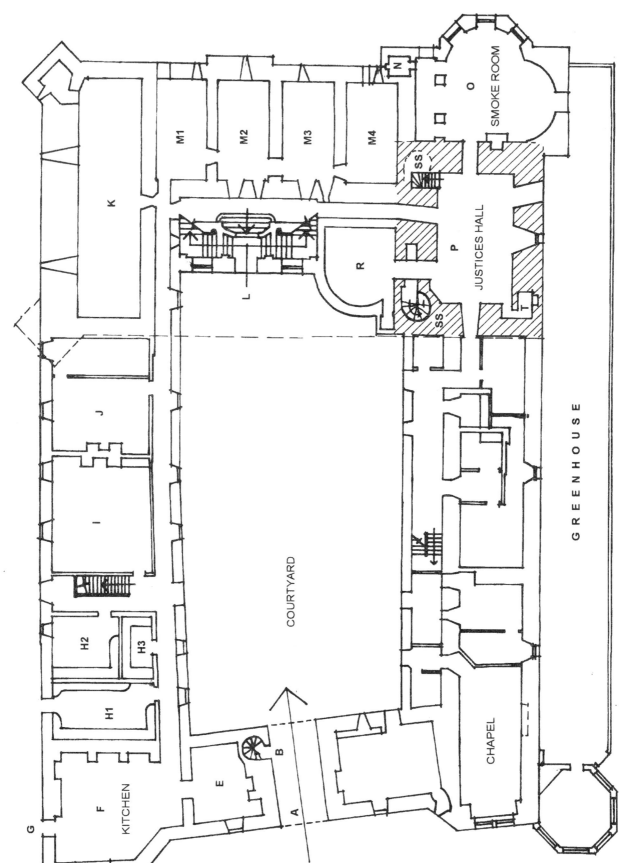

GROUND FLOOR PLAN OF WORKINGTON HALL - SEE NOTES BELOW

F
KITCHEN
G
H1
H2
H3
I
J
K
E
B
A
COURTYARD
L
M1
M2
M3
M4
SS
N
O
SMOKE ROOM
R
SS
P
JUSTICES HALL
T
CHAPEL
GREENHOUSE

NOTES TO DRAWING ABOVE

A - Main semi-circular arched gateway, with barrel vaulted stone ceiling, facing almost due west, built in the late 15th century. The iron gates which once hung at the entrance (until around 1870), were reputed to have been brought from Galloway's Carlaverock Castle, in August 1570.

Leading through to the main courtyard, originally thought to be around at least a metre lower, than today. In the corner of this courtyard, once hung a large iron bell, that was rung to let the family know when their meals were ready.

B - Stone spiral staircase, rising to Tower Room above.

E - Sculery room.

F - Main kitchen added in late eighteenth century possibly by John Carr. The ceiling height of this room was exceptionally high, perhaps 9m. On the east wall are three large fireplace recesses. In one hung a jack or spit, on which half sides of beef were roasted over an open fire. In another opening was likely to be a cast iron hobgrate, with side bread oven. Within this kitchen the cook, servants and kitchen hands would labour to prepare vast and lavish meals for hall guests, sometimes said to have numbered upto a hundred. Generally the fires and ranges were kept burning all day, providing warmth in the winter, but making the kitchen a stiflingly hot place to work in summer.

G - door out to Kitchen yard and outbuildings.

H1, H2, H3 - Adjacent to the kitchen were three main larders or store rooms. One was thought to be the Butler's room, where some of the halls fine china and glasses were kept. Another led to a cold store, where the meat and game killed in the hunt, were hung from the ceiling on hooks.

I - Servant's Hall or dining room. Once contained a very large whitewood table, at which all the servants sat for their meals. On the wall was a card of rules and mottos, one read "Waste not, want not". It is thought that when the family were in residence, often there were upwards of 20 servants and 2 butlers, employed at the hall. In 1851, there was at least a Butler, Under Butler, Cook, Ladies maid, Housekeeper, Housemaid and Kitchen maid actually living-in at the Hall.

J - Housekeeper's Room

K - Fifteenth century cellars and the area that may have once been occupied by the ancient hall kitchen. The outside north wall is 2.3m thick, with narrow windows, obviously substantially built to resist attack. Externally on the north wall,

there is evidence of a pointed arched doorway. In the north east corner is a projected turret, positioned so the entrance, could be defended. Shown dotted is a similar turret to the north west corner of this room. There is evidence to suggest this may have been the corner to a smaller courtyard.

L - The late eighteenth century Main entrance to the Hall, added by John Carr. Leading down to the early fifteenth century cellars, and up to the Salon.

M1, M2, M3 - Three cellars, with stone barrel vaulted ceilings, likely to date from around 1404. Used as storerooms, to stockpile food and supplies, so the fortified hall could be almost self-sufficient when under siege. One or more of these rooms may well have been utilised as dungeons, for the confinement of prisoners.

M4 - Here is thought to be the Barbican, or outer fortified entrance to the original fourteenth century pele tower. It's ceiling is also stone vaulted

N1 - Turret, similar to that in K above.

O - Smoke room, with bay window overlooking the park below. Added to the South east corner of the old Hall structure, by John Carr in the late eighteenth century.

P - The oldest part of the Hall, the pele tower, later called the Justice's or Judge's Hall. The rough rubble walls to this ground floor section are over 2.1m thick. Originally, this room would have had a stone vaulted ceiling, remains of which are still visible. In the west corner is a stone spiral staircase, rising anti-clockwise, built into the thickness of the wall. There is also a suggestion that another similar staircase existed in the north corner. (both are marked SS) Adjacent to the foot of this staircase was the original entrance into the tower. In the south corner is what appears to be the original lavatory or garderobe. The thinner upper walls of the pele tower, are unlikely to be the original fourteenth century walls. It is thought they were pulled down, and rebuilt at just 750mm thickness, at the time John Carr greatly remodelled the hall..

R - Basement or cellar, under semi-circular staircase, added by John Carr in late eighteenth century. Reached by new opening from Justice's Hall.

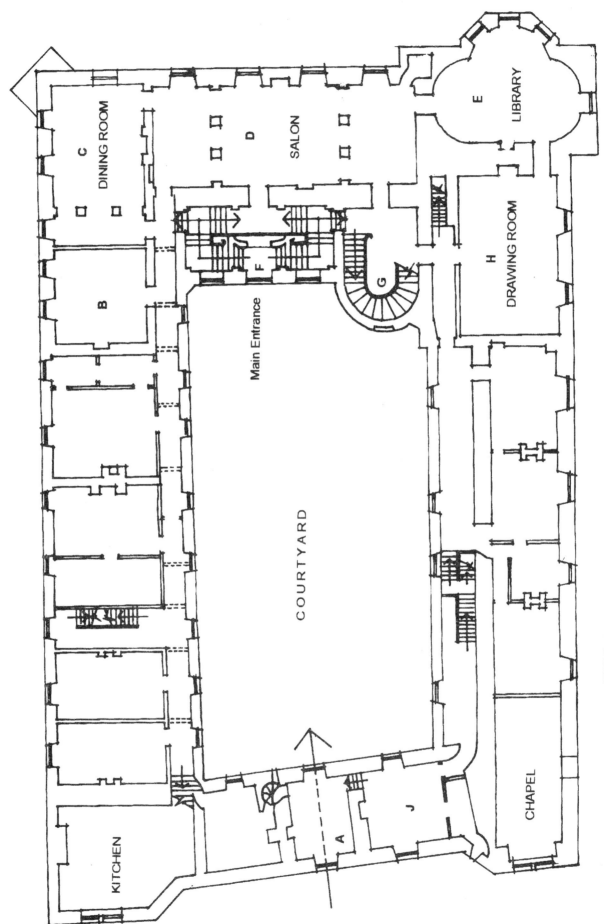

KITCHEN

DINING ROOM C

B

COURTYARD

Main Entrance

D SALON

F

G

E LIBRARY

DRAWING ROOM H

A

J

CHAPEL

FIRST FLOOR PLAN OF WORKINGTON HALL - SEE NOTES BELOW

A - Tower Room, above main gateway.

B - This is the area once occupied by the bedroom where Mary Queen of Scots slept in May 1568. (see chapter eighteen) Unfortunately, the walls of this part of the hall, which contained the actual bedroom, were later pulled down. What we see today, are the remains of the north wing, added by John Carr in the late eighteenth century. Despite the alterations, the room has always been referred to as "Queen Mary's" bedroom. In later years this room was also used as a drawing room.

C - The Dining Room, added by John Carr, in the late eighteenth century. Like the other Carr rooms, the primary feature of this room was its highly decorative *"Adam style"* plasterwork, particularly its cornice, with fine dentils and corbels. In 1947, after years of neglect and the discovery of dry-rot in the hall, attempts were made to protect and retain this delicate plasterwork. But the old Workington Borough Council failed to prevent further decay, and by May 1965, virtually all Carr's priceless work had been lost forever.

Around the walls of this room were once fifteen very clever wall paintings, made to resemble bias-reliefs plasterwork. These were thought to have been painted by a young painter, who John Christian Curwen encouraged. He had paid for him to study in Rome, but he sadly died on his journey there. In 1947, although some panels were painstakingly removed with little damage, they too were lost through being badly stored.

Carr was also responsible for detailing some of the hall's magnificent joinery work, including the Corinthian columns and semi-circular arches in this room. He also installed a fine carved white marble mantle piece and fire surround, flanked either side by columns of Blue John Derbyshire Spar. A pair of double doors enter into the Salon.

D - The Salon again added by John Carr, in late eighteenth century. Previously it is thought to have been the site of the Aula or Great Hall. The Salon was entered through a massive Mahogany door, off the main staircase. This and all the main doors throughout the hall, are believed to have been made from Spanish mahogany taken from a shipwreck, on the Workington shore. On the east outside wall, between the two central windows was the fine detailed white marble Corinthian fireplace.

The Salon, also had two rows of columns, similar to those in the dining room, together with some equally fine Carr plasterwork.

It also accommodated a full-size billiard table. Off the south east corner of the Salon, was a small room, thought by some to be a powder closet, used when people powdered their hair white.

In 1947, when Isabel Mary Curwen gifted the hall to the Borough Council, she particularly wished this large elegant room to become the Council Chamber.

E - The Library, also added by John Carr. Almost elliptical in plan, with a bay window, overlooking the park below. The walls were once incased from floor to ceiling with a treasured collection of books, many bound in matching calf leather. John Christian Curwen who assembled much of the valuable library, is said to have kept it locked while he was away from home. The only person with a key, was his agent Charles Udale. Here also was another beautiful carved white marble mantle piece and fire surround very similar to that in the Dining room. In 1946, the Borough Council hoped to use this room as the Committee Room, after it had been converted into the Town Hall.

F - Staircase and gallery or landing above main entrance. The ceiling of this entrance hall had a semi-circular vaulted plaster ceiling, with it's ribs being enriched with floral decoration.

G - Finely proportioned, open, geometric semi circular staircase, with metal balustrade. Leading to a suite of bedrooms over the Salon, Library and Withdrawing Room. Lit from above by iron-framed circular lantern light, set in another finely decorated *"Adam style"* plaster ceiling, by John Carr.

H - Withdrawing Room (or Drawing room) occupies the area, formerly the solar, or upper floor of the fourteenth century pele tower below. As you pass from the Library into this room, you appear to move along a corridor. You are actually passing through the only remaining original first floor (2.1m thick) wall of the ancient pele tower.

On the walls of this room once hung four large Elizabethan mirrors, in richly gilded, carved wood and copper frames. In a small glazed cabinet was displayed some precious heirlooms of the Curwen family. The most famous of which was the small agate drinking cup, given by Mary Queen of Scots.

J - Tapestry Room.

CHAPTER TEN

COAL INDUSTRY

UP until the latter part of the nineteenth century, the coal industry was of primary commercial importance, to much of West Cumberland. Without the progress in coal production, it is unlikely that the town and port of Workington would have seen any major development.

The coal measures or seams, under the town were created in what is usually referred to as the *Coal Age* or *Carboniferous* period. This lasted 65 million years and ended about 280 million years ago. Then much of the world was covered with luxuriant vegetation growing in swamps. Many of these plants were types of ferns, some as large as trees. This vegetation died and became submerged under water, where it gradually decomposed into peat. As the Irish Sea advanced and receded in cycles over West Cumbria, it deposited heavy layers of sandstone, shale, and other rocks on top of each peat layer.

The pressure of these overlying layers, the movements of the earth's crust and sometimes volcanic heat, acted to compress and harden the deposits, thus producing coal. Workington's high-quality coal deposits are found primarily in many thin strata or layers, some no thicker than a few feet. Because they are quite thin, the greater portion of these seams are unworkable. However, the main band, called the *Great Coal* seam is around ten feet (3.0 metres) thick.

The Workington coalfield is simply only part of the much larger West Cumberland coalfield. It extends from Salterbeck to the River Derwent, and from Workington Hall and the Scaw Road area in the east, westward to an unknown distance under the Solway. To date, it has only ever been proved for about a quarter of a mile passed the low water mark.

Basically, these various thin layers or seams of coal do not lie horizontally, under the town. They tend to slope downwards towards the sea. Many millions of years ago, a number of faults or fractures have also split and displaced some layers. This has resulted in some of the richer and thicker coal seams being closer to the surface, in some parts of the town, whilst much deeper elsewhere.

Workington has around eleven workable seams, each of which is generally known by a name. These are Brassey (1.2m approx thickness), Kennel (1.2m) Metal Band (1.0m), Fiery (1.2m), Moorbanks (1.05m), Little Band (0.95m), Great Coal (upto 3.35m), Workington Yard Main

ABOVE - a generalised section showing the coal seams under Workington. For approximate thickness of each seam see text right. ■

(0.68m), Hamilton (1.2m), Udale (0.9m), Virgin (1.2m). Virgin was the lowest coal seam occurring about 300 feet (90m) below Hamilton. A basic geological section across the Workington area is shown right. This clearly shows how some seams are found at different depths, where the faults have occurred. In the Moss Bay area around Jane pit, the Great Coal seam is found quite close to the surface, whilst it occurs much deeper towards the centre of the town. Generally, much of the past coal production has been from the Great Coal and Moorbanks seams. Next in order are the Hamilton and Workington Yard bands.

Archaeologists have uncovered evidence that the Chinese may have used coal for smelting copper more than 3,000 years ago. Without a doubt, the Romans would have found and made use of the coal in West Cumbria. In England, it is certainly known that they used the coal around the third century AD. The ancient Britons dug coal even earlier. Stone axe-hammer heads and fint axes of many types have been found in coal seams. In the Workington coalfield, there are perhaps at least four recorded finds, which could suggest such very early coal working. Close to the old Harrington Road cemetery, a bronze age stone axe-hammer was found. Whilst similar prehistoric axes have been dug up at Schoose, Winscales and Seaton.

In the early part of the 13th century, people in the North East of England also collected coal that was washed ashore by the waves. This *sea coal* was sent to London, where metal-smiths used it as fuel to fire their forges. It is safe to assume, that local people on our coast would then also have gathered sea coal, from our beaches. We know that in January 1569, Henry Curwen supplied *"30 horse loads of sea, or stone coal"* from Workington, to the German copper miners at Keswick.

During the Coal Strike of 1912, W. C. Lawrie also recorded coal being gathered by hand around the Banklands area and on Windscales Moor. His photographs graphically illustrate how large outcrops of coal once existed very close to the surface. Similar exposed seams would have occurred in other parts of the town. Without a doubt, this coal would have been easily exploited by much earlier inhabitants of the district, many centuries earlier.

Around 1630, Patricius Curwen is thought to have opened the town's first pits and began to commercially exploit the coal reserves under the town. These very earliest mines would have had very shallow workings. By a drift into a outcrop, coal may have been almost quarried, more than mined. These entrances to drift mines, called *day-holes* or *bear-mouths* would be cut into a hill side or river bank. No major machinery was required, even if it

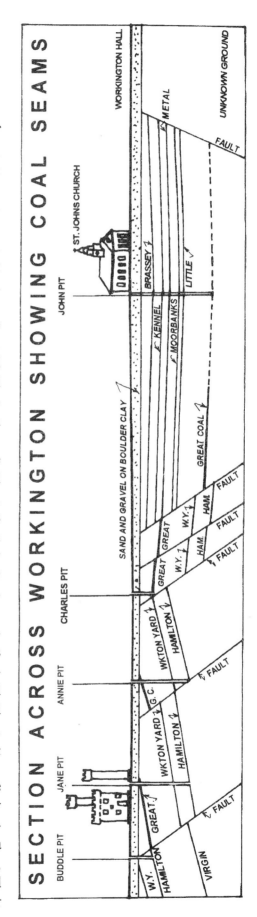

SECTION ACROSS WORKINGTON SHOWING COAL SEAMS

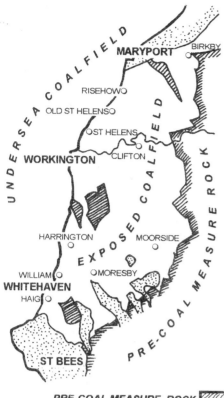

PRE-COAL MEASURE ROCK

COAL FIELD

NEW RED SANDSTONE

COLLIERIES & PITS   o

**WEST CUMBERLAND
COAL FIELD**

[01] In 1842, the employment of
women and children underground in
the pits was prohibited by law. ■
[02] William Rollinson in his *"History of Cumberland & Westmorland"*
provides an insight into the then
"clearly horrific" and unsatisfactory
conditions of child labour in the town's
pits. He tells us of James Wilkinson,
who at the age of just seven (in 1804),
is made an apprentice *"coal hewer
and engine man"*, at John Christian
Curwen's collieries. The term of his
lengthy apprenticeship is 14 years, for
which he would first receive just five
shillings (25p) a week, rising to seven
shillings (35p) in five years. It was
then recognised that it took at least a
"dozen" years to train a skilled experienced hewer. Until he is *"of fit age
and strength"* to work at the coalface,
he was employed *"in attending to trap
doors, cleaning of roads (tunnels) and
drawing horses under ground"*. ■
[03] Some of these Boulton & Watt
engine were likely to have been installed at the Curwen's Harrington
colliery. ■

had been available. Ground water would simply naturally flow from the workings and with such shallow workings, ventilation was only a minor problem.

Up until at least 1750, records suggest that such a open-cut method was adopted and used at the Chapel Bank workings. Later, at least one day-hole was thought to have been retained, possibly to aid the ventilation of Union pit. This provided a vital means of escape, for many miners when the pit was flooded and lost in 1837.

Early working conditions in the coal mines were not good and safety was then often of little concern to the mine operators. The work was done entirely by hand, men (called hewers or haggers) crouched in the narrow seams, digging the coal away from the walls with picks. Some hewers were paid at piece-rates, sometimes filling 20-25 baskets each six or seven hour shift. These baskets were called *Corfs* (or *Korves*), each is thought to have contained anything upto 12 stones (76kg).   Long before the use of wagons on rails, women and children [01] dragged these baskets to the surface, crawling on their knees through the low passages. Young children sometimes dragging the equivalent of almost a man's weight. It was also quite common for children, as young as seven, to be employed to carry the lighted candles for the miners. On the surface, children would also work sorting coal from the rock. Sometimes working 12 to 14 hours a day, six days a week.[02]

The oldest colliery areas of the town were at Banklands and Chapel Bank. William Whellan wrote that *"About the year 1722 the coal pits were described as from forty or fifty fathoms* [about 72-90 metres] *depth, having generally only two or three workable bands.....The number of persons employed was about 600."* By 1829, the shaft at Isabella pit was 275 metres deep, with most of the other pits generally being upto 180 metres deep. These deeper mines could only be opened up with the arrival of more efficient steam power. In 1765, Gabriel Jars tells us that early steam engines had been then employed at Workington pits. They were used to pump seepage water out of the pits, ventilate the workings and to raise containers of coal through shafts. Often these steam engines were then listed or described in the early records as *"fire engines"*. By 1789, the Curwen family were to acquire around eight or nine new and improved *Boulton & Watt* steam engines.[03]   Marshall & Davies Shiel in their book, *Industrial Archaeology of the Lake Counties*, suggest that the town's first *James Watt* winding engine was installed at Hope pit, by John Christian Curwen in 1789. The Curwen records of 1792, show show there were engines at Hope, Elizabeth, Charles and Old Engine pits. In 1814, John Buddle the eminent mining engineer, [01] recorded that there was *Boulton and Watt* engines at Isabella, Lady and Union pits, with a *Heslop* engine at Church pit.

The Heslop engine was patented in 1790, by Adam Heslop of Workington (Patent No 1760). The earliest of these engines are thought to have been built by Seaton Iron Works, at Barepot. A 1792 drawing (by Simpson Penrice) of a *Heslop* engine exists in the Curwen papers, showing also its adjacent steam boiler. This was ordered by John Christian Curwen, although we have no accurate indication where it was erected. The Curwen accounts suggest that Heslop engines were also once installed at John Pit (in 1793) and Charles Pit (1794). Later the Curwen's are then known to have had a *Heslop* engine at Isabella (later moved to Jane pit), and others in their Harrington colliery. These were not necessarily new engines, it is quite likely that when a pit was closed the engine was simply dismantled and re-sited at new workings. At least fifteen other *Heslop* steam engines were employed eleswhere at other West Cumberland pits, but few examples are known further a field.

Adam Heslop (d.1826) was the son of Thomas Heslop (d.1785), a Scottish blacksmith, who settled in Workington. Together with his two brothers Thomas (d.1834) and Crosby (d.1835), he went to work at Seaton Ironworks. (see chapter twelve) After then spending some time in Shropshire's Coalbrookedale, he later returned to the town, inventing and patenting his steam engine in 1790. Around 1798, they established a new company based at Lowca Ironworks, just south of Harrington. In partnership with several others, they traded as *Heslop, Johnson, Millward & Co.* (see sketch of *Heslop* engine overleaf)

Inadequate ventilation in the early pits made mining an extremely hazardous occupation. Highly flammable methane gas or *firedamp* emanating from the coal strata, it was difficult to detect and as a result, large fatal explosions were quite common. The gas being easily ignited by the candle flame or even a spark from the miners tools.

Around 1765, after French metallurgist Gabriel Jars visited Workington, he wrote an extremely valuable account of the problem. A translation of his notes, published in french begins; *"The bad air in these English mines is called "foul-air". Mines of Whitehaven and those of Workington are always prone to bad air, that can cost the lives of a very big number of workers. Six weeks before my arrival, some workers were wounded dangerously, and during my stay there were two killed and several burnt in the mine of Workington. This air is more dangerous as it ignites. The flame of a candle lights him very comfortably."*

JOHN BUDDLE
(1773-1843)

Buddle was the eminent mining engineer, employed as a consultant by John Christian Curwen. (see notes below) ■

[01] Between 1814-1823, John Buddle (1773-1843) an eminent consultant mining engineer from the north east; was appointed by John Christian Curwen, to provide detailed annual reports on the Workington pits . Buddle also greatly assisted Sir Humphry Davy with the development and testing of his miners safety lamp.

ADAM HESLOP'S "ROTATIVE" STEAM ENGINE

Invented by **Adam Heslop** of Workington **Patent No** 1760 (dated 17th July 1790)
This illustration is based on engine formerly at Low Wreah Pit, Whitehaven.
Still working when moved to **Patent Office Museum** in Spring 1879,
being donated by the Earl of Lonsdale. Formerly on
permanent display at the **Science Museum,**
but was dismantled in the late 1980's
and is now in storage,
in Wiltshire.

A - *Hot (or Receiving) cylinder*
B - *Main beam*
C - *Cold (or Working) cylinder immersed in cold water tank*
D - *Value beam*
E - *Connecting rod*
F - *Flywheel*
G - *Timber frame*

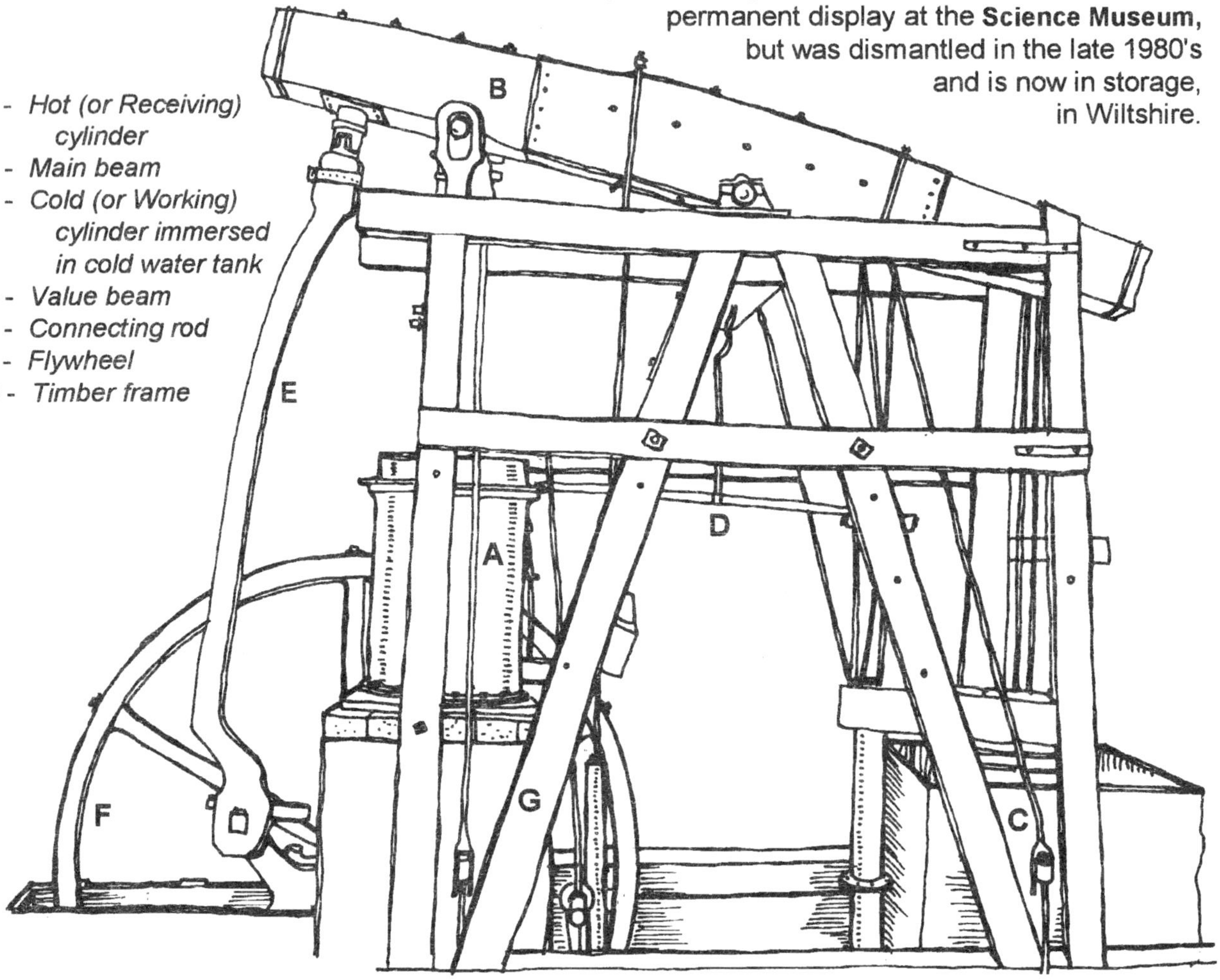

Adam Heslop did not infringe the earlier James Watt steam engine patent, by adopting two cylinders **(A & C)** either end of the main beam. Steam from an adjacent boiler (not shown above) was admitted into the Hot (or Receiving) cylinder **A**. As the main beam **B** rises, a value is opened, allowing this steam to pass from the hot cylinder **A**, to the cold (or Working) cylinder **C**, under the other end of the beam. The reducing pressure in **A**, pulled that end of the beam down. As the cylinder **C** is immersed in cold water, there the steam was condensed, thus creating a vacuum and drawing that end of the beam downward.

A system of values, each connected by rods to the beam **D** open and close, with the rocking motion of the main beam. Whist one allows the steam to pass from **A** to **C**, another closes off the steam supply into **A**. The return stroke reverses the process, and also allows the condensed steam to drain from **C**. Later Heslop engines had pumps added to aid these processes and increase efficiency, again operated by the movement of the beam.

The connecting rod **E**, fixed to the main beam **B**, then turns the flywheel **F**. This in turn operated the winding gear and pumping machinery in the pit shaft. This *"curiously bent"* connecting rod was considered a common feature of the Heslop engine, although it is not clear why it was so shaped. Originally, the main beam would have been much simpler, the *"hog-back"* shape of the above sketch, is a much later development. The main beam of this Science Museum engine, appears to have been prone to splits and fractures, and has been strenghtened by adding a patch of two pieces of old boiler plate, around its pivotal point.

The flywheel **F**, was later made from wrought iron, but the earliest were likely to have been cast iron. The pistons of earlier engines may also have once been connected to the main beam, by chains. Then the main beam was likely to have had curved or arched ends. ∎

Jars also quite graphically recorded how the miners reacted when an explosion of gas occurred underground. *"If one has the time the best means to avoid being killed, is to fall to the ground (on ones stomach) and to put your head as far as is possible into the mud, on the ground. Amongst those who die there, are some who appear hardly burnt; but others are roasted entirely; others don't have any outside injury. The effects of this gas or bad air are singular fate. One can compare them to an explosion of gunpowder that suddenly draws circulation of air that all of a sudden. People found close to the actual explosion are roasted, or at least burnt; others through a sudden loss of air are invariably choked, if they don't get to a supply of air or fresh air does not arrive while they lie face down in the mud.*

One believes that when there is an explosion of the gas less workers are killed by fire than the bad air. I spoke to a minor master (foreman), who has been burnt four or five times, and that carries some of the very obvious marks on the face and hands; he told me he always avoided the return of the bad air, by throwing himself flat on his stomach on the ground and push his face in the mud. Two of the workers who perished two days before my trip down the mine, worked with this minor master, (of which one has just spoken), were killed by the return of air, and were not at all burnt, while others suffered burns, but without danger to lose life."

With this almost constant threat to the safety of the miners. Many experiments were carried out to find alternative safer forms of lighting, when candles proved far too dangerous. One method invented by Charles Spedding [01] of Whitehaven, was known as the *steel-mill*. Basically, this device contained a steel disc, which made to revolve rapidly by turning a handle. It was then moved in contact with a piece of flint, and a stream of sparks was created, emitting a *"glimmering"* light. Jars' called it a *"flint-mill"* and noted that *"with the help of one of these mills, a man can illuminate five to six workers at the pit face, while pushing this machine on the one hand against his stomach, or another stationary place, with the other hand he quickly turns a cranked handle."*

Although it was relatively safer than the naked flame of a candle, it produced less than two-thirds the light and was quite expensive to operate. John Buddle claimed two boys had often to be employed to take turns to rotate the handle, as one would soon tire. Jars' also noted that it was not totally safe when there was a particularly high concentration of gas present. It's sparks themselves being capable of causing an explosion. But he did tell us that Spedding's steel mill provided something of an early warning to the miners. When the air was bad, he wrote *"the sparks don't*

[01] Carlisle Spedding was the son of Edward Spedding and brother of John Spedding, all three of which were agents for the Lowther estates, Carlisle between 1730-55.
His *"steel mill"* invented around 1730, despite its dim light and safety problems became widely used in many local coal pits, until the arrival of the Davy's safety lamp. A model of what Gabriel Jars called a *"flint-mill"* is displayed at the Beacon Heritage Centre, in Whitehaven. Carlisle Spedding sadly (and a little ironically) died in a gas explosion in August 1755. ∎

give any gleam. *Workers quickly leave this place, otherwise they may perish. There are some who are extremely sick and may fall unconscious. Some pass out or choke furiously and must be moved quickly to the fresh air"*.

Accidents such as this highlights another major safety problem, often overlooked by historians. As safer methods of lighting were developed, the gas in the mines did not just simply disappear. Often it became just as dangerous and could choke the miners and kill even without ignition. Again Jars' wrote *"one always puts together several workers to work in one same place, and they have to call out to one another every five to six minutes; if a call is not heard, the others can transport the unconscious person to fresh air. The effect of the gas in those cases, can make the miners sick for many days"*.

Only powerful pumps or an efficient system of ventilation could really clear this build up of deadly, often fatal gas. At Workington, Jars said a supply of fresh air was *"pumped down into the workings by a fire engine (steam engine)"*. Using a system of *"large ducts* [01].....*which are extended down the tunnels of the mine as work advances, a very sufficient circulation of air is supplied to allow the miners to work in safety"*.

He also described how *"several ducts and a lot of doors"* were then used successfully in Whitehaven mines; *"to introduce a circulation of fresh air in several places"*. Unfortunately the basic layout of Whitehaven collieries was then quite different from those at Workington. Here openings were almost on the same level, and it was very difficult to achieve a good through draught into the workings. Several other experiments were tried, including one at Union pit in 1814. William Swinburn (d.1825), the agent for Christian Curwen, attempted to solve the problem by building a mechanical ventilator. John Buddle mentioned it in his 1816 report of the Curwen pits. Commenting that a small furnace, at the bottom of the pit would be more efficient, furthermore he concluded *"inflammable air does not prevail in much of Union's workings"*.

Occasionally, gas levels in certain parts of the pit could not be adequately cleared and as a last resort that area was sealed off and abandoned. Jars recounted that for this reason, some of the *"best quality seam"* at Workington were then *"not presently worked"*. He elaborated by saying *"The old workings contain a very big quantity of bad air. When this is piped out of the workings, if one puts a light to the end of the hose, it will burn perpetually with a flame of about a foot of height. One extinguishes it comfortably with a stroke of a hat.....The flame is some bluish and of a colour of the one that gives reminds me of wine"*.

"The old workings contain a very big quantity of bad air. When this is piped out of the workings, if one puts a light to the end of the hose, it will burn perpetually with a flame of about a foot of height. One extinguishes it comfortably with a stroke of a hat .....The flame is some bluish and of a colour of the one that gives reminds me of wine".
Gabriel Jars (c.1765)

[01] These ducts would initially be constructed from timber, but later cast iron was certainly more commonly used. ■

Jars also noted that very occasionally if an explosion of gas actually ignited the coal in the mine. Then those pumps draining the workings were stopped, to allow the water level in the mine to rise upto the place of the fire, so extinguishing the blaze.

Real progress was not made until after 1815, with the invention and development of the safety lamps by George Stephenson and Sir Humphry Davy.[01] As pumping technology had also dramatically increased, ventilation had become greatly improved. For the first time, miners could now work in relative safety, although candles were still often used when firedamp levels were thought to be low. Consequently, frequent and often fatal accidents were still to occur, until the safety lamp was made compulsory around 1819. At this time, *"any hewer or other worker"* at the Whitehaven collieries, found not using his safety lamp, was instantly fined five shillings (25p). Not a large amount by today's standards, but then it equated to almost half a day's pay.

In 1778, Henry [v] Curwen's *"collieries upon the estate are valued at about £5000 a year clear of all expenses"*.

Around the middle of the 17th century, small horses were now introduced into coal mines to pull sledges, and later wheeled carts along oak rails to the mine shaft. Michael Finn in his *History of the British Coal Industry* suggests it was 1800 before iron rails were used underground in the Curwen pits. We know from John Christian Curwen's notes that he was using colliery horses, from before 1801. His 1809 *President's Report to the Workington Agricultural Society* tell us that he had fed the horses, both at Schoose farm and at his collieries, on steamed potatoes as a substitute for hay. Commenting that this *"had greatly mended the condition of his work horses"*. He afterwards, increased potato production at Schoose, as he felt it essential to the good working of his pits. Sometimes upwards of *"175 stones"* of potatoes were steamed daily, to feed the horses. He continued to feed hay, but grew both as it was seldom that both crops failed, at the same time.

In 1688, Thomas Denton wrote that the Curwen's then had *"a colliery worth £200 a year"*. For around the four years following Henry [v] Curwen's death in June 1778, his estate, including his collieries were managed by his executors. Isabella, his daughter and heir being then only thirteen years old. His executors now recorded his *"going collieries upon the estate are valued at about £5000 a year clear of all expenses"*. At least seven Curwen pits were then working, producing a total of around 1000 tons of coal each week. These were Old Engine, Crosthwaite, Ellerbeck, Udale, Bella, Newlands and Hope. It was Charles Udale, the Curwen agent, who took over the day to day management of the late Henry [v] Curwen's col-

[01] Sir Humphry Davy (1778-1829), was the renowned British chemist and inventor, and is probably best known for his miner's safety lamp. In March 1816, his lamp was successfully tested at William Pit, Whitehaven, regarded then as one of *"the most dangerous in the kingdom"*. The safety lamp later adopted in many of the local mines was believed to be the *Marsent* type. ∎

162

lieries, until John Christian married Isabella in Oct 1782. In addition the Anthony Bacon's Banklands Colliery, would also have been in production.

In the twenty or so years before 1795, There were at least fourteen pits in the town, mainly working coal from the Moorbanks seam. Many of these were active for only a short period, sometimes as little as a few months, and it was seldom more than a few years before being abandoned. In this period over 431500 tons was extracted from this seam.

From 1792, there were nine pits in the parish belonging to the Curwens. These were Old Engine, Bella, Udale, Henry, Hope, John, Elizabeth, Walker, and Charles Pits. Issac Fletcher in his *Archaeology of the West Cumberland Coal Trade*, suggests that annually John Christian Curwen was then exporting around 100,000 tons of coal from Workington. However, the Curwen Colliery accounts appear to show production from his pits, then amounted to just half that figure.

From Jan 1803, John Christian Curwen leased the *Rectory and Tithes*, [01] from Rev. Peter How (then Rector of St. Michaels). This 99 year lease is said to have given him the right to mine and quarry all *"coal stones"* from the Glebe lands, around the south of the estuary, including Crossfitts. In return Christian Curwen could collect all tithes, but would pay the church £480 per year and *"refrain, sustain and maintain the chancel of the church"*. This latter condition was a fairly standard clause in similar leases. He would generally also have to appoint and pay the vicar and provide the communion wine and bread.

In 1817, John Buddle advised John Christian Curwen to sink Isabella pit, deeper to the Great Coal seam. He also suggested working Lady and Church pits was unproductive, and should be discontinued. The following year he also proposed sinking a new pit, to reach what was thought to be the Great Coal seam isolated, by the fault south of Union pit. (see section on page 155) John Christian Curwen, later named this new pit, Buddle, after his famous mining engineer.

Between 1817-19, there were now only four working Curwen pits, in the town. These were Lady, Union, and Isabella pits, which formed what was generally referred to as the Chapel Bank colliery, and the other was Church pit. By January 1820, a crisis was reached in John Christian Curwen's pits. Production was not at all high, [02] and expenses were spiralling out of control. Christian Curwen having heavily mortgaged much of the family assets, now found himself deep in debt, . Oliver Wood in his book *West Cumberland Coal* suggests his debts

Around 1792, there were nine working pits in the town, belonging to the Curwens. These were Old Engine, Bella, Udale, Henry, Hope, John, Elizabeth, Walker and Charles Pits.

[01] The *Tithe* - was a form of tax, paid by each inhabitant of a parish, on their earnings or produce. It was usually intended for maintaining the church and it's parson. The *Rectory* - was the ancient word which generally referred to the *"parish church and the spiritual living"*, with all its rights, tithes and glebes. (it's meaning was quite different to today's rectors house or vicarage). ■

[02] Workington Harbour export figures suggest that coal production had dropped by as much as 45% between 1800-1816. ■

may then have been as much as £120000. Christian Curwen met John Buddle for *"mature deliberation"* on *"the state and prospects"* of his collieries. Church and Lady pits were to be laid off, except for small amounts of coal which could be safely removed from the pillars. Work was also to be suspended at Union for essential repairs to be shaft. Leaving just Isabella pit in constant production, till 1824.

Meanwhile, the sinking of the new Buddle pit was continuing. It was hoped they would soon reach the productive Great Coal seam, believed to lie at around 58 metres. But soon after it was discovered that this seam simply didn't exist here, due to yet another fault. Reluctantly, the work too was also suspended, as John Buddle himself advised *"there does not seem any reason to proceed".*

In the summer of 1836, at Lady pit they started to work a *"ten foot deep"* (3.0 metres) coal seam, to a distance of about 1370 metres out under the Irish Sea. Records state that this was not the Great Coal seam, but referred to as the *"Camperdown"* band. The mining method adopted at Lady pit, was the *"rooms"* or *"bord and pillar"* system. Where the coal was cut away, with pillars of coal left to support the roof. Matthias Dunne [01] in his 1852 book *Winning and Working of Collieries*, described how the width of coal workings here was upto about five yards, and the pillars between, seven to eight yards (7 to 7.3m). Concluding that it *"was barely sufficient to support the roof unbroken"*. Apparently, this coal seam also began to rise rapidly at this point. As mining proceeded the workings were now little more than 27 metres beneath the sea bed. Around only 7 metres of which was rock, with the rest simply loose sand, gravel and mud.

For almost a year, the mine suffered several roof falls and the miners were in continual danger of drowning, due to major flooding. The large steam engines were employed twenty four hours a day, pumping upto a thousand gallons of water a minute, from the colliery working upto 244 metres below the surface.

Despite these hazards, the management recklessly pressed forward production. Until the evening of Friday 28th July 1837. When at around 8.45pm the sea finally broke through. In less than ninety minutes, the three Chapel Bank pits all connected underground, were almost instantaneously filled and lost forever. There were 57 men and boys in the mine, of which thirty did manage to escape from a *day-hole*, [02] close to some cottages at Chapel Bank.[03]

Overleaf is a list of twenty-seven miners who died in the flooding. The list, includes three generations of the Creen family, Thomas Creen was killed as was his son

[01] Matthias Dunn was the Government mine inspector for Durham, Northumberland, Cumberland & Scotland. He had also been appointed to direct the Curwen mines between 1833-36, purely in an advisory role. Obviously he would have acquired an intimate knowledge of the Chapel Bank colliery. It is believed that he had appointed Ralph Coxon, to manager the pits, but later resigned after a dispute. ■

[02] A day-hole (often also called a bear-mouth in Cumberland) is a sloping entrance into a mine or an opening cut into a exposed outcrop (a coal seam exposed on the surface).

[03] Chapel Bank Farm and cottages were situated to the west of the new road, over the Main railway line, at the bottom of Annie Pit lane. Almost opposite Derwent Howe stores of Halfords and B&Q. ■

CHAPEL BANK DISASTER
28 JULY 1837

The following is a list of those who died, when the sea flooded Isabella, Union and Lady pits. - Thomas Allison, John Brough, Jonathan Brough, Hugh Cain, Richard Craney, Thomas Creen, Robert Creen, Thomas Creen jun., Martin Darling, Thomas Ditchburn, Philip Dobson, Daniel Frill, James Gambles, William Hayton, Thomas Huids, Thomas Johnston, John Magee, George McKitten, Robert Mountjoy, John Mulligan, Robert Mulligan, Jeremiah Murrow, Joseph Sharp, John Sides, William Stubbs, William Wilkinson, John Young. ■

*Dark is the mine and drear below
We hang upon a breaking cord
Hear us, as down the pit we go,
Save, or we perish, - gracious
    Lord.
Oh! save us from the hurtful air,
from spreading fire, and rushing
wave.
But chief, good lord, in mercy
    spare
from the proud sinner's hopeless
    grave.*

A Collier's Pray, reprinted from the West Cumberland Times in 1835.

Robert, and his grandson also called Thomas. Twenty eight colliery horses were also lost.

The three pits at Chapel Bank, then owned by Henry [vi] Curwen, were the only pits working in the town, at the time. The truly frightful loss of life not only cast a dark gloom over the townspeople, but several hundred miners were thrown into instant unemployment. Although a few were taken on and re-employed at the Curwen's Harrington pits. The whole town suffered the effects of the disaster, including the harbour, where revenue fell dramatically.

At the time of the accident, the Chapel Bank Colliery manager was Ralph Coxon, from Newcastle. Much has been written about his apparent disregard for the safety of his miners, in his relentless quest to meet the growing demand for coal. Many local people blamed Coxon entirely for the disaster, and a lynch mob armed *"with rifles, revolvers and sticks"* went in search of him. He escaped the murderous crowd and disappeared, having also been dismissed by Henry Curwen. For many weeks, the question of blame, brought an exchange of letters in the local newspapers. Some believed he had been treated harshly, being denied a hearing at the investigation. Curwen, himself was even condemned *"for his love of gain, having counselled the destruction of his own mines"*.

The extensive scale of the workings lost in the deluge of these three pits, is difficult to imagine. The far-reaching maze of underground tunnels alone, stretched out under the Solway for around twenty miles in length. Matthias Dunn estimated that the fracture on the sea bed measured around 80 by 30 yards (74 x 27 metres). The consequent loss to the Curwens was to be almost irreparable, and immediately affected several members of the family. It was then almost impossible to insure a coal mine against such a loss, because of the great risks involved.

Poet Laureate William Wordsworth (whose son John was married to Henry [vi] Curwen's daughter Isabella) wrote how his son's income was now *"much reduced"*, by the *"sea having swallowed up his father-in-law's coal pits"*. So much so that *"he therefore feels it necessary to endeavour to procure a couple of pupils, who could afford to pay rather handsomely for the advantages they would have under his roof"*.

Within ten days, the abandoned shaft at Buddle pit was reopened, and sunk deeper in the search for richer coal seams. Spirits rose two months later, as the miners reached the Hamilton seam. It was found to be around 1.6 metres thick and some production recommenced. Some coal still available at the Great Coal seam was also mined from the Moorbanks Engine workings, and areas of coal below this seam were also extracted.

Buddle and Jackson were likely to be the only pit to be working in the town, until Jane pit began production around 1846. High Hope pit was sunk around 1854, but proved unprofitable and was closed in 1858. By then exports of coal to Ireland were becoming unprofitable, for it sold in Dublin for only about 7 shillings (35p) a ton.

Around November 1875, the demand for West Cumberland coal again slumped, the cost of extraction was simply far too high. The rapidly growing railway system now also brought supplies of cheaper Scottish coal, into the area. The mineowners in an effort to remain more competitive, attempted to reduce the miners wages by around 15%. A fourteen week strike ensued, the men returning with a 10% wage cut. The town's coal industry was permanently and seriously affected, and never really recovered from this crisis. During the strike, Scottish Coal proprietors had stepped in and grabbed an increased their market share. Later in 1875, when Annie Pit closed, mining ceased completely in Workington. It would be 64 years before it recommenced at the nearby Solway colliery. Coal was still to be mined elsewhere in West Cumbria, for another hundred years.

Today, all that exists in Workington, to now remind us of our once rich coal trade, are the two chimneys and the castellated oval engine house of Jane pit. [01] Situated at the corner of Moss Bay Road and Annie Pit Lane. Now of course listed and protected for their historical and architectural interest, as an Ancient monument.

[01] In 1883, eight years after Jane Pit was closed an article in the West Cumberland Times, gave a dreary description of the mine - *"the machinery is rheumatic, and the engine house, castellated chimneys and all, look as frowzy as a drunken man who has slept in a haystack."* A century or so later, despite the walls being preserved from further decay. The recent needless and senseless addition of spray-paint graffiti, now also gives the impression of a quite gloomy and dispiriting structure.

FURTHER NOTES ON WORKINGTON'S COAL PITS & COLLIERIES

Numerous old coal pits are known to have existed in and around Workington. Though now accurate identification of sites is sometimes doubtful. Below is a list of 46 pits, together with locations where known, and some additional notes. By comparison today (1998) there remains just thirty deep coal mines throughout the country, none of course in in Cumbria.

ALEXANDER PIT
OS map ref - E:299350 N:528500
Mentioned by Lancaster & Wattleworth in their History of Iron & Steel in West Cumberland. Said to have been located between Main Rail line south of the Station and the west end of Barnes Road.

ANNIE PIT
OS map ref - E:299650 N:527950
Situated about 3 furlongs from New Yard. Sunk by William Irving, who had leased the royalty from Henry [vi] Curwen, in 1864. Here the coal seams of Hamilton and Workington

Yard were found to rise to the north east at a slope (or angle) of 1 in 47. Production continued till Walker's death in 1872; whereupon H.K.Spark of Darlington, took over the lease. It was Workington's last working pit, when it was closed in 1875. The Workington Colliery Company took over the lease of these royalties shortly after. It was their intention to re-open Jane and Annie pits, but the company collapsed soon after.

BANKLANDS COLLIERY
This colliery is said to have included John, Elizabeth, Hope, Henry, Old Engine, Crosthwaite and Bowness or Well and other pits. (see separate entries) The earliest record of any workings here is in the harbour trustees records of 1722, where John Porter is shown as proprietor of the "Banklands Collieries". Little is known of the pits and their production, but Porter is known to have served as a harbour trustee, until at least 1733.

The Banklands Colliery Co. were working the area, around 1770. For an early lease exists, dated July 1771, which details Henry Curwen granting permission to Rev. William Mence, of St. Michaels, Winchester, *"a partner in the colliery called Banklands"*, for the laying of a waggon-way from Banklands to Workington Quay. One condition was that Curwen had the rights to extend it to his Moorbanks colliery, and have running powers over the Banklands track. The Company also had to make and erect three additional coal hurries on the quay. No company accounts appear to have survived to give us an accurate record of production, we can assume they were not too successful, as the company was to be formally wound up in summer of 1775.

Banklands may then have been purchased for £4400, by Anthony Bacon MP of London. He is certainly shown as proprietor in the 1784 Bailey's *Northern Trade Directory*. Bacon was then also actively engaged in the tabacco trade in Whitehaven. At the same time, he was suspected of dealing in slaves, and is thought to have amassed a large fortune from this activity.

Between 1792-5, the Curwen accounts, show a William Walker paid the tonnage duty for Banklands coal shipped from the harbour. Walker was the agent for the trustees of Anthony Bacon, and continued to work Banklands, after his death. During this period there were five pits in production here, which averaged 14156 wagons a year (42468 English tons). Records also shows that Banklands paid £100 per annum, to the Curwens, for wayleave over the waggonway to the harbour. We can also deduce that around 42 wagons of coal a day, were brought down from the Bankland's pits, over the waggonway, to be loaded into ships.

It was advertised for sale in December 1795, as being part of the estate of the late Anthony Bacon. However, at this time the sale particulars, show it let to William Monteath, as tenant, at a rent of £40 per year. With this intimate knowledge of production figures, it is little surprise that the new purchaser, was John Christian Curwen. His accounts reveal he paid £6300, for the colliery in 1796. By 1800, annual output had fallen to just over 31500 tons, but there was now seven active pits; with Elizabeth, Crosthwaite and Hope producing over 6100 tons each.

Some have also grouped Church pit into the Banklands Colliery. By 1818, when the Chapel Bank Colliery became fully developed, production had almost ceased at the Banklands pits. These were now abandoned and filled in, Church pit was the last to close, around 1820.

BANKLANDS ENGINE PIT
North of Bella Pit, near the Roman Catholic Church at Banklands, may have reached the Great Coal seam, but the greater part of the output appears from the Moorbanks and Metal seams.

BELLA PIT
OS map ref - E:300250 N:527700
Situated approx.170 yds. north east of Laverock Hall. The shaft reached the Great Coal seam, 3.2 metres thickness at a depth of 103m. The Little Main, 1.8m thickness, occurs at 57m, whilst Moorbanks, 0.7m., lies 6.3m higher. Shown in the Curwen records as working in the summer of 1787, but closed by April 1797.

BOECLOSE or BOCCHOSE PIT
Exact location is not known, but appears to have been part of the Chapel Bank Colliery. Mentioned in the lease of August 1770 to Messrs. Stanley, Hodgson, Falcon and Stead. Upto then it had been worked to at least the Fiery or "Firy" band. Very little further is known, apart from this single reference.

BOTTOM PIT
Referred to occasionally in the Curwen records, may be another name for the Moorbanks Great Engine pit. Although this is difficult to confirm either way. (see Moorbanks Great Engine pit notes)

BOWNESS PIT (see WELL PIT)

BUDDLE PIT
OS map ref - E:299400 N:527750
Located about 500 feet south-west of Jane Pit. Named after the prominent mining engineer John Buddle, who advised the Curwen's on their pits between 1814-23. Sunk originally, to about 40 metres in 1819-20, to reach the Great Coal seam. But unfortunately, due to a fault this coal measure, was discovered not to exist here. No real quantity of coal was extracted, before the shaft was abandoned, in the summer of 1820. Reopened up after the flooding and loss of the three pit of Chapel Bank Colliery in 1837.

Initially, production was restricted by the constant ingress of water into the workings, until extra pumping equipment was installed in the summer of 1838. It was likely the only pit left working in the town, upto about 1847, when the nearby Jane pit, came into production. It's lowest workings were at about 78 metres. Reached the Hamilton coal seam at 49 metres, which was found to be around 1.7 metres thick, and is believed to extend as far as Harrington. Some of the Great Coal seam was also extracted, left near the abandoned Church pit, reached across the fault, east of Buddle. (see section on page 155).

Was listed by William Whellan as one of only three working pits in the town around 1847, the others being Jane and Jackson pits. The Curwen records suggest that flooding became a major problem in this pit, detailed notes exist of water levels in the workings, and attempts at pumping operations, carried out in the spring of 1853. Buddle was subsequently closed and abandoned later the same year. Buddle pit received its name from John Buddle (1771-1843), the consultant mining engineer, employed by John Chris-

CHAPEL BANK PIT
OS map ref - E:298850 N:528475
See Union pit - often also called Chapel Bank pit. It is also very likely the site of some of the earliest coal workings, in the town.

CHAPEL BANK COLLIERY
Chapel Bank is perhaps the oldest area of the town to be commercially mined, on any scale. Exactly when this colliery was opened up is unclear, but records show that up until at least 1750, coal was being worked by the open-cut method. The Curwen family later, developed the site, laying a wagon way to the harbour, and installing a steam "fire" engine before 1770.

In August of that year, Henry Curwen rented the colliery to Edward Stanley (merchant), John Hodgson (ropemaker), John Falcon (ships carpenter) all of Workington, and John Stead (engineer) of Newcastle. The eleven year lease was for the working of coal to just the Moorbanks seam, on the Chapel Bank estate, then the property of Robert Gibson, and excluded the Frostoms area.

The success of this partnership was short lived for within two years, we find that they have surrendered the lease, back to Curwens. Up until 1777, the colliery was worked by a new partnership between Henry Curwen and William Hodgson, with profits being divided equally. Each year the partners average earning were £195 each. Interestingly, the four original 1771 partners, crop up again in April 1778, when they received what appears to be William Hodgson share of the profits, divided equally between them.

In 1782, following John Christian Curwen's marriage to Henry Curwen's daughter Isabella. He devoted much of his time to developing this colliery. It was Christian Curwen who opened up Lady Pit, Union Pit and Isabella Pit. (see notes below) Coal production here was to last further fifty years. Until the three pits, which connected underground, were flooded and lost, *"owing to an eruption of sea"*, on 28th July 1837.

"The Chapel Bank Colliery is yet, and ever must remain, under water, as also the bodies of the people. From the magnitude of the breach of the strata under the bed of the sea, assurely no engine power can ever be made effective in draining of these workings." - Matthias Dunn (Mines inspector) 1852.

In 1836, a year before the disaster, the output from this colliery (with its three pits) was 1500 tons a week.

CHARLES PIT
OS map ref - E:299900 N:528100
Located near to the Harrington Road cemetery, about 600 yds north-north west of Laverock Hall. Sinking started around February 1791, may be on the site of the earlier unproductive Duke pit. First coal raised in July 1791. Appears that no real productive seams were found, until the Great Coal seam, was reached at 43 metres depth, found to be 3.35 metres thick. Production appears to have ceased in February 1796. Very likely to have been named after the Curwen agent, Charles Udale.

CHURCH PIT
OS map ref - E:299750 N:528600
Situated close to where Queen Street now stands. Opened up in 1792, with production beginning April 1793. Sunk to at least the Moorbanks seam (1.7 metres thick) at 37m, before any really productive coal band was found. Production ceased in November 1795, but the pit was re-opened many years later. Certainly open in 1814, as John Buddle mentions it in his reports of the Curwen pits. Then he estimated that there was then still 1.2 million *"waggons"* of coal available at Church pit. A Workington coal waggon was believed to hold "6 baskets or 44 cwt" (2.2 tonnes).

He also records that there was a patent *Heslop* winding engine, which was also employed pumping water, but not simultaneously. Its hot cylinder was 25¾ ins diameter (653mm) with a 30½ ins (775mm) stroke. Whilst its cold cylinder was 22ins (559mm) dia, 38ins (965mm) stroke.

Water was also raised by a horse-gin or horse-engine crank, built by Thomas Penrice, which Buddle described as a *"excellent machine"*. Output here in 1816 was recorded at over 9300 tons. Sometimes this pit is grouped into the Banklands Colliery (see entry). Was certainly still working 1814, but was drowned out by a roof fall and abandoned in March 1821.

CROSTHWAITE PIT
Situated almost due west of Stonyhaugh House, close to where Moorclose Farm once stood. Worked the Moorbanks seam between November 1779 and April 1791, extracting nearly 94300 tons. Production ceased here in April 1791, while the pit was sunk deeper, restarting in June 1793. (likely to also have also been worked upto 1840, but not continuously).

DUKE PIT
Location unknown. Sinking of this pit is shown in the Curwen records as having commenced in May 1788. No coal appears to have ever been raised here, and it is not mentioned after January 1790. It is unclear wether it was abandoned or simply renamed, possibly later to become Charles pit.

ELIZABETH PIT
OS map ref - E:299950 N:528600
Situated in an area, about 360yds west of John Pit, (now Vulcans Park). Shown in the Curwen records as commencing production in October 1790. Believed to have not reached the depth of the Great Coal seam, but worked the Moorbanks seam at 127 metres. Here none of the coal seams were found to be no thicker than *"a couple of feet"* - 0.6 metres. Closed around August 1802, being described as being *"all robbed out"*.

ELLERBECK PIT
Situated about 300yds north of High Hope pit. Worked the Moorbanks seam between January 1782 and May 1791, extracting nearly 85334 tons. Pit was sunk further and was believed to have also worked Great Coal seam (3 metres thick) at around 45m depth. Production seems to have ceased here in the summer of 1791.

FOX PIT
Location unclear as the records here a quite vague, there is a suggestion that Fox Pit, could have been a early trial pit, which was began in January 1788. Only to be later abandoned a few months later. It may also have been very close to the site of Henry pit, and possibly even the same pit, simply renamed.

HENRY PIT
OS map ref - E:300100 N:527450
Situated around 200 metres, to the south west of Bella Pit. Some records show that this pit was originally called New Engine pit, others perhaps link it to Fox pit. It is quite likely that it renamed Henry pit, around the time of the death of its proprietor Henry Curwen in June 1778. Working had certainly commenced here in November 1776. Records certainly show that in the period upto February 1785, over 63200 tons was extracted from the Moorbanks seam. It is was also sunk deeper in May 1788, with production re-

starting in August 1789. Worked the Great Coal, 3.0m thickness, at around 60m. Sunk further again, to at least 155m, where it was believed also to have worked the Hamilton seam (0.85m thick). The actual date production ceased is not clear, but it was still working in 1804. Handwritten notes on the original plans state *"discontinued working on account of water"*.

HIGH PIT
OS map ref - E:300250 N:527870
Also sometimes referred to as Robinson Pit. Located in the Newlands area, north of Bella Pit; may have reached the Great Coal seam, but the greater part of the output appears from the Moorbanks and Metal seams. Worked the Moorbanks seam between 1771-90, although its actual dates of operation are not clear, extracting nearly 8000 tons.

HIGH HOPE PIT
Situated around 750yds south-south-east of where Moorclose Farm stood. To south of the Old Ellerbeck Poorhouse and just north of Low Scaw. This pit is quite likely on the site of earlier mines The Curwen records suggest work began on sinking a new shaft here in the summer of 1853. Believed to have worked the Hamilton seam. Closed as unprofitable in 1858. Believed to be worked by one of the Penrice family.

HILL PIT
Location unknown. Worked the Moorbanks seam between October 1775 and July 1777, extracting over 4340 tons.

HODGSON PIT
Location unknown Records show here the Moorbanks seam was worked for just three months, upto February 1780, extracting just 242 tons. May well have formed part of the Chapel Bank Colliery (see entry), leased in August 1770 to Messrs. Stanley, Hodgson, Falcon and Stead.

HOPE PIT
OS map ref - E:300100 N:528400
Situated about 400 metres almost due east of Church pit, mid way along Brown Street, off Vulcans Lane. Work began on sinking this pit in August 1786, with its first coal raised in June 1787. Much of this early production being sold to the Seaton Ironworks, at Barepot. Reached the Great Coal at 175.5 metres, found to be around 1m thickness. Original sections through this pit show the shaft was also sunk through Brassey, Kennel, Metal, Firey, Moorbaks and Little Main bands, all would have been quite productive being from 0.5m to 1m thickness. Curwen records also show coal was certainly being mined here from September 1855 to March 1858.

ISABELLA PIT
OS map ref - E:298650 N:529150
Situated on the shoreline, to the south of River Derwent, almost due west of the old dock or harbour. Thought to have been named after his only daughter Isabella (1787-1803), who had died age sixteen. Although others suggest it was named after his wife or even his first granddaughter, who was born in November 1806.

John Christian Curwen, began sinking this pit in 1808, reaching the Moorbanks seam, four years after; at about 162 metres. The pit shaft was around 4.9 metres diameter. In 1816, the pit was deepened to what should have been the Great Coal seam level, (reached in 1818) at about 230 metres. This seam, which elsewhere in the town was upto 3.0 metres deep was *"nipped out"*, to virtually nothing. This was a bitter disappointment after an expenditure of upwards of £50,000. Sometime later, the Great Coal band, was ultimately discovered in its normal thickness, by cutting horizontally through the nip, for a distance of over 460 metres. Some of the Little Main was extracted at Isabella, whilst a considerable amount of Moorbanks seam was mined, both on the land side and under the sea.

By 1829, output here was over 24200 tons; the workings being about 92 metres deep, then drained by a 160 horse power steam engine, erected in 1811. A new *Boulton & Watt* patent *"double powered"* 40 HP steam engine was installed before 1814. With a 66 inch (1.7m) cylinder and 9 foot (2.7m) stoke, capable of 12 stokes a minute, it could lift 40 tons of coal in 12 hours. It was made by Fenton & Murray of Leeds and was then said to be the most powerful ever erected in Cumberland. H.A. Fletcher tells us that a *Heslop* engine (with a cast iron main beam) was also installed at Isabella. It's hot cylinder was 36ins (914mm) diameter, with 30ins (762mm) stroke, whilst its cold cylinder was 22¼ ins (565mm) dia. 42ins (1067mm) stroke. Much later, probably after the flooding at Isabella, this steam engine was thought to have been moved and re-employed at Jane pit.

In the undersea areas, near Workington, difficulties arise from the absence of data about the levels of the workings. Although it could be as much as 780 feet below sea-level. Worked between 1808 to 1837. Part of the Chapel Bank Colliery, which also included Lady and Union pits, flooded and lost forever, in July 1837

JACKSON PIT
Situated almost midway between where the Westfield and Moorclose farms, once stood. Working in 1846. Was listed by William Whellan as one of only three pits in the town in 1847 (working) and 1860 (idle), the others being Buddle and Jane pits. But Jane Pit was the only one working in 1860.

JANE PIT
OS map ref - E:299550 N:527800
Located between the Ellis sports ground and Moss Bay Road. The castellated chimneys of the engine house can still be seen today. William Whellan in his History of Cumberland describes then as having *"as pleasing an appearance as it is possible for chimneys to have"*.

The sinking of Jane pit was commenced in 1843. It reached the Hamilton coal seam (in 1846) at 135 metres, which is believed to extend as far as Harrington. By 1851, the output from Jane and the nearby Buddle pit was 20000 tons. Isabella is listed by William Whellan as one of only three pits working in 1847; Buddle and Jackson pits the others. By 1860, Jane was the only pit left working. Buddle had closed and Jackson was lying idle. Production, on a small scale, continued to 1864. The royalty was then leased by the Curwens to William Irving, who afterwards sunk nearby Annie pit. Exactly when production ceased at Jane is not clear. H. K. Spark of Darlington, took over the lease after Walker's death in 1872. It appears much of the coal was extracted from Annie pit, whilst pumping was continued at Jane until at least 1875. The Workington Colliery Company took over the lease of these royalties around the same time, with the intention of re-opening the Jane and Annie pits. But the company collapsed soon after.

JOHN PIT

OS map ref - E:300300 N:528600
Located about 80 yds. south east of Central Square. Shown in the Curwen records as commencing production in April 1790. Generally worked the Brassey, Kennel, Metal & Moorbanks seams, to about 109 metres depth, some to exhaustion. Each band was around 1 metre thickness. Here the thickness of the Great Coal band, about 200 feet below Moorbanks, reduces to an unworkable seam, from its depth of around 3 metres, under other parts of the town. Original plans of the workings indicate that the workings, to the north of John pit, extended at least to the old mill race which runs through the Cloffolks.

Around 1800, the Curwen family were forced to pay compensation to the Lowther family, who owned the Cloffolks area. As it was found that John Pit workings had encroached onto this land.

LADY PIT

OS map ref - E:298530 N:528650
Situated south of Isabella pit, on the shoreline below where How Michael once stood. Opened up in the summer of 1793, into production by May 1795. The shaft was around 3.35m diameter, and sunk to at least 157 metres depth, where what is believed to be the Great Coal seam (1.1m thick) was found at 149m depth. Although some geologist tend to dispute the existence of this coal measure here. It was here that the workings extended around 1370 metres out under the sea. Issac Fletcher tells us that "At Lady Pit, large pumping and winding engines were erected and all equipment was the best of day". In 1814, John Buddle wrote the engine was a Boulton & Watt double powered Steam engine with 21" (535mm) cylinder.

Output in 1829 was over 15400 tons. Worked by the pillar method. John Buddle in his 1817 report of the Curwen pits, comments that the roof was a very indifferent "blue slate". Suggesting not too much coal should be removed, as sufficient should be left to support this unstable roof. Production at Lady pit was limited around 1820, except for what could be safely removed from the pillars supporting the roof. In 1823 there an underground connection was made between Lady and Isabella pits to aid ventilation of the workings. Seventeen years later on 28th July 1837, whilst extracting coal from the Camperdown seam, very close to the sea bed, there was a roof fall. The entire Chapel Bank Colliery, which also included Isabella and Union pits, was flooded and lost forever.

LANE PIT

Location unkown. Worked the Moorbanks seam between July 1780 and June 1781, extracting 1692 tons.

LANTY PIT

Located to the north of Bella Pit.
May have reached the Great Coal seam, but the greater part of the output appears from the Moorbanks and Metal seams.

LOW HOPE PIT

Located on the east side of Vulcans lane, about 250yds southwest of Central Station. reached the great Coal seam, 3'5" thick at 589 feet. Working around 1800.

MOORBANKS GREAT ENGINE PIT

OS map ref - E:300000 N:527850
May have also been referred to as the "4ft Coal" Engine pit.

Situated just south of the Victoria (Islay Place) Infants School. In the Curwen records, may also have been referred to as Bottom pit, although this is quite difficult to confirm. Situated close to the railway and road 300yds north-north west of Laverock Hall. Production started here before 1771. Shown in the Curwen records as working in the summer of 1787. After passing through about 150 ft of boulder clay, the Moorbanks seam, (0.7m thick) was reached at 49m, the Little Main band, 0.5m thick at 60m, and the Great Coal, 2.4m at 106m. Close to the level at which the Workington Yard seam was expected in the shaft, a fault, up west, was encountered and beneath the Udale seam of Workington. Records indicate the working of the Moorbanks seam between January 1788 and January 1795, extracting over 7830 tons. Production had ceased here around 1801-1820, but was re-opened up after the flooding and loss of the three pit of Chapel Bank Colliery in 1837; finally abandoned again around 1840.

Around 1771, a wagon way was laid from this pit to the quay, so ships could be loaded efficiently in the harbour. The track ran through "High Frostoms, 100 yards on the east side of Mr John Street's house, and by the west end of a place called Mire, and thence to the harbour". This description of the route of track is taken from original lease, dated July 1771, in Curwen papers at Whitehaven Record office.

NEW ENGINE PIT

See Henry pit - This was the former name for what was later and more commonly referred to as Henry Pit.

NEWLANDS PIT

Situated north of Bella pit, there were at least two, possibly three pits called Newlands. One worked the Moorbanks seam between May 1778 and April 1785, extracting over 19910 tons. Another worked the same seam between December 1786 and August 1787, extracting just over 2600 tons. At either or both of these pits, the Great Coal seam may have been reached, but the greater part of the output appears from the Moorbanks and Metal seams.

OLD ENGINE PIT

Situated very close to where Laverock Hall once stood. Commenced around 1771 and worked the Moorbanks seam, upto 1783, extracting over 45100 tons. Shown in the Curwen records as also working in the summer of 1787.

RISE PIT

Location unknown. Worked the Moorbanks seam upto around 1774, extracting over 10200 tons.

ROBINSON PIT

It appears that High pit was sometimes also referred to as Robinson Pit - see High pit. The Curwen records show some production here from 1796-1797. There maybe also be some connection between this pit and Charles pit, which ceased work in February 1796, It could have been just a simple name change, but the association is really quite unclear.

SCHOOL HOUSE PIT

Likely to have been situated on High Street, close to the old School House Field, shown on the Schoose Farm plan (see page 200). Work began on sinking this pit in December 1804. Little else is known.

SCHOOSE PIT

There are no records of the workings east of what is referred to as the Great Upcast fault, close to Workington Hall. But there is some evidence, to suggest small scale workings around Castle Gardens and Schoose.

SMITHY PIT

Located north of Bella Pit, near the Roman Catholic Church at Banklands. May have reached the Great Coal seam, but the greater part of the output appears from the Moorbanks and Metal seams.

STEPHEN PIT

OS map ref - E:300400 N:528250
Situated just to west of the Roman Catholic Church, close to St Josephs School. May have reached the Great Coal seam, but the greater part of the output appears from the Moorbanks and Metal seams.

SUNNYSIDE TANNERY PIT

Actual location not clear, may have been close to Stainburn Road, north east of where Cuckoo Arch once stood. The Curwen records show that coal was worked here in 1762. The working were relatively shallow to just around 32.5 metres depth.

THOMPSON PIT

Located to the north of Bella Pit. May have reached the Great Coal seam, but the greater part of the output appears from the Moorbanks and Metal seams.

UDALE PIT

OS map ref - E:300550 N:527500
Situated about 400 yards east of Henry pit. Believed to have reached the Great Coal seam (0.9 metres thick) at a depth of 72 metres, below the surface. No other productive seams of coal appear to exist at this pit. Udale pit field is shown on the Schoose farm plan on page 200. May have started around 1782, the Curwen accounts record it working in the summer of 1787. Production appears to have ceased in October 1794.

UNION PIT

OS map ref - E:298850 N:528475
Sometimes mistakenly referred to as Unicorn pit. Located very close to Chapel Bank Farm. In October 1795, the local newspaper records that John Christian Curwen *"marked out a new pit"* and named it Union pit. The ceremony was *"in the presence of a most numerous and respected assembly of the principle inhabitants"* of the town. In July 1798, reached the Great Coal seam at about 105 metres. Output in 1799 was over 11000 tons. This main band of coal appears to be the lowest worked here, although borings reached the Workington Yard and Hamilton seams. Union pit had a Boulton and Watt winding engine, which was also used to drain the pit. It was capable of upto 32 strokes per minute and had a 50½ inch (1.28 m) cylinder and generally ran for around 15 hours a day.

John Buddle in his 1816 report of the Curwen pits told how coal was conveyed underground in tubs from several workings, *"on trams drawn by men"*. It was then turned into baskets and drawn up a sloping tunnel, by horses. He also commented that the pillar method of working in the pit, was very unproductive. Only about a third of the coal was being extracted whilst the remainder was being left to support the roof. He suggested that the Curwens could increase production by over 12%, by reducing the pillars, and still work in relative safety.

Worked only the main band from the summer of 1820. Production at Union was suspended in the summer of 1822, for shaft repairs and for the installation of a new steam pumping engine. Part of the Chapel Bank Colliery, which also included Isabella and Lady pits, flooded and lost forever, in July 1837.

WALKER PIT

Located about 350 yds west-north-west of Bowness pit. Listed as one of eleven Curwen pits, in production around 1790-1, but ceased in March 1792. Here about 16.5 metres of boulder clay occurs over the Main Bank Rock, whilst the Great Coal was found to be 3.35m thickness at a depth of 35m. Which is quite close to the surface, by comparison with other areas in the town.

WELL PIT

Also once thought to have been referred to as Bowness pit. Situated to west of Old Poorhouse, and on west side of Moorclose Road. Worked the Moorbanks seam between July 1774 and April 1777, extracting over 20100 tons. Likely to have laid idle for several years, before being re-opened in June 1799.

WILSON PIT

Situated about 160 yards north of Bowness pit, to the North of Bella Pit, near the Roman Catholic Church at Banklands. Worked the Moorbanks seam between June 1774 and October 1782, extracting nearly 68600 tons. May have also reached the Great Coal seam, at around 114 feet, but the greater part of the output appears from the Moorbanks and Metal seams.

WORKINGTON COLLIERY COMPANY

This company was formed in December 1875, for the purpose of *"acquiring the collieries in Cumberland, the property of H. K. Spark esq., of Penrith"*. Mr Spark leased the royalty covering the closed Jane and Annie pits, which he had acquired after the death of William Walker in 1872. Newspaper reports state that Thomas Pattinson Martin, the companies mining engineer, was in Workington around Christmas 1875, to investigate the workings. Production never appears to have recommenced from these two pits, before the company collapsed and ceased trading.

RULES AND REGULATIONS

TO BE OBSERVED IN

LOADING the COALS of HENRY CURWEN, Esquire,

AT WORKINGTON.

1.—Each Vessel to have the turn of loading Coal after her arrival next to the ship in the Harbour laden before her the preceding voyage, and Vessels not arriving until their regular turn of lading is past to have Coal after the Vessel then taking. Vessels taking Mr. Curwen's Coal at Harrington to have a turn here from the date of their last loading there.

2.—Vessels taking on board any other Coal or Culm (without reference to quantity) and delivering or landing the same in Ireland, Scotland, or the Isle of Man to be deemed Strangers.

3.—Vessels leaving the Coal Trade for any other Trade for the space of Six Months to be deemed Strangers.

4.—Vessels arriving with Materials for the Collieries to have a turn after the Vessel then loading.

5.—New Vessels built at Workington to have a turn on the fourteenth day after launching, if they accept it before leaving the Harbour. Vessels purchased at any other Port by an Inhabitant of Workington or Harrington to have a turn Thirty Days after their arrival; and any such Inhabitant losing his Vessel at Sea or otherwise, and purchasing or building another at any other place, to have a turn Fourteen Days after her arrival. The days of launching and arrival to be reckoned as one.

6.—No Waggon to be stopped at the Quay without the consent of Mr. Curwen's Agent, and if the first Vessel is not ready, or the Master refuses, to take the Coal then down they must be offered to the next Vessel in turn, and so on progressively until some one will take them, and such Vessel taking such Coal shall be then loaden out.

7.—All Vessels must be entered for Coal at the Fitter's Office within Twenty-four Hours after their arrival, and a list of such entries will be kept there for inspection, with the dates of their last loading, and if any valid objection can be made to any of such Vessels taking Coal, it must be made in sufficient time to allow it to be examined and settled before the Vessel then loading be finished. Any Person neglecting to obey this Rule cannot afterwards be attended to.

James Kirkconel, Printer, Workington.

❧ CHAPTER ELEVEN ❧

SHIPBUILDING

At Workington - *"Next in importance to the coal trade is that of shipbuilding"*
William Whellan (1860)

The measurement of ship size's in tons, has nothing to do with the actual weight of the ship, but refers to its cargo carrying capacity. The origin of ton, in ship measurement appears to have come from the word 'tun', meaning barrel, as used to transport wine. A ship was described as holding so many tuns or the equivalent in size or weight.
The early method of fixing the tonnage of a vessel was quite vague, but became progressively more accurate after 1660. Several Acts of Parliament (upto 1854) followed to fix a reliable formula, each system differing from the previous one. Whilst tonnage values are included throughout this chapter, accurate comparison with earlier or later sizes of ship is almost impossible. As a rough guide, tonnage shown prior to 1835, would equate to approx. two-thirds of tonnages, after that date.

[01] No bridge existed over the South Gut, onto the Merchant's Quay from Church Street, until 1846. ■

PROBABLY before any recognised shipyards existed at Workington, ships needing repairs, were simply grounded at low tide. More than likely on the south bank of the Derwent, north of what is now Merchant's Quay. An 1798 account in the harbour records, tells us, *"ships ever since the memory of any man living have always been laid upon this bank for repair, and the men with materials, have always gone over the cloffolks"* [01] From the very earliest times, when a new boat or ship was required. The shipbuilder would use the same reasonably level piece of land, beside water deep enough so the ship could be launched.

Then (and for centuries later) wooden ships were built with an almost total lack of machinery. The shipwright worked the hull of the ship with his adze, a form of axe. Whilst planks were cut in a saw pit, one man standing above to guide the cut, the other in the pit, pushed the saw up and down. Traditional shipbuilding developed into a skilled and intricate craft, passed down from one generation to another.

In 1794, prior to the start of construction of the Dock Quay, there was just one shipbuilding yard, at the seaward end of the South Quay. It was then located on Glebe or Church land, leased from the Rector of Workington, to a consortium or co-operative of local merchants, mariners, joiners etc.; *"for the liberty of building and repairing ships and other vessels, above the high water line"*. When exactly it was first established is unclear, but it is shown as *"existing and being used at present"* in a 1767 lease.

This lease lists those involved, describing them as *"joint traders together"*. They were John Whiteside (mariner), William Watts, John Ellwood (both gents), Henry Allison of Seaton (mariner), John Peile (timber merchant), Alexander Jones of Egremont (gent), Richard Bell, John Wood (both ships carpenter), Joseph Hurd, John Thompson and Adam Thompson (all mariners), Joseph Osbourn (joiner).

Exactly, how such partnerships were constituted is not clear, but they are often referred to as the *"Company of Shipbuilders"* in later documents. It would appear that ships were usually repaired and built by individuals or a couple of members of the consortium. They would no doubt use the facilities of the jointly leased yard. Perhaps calling upon the skills and services of other members. But their level of involvement and how they were paid is also a mystery. No early accounts seem to have survived to tell us more.

Upto 1771, John Wood [01] is shown as building two ships, (average size 160 tons) in this yard, Whilst between 1784-87, John Ellwood launched three vessels (average size 164 tons). Because of the shortage of information, we must assume that this is not a complete list of new ships launched. This rather small yard may then also have simply concentrated on the repair of older vessels, rather than the construction of new ships.

The 1767 lease initially for twenty-one years, was renewed again in 1787, by the Rector. A list of the partners in this new lease is shown right. Their shipbuilding yard (or *"timber yard"* as it was often then called) being made up of two areas, referred to as the inner and outer yards; these are shown on the plan below.

In 1794, when work began on the new Dock quay , the shipyard was moved a little further west. Instead of

THE 1787 COMPANY OF SHIPBUILDERS IN WORKINGTON

The 1787 Company of Shipbuilders, taken from those mentioned in the lease of the shipyard at Crossfitts, from the Rector of Workington. It included: Henry Fawcett, Henry Gaitskole, Joseph Hurd, William Watts, John Smith, Adam Thompson, William Cragg, (all listed as "gent") Wilton Wood (shipcarpenter), Bowman Crosthwaite, Joseph Hayton (both mariners), John Ellwood, Richard Askew (both merchants), Julia Green of Cockermouth (widow), John Hodgson, John Bowe (both curriers), Benjamin Crosthwaite of Harrington (gent), Roger Fleming of Whitehaven (gent) and Jacob Fletcher of Liverpool (merchant).

[01] John Wood is thought to have been related to the Wood family of shipbuilders from Maryport. He launched his first vessel "Diamond", a 140 ton brig. Followed by "Vine", 150 tons, both completed in 1750

LEFT - Plan of the Shibuilding yard, leased to the *Company of Shipbuilders*, prior to 1794 and the construction of the Dock Quay. The later shipyards 1 and 2 are shown dotted. (see plan overleaf for more details).
WH1 - Customs Watch House, later moved. CH - Coal Hurries. SB - shows the sand bank which built up against South Quay, restricting the entrance (E). ∎

just a single shipyard, two separate areas were now laid out, both allowing vessels to be launched directly into the new dock. These are shown as Shipyards 1 and 2, on the plan below. Those remaining partners from the *Company of Shipbuilders* now appear to have occupied yard 1. Which was then the smaller of the pair, extending only from the dotted line. (on the sketch opposite) Wilton Wood (1756-1803) was still very much involved and was joined a little later by his son, Kelsick Wood. [01]

The larger shipyard 2, which had a 225 ft (68.5m) frontage onto Dock Quay, appears to have remained vacant and undeveloped till November 1803. Then it was let jointly to William Wallace (shipbuilder), Robert Steele, Joseph Wallace, Henderson Borrowscale and Joseph Walker (all mariners). [02] In May 1823, this partnership was to be dissolved by mutual consent. Afterwards William Wallace appears to have continued to occupy the site, principally as a sole trader, till at least 1828.

William and Joseph Wallace were brothers, their father being also William Wallace, a Seaton mariner. He is

[01] Wilton Wood was the son of John Wood (see previous page). In February 1795, Wilton Wood & Co launched a ship called *Derwent*. ■
[02] *William Wallace & Co* built the Alexander (450 ton copper bottomed vessel) for Captain Vickers of Liverpool, launched on 17 February 1814. Intended for the Quebec trade, it was pierced (or armed) with 20 guns. Much of the town (including school children) then turned out to watch the spectacle of a new ship being launched, and afterwards joined in the celebrations. This particular day was quite unusual for the Cossack (500 ton copper bottom), was also launched from Michael Falcon's yard. ■

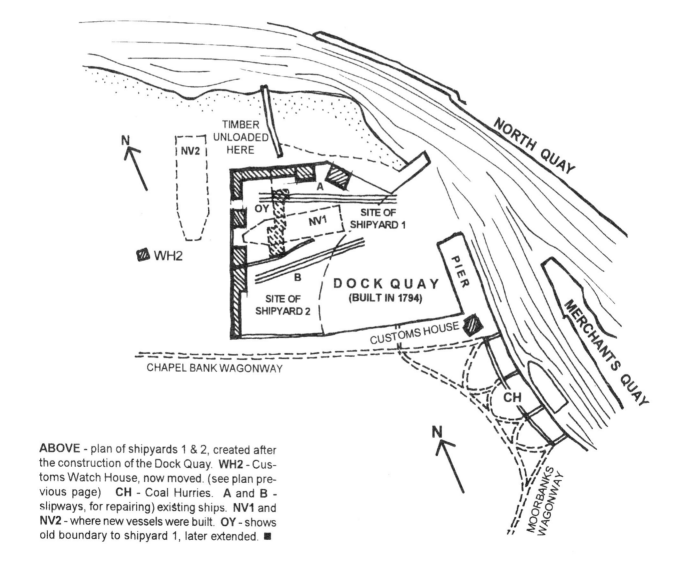

ABOVE - plan of shipyards 1 & 2, created after the construction of the Dock Quay. WH2 - Customs Watch House, now moved. (see plan previous page) CH - Coal Hurries. A and B - slipways, for repairing) existing ships. NV1 and NV2 - where new vessels were built. OY - shows old boundary to shipyard 1, later extended. ■

thought to have died when the brig *Lady Mary*, was ship-wrecked near the entrance to Liverpool harbour in 1766. Joseph (1765-1852) obviously followed in his father's footsteps by going to sea.   Whilst William (1767-1832) is recorded as a *"ships carpenter"*, when he married Mary Court, at St. Michael's Church in November 1788.

Unfortunately in 1830, William was made bankrupt and forced to cease trading. His home, all tools, materials and goods being sold off by auction in August that year. Included in the sale was the *"new ship now standing"* in his yard, together with a *"good brigantine"* called *Industry* (94 tons built by Wallace in 1828); and the schooner *Despatch* (53 tons, Wallace also built in 1829). At this time he is shown as living on the west side of Priestgate (now Church Street). During the twenty seven years he had occupied shipyard 2, he is known to have built some 55 new ships, (average size 175 tons).

At the end of the 1787 lease of shipyard 1, it was re-newed once more for a further thirty years, by Wilton and Kelsick Wood and others.   Unfortunately the other part-

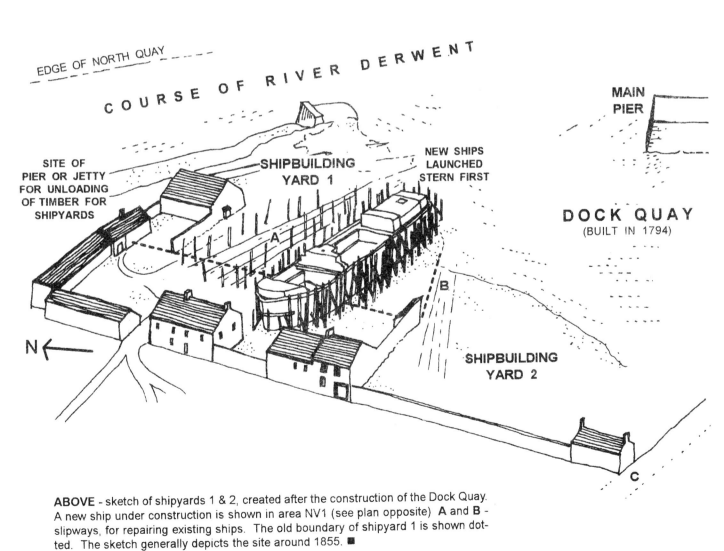

ABOVE - sketch of shipyards 1 & 2, created after the construction of the Dock Quay. A new ship under construction is shown in area NV1 (see plan opposite) **A** and **B** - slipways, for repairing existing ships. The old boundary of shipyard 1 is shown dotted. The sketch generally depicts the site around 1855. ∎

Hutchinson in his 1794 *History of Cumberland* records how *"every ship of an hundred tons"*, built at Workington, then cost £1500 and *"so in proportion"*.

[01] The Curwen Accounts from 1794-8 record that Wilton Wood may have also traded as the *"Low Yard Timber Co"*. This suggests that shipyard 1 may have become known as the Low Yard. Some credence is added to this assumption, when we find in a later Charles Lamport lease of shipyard 2, the site being referred to as the *"High Ship Yard"*. ■

[02] A snow is a vessel with two large masts, resembling the main and fore masts of a ship, and a third jigger-mast (smaller mast) abaft or nearer it's stern. It's main mast carried a try-sail (a smaller sail). ■

[03] In 1811, both William Peile and Kelsick Wood are recorded in a lease of land at Harrington, from the Curwen's, for a shipyard. Around 1821, Kelsick Wood is thought to have ceased to build ships at Workington, but continued at Maryport, with his nephew. Here we know he constructed the *Irishman*, a 90 ton brigantine The first ship for the new Carlisle Canal, which was under construction. ■

ners were not specified, but are likely to have later included Thomas Peile. [01] Harbour records show K. Wood, Peile & Co., launched their first ship from this yard in 1809. It is thought this was the *Stamper*, a 184 ton snow. [02] Upto1821, this group, which also had shipyard interests at Harrington, [03] went on to build around 42 new ships (average size 186 tons), at Workington.

Previously in the period 1788-1808, Wilton Wood & Co. are shown as launching around 28 new vessels, (averaging 177 tons). One particular ship the *Edward*, a 127 feet long snow, had a remarkable long life. Built in 1797, it gave over eighty years continued service before being wrecked on it's homeward journey from the Black Sea, off Carthagena in December 1880. The majority of ships built by both Wilton & Kelsick Wood were principally for the North Atlantic trade routes and the coal trade.

After *Workington Enclosure Act* (1809-15), John Christian Curwen became the new owner of the Glebe or Church lands, to the south of the estuary. He then allowed those who occupied shipyard 1, to also use the adjacent land extending westward, towards the site of John's Pier. New ships were also built in this area (marked NV2 on the plan - see page 174). Shipyard 1 was now also enlarged, to allow larger ships to be accommodated. Most of the old buildings (shown dotted and marked OY on plan) were now replaced as the yard was reorganised, its western boundary wall, being brought in-line with that of shipyard 2.

By Jan 1824, when Christian Curwen renewed the lease, the *Company of Shipbuilders* now had a membership of between thirty and forty traders. It's principal partners now being Thomas Peile, William Peile and John Thompson. As well as granting them the usual privilege of launching vessels into the new dock, they could also load and unload timber on a small pier or jetty, just north of the shipyard, on the south of the Derwent. Occasionally, this small jetty (extended in 1837) was also referred to as the South Pier, on old plans and maps.

This pier was for the exclusive use of the shipyard, and now allowed considerably larger vessels (usually carrying timber) to be unloaded. When they would not normally had access to the South Gut. It was estimated that an additional four feet (1.2m) of water could now be obtained here. A newspaper report from the *Cumberland Pacquet*, reported how *"the Ann Blair from Quebec, drawing 13.5 feet, docked in a 17'0" tide. Whilst the "Christiana" from Sierra Leone, with a load of teak wood, drawing 16'0" entered on 13 June, 1837"*. Matthew Patten (b1807) and who became an apprentice mariner in 1820, recalled how Peile &

Company imported much of their timber from Quebec.

Before the importation of foreign timber, English Oak, the best and most plentiful of our native hardwoods, was the primary ship building material. Between 1000-1500 oak trees were needed to build even a standard vessel, whilst much more was required for the larger ships. In each ship yard, the timber had to be stacked clear of the ground, to season well before it could be used. Hence many of the early shipyards were often also called *"timber"* yards. Much of the English Oak used at Workington, was brought from Chepstow, via the Bristol Channel.

Unfortunately, ships built of oak suffered greatly from decay, both from fungal attack and wood boring insects, such as the teredo worm. All oak vessels required constant and often extensive repairs. Although providing valuable additional work for the shipyards, the cost to their owners and the loss of trade, while the repairs were being undertaken was often considerable.

The use of the tropical hardwood teak, imported mainly from India and Africa, provided not just a degree of resistance to insect attack, but was also hard and durable. Despite it's introduction, Falcon's yard in the town was one of the few who still preferred to use English oak, to built their ships.

In the next twenty years or so, upto 1832, Thomas Peile and Co., launched around 35 new ships (average size 154 tons). They were then joined by Issac Scott,[01] the partnership then being known as Peile, Scott and Co. Between 1833-69, this group are thought to have built 14 new ships (average size 316 tons). Interestingly, most vessels were now almost twice the size, of those built just twenty or so years earlier. When the *"visitation committee"* for Lloyd's Register visited the Peile, Scott and Co's Workington yard in 1851. It was very impressed, commenting that; *"It seems scarcely possible to produce a finer standard of naval architecture"*.

Much of the credit for this accolade, was due to Jonathan Fell (1800-1870), the son of the Maryport shipbuilder Robert Fell. [02] He designed and oversaw much of the later ships launched by Peile, Scott and Co. Before going on to build many other new vessels, under his own name. In 1839, he had also developed and patented some quite revolutionary and improved methods for building his ships. Some of these methods being adopted throughout the industry.

He had rapidly gained a reputation for building larger and larger ships. Only months before Lloyd's visit, he had completed the *Sea Horse*, a 900 ton, 180 feet long ship. The local newspaper reported how Fell was now in

[01] Issac Scott (1812-75) lived at 39 Brow Top. ■
[02] Between 1805-1819, Robert Fell is also credited with building at least four new ships at Workington, although the shipyards he used are not clearly defined. ■

Harrington & Workington Shipbuilding & Ropemaking Co.

Below is a list of the H&WSRC's proprietors, taken from their Deed of Constitution, dated 8 June 1837: Richard Watts (Clifton House), William Peile (Harrington), Issac Scott, Richard Thompson, Jacob Holliday, Jonathan Fell, Edward Smith, Henry Grayson, Joseph Thompson Snr, Jane Swinburn, Isabella Falcon, Eleanor Priestman, Mary Peil, Ann Kirkconel, John Smith, William Fell (all of Workington), Benjamin Crosthwaite (Harrington), William Hurd (Whitehaven), Caleb Fletcher, Robert Russell, John Nelson Wood, Elizabeth Wood (all of Liverpool), Sally Scaife, Henry Blake (both of Maryport), Elizabeth Gaitskell (Yearton), Jain Fawcett (Keswick) and John Duncan (Manchester).

[01] One of the few vessels thought to have actually been built by the H&WSRC was the Volunteer. A 783 ton ship (or 855 ton under old system of measure) launched 18 August 1860, and built for Bushby & Edwards of Liverpool. It is thought to have been named in honour of the many volunteer forces then being formed around the country. The 4th Cumberland (Workington) Artillery Volunteer Corps fired a five gun salute at the launch, from their battery close to How Michael.

the *"proud position"* of having launched *"three times consecutively the largest vessels in the country"*. The *Sea Horse*, like other really large ships was built on the land between John Pier and shipyard 1, being launched stern first into the Derwent estuary. This site and north of Merchant's Quay (SY3 on the harbour plan on page 97) were the only part of the harbour with water deep enough, for a successful launch. Between 1834-69, Jonathan Fell is credited with building 35 new vessels (average size 451 tons).

The town's *Company of Shipbuilders* had now operated continually for over sixty years. It's present members now included not just several sons, but also some grandsons of the original partners. As well as building and launching over 110 new ships, almost two every year. It had also provided a skilled workforce and facilities to repair hundreds of other vessels.

By the summer of 1837, it was proposed to reconstitute this rather informal co-operative, into a new limited company. It was to be called the *Harrington & Workington Shipbuilding & Ropemaking Company* (H&WSRC), with a capital of 25000 shares of £10 each. It's twenty seven initial proprietors all *"shipbuilders, shipowners, ropemakers, ships' blacksmiths and other dealers"* are listed left. The company is believed to have initially operated in Workington, from the Peile, Scott & Co's shipyard 1. But sometime prior to 1851, is also thought to have occupied shipyard 2, formerly occupied by William Wallace,

William Whellan in his 1860 history, believed the *H&WSRC* to have commenced trading as early as 1773. But the company does not appear to have been formally registered until October 1856. He may have mistakenly grouped together the older *Company of Shipbuilders* with its more recent *H&WSRC* counterpart. Whilst there are obvious links, his assumption is thought not altogether accurate. The earliest reference to the *H&WSRC*, in harbour records, is not until its 1837 *Deed of Constitution*. Whellan does however tell us that the company in 1860, *"employ 150 hands in the various departments of their business"*.

The transition to this new company was not altogether successful. Many of its proprietors appear to have continued to trade on their own account. Peile Scott and Co. and Jonathan Fell, both continued to build new ships, very much as before. There appears to be few specific references to the company launching vessels, most were usually registered under individuals or groups of the company's proprietors.[01] The company went into voluntary liquidation in the summer of 1869, being formally wound-up in May 1877.

In addition to shipyards 1 & 2, on the Crossfitts area of the harbour, there was then also another at the eastern end of the South Gut. It was immediately east of (what is now) the main railway line, north out of Workington (Low) Station. Much of its site was swallowed up when the viaduct, across the railway was built around 1886, whilst the remainder is now occupied by the *Railway Club*.

The exact date this yard was established has not been determined (it is shown as SY4 on the harbour plan on page 97). Often it was generally referred to as the *"High Yard"*. It may well be the site of Workington's first shipyard. For many years it was operated by the Falcon family, and is thought to have been initially established by Michael Falcon (c1700-1771). This Michael Falcon, (the son of Capt. Thomas Falcon of Whitehaven), was the first of four generations of Falcons, associated with shipbuilding in the town.[01]   The late Denis Hepburn who spent much of his life researching shipbuilding in West Cumbria, believed they built the earliest recorded vessel at Workington. It was the *Hope*, built for Seaton Colliery in 1733. [02] His unpublished notes attribute the vessel to Michael Falcon (c1700-1771), believing it to be built at his High Yard, upon the South Gut.

Despite the majority of other shipbuilders in the town trading happily as a consortium, the Falcon's appear to have initially remained quite independent. Harbour records suggest that between 1760-1832, John Falcon and his son Michael (1761-1838) built around 59 new ships (average size 177 tons); not all of them at their High Yard.

Shipowners were beginning to demand larger and larger new vessels. The location of this Falcon shipyard, seriously restricted the size of ship that they could either built or repair. The depth of water in the South Gut, was often hardly sufficient to launch smaller vessels, even at the high spring tides. It's scarcely surprising that as harbour trustees, the Falcons appear to have constantly pushed for this channel to be cleared and deepened.

In order to remain competitive, Michael Falcon and his son, together with David Fletcher, James Harding, William Wallace, Thomas Falcon, and A. Crosthwaite agreed to jointly erect a new *"Morton patent slip"* [03] on the north side of Merchant's Quay (SY3). The agreement with the landowner, the Earl of Lonsdale, was dated 8 November 1825. Around a decade earlier Falcon is also thought to have agreed to share shipyard 2, with William Wallace. Although the precise details of their agreement or exact dates are not clear.

Despite these arrangements some ships were still built

"Michael Falcon (c1700-1771) was the first of four generations of Falcons, associated with shipbuilding in the town".

[01] At least two other later Falcon's, all shipbuilders, were also called Michael, being the grandson and great-grandson respectively of Michael Falcon (c1700-1771). Basically, Michael Falcon (1792-1858) was the son of Michael Falcon (1761-1838). His father was John Falcon (1731-1780), the son of the first Michael Falcon (c1700-1771). ■
[02] The original *"Hope"* was thought to have been lost in the Baltic, around 1746. At least three other ships, also called *"Hope"* were later to be built at Workington shipyards. ■
[03] The *"Morton patent slip"* was invented and patented by Thomas Morton in 1819. It's operation allowed vessels requiring repair or overhaul to be dragged out of the water, up onto dry-land. They were drawn up by means of a *"capstan and railway"*, into the shipyard. Workington had at least three such slipways, one located on the northside of Merchant's Quay and others in shipyards 1 and 2. Each *"patent slipway"* was approx. 123 feet long. New ships which obviously took longer to build, were generally assembled on other more simpler slipways. To use these Morton slips for new vessels was considered uneconomic, as it greatly restricted the range of repair work that a yard could undertake. ■

at Falcon High Yard (SY3), probably until the construction of the Whitehaven Junction Railway.[01] John Waite, the town's Customs Officer between 1831-40, clearly shows the site as a *"ship building yard"* on his town plan produced around 1835. Sergeant C. Hall in his 1883 *Inductive History of Workington* records how it was believed that the last ship to be built on this old site, was a brig which was named after *Falcon*. A closer look at the harbour records casts some doubt on this assumption as the only vessel of that name, despite being a brig of 135 tons, appears to have been launched from the yard as early as 1790, thirty or so years earlier.

Interestingly, the road that now runs along past where the old Falcon's High Yard stood, is known today as Falcon Street. The site was subsequently purchased after for the Whitehaven Junction Railway. After the track to Maryport was first laid (1846) and before the erection of the viaduct (some forty or so years later), Hall say the site became a simple, but *"pretty flower garden"*.[02]

Around 1833, Michael Falcon (1792-1858), the fourth generation of the family entered into a further partnership with James Alexander (1799-1881). They jointly leased Shipyard 2, which is thought to have laid vacant following the bankruptcy of William Wallace. The first vessel they built together was the ship, *Francis and Mary*. Up until 1840 when the partnership was dissolved, they went on to build a further 13 (average size 183 tons).

James Alexander [03] then continued trading from the same yard until 1849. In this time he is thought to have build at least seven ships, on his own account. In September 1845, he launched the *Christabel*, a 335 ton Barque, the first vessel for Liverpool's famous *Lamport & Holt* line, founded that same year. [04]

In 1849, Charles Lamport,[05] the brother of William James Lamport (founder of the Lamport & Holt line), acquired James Alexander's lease of Shipyard 2. Upto 1866, of the twenty seven vessels he built at Workington, five were commissioned by his brother's shipping line. (these are listed opposite) Many of his larger ships, two of which were over a thousand tons, were built on the Merchant's Quay shipyard (SY3). He had taken a lease of this site around 1851. Around the same time, Lamport rented the old Isabella Pit buildings, on the shoreline. These had laid vacant since the flooding of the Chapel Bank colliery in 1837. Here he created a sawmill, although it is not known if he adapted any of the old pit engines or machinery.

Between 1849-1866, he built twenty seven new ships at Workington. The average size being nearly 560 tons,

[01] For more details of the Whitehaven Junction Railway (see chapter fifteen) ■

[02] The author Sergeant C. Hall was thought to be the pseudonym of Alfred Hall. In 1883, he wrote a brief history of the town, published (over several weeks) in the *West Cumberland Times*. The accuracy of much of the work is questionable, as it is embroidered with some obvious purely fictional material. ■

[03] James Alexander (1799-1881) is thought to be the son of Patrick and Mary Alexander. He was christened at Harrington on 13 May 1799. When he died on 10 April 1881, he is shown as living at Derwent House, 7 Brow Top, Workington. Alexander is credited with building the "Workington", a 150 brig, 73 feet long, 18.75 ft breath and 12.5 ft depth, launched on 2 Nov 1840.

[04] The Lamport & Holt Shipping Line, was founded in Liverpool, by William James Lamport (d1874) and George Holt, in 1845. They initially handled general cargo, exploiting the then undeveloped trade routes to Argentina. Gradually, moving principally transporting live *"cattle on hoof"*. By 1880, they had pioneered the transfer of frozen meat. The company traded for over a century, before it was absorbed into the *Blue Star* line. Blue Star are now part of P & O. Line. ■

[05] Charles Lamport (1817-1902) was the son of William Lamport (b1770), a Liverpool Unitarian minister. Both his brother, George Holt and himself were members of the same Unitarian church in Liverpool. He moved to Workington around 1849, when he acquired Alexander's lease. The 1851 census shows him living in Park End Road, then of course called the Row. He is thought to have retired around 1866, and later moved to Blinton, in Somerset. Lamport died on 23 April 1902 at Alassio, Italy, aged 85. ■

although two were well over a thousand tons each. For every new ship he launched, Charles Lamport would donated five pounds to the Workington Mechanics Institute. His only condition was that his apprentices be allowed access to the Institute facilities.

By 1851, Charles Lamport's shipyards employed 107 men and 62 boys. He obviously continued to maintain the town's impressive reputation for quality shipbuilding. By 1860, William Whellan recorded that *"The establishment of Charles Lamport, Esq., is well and favourably known, and affords employment to about 120 hands on an average."* That year he launched the *Sebastian Cabot*, a massive 1009 ton ship, built on the Merchant Quay yard (SY3). It was 180 feet long, 32 feet breath and 21ft depth. At it's stern was an elaborate carved *"emblematic"* design of the *"British Lion supporting the world"*. The launching ceremony was performed by Edith, daughter of Charles Lamport. [01]

In July of the same year, he also completed the first *"ship of war"* to be built at Workington. It was the 268 ton *Speedy*, a wooden gun boat of the *Britomart* class. Measuring 120 feet long, 22 feet breath and just 9.5 feet depth, it was armed with two 32 pound and two 68 pound guns. It's launch was attended by forty members of the 7th Cumberland Rifle Corps, in full dress uniform. Charles Lamport being then captain of this volunteer regiment. Before the vessel slid down the slipway into the Derwent, a salute was fired across its bows. *Speedy* was to remain in active service for almost 30 years.

Although this was the town's first actual warship, adding gun emplacements to vessels was quite common to the local shipyards. In 1779, Ellwood and Co., built the 400 ton *Tyne*, with two decks pierced for 30 guns. Whilst a couple of years later they launched the 500 ton *Tartar*, armed with twelve 9 pound and six 12 pound guns between decks. Some form of defence was rapidly becoming essential for nearly every ship that put to sea. Around this time, even in the Irish Sea, there was the constant threat of attack. It came not just from the French and American fleets, but piracy was also quite rife around the Solway and beyond.

Ships and their cargoes were often seized by pirates, and released only after a substantial ransom was paid. The *Cumberland Pacquet* of August 1781, reported how three Workington ships, the *Trydal*, *Lowther* and *Speedwell* were all captured while on short voyages to Cork, in Ireland. They suspected the pirate ship was a *"Priatical Cruizer"* with an Irish crew, commanded by a noted smuggler called Kelly. All three ships were eventually safely released, but only after payments of upto £450 per vessel were paid.

LAMPORT & HOLT SHIPPING LINE

List of ships built at Workington, for the Lamport & Holt line:
Built in 1845, at James Alexander's shipyard was the *Christabel* (335 ton barque)
Built at Charles Lamport's shipyards were the *Cathaya* (407 ton ship, built1850), *Blencathra* (466 ton barque,1856), *Coniston* (204 ton barque,1857), *Glaramara* (475 ton barque,1857), *Chalgrove* (509 ton barque,1862). ■

[01] Denis Hepburn recorded in his unpublished notes that traces of the shipyard slipways (SY3) were still visible north of Merchant's Quay in 1974. (see plan page 97). ■

It was often common for several ships to also travel in convoy, being closely guarded by a private armed vessel, paid for at great expense by the shipowners.

At the 1851 *Great Exhibition*, West Cumberland was represented by a fine replica scale model, an exact copy of the *Dinapore*. [01] The three masted merchant vessel, built at Charles Lamport's yard, was launched in April 1851. The expertly constructed model measured ten feet (3m) in length, and took twenty weeks to build. Each timber of the little vessel was made to correspond with the larger ship, although one side of the model was left open to show the frame-work and interior.

Today, tucked away at the top of Wilson Street, once one of the towns main shopping areas, is an old drinking fountain presented to the town by Charles Lamport. In 1859, the fountain with a polished pink Peterhead granite basin was originally sited on the corner of Sanderson Street,[02] now occupied by the Midland Bank. Around 1865, when these bank premises were built (for the *Cumberland Union Banking Co*) it was relocated to Wilson Street. First it was placed against the gable end of house number 46. This grocers shop once stood alone, almost at the top of the street, in the centre of this narrow thoroughfare. When it was later demolished, the fountain was moved for a third time, and fixed to a small section of new stone wall.

Charles Lamport was also responsible for building Hawksley Terrace, located where Belle Isle Street joins Gladstone Street. This row of seven neat terraced houses, were named in honour of Thomas Hawksley, the engineer responsible for Workington's first waterworks. [03] Completed prior to 1863 and before Gladstone Street was built, these houses then stood at the end of a quiet cul-de-sac, surrounded on three sides by just open fields.

Richard Hellon is also credited with building two new ships between 1825-26. One of which was the *Rob Roy*, a 33 ton sloop. Whilst a J. Wilkinson and a J. White are also known to have built vessels at Workington, in 1822 and 1827 respectively. Unfortunately very little else is known of these three individuals and where they traded from.

Workington shipbuilders built many elegant Clipper ships. [04] Four such vessels, Charles Lamport's *Whinfell*, and Jonathan Fell's *Melbreak*, *Corea* and *Belted Will*, featured prominently in the China Tea Races. These annual races ran from Shanghai to London, and attracted huge interest from the general public. The masters, owners and builders of the fastest vessels each acquired great prestige, honour and acclaim. Clipper ships was remarkably

[01] The *Dinapore*, launched on 18 April 1851, was a 693 ton ship, measuring 150 feet from *"bowspirt to taffail"*. The vessel was built for the Liverpool company of W.S. Lindsay & Co., who later also acquired the scale model, which went on display at their offices. ■
[02] Sanderson Street has now almost disappeared from Workington's street plan. This short street originally curved from Pow Street, around the present Midland Bank site, to join Washington Street, in line with the old Presbyterian Church. An inscription on the drinking fountain reads *"Presented to the town - 1859 by C. Lamport Esq"*. ■
[03] For details of Workington Waterworks see chapter seventeen. ■
[04] Clippers were the fastest wind-driven ships ever built. These sharp bowed vessels, with extremely narrow hulls, were designed for speed rather than cargo carrying capacity.
The clipper had a graceful sheer (an upward curve of the lines of the hull as seen from the side), a simple, high-arched stem fitted with a figurehead, a square or a round stern, rather low freeboard when loaded, and an extremely large sail area, designed for speed.
They were employed principally in the tea trade, sailing to the China, India, and the other main Asian producers. Tea had been introduced to Britain in 1657, and had rapidly became our main beverage, far more popular than coffee. ■

fast, and claims for speeds from 16 to 18 nautical m.p.h were quite common, exceptional speeds of up to 20 knots were also sometimes recorded. The clipper *Corea* (581 tons) built by Jonathan Fell in 1859, competed in the tea race of 1872-3. Recording a time of 116 days from Shanghai, just hours behind the winner. Whilst another Fell ship, the *Belted Will* (773 tons) built at the yard of Peile, Scott & Co., made the trip in 109 days, being beaten by just one day.[01]

Another Charles Lamport vessel the *Scawfell*, a 825 ton ship, was built specifically for the tea trade. Launched on 30 March 1858, every beam was constructed of teak, strengthened with diagonal iron braces. Beneath its decks could be *"stowed"* a cargo of over 1020000 lbs (or 462668 kgs) of tea. [02] A half model of the hull and two fine paintings of this ship, built for Rathbone Bros., [03] can be seen at the Merseyside Maritime Museum.

On 9 January 1883, the *Scawfell* was abandoned with seven feet of water in her hold. Her demise was blamed on her pumps being choked and blocked with coal from her cargo. She was subsequently lost about 250 miles west of the Bay of Biscay.

From early in the nineteenth century, Britain was the world's major sea trader and carrier. This spawned a huge demand for quality new vessels. In little over a century from 1760, Workington's shipbuilders built and launched around 330 new ships. Averaging over three each year, and providing valuable employment for generations of shipwrights, caulkers, joiners, carpenters, pitch-heaters, sawyers and labourers.

But by 1870, the town's proud and renowned shipbuilding industry went into a rapid decline, a recession from which it never really recovered. [04] Charles Lamport had now retired, Peile, Scott & Co had ceased to trade and Jonathan Fell had died. The era of the large and graceful clipper ships (and sailing ships generally) was dealt a grievous blow by the introduction of the much more economical steamships. The shipyards, which produced traditionally wooden vessels also faced a bleak future, with the more widespread introduction of iron-clad ships. Steel became an ideal material, as larger and more economical vessels were demanded by the highly competitive shipping lines. Improved ship speed and economy lay in further developments of the compound engine and boiler. Workington's remaining shipbuilders were no longer skilled enough or equipped to handle these new materials or innovations in design. [05]

[01] The *Belted Will* launched on 2 July 1863, was a three masted Barque, 186 feet (57m) long, 32 ft (9.8m) breath, 20 ft (6.2m) depth. ∎
[02] Today, this quantity of tea would make over 148 million cups (equivalent to 80% of Britain's daily consumption). However, the *Scawfell* did not just carry a cargo of tea. In April 1858, it is recorded as carrying iron to Liverpool, for the *Workington Haematite Iron Co.* ∎
[03] *Scawfell* was originally built for Rathbone Bros., of Liverpool, but later passed to Wilson and Blain of South Shields in 1872. Hutchinson's of Newcastle later acquired the vessel in 1880. ∎
[04] Between 1870 and the First World War, shipyards nationally went through radical changes. With the rapid introduction of *"steel and steam"*, many smaller yards became uneconomical and were simply forced to close. By then only 6% of Britain's total shipbuilding output lay outside the major centres of the Northeast and the Cylde. ∎
[05] Although some repair work continued, only one new ship appears to have been launched in the period upto 1882. Shipbuilding was now to be continued only by R.Williamson & Sons, who had moved their entire operation from Harrington to Workington, a year or so earlier. ∎

In 1786, Statuary Registration of British Ships became compulsory. Shipping registers provide a host of information, including full details of ownership of vessels, their dimensions, crew and history. From 1786-1839, those registered at the port of Workington are included in the Whitehaven list, as they then administered the West Cumbrian Coast. Workington's own register began on 22 March 1839. Readers may consult the originals (upto 1959) by visiting Whitehaven Record Office. ∎

CHAPTER TWELVE

IRON & STEEL INDUSTRY

THE town's first ironworks was established at Barepot, (sometimes also found spelt *"Beerpot"*) on the north bank of the Derwent, just upstream of Workington Bridge [01] Here in 1763, William Hicks, Robert Watters, John Ponsonby, William Skyrin and Richard Dearham [02] are said to have built what became generally known as *Seaton Iron-works*. Hutchinson in his 1794 History of Cumberland, tells us that the *"eminent engineer"* Thomas Spedding of White-haven, was actively involved in the enterprise. For he is credited with planning and building the works, which included one of the first blast furnaces in Cumberland. However, other accounts suggest it was James Spedding who established the plant. [03] Then it is also recorded that the works traded as *Spedding, Hicks & Co.*

Gabriel Jars recorded the first description of the plant in 1765. He was the same Frenchman who wrote extensively about the collieries in Workington and Whitehaven (see page 157). Then there was already one blast furnace in production and another under construction. The pig iron produced here being converted into quality wrought iron. [04] The iron ore used was noted as being the same as that smelted at Clifton. Sugden in his 1897 *History of Arlecdon & Frizington* comments this was bought overland by pack-horse from the Frizington district.

Interestingly, the fuel being used in this first Barepot blast furnace was charcoal, thought to have been brought south from Scotland. But Jars also mentions that it was planned to fire the new furnace with coke, to solely produce cast iron. If coke supplies were not also to be purchased elsewhere, it is not exactly clear how this coke was then to be produced. Perhaps they were to adopt a similar method to that used at nearby Clifton. Here heaps of coal were laid upon a thick base of sandstone slabs, then it was covered with earth and lit. By adjusting it's rate of combustion, the heap of coal became carbonized. In much the same way as charcoal is traditional produced from timber.

In October 1779, a *Spedding, Hicks & Co.* advertisment from the *Cumberland Pacquet*, tells us they were then still supplying both *"charcoal and coke pig irons"*. This may suggest that the company had yet to establish an adequate method of producing their own coke on site, and were continuing to purchase charcoal. Certainly by 1812, coal could

[01] Workington Bridge crosses the River Derwent from Hall Brow to the foot of Calva Brow. ■

[02] These are the five people listed on what appears to be the original lease for the erection of an ironworks at *"Barepotts meadow and Holegill"*, near Workington (dated 8 March 1762). It is contained in the Lowther papers, deposited at Carlisle Record Office. Another name which is occasional connected with founding the works is Benjamin Ravencroft died c.April 1778.■

[03] Lancaster & Wattleworth in their 1977 history of *The Iron & Steel Industry of West Cumberland*, suggested it was James Spedding (1720-88) who was responsible for the construction of Seaton Ironworks, and not Thomas. They felt that James (then also the agent for the Lowther family) was clearly very prominent in the scheme, and no suitable Thomas Spedding can be found amongst their family records. The executor's memo books of James Spedding, (who died in 1788) seem to add some credence to their suggestion. He clearly then had a very large and active interest in the works.■

[04] Pig iron (produced in a blast furnace) contains impurities that weaken the iron and make it difficult to forge or work. It was usually only suitable for casting in the foundry. Wrought iron (almost pure iron) is produced by reheating the pig iron in a puddling furnace, to oxidise away the impurities. ■

now be converted in a row of four or five beehive shaped coke ovens, located on the hillside overlooking the works.

By 1794, Hutchinson provided some further details of the works, now obviously expanded. There was still two blast furnaces, but now there was also *"a mill for slitting and rolling bar iron, a double forge for refining and drawing of bar iron, a foundry with several small furnaces, wherein they make cannon and cast iron work of all sorts; a boring mill for boring cannon cylinders, etc., a grinding house and turning house and many other conveniences suitable for carrying on very extensive iron manufacturing"*.

From around 1775 to after the Napoleonic wars, Seaton Ironworks is known to have manufactured many cannons. At the time all English shipping was in constant danger of attack. Not just from the hostile French and American navies, but also they risked confrontation from marauding pirate ships; even close to home in the Solway Firth. It now became quite common for the Workington's shipbuilders to add cannons to their new ships, no doubt the ironworks supplied many of these. [01]

The works then employed several hundred local people, busily producing castings and iron work of all descriptions. Their advertisements proudly boasting that they could manufacture almost any *"article in the Cast Iron way, in the neatest manner, and on the lowest terms"*. Although their largest customers were likely to be the local shipbuilders and collieries. They also made an extensive range of general household items; such as frying pans, griddles, pye pans, tea kettles, clothes irons, stoves and grates. The general public could purchase these, by calling at the Barepot works or from their warehouse in Whitehaven.

The Curwen's accounts show *Spedding, Hicks & Co.*, supplied their collieries with numerous more industrial items, such as bar iron, bogie wheels, nails, hoops, pistons and cylinders, boiler plate and barrow wheels. They also provided quite large quantities of both fire and common bricks. Where these were manufactured is unclear, as there appears to be no record of a brickworks on the Barepot site. Perhaps they came from the brickworks at Camerton.

By 1791, the company now trading as *Spedding, Hicks, Senhouse & Co.*, also began to produced parts and assembled the *Heslop* rotary steam engine (see page 158). It is thought Adam Heslop who patented his invention in 1790, become a employee at the works, perhaps to supervise it's construction. The Barepot works may well have then manufactured these first steam engines under licence. Unfortunately, there is no record of the actual arrangement he had with the proprietors. In 1798, Heslop resigned inorder to continue to build his engines elsewhere, forming a new company *Heslop,*

".....English shipping was in constant danger of attack.....they risked confrontation from marauding pirate ships, even close to home in the Solway Firth".

[01] As more and more local ships were seized or attacked. Spedding, Hicks & Co. often advertised their cannons "of all sizes, cast solid from metal, all of the best quality", in the local newspaper. They insisted that each could be tested fired, "in the presence of any person the purchaser may appoint". It is said they were loaded and fired across the River Derwent, into the steep hillside below Stainburn.

Milward & Co., [01] They erected their own new works at Lowca, near Harrington, leasing the land from John Christian Curwen.

In August 1813, a further advertisment in the *Cumberland Pacquet,* tells us that the Seaton company had recently *"extended their Brass & Cast Iron foundry",* but the actual extent of this work is not recorded in detail. It is however revealed, that they were now also manufacturing *"stoves for churches, shops, ships etc, Cast iron ploughs",* and could supply Camerton cokes. Just over a year later, the works were again advertised for sale. From the auction particulars in the *Cumberland Pacquet,* we are able to obtain a better description of the plant. The works now consisted of *"A blast furnace capable of making 30 to 40 tons of iron per week",* [02] said to have been substantially rebuilt the previous year. Together with *"ovens for coking coal, a large foundry or moulding house for both iron and brass, a double forge, refineries and slitting and rolling mill".* It was now being sold by proprietors *Speddings, Dickinson, Russell & Co.* It was suggested that its principal partners now wished to retire. But in truth it was more likely that activity at the works had been declining for some time. This being the true reason for wanting to dispose of the plant. As no financial accounts of the company have survived, the true state of business remains a mystery.

Certainly, the likelihood of poor profits may explain why no purchaser was forthcoming. Finally at the beginning of June 1819, it was sold at auction to *Heslop, Milward, Johnson & Co.* So Adam Heslop, who had left the Seaton Ironworks over twenty years earlier, and set up a new foundry at Lowca; now returned to take control of his old workplace, where his first steam engines were built. [03] Adam was in partnership with his brothers Crosby and Thomas Heslop. Their large gravestone in St. Michaels Church records, that all three had died by Christmas 1835.

Around 1837, *Seaton Ironworks* was sold again, this time to *Tulk, Ley and Company.* At the same time, they also purchased Heslop's *Lowca Ironworks.* That same year, Tulk and Ley took a lease on the iron ore pits at Yeathouse (Frizington). Obviously with their own blast furnaces, they would wish to secure a cheap and constant supply of iron ore. Lancaster & Wattleworth tell us the partnership was made up of John Augustus Tulk (the principle shareholder) and James Peard Ley (of Bideford). Despite major partnership problems the company appears to have continued to operate the Barepot works until around 1851. During this period they may have also rebuilt and upgraded its blast furnace, and added a rail connection into the plant, from the newly opened Cockermouth & Workington Railway. No records of their

[01] Readers may find some confusion occasionally arises in some other accounts of Seaton Ironworks. Often we find Heslop, Milward & Co., being then assumed to be the proprietors of the works. However, the company did not actually acquire the plant until the summer of 1819. (detailed later) Obviously this mix-up may stem from Heslop then working at Barepot, having his first engines made there and eventually becoming it's owner, some twenty years later. ■

[02] In 1813, the pig iron smelted at Seaton Ironworks sold for around 8s-6d per cwt (hundredweight) or the equivalent of £8.50 per ton. ■

[03] Lancaster & Wattleworth in their history of *The Iron & Steel Industry in West Cumberland,* tell us that the partners in Heslop, Milward Johnson & Co., were Adam Heslop, Crosby Heslop, Edward Johnston (of Moresby), Thomas Milward (of Parton), Mary Stead (of Waverbridge) and Betty Ritson (of Appleby). ■

output at Seaton Ironworks seem to survive. But in 1849, we know they mined around 15000 tons of ore from their two pits at Yeathouse.

From 1852, the plant was taken over by the partnership of *Henderson & Davis*. [01] They were known to have then converted and adapted Barepot into a tin plate manufactory. Tin plates were made from successively re-heating and rolling wrought iron bars into thin sheets, then coating their surfaces in a film of tin. The tin protected the iron against rusting and corrosion. They also erected the *Derwent Iron Works*, on the south side of Stanley Street, next to where the Gas works was built. It was sometimes also called the *Quayside Ironwork* and later the *Derwent Tin-plate Works*. It had no connection with the later *Derwent Haematite Iron Company*, established around 1874.

Lancaster & Wattleworth recorded that by 1860, the lease of *Seaton Ironworks*, which then employed 120 men, was now acquired by *Samuel Wagstaffe Smith*. Whellan in his 1860 history suggests it may now have been re-named the *Quarry Ironworks*. Although we can discover no further reference to the plant under that name. Locally, it was certainly still known as *Seaton Ironworks*. For around the next five years, Smith continued tin plate production and also resumed smelting iron. Within twelve months the workforce had increased to nearly 195. But work was then not continuous, for in June 1861 they were all laid off *"in consequence of a stagnation of trade"*. From 1865-70 the plant was believed to have been ran by *Samuel Sandys Briggs*.

The *Derwent* or *Quayside Ironworks* in Stanley Street, was principally a puddling furnace and rolling mill. It too was established before 1853, by *Henderson and Davis*. As previouly mentioned, they also held the lease of *Seaton Ironworks*. Here pig or cast iron was converted into bars of wrought or malleable iron, before being sent across to Barepot, to be transformed into tin plate. The plant was powered by a 60 H.P. steam engine which was then capable of finishing upto 70 tons of bars weekly.

Around 1860, the quayside works were let to James Spence and Fredrick Worthington (of Liverpool). But production was to continue here for only a further couple of years, before the plant was advertised for sale again. In March 1861, the works suffered some employee unrest, which perhaps ultimately signalled the end of this company; and today clearly highlights how much progress has since been made towards improved labour relations. After the *"puddlers"* (puddling furnace workers) had their requests for a pay rise rejected. They apparently immediately went on strike, bringing production to an abrupt halt.

[01] Tulk and Ley continued to operate Lowca Ironworks till around August 1857, when their partnership was dissolved by the courts. ■

[02] Samuel S. Briggs was to run both sites again, trading as the *Lonsdale Haematic Rolling Mills*. But in 1869 the tin plate works and mills laid idle for many months, as attempts were again made to sell the works. By the spring of 1870, the business was acquired by William Ivander Griffiths. Production was resumed but rapidly declined around a decade later. After passing to the *West Cumberland Haematite Iron & Steel Co.*, The plant at Barepot was finally dismantled around 1899. ■

[01] The *Whitehaven Junction Railway* is now the main railway line, from Whitehaven north upto Carlisle. (see page 208) ■

[03] The *Workington Haematite Iron Company Limited* was incoporated in November 1856. It's initial share capital amounted to £25000, consisting of fifty shares of £500. ■

[03] The blast furnace was now a massive tall masonry structure (the construction of modern types is now quite different again). Into it's hollow centre was dropped the iron ore (haematite), the fuel (coke) and a flux. By means of bellows or fans, an air-blast was then introduced near the foot of the furnace (later blowers and blowing engines were used). This generated an intense heat melting and fusing it's contents together. When sufficient molten iron had collected at the foot of the furnace, it is then allowed to flow out into pig iron moulds (called *"beds"*). The slag or molten waste materials were also separately drawn ran off, to be tipped along the shoreline. The furnace was usually kept full with fresh materials, so it was alight or "in blast" almost continuously. ■

The ringleaders of the dispute, James Rodgers, John Leonard and Robert Livingstone were quickly arrested and sent to Carlisle gaol Each was sentenced to serve six weeks hard labour. By today's standards, this severe punishment sounds somewhat bazaar and peculiar. But it was rightly imposed as the workers had acted illegally, by ignoring a rule of the works which stipulated fourteen days notice of any strike. Although the remaining puddlers wisely restarted work *"without delay"*, production was to cease again quite soon after. The Quayside works was to lie idle for almost the next five years. Lancaster & Wattleworth believed the lease of this site was then eventually also acquired by Samuel Sandys Briggs.

In addition to the Seaton and Quayside ironworks, there was also a foundry at New Yard, run for a time by the Curwen family. *New Yard* was west of the Whitehaven Junction Railway line [01] as it crossed Annie Pit Lane. Today, it's site is best described as being just south of the Derwent Howe Retail park. Here iron and other metals were cast into many different items. Within the Curwen Papers are extensive records of these castings. It is later shown on the 1863 OS plan as a *"bar iron"* foundry. In March 1861, it is thought to have been acquired by *Kirk Bros*. A report from the *Cumberland Paquet* tells us that this new company was formed by Peter & Henry Kirk, and were *"to commence smelting ore at the New Yard works"*.

North of the River Derwent at Oldside, was the *Workington Haematite Iron Company's* works. [02] This plant was located west of the main railway line north to Maryport and began production in mid February 1858. When first opened there was just two blast furnaces [03] located to the south of the site. Together with around sixty six small coke ovens, built to the *"newest and most approved principles"*. Each capable of converting nearly six tons of coal. Built around the south west corner of the site, were the offices, stables and two rows of terraced workers cottages.

There was also a large *"heavy quadrangular building"*, housing a massive 200 H.P. steam engine. This vast beam engine provided the powerful air blast into each furnace; and had a huge 22 ft (6.7m) diameter flywheel, which alone weighed around 15 tons. The beam itself was at least 36 ft (11m) long, and gracefully rocked as the cylinders moved at upto 16 strokes per minute; forcing 18000 cubic feet of air into the base of the furnaces. The scale of this steam engine is now quite difficult to comprehend. Its basic appearance would have been very similar to Heslop's earlier engine (see page 158). Although it was very much larger and technically it's operation was then so much more refined.

Within two years, there was two further massive stone

stone blast furnaces and the site employed around 100 men. A sketch of the plant is shown below. Initially the works were built and managed under the supervision of a Mr Thorburn. Later, Joseph Smith held the post for almost twenty years, until the plant was sold around 1879. Work on building two additional blast furnaces and a further additional powerful steam engine began in the spring of 1860. The ironworks also had a connection to the Whitehaven Junction Railway and a further line looping south to link the plant to the Lonsdale Dock.

It was at this Workington ironworks that the prolific inventor Henry Bessemer (1813-1898) finally discovered an ideal source of quality pig iron to use in his revolutionary new steel-making process. In 1855, he had discovered that by blowing a blast of air through molten pig iron, he could oxidise away it's naturally occurring impurities to create steel. He soon realised his invention could be scaled-up to manufacture larger quantities of relatively cheap steel, with very little effort. Something that had simply been impossible to achieve until then.

Today, we take steel very much for granted. But as Bessemer comments in his autobiography, before he made his discovery *"there was no steel suitable for structural purposes, ships, bridges, railway rails, tyres and axles were constructed of wrought iron"*. The use of steel was then confined to just *"cutlery, tools springs, and the smaller parts of machinery"* as it's manufacturer was *"long and costly"*.

Henry Bessemer came to Oldside, soon after starting to build his Sheffield steel works (opened 1858). He was fully aware that West Cumberland mines produced *"the purest iron ore which this country possessed"*. But there was a problem with the quality of pig iron then produced from Work-

BELOW - is a sketch based on an old print (drawn approx. 1867) of the *Workington Haematite Iron Company*'s plant at Oldside. By 1861 there were six tall massive stone blast furnaces or *"skiddies"*. The works then providing employment for over 100 men. Raw materials were brought up to be loaded into the top of the furnace, by hoists, which closely resembled a *"pit-head"* structure. The moulded pig iron, often simply called *"pigs"* can be seen stacked in the foreground.

The stream of gases were then allowed to freely escape, and be burnt off from the top of the blast furnace; often they could reach temperatures of 500° C. The volume of gas produced was enormous and as it gushed from the chimneys it carried vast clouds of fine dust into the atmosphere. No doubt this was a constant irritation to the townspeople.

Today, this airborne pollution would simply not be tolerated. In the later furnaces built at the adjoining West Cumberland Ironworks, these gases were re-circulated back to the foot of the furnace. These six open-topped furnaces were demolished around 1877. The tall chimney from the furnace of the engine house was around 125 ft (38 m) tall and had an internal diameter of around 2 metres.

HENRY BESSEMER
(1813-1898)

[01] It appears this flux material then used in the Workington blast furnaces, was infact *"a reddish brown furnace waste"* brought from the Black Country (Staffordshire) as ballast in empty ships, returning to Workington harbour. (see page 96) The owners of the ironworks obviously found the material to be suitable, as well as no doubt extremely cheap. ■

[02] The major problem at the *Workington Haematite Ironworks* was their older style, open-topped blast furnaces which soon became obsolete and expensive to operate. As they failed to upgrade the plant, it was always going to be difficult for them to compete with more advanced and modern furnaces. The works were to be later rebuilt and production continued till around 1930. They traded from 1879-1901, as the *Workington Haematite Iron & Steel Company Ltd.*, with Bessemer iron still being a major product. In 1909 they were amalgamated into the *Workington Iron & Steel Company Limited*, although the site was often also referred to as the *Oldside Iron & Steel Works.* ■

[03] The West Cumberland Haematite Iron Co was incorporated in November 1860. ■

ington's blast furnaces. He was surprised to find that the smelted iron had a high phosphorus content, making it unsuitable for his process. Bessemer toured the works, taking samples for analyses of all the raw materials, and discussed the problem with furnace managers. Initially, it was a mystery how such pure iron ore could become contaminated during processing. Then, he discovered that the flux (or cinder) added to aid the blast furnace operation, contained the phosphoric impurities.[01] Bessemer simply switched to another flux, and later wrote *"I now feel certain we would soon have thousands of tons of British iron suitable for the production of steel by my process".*

Suddenly, this virtually phosphorous free *"Bessemer pig"* iron, became a much sort after major world wide commodity. Initially, only smelted here in Cumberland and Furness, it brought a boom period not only for the local ironworks and iron ore mines, but also greatly benefited the local railway companies and ports. From which it was transported to numerous Bessemer steel plants, across Europe and North America. But booms are invariable followed by slumps, and by 1877 work had ceased at Workington's first major ironworks. [02]

Also at Oldside, situated opposite the *Workington Haematite Ironworks* (directly across the main railway line), was the *West Cumberland Haematite Iron Company.* [03] Work began on this site in March 1860, four improved blast furnaces being initially built to take advantage of the growing demand for Workington's Bessemer pig iron. The design of these new furnaces benefited greatly from advances in recent technology. The quality of the smelted iron was now better regulated and controlled, with production here being far more economical, than at their neighbours older furnaces, on the opposite side of the railway.

The overall appearance and construction of these blast furnaces, *"first blown"* in November 1862, was quite different. Instead of the massive masonry structure, they were now almost totally encased in thick steel plate. The hot gases which belched out from the earlier models, were now recirculated to the foot of the structure to pre-heat the air-blast. Much of the initial building work was carried out by Messrs. Telford. Along the southern edge of the site were twelve workers cottages built for the company, in the summer of 1860, by Mr Frazer of Harrington.

The first slag waste from these furnaces was deposited in two large banks or heaps in the south east corner of the works, beside the main road to Maryport. Later it was poured upon waste ground and coastline to the north west, near St. Helens Colliery. Layer upon layer was laid here greatly remodelling the landscape forever.

Within two years, the plant was extended to the north to now include puddling furnaces and a plate mill. [01]   With the company now producing upto around 2000 tons of *"Bessemer"* quality pig iron each week, their next obvious step was an expansion into steel making themselves, at Oldside. Work began on building a steel plant, with four Bessemer convertors in the autumn of 1870; the first steel being produced in mid November 1872.   Much of this early steel from Oldside was cast into large bars (called *"ingots"*), then rolled into flat plates and railway lines.   A few months earlier the company had been restructured and renamed *The West Cumberland Haematite Iron & Steel Company Limited.* [02]   By 1883, they employed over 1400 local people, and had six blast furnaces.

The 1863 OS plan shows that there was then only the relatively small New Yard foundry and Quayside Ironworks south of the Derwent. With the enormous demand for iron and steel, several enterprising local people attempted to form new company's to also begin smelting ore.   A report from the *Cumberland Pacquet* in October 1860, tells us that one such new iron company *"under the auspices of Mr Guy"* had raised capital of £8000 and their plant near New Yard should be operational shortly.

It was perhaps 1872 before the *Moss Bay Haematite Iron & Steel Company* commenced production and 1874 before the *Derwent Haematite Iron Co.,* smelted it's first iron. Further accounts of these two companies, together with later developments are outside the period covered by this volume of the History of Workington.

"The works are more eligibly placed for the manufacture of Bessemer steel, than any other"
West Cumberland Haematite Iron & Steel Co. Ltd.
(1872 prospectus)

[01]   The plate mill and wrought iron furnaces were officially opened on the 24 May 1865.■
[02]   The transfer to the *West Cumberland Haematite Iron & Steel Co. Ltd.,* was officially completed on 30 September 1872.   It's initial share capital amounted to £600000.   It is said they paid the shareholders of the old company around £485000 for the Oldside plant.   The fortunes of the new company fluctuated, before being wound up in 1892.■

"It has employed hundreds, and fed thousands, and made me a fair return - This is the real comfort of being a farmer".

John Christian Curwen (1812)

[01] Like many before, Emily Mitchell in her account of *Agriculture in Cumberland*, believed the agricultural history of Workington was built around John Christian Curwen. (see page 50) She wrote *"Once his interest in agriculture was aroused he followed it with a zest and vigour that never flagged for thirty years"*. ■

[02] John Christian Curwen's descriptions of the common or waste lands surrounding Workington, was written around 1812. ■

❧ CHAPTER THIRTEEN ❧

AGRICULTURE

THE physical conditions of West Cumberland, especially it's soil and relief, tend to make farming deferent from the surrounding inland districts. In an area, very similar to that occupied by the West Cumberland coalfield the soil is chiefly boulder clay, often quiet variable in quality. Due to it's high moisture content, this soil is often best defined as *"cold and late"*. Late in so much that the main growing season commences sometimes weeks, after the adjoining Cockermouth area. There the soil is generally a loam-covered limestone, which provides the superior farming conditions. Furthermore, the general physical geography of the coastal strip, tends to expose it to more inclement weather.

The heavy soils of the Workington area, have resulted in the adoption of predominant dairy farming and stock raising husbandry. Today nearly half of the area is permanent pasture land. However, in the early nineteenth century, due without doubt to the great influence of John Christian Curwen, [01] arable cultivation of crops such as wheat, oats, potatoes and turnips was far more widespread.

Developments over the centuries, due to improvements in production methods, means of transport, marketing facilities and external factors such as government legislation and subsidies, may have brought about substantial changes in agriculture generally. But the physical conditions of the land today, are very much the same as Christian Curwen's time.

As the Industrial revolution generated massive strides forward in science and technology. It also stimulated new and improved farming methods, superior crops and a better knowledge of stock breeding and management. So too the population also rapidly increased, and thus did the demand for food. But much of the English countryside, lay *"barren and unproductive"*, used for grazing *"a few miserable sheep"*.[02] It was then farmed using the out of date, inefficient and wasteful *"open field"* system. The land of the eighteenth century farmer was often not fenced off from that of others. His actual holding was often not compact, being scattered among his neighbours' holdings, separated by only a strip of unploughed land. Growing winter root crops such as turnips was often out of the question, as then town's cattle were turned out onto the common to get what food they could from the waste.

As major reform became a necessity, the national *Board*

of Agriculture was formed in 1793, and the *General Act of Enclosure* [01] passed through Parliament in 1801. Previously any common land (or *"wastes"* as they were often called) had been enclosed by private acts or mutual consent. This new act made the often complicated process very much clearer, and also so much cheaper. Now it was accessible to almost every town and village throughout the country.

As these common lands were now essentially converted into private property. Each old, often scattered holding was carefully measured and reallocated into a more concentrated form, tithe or glebe (church) lands were also restructured. Any remaining land was often sold off at auction to the highest bidder. New boundary hedges and fences had to be set up at the cost of the farmer. If we look at the original 1809 *Workington Enclosure* (or Award) map, [02] it is interesting to note that the position and lines of the majority of these fences, are almost identical to those still seen in fields today.

So the town obtained the basis of a better system for arable farming. Although recorded as a major step forward in agriculture, the enclosures also had certain disadvantages. Small struggling farmers, with little capital, could often not afford the expense of enclosure. To get the best out of the land, more had to be put in, it needed marl (or manure) and often costly drainage. Many failed altogether, others simply took work as agricultural labourers, others left farming and sort work in the collieries.

The wealthy Lord of the Manor, John Christian Curwen was one farmer, who did not have to worry about a lack of capital. He of course, obtained a generous allocation of new farm land. Almost immediately he enclosed an area of seventy acres near Ellerbeck, and began *"paring and burning"* off the existing vegetation, principally gorse. Afterwards lime and ashes were spread over the entire area, before being ploughed in. His 1809 report to the *Workington Agricultural Society* [03] tells us that he *"commenced ploughing on 25 July 1809, with eight teams of oxen, which remain on the field from seven in the morning till six at night, having two hours rest at dinner"*. The land was then sown with it's first crop of wheat. The following year, after being deep ploughed and drained, it was planted with turnips. Accompanying the report was a costing of the work. It showed two men were employed to plough, for 2s.6d. (12½p) a day each; whilst the women who the cut grass to feed the oxen, were paid two shilling (10p) a day each. [04]

Christian Curwen concluded his report by emphasizing the general advantages of the enclosures. *"It will give great employment to a number of hands, increase the produce, and diminish the distance from which the town of Workington is supplied with the necessaries of life"*. Previously a great deal

[01] One obvious reason for the 1801 Enclosures Act was the events of the Napoleonic Wars. John Christian Curwen wrote how during this period *"the whole of Europe was distressed and many of the most fertile districts destroyed"*. As a result of the enclosures farming in Britain rapidly improved. So much so that when Napoleon blockaded Britain and attempted to starve the country into surrender. We were then capable of growing much of our food.
The commons of the old townships of Workington and Winscales were enclosed under an Act of Parliament, passed in March 1809. (amended in 1815) Whilst similar acts for Stainburn, Great and Little Clifton followed in 1812 and 1814 respectively. ■
[02] Hutchinson in his 1797 *History of Cumberland* tells us that perhaps 20% of the farm land (in the Parish of Workington) are *"Commons"*, used for grazing cattle and some sheep in the better drained areas.
[03] The *Workington Agricultural Society* was founded by John Christian Curwen in Oct 1805. When the rules of the society were formulated and Christian Curwen elected president. The society had *four districts Keswick, Wigton, Egremont and Cockermouth (which included Workington). The President's Reports were published annually from 1806-1814, and included a full list of members. One of it's most eminent subscribers was the Duke of Cumberland, appointed Patron in 1811.
* *The Isle of Man Agricultural Society also became part of the Workington Society, after it's formation in November 1806.*
[04] These figures point to a weekly wage (in 1809) for a male farm labourer of just 75p, with a female earning 60p. The working week consisted of six days, working nine to ten hours per day. ■

of Cumberland's grain had been expensively imported. Now he foresaw that with little *"waste left uninclosed"*, there would soon be a *"considerably quantity of grain to spare"*.

The earlier generations of the Curwen family, as Lords of the Manor, had always been the town's principle farmers. Despite some barley, corn, oats, and wheat being obviously grown on a small scale. Much of the land, was poor quality and only then really suitable for meadow and pasture. As a result, the family placed much more importance on breeding and raising of livestock Thomas Denton (in 1688) recorded that the Curwens *"breads yr largest cattle and sheep in all the county, worth £200 a year"*.

Some early historians suggest that the majority of cattle in Cumberland, were then principally all black; distant descendants of the whole-coloured cattle of the Celtic tribes. But it is difficult to accurately determine what breeds of cattle were then raised by prominent landowner Henry [iii] Curwen. There were no recognised breeds as today, cattle of many types was distributed all over Britain.

Around eighteen years before the enclosures, Christian Curwen had began his often radical and innovative approach to agriculture.[01] He had already began to reclaim some poor quality pasture land by ploughing, adding fertilizer and laying drainage. By 1802, he could now grow good crops of wheat, *"barley, potatoes and fine oats"* [02] on nearly 25% of his lands. Oats being an essential foodstuff for both his farm and colliery horses. By the year of the enclosures, he could boast that almost 85% of his land was already devoted to arable farming.

He also admitted that he had *"in consequence of his attendance on his parliamentary duties"*, the opportunity to closely study other agricultural practices all around Britain and on the continent. On his return to the town, he would test many aspects of this newly acquired knowledge. As well as spending three to four hours a day on his farm, he read extensively. No doubt upon his shelves of his treasured library at Workington Hall, was Arthur Young's famous *Annals of Agriculture*. [03] Henry Lonsdale recorded in his 1867 *Worthies of Cumberland*, that Christian Curwen, like his predecessors such as Young, was destined to *"set an enlightened example to a great body of English and Scottish agriculturists"*.

Trees were planted to provide shelter and warmth to his fields, *"by breaking and interrupting the force of the winds"*. He obtained samples of many different types of barley, wheat, mangels, turnips and swedes, and carried out carefully recorded trials. Several varieties of rye grass were also cultivated, until a good prime pasture for grazing stock was perfected. He also assessed the benefits of different types of

[01] Between at least 1782-8, Christian Curwen and his new wife Isabella Curwen had actually lived away from the estate, at Unerigg Hall (Maryport); while Workington Hall was being substantially renovated and improved. If we examine John Christian Curwen's original account books, now deposited at Whitehaven Record Office. We can deduce that he commenced a active interest in farming from around 1792. Previously the accounts suggest little (or no) activity. Certainly in these early years activity was also never really great. Some credence is added to this assumption, when we read in his 1812 *President's Report* to the *Workington Agricultural Society*, about his *"exertions of the last ten years"* upon his farm. ■
[02] William Hutchinson in his 1797 *History of Cumberland*, gives this description of the towns crops, further accounts exist in the 1811 *Presidents Report*. This report also includes a detailed analysis of what was grown (per acre), in each year from 1802-10, at Christian Curwen's Schoose and Moorclose farms. ■
[03] Arthur Young (1741-1820) was the distinguished agriculturalist and agricultural author. He like John Christian Curwen had travelled extensively throughout Europe. Appointed the first secretary of the Board of Agriculture, founded in 1793 (later to become the Ministry). As a contemporary of Christian Curwen, we know Young took an interest in the *Workington Agricultural Society* as he is often quoted and listed as a member. We know also that Christian Curwen attended many lectures at the Board of Agriculture. In 1770, Young had published an account of the agriculture, manufacturers and population of Cumberland & Westmorland. His famous *Annuals of Agriculture* were published from 1786-1804. It is quiet likely Christian Curwen modelled his own annual President's Reports, on Young's earlier writings. ■

feed, (such as turnips, linseed oil-cake and steamed chaff) for both his *"milch"* or dairy cattle and fattening his other stock. Setting up a quite innovative *"Chaff Steaming Apparatus"* at Schoose. [01] In further experiments, he feed carrots and steamed potatoes to his farm and colliery horses, instead of oats and to supplement their winter feed.

Around 1809, when a flock of Merino sheep was first brought over from Spain by Sir Joseph Banks. Christian Curwen wrote to the famous naturalist, asking to participate in his experiments. The fleece of the Merino produces a very fine, close-set silky wool. Considered much superior to the native sheep, then reared in Northern England. At the time over £1.5 million of this fine quality wool was imported annually into Great Britain. If the Merinos could be successfully bred and reared here at home, Christian Curwen commented that once again it would reduce our *"reliance upon foreign countries"*. Tests were considered almost a failure, until the Merinos were crossed with the native sheep. Later it was found that they were then able to survive well in our climate and the fleece was equal in quality to that produced in Spain. His notes also reveal how he carefully compared them to his existing South Down flock, and calculated the profit each produced on fleece, carcase, tallow etc.

Short-horned, Hertford, Sussex, Galloway, Glamorgan and Long-horned cattle were also selected from the best available stock. Over a twelve month period, they too were fed on controlled amounts of different dry and *"green"* foods; including straw, grass, clover, turnip and carrot tops. After twelve months, all the feed costs, and weight gains of each species were carefully assessed. The Short-horned cattle showing potentially 25% more profit than the next best.

This was the breed later adopted for Christian Curwen's dairy at Schoose Farm.[02] In 1810, he had 22 Short-horned cattle producing more milk than 35 Devon and Long-horned cows, had in the previous year. The farm accounts clearly show each Short-horned *"milch"* cow would consistently yield around 8600 pints (4887 litres) of milk each year. [03]

By 1812, Christian Curwen commented that his dairy at Schoose, was a *"complete"* success, nothing had *"afforded him equal gratification"*. He estimated that his *"better fed"* cows each produced upto 20% more milk, than others in urban areas such as London and Liverpool. He also received *"most heart felt pleasure"* by observing *"the benefit received by the community from a regular supply of milk"*. Being extremely conscious that *"good and wholesome"* milk, both greatly improved the health of his townspeople, and actually saved lives. In 1810, Christian Curwen noted that three years earlier, not a single *"milk cart was known in the town....they are now met in ever part of it"*.

In 1812, John Christian Curwen wrote that his dairy at Schoose, was a *"complete"* success, nothing had *"afforded him equal gratification"*.

[01] "Chaff" is the husk or straw waste left after the grain has been thrashed. Christian Curwen's Chaff Steamer was capable of steaming 24 stones (336 lbs) of chaff, in four hours using around 6 stones (84lbs) of coal for the boiler. ■
[02] Christian Curwen choice of Short-horned dairy cattle was no doubt influenced by Thomas Bates. As well as being a member of the *Workington Agricultural Society*, he also became the country's premier short-horned breeder. Establishing dairy breeds whose ancestors have become the foundation of some of today's best stock. ■
[13] In 1810, Christian Curwen sold his milk (directly to the public) for *"2d a quart"* the equivalent of less than ¾p per litre. Today (1998) we would expect to pay at least 39p per litre. ■

"Such is the change, within the space of three years, that, from there not being a milk cart known in the town, they are now met in every part of it."
John Christian Curwen (1810)

[01] John F. Curwen in his *History of the Ancient House of Curwen* records that Christian Curwen received two gold medals from the Society of Arts & Sciences, for his *"achievements in agriculture"*. The first (in 1807) was for feeding carrots to horses, as a substitute for oats. His second was for his successful dairy cattle feed experiments, mentioned above. ■
[02] The Luddites, active from 1811-16 originated in Nottingham. Although the riots spread through Yorkshire, Cheshire and Lancashire. There is no apparent evidence to suppose that the group was active locally or any machinery was wrecked. ■
[03] Christian Curwen's farming ideals are obviously reflected in the motto adopted by *Workington Agricultural Society* (founded in 1905) - *"The Prosperity & Security of Great Britain"*. ■
[04] In 1811, John Christian Curwen had around seventy farm and colliery horses. ■

Anxious that others should share his success, he addressed the *Society of Arts & Sciences* in London. Boldly telling them of the benefits he had achieved through *"adopting a different mode of feeding the milch cows"*. Distressed at the current mortality rate of people in the cities, particularly amongst children of the *"lesser"* classes. He urged others to make similar striking and important changes in their dairies. Inorder to provide a plentiful supply of milk, the *"prime necessity"* in every community.[01] He also invited anyone to visit and view his successful model dairy at Schoose.

On various types of ground, he tested oxen (first purchased in 1808) for pulling the plough. Recording their performance carefully and again closely analysing feed costs. He concluded they were *"as docile as horses"*, cheaper to feed and ploughed better than horses, except on really hard rough ground. Furthermore, the ox could be turned into meat when they became too old to work. Eventually, the horse would supersede the oxen by his greater speed, just as the tractor replaced the horse.

As the machine-recking *"Luddites"* protested that unemployment was caused by the increased introduction of machines. [02] Christian Curwen extolled the virtues of the machinery on his farm. He was passionate about new machines and *"human ingenuity"* involved in their design. Feeling that *"a nation should hail every attempt to lessen the labour of agriculture"*. The motives of his enthusiasm were not particularly directed to reducing his labour costs. He was more interested in ensuring sufficient home-grown produce could be cultivated, to make the country self-sufficient. Britain was at war again with France, and Napoleon was attempting to put a stranglehold on food imports. [03] At Schoose, he tested and employed many new machines and implements. These including his chaff and potato steamers, chaff and straw cutters, many types of plough, threshing and hay-making machines driven by horse and the wind, and a crushing-mill for producing bone meal.

He also believed in the application of science to agriculture, feeling a knowledge of even basic chemistry was likely *"to produce most beneficial results"*. Christian Curwen had attended several *Board of Agriculture* lectures given by the eminent chemist Humphry Davy; and freely adopted many of his observations. Particularly his recommendations on the different properties of manures and how best they should be applied. At Schoose during this period, a massive 2600 tons of home produced manure was distributed annually, over his land. This manure was a mixture of horse [04] and cow dung, and street rakings acquired from the town. He also experimented with collecting the cattle urine from his dairy, and spread it over his fields.

More importantly Christian Curwen, a real lover of agriculture, was totally unselfish with his knowledge and wisdom. His enthusiasm is so clearly evident in the extensive president's reports to the *Workington Agricultural Society.* Each was published annually, inorder that each member could learn from his successes (and his failures). He professed that *"the interests of agriculture were the interests of humanity"*. On 28 September 1810, in recognition of his services and *"as a mark of respect and esteem"*, the society presented Christian Curwen with a large engraved solid silver salver.

John Christian Curwen was also responsible for carefully planning and building much of Schoose farm. [01] Unlike other typical Georgian model farms attached to serve a large mansion house. Schoose was very much bigger, designed to be both a model experimental farm and a commercially viable business. Quality crops and stock had to be produced efficiently and sold at a profit. Schoose (also sometimes referred to as *Hall Farm*) was not really developed until at least 1795. It was certainly shown as only a very small cluster of buildings on Thomas White's 1783 landscaping plan, for the Workington Hall estate.

He later also built Cuckoo Arch, inorder to provide a easier route between Workington Hall and Schoose Farm. , This semi-circular arched bridge once spanned the main road to Stainburn (now the A66), a little east of the entrance to Stainburn School. Constructed from the same pale yellow stone as the Hall and St. John's Church, it became perhaps one of the most photographed structure in Workington. Several legends surround the arch, one quite foolishly suggesting it's origins to be Elizabethan, but clearly the bridge displayed obvious Georgian architectural features. (see photograph on page 104) It also does not appear on Thomas White's 1783 detailed plan of the Hall estate. Then the track appeared to simply run down an incline and then cross the main road on the same level, before climbing up the opposite bank towards Schoose.[02]

Between 1805-21, Christian Curwen allowed the *Workington Agricultural Society*, to use Schoose for their annual show. Sir Frederick Chance tells us it was *"unrivalled in character and extent"*. [03] It was certainly one of the earliest, if not the first such annual show in England. The first *Royal Agricultural Show* did not take place until July 1839, nearly thirty four years later. Upwards of eighty cash prizes, usually five guineas (£5.50) each were presented each year. Almost every aspect of farming was judged, from best stallion, foal, tup or heifer to the best shepherd, ploughman, drainage, turnips and flax. The best managed farm in the district recieved a prize of ten pounds.

[01] Schoose, still a working farm, is located off the top of High Street, just before Castle Gardens. Many of the original buildings, erected by Christian Curwen still exist, including the tower of his windmill and the castellated gatehouse to the farmyard. Today (1998) it is worked by the Bowe family, who began farming here in 1934. In 1997, they purchased Schoose from the Curwen family. ■

[02] Cuckoo Arch was located around 155 metres from the entrance to Stainburn School. This once impressive landmark also became something of a status symbol for the Curwen family, reminding those approaching the town of their importance. With the rapid increase in traffic, the narrow opening of the bridge eventually became something of a hazard. It was demolished in 1931, being blown up on a quiet sunday morning. Today, it's site can still clearly be identified by the remains of the stone bridge support, on the north side of the road. A closer look will reveal much more of this end of the arch, now obscured by the undergrowth. ■

[03] Henry Lonsdale records the events of the first meeting of the *Workington Agricultural Show* in his 1931 book *Some Notable Cumbrians*. Held in October 1805, it occupied two days. On the first day was the show, followed by a dinner (for 460 people) and grand ball, hosted by Isabella Curwen (John Christian Curwen's wife). Amongst the honoured guests were the Dukes of Norfolk and Bedford, Bishop Llandaff and Sir John Sinclair. On the second day, at the Assembly Rooms (in Portland Square) Christian Curwen read the first of his *President's Reports*, later to become an essential feature of future shows. The Duke of Bedford is said to have been so impressed with Schoose farm, that he later copied many of Christian Curwen's ideas; and erected a similar (but larger) model farm. Staffed with Cumbrian farmers and ploughmen. ■

One of the obvious advantages of having a farm quite close to the town, allowed Christian Curwen to easily *"muster"* (without giving extra wages), several hundred people for the harvest or hay-making. This workforce being usually roused by the bellman or town-crier, calling out *"Shearers for the Squire"*. Generally, these *"shearers"* would cut between 30 to 40 acres each day. The wheat was then stacked to dry, in around 50 *"stooks"* per acre, dotted around the field. [01] Then of course the crop was cut entirely by hand with only a sickle or scythe.

After the harvest was *"brought home"* or got in. It was usual for a celebration at Schoose Farm. Christian Curwen tells us that it was attended by *"all my work people"*, upwards of three hundred of both sexes, spent a few hours in *"great festivity and good humour; rejoicing the labours of harvest were concluded"*. [02] His later comments are quite enlightening, and portray quite a delightful scene of the celebrations. *"What can be more gratifying than to contemplate joy, and light-heartedness widely diffused - Independent of the advantages of education,.......the children of the very poorest people are taught to dance. The moment the music is heard, the fascination becomes general, the hours pass gaily on"*

As many older readers will recall, local casual workers were also employed to harvest the potato crop. The traditional time for *"Tattie picken"* being the first weeks in October. The farm accounts of 1809-12 record upto almost 2000 stones (28000 lbs) of potatoes, were generally picked per acre at Schoose. Each year around fifty acres of potatoes were cultivated and produced an estimated income of around £800. However, rather than all being sold at market, a large proportion were stored and later steamed for cattle and horse feed. Potatoes also then formed the basis of the diet of many poorer townspeople. With their meagre incomes, few could actually afford meat or anything more substantial. Occasionally, when there was a shortage of potatoes in the town's market. Christian Curwen would make available sufficient supplies, so his townspeople did not suffer and starve. He described this as affording *"a most salutary relief"* to the poor. [03]

But when a really poor harvest resulted in a big shortage of potatoes in the town, even his stocks could have been quickly eroded. Anxious that it was essential to retain at least some, to feed his cattle and work horses. He would often wisely sell turnips instead, at *"2d a stone"* (0.13p/kg), from the Hall yard. This he hoped would lessen the demand for his valuable potatoes, keep his horses working and still provide a cheap food for the poor.

It is said that John Christian Curwen earned the reward of being called the *"Father of Cumberalnd Agriculture"*. Cer-

[01] The actual size of a *"stook"* (or stack) of cut wheat or any other crop is a little difficult to determine, no accurate measure appears to exist. It is thought to have weighted around 60 pounds (or 27 kg). Another measure was the *"bushel"*, although its size generally varied depending on the region and often what type of crop was being measured. Locally (in 1855), a bushel of wheat weighed 14 stones (or 89 kg), a bushel of oats 9 stones (57 kg) and barley 12 stones (76 kg). ■
[02] The 1809 Curwen farming accounts show the harvest (from Schoose and Moorclose - a total of around 260 acres) was nearly 14000 stooks of wheat. This grain being sold for around £5200.
[03] In May 1812, Christian Curwen recorded that he had sent *"900 stones"* (27775 kg) of potatoes (each week) to the Workington market, for the last nine weeks; as there was *"a failure of supply"*. Potatoes then sold for *"5d per stone"* (0.32p per kg). John Bowe the present farmer at Schoose, cultivates approx 30 acres of potatoes, and sells them for around £1.20 per tonne (or 12p/kg). At the supermarket, one would expect to pay at least 30p/kg for potatoes. ■

tainly, his strong impetus and good farming set a wonderful example not just to our county farmers, but to many others throughout Britain. Without question his detailed reports for the *Workington Agricultural Society*, were an excellent chronicle of agricultural progress, almost unique in their length and detail. John Christian Curwen stands tall amongst other distinguished agriculturists, including the Duke of Bedford, Arthur Young, Sir John Sinclair (of Edinburgh) and Thomas Coke (of Holkham in Norfolk). All of which are listed as members of the society, and are known to have attended the first *Workington Agricultural Show*, in October 1805.

As Christian Curwen advanced in age, he can be forgiven for allowing his agricultural activities at Schoose, to fall into sad decline. After November 1814, he didn't issued another comprehensive President's report, and the last Agricultural Show at Workington took place in 1821. In August 1826, he was to sell, without reserve, all his valuable stock of short-horns, for just a fraction of their real worth. Today, apart from Christian Curwen's extensive agricultural writings, the existing fine stone buildings at Schoose Farm, remain as the only real monument to our *"Father of Cumberland Agriculture"*.

ABOVE - logo of the *Workington & District Agricultural Society*, reformed in 1946. Sadly it no longer exists. ■

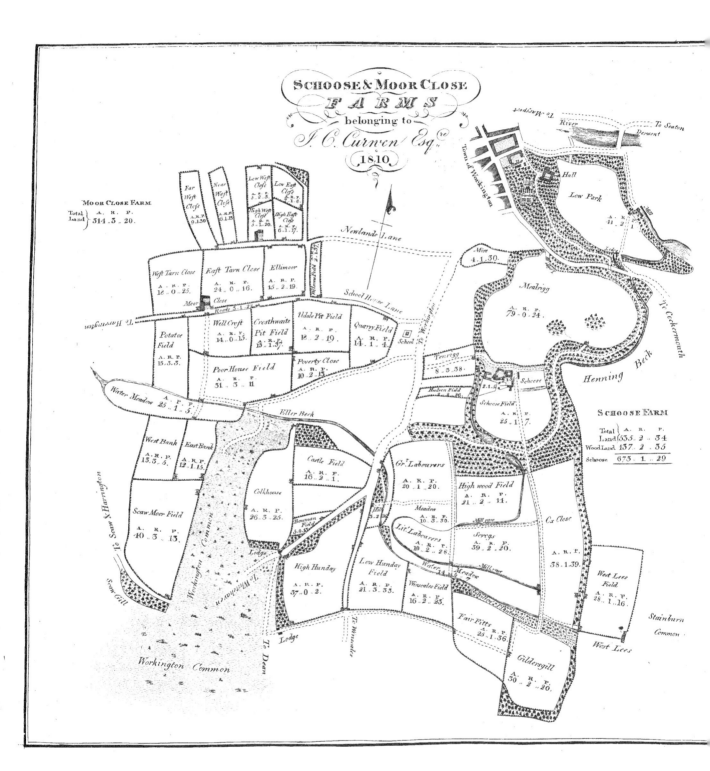

SCHOOSE & MOOR CLOSE
FARMS
belonging to
J. C. Curwen Esq.re
1810

MOOR CLOSE FARM
Total Land } A. R. P. 314 . 3 . 20.

Far West Close A. R. P. 9 . 1 . 36
Near West Close A. R. P. 6 . 1 . 15
Low West Close A. R. P. 5 . 2 . 3
Low East Close A. R. P. 2 . 1 . 6
High West Close A. R. P. 5 . 1 . 20
High East Close A. R. P. 6 . 1 . 17

West Tarn Close A. R. P. 18 . 0 . 25
East Tarn Close A. R. P. 24 . 0 . 16
Ellinoor A. R. P. 15 . 2 . 19

Moor Close
Road 5 . 1 . 22

To Harrington

Potatoe Field A. R. P. 15 . 3 . 3.
Well Croft A. R. P. 14 . 0 . 15
Cresthwaite Pit Field A. R. P. 13 . 1 . 37.
Udale Pit Field A. R. P. 18 . 2 . 19
Quarry Field A. R. P. 14 . 1 . 4.

Poor House Field A. R. P. 51 . 3 . 11
Poverty Close A. R. P. 10 . 2 . 13

Newlands Lane
School House Lane

School To Workington

Water Meadow 25 . 1 . 5.
Eller Beck

West Bank A. R. P. 13 . 3 . 6.
East Bank A. R. P. 12 . 1 . 13

To Scaw & Harrington

Scaw Moor Field A. R. P. 40 . 3 . 13

Workington Common

Scaw Gill

Castle Field A. R. P. 16 . 2 . 1.
Cokhouse A. R. P. 26 . 3 . 25
Bowman Field 5 . 0 . 39

Lodge

High Hunday A. R. P. 37 . 0 . 2.

To Dean
Lodge
To Winscales

Low Hunday Field A. R. P. 21 . 3 . 33.
Winscales Field A. R. P. 16 . 2 . 25.

Gr.t Labourers A. R. P. 20 . 1 . 20.
Meadow A. R. P. 10 . 3 . 30.
Lit.t Labourers A. R. P. 10 . 2 . 28
Water 14 Meadow

High wood Field A. R. P. 21 . 2 . 11.

Scroggs A. R. P. 59 . 2 . 20.
Mill race
Mill race

Ox Close A. R. P. 38 . 1 . 39.

Fair Fitts A. R. P. 25 . 1 . 36.

Gildersgill A. R. P. 30 . 2 . 20.

West Lees Field A. R. P. 28 . 1 . 16.

West Lees

Stainburn Common

Town of Workington

To Maryport
River
To Seaton
Derwent

Hall
Low Park A. R. P. 41 . 1 . 1
Lodge

To Cockermouth

Mire 4 . 1 . 30.
Mealrigg A. R. P. 79 . 0 . 24.

Henning Beck

Tenrigg 8 . 3 . 38.
Huden Field 26
Schoose 2 . 1 . 5

Schoose Field A. R. P. 25 . 1 . 7.

SCHOOSE FARM
Total Land 535 . 2 . 54
Wood Land 137 . 2 . 35
Schoose 673 . 1 . 29

CHAPTER FOURTEEN

EDUCATION - SCHOOLS & LIBRARIES

IN Sir Patricius Curwen's will, made just a few days before his death in December 1664, he bequeathed £10 towards the erection of a school-house, in the parish of Workington; *"in such a convenient place as his wife and executrix should think fit".* He also left the annual sum of £6.6s.8d to pay the *"schoolmaster or schoolmasters as should be appointed and elected by the ministers of Workington and Harrington."*

Not long after, it appears this school was erected, by his executors, *"upon part of the wastes* [01] *adjoining the town of Workington".* Unlike today, it was not compulsory for any child to attend school. There was also no established standard curriculum in any schools. It was the schoolmaster who made the decisive decisions on what and how lessons were taught. Those who did attend would only have received a very basic level of education; usually adapted and developed to meet the needs of the local agricultural based economy.

Also included here was a *Grammar School* [02], kept by a master; who received his appointment and salary from the Curwen family. Unlike the more famous and established grammar schools of St. Bees, Carlisle and Hawkshead. It was likely to have been simply an extension of the present school. Here the brighter pupil could receive a more classical based education, perhaps for university entry. He was also likely to have been taught by the same schoolmaster, in the same classroom.

The site of the school building was on High Street, almost opposite the Travellers Rest. (see plan on previous page) Thomas [v] Curwen in his will, dated 18th December 1672, also *"granted and bequeathed"* for a term of 21 years after his death, the *"three closes or inclosures known as Colker Close, Dobby Miller's Close and Moor-close....within the fields of Workington",* for the better encouragement of the schoolmaster of his late brother's school.

Actually, the subsequent schoolmasters enjoyed possession of these *"three closes"* for far longer than the initial 21 years. It was 1724 when *Galloping Harry* Henry [iii] Curwen took back the land for the family. Court action followed by the ministers and churchwardens of Workington. Who felt they should hold title, for the benefit of their school's charity. Before the case was heard, Henry Curwen was to die, and the suit was never revived.

"Train up a child in the way he should go, and when he is old he will not depart from it"
John Christian Curwen (1808)

[01] *wastes* - was generally another word for the common lands. The common at Workington were enclosed under an Act of Parliament in 1809. (see chapter thirteen) ■
[02] The term *Grammar School* was used to describe a certain type of school, which taught the more established classical and mathematical subjects, principally to prepare pupils for university entry. ■

The schoolmasters continued to hold the land, totalling about 70 acres, up until 1798. Then Joseph Winder,[01] the present schoolmaster, leased the lands, to John Christian Curwen, the then owner of the Workington estate, for the yearly rent of £42. This arrangement continued until the schoolmaster's death in 1803. Then John Christian Curwen appears to have discovered that he was likely to own the land afterall. He assumed full possession again.

However, he did not let the school suffer, for he appointed Rev. Anthony Dalzell [02] as the new schoolmaster, giving him a annual salary of Ten guineas (£10.50). Henry Gladders was also thought to have been employed to assist Rev. Dalzell. His lengthy *President's Reports* to the *Workington Agricultural Society* reveal how Christian Curwen farmed Moorclose lands, until at least October 1812. Then they were rented off, inorder that Christian Curwen could concentrate his activities at Schoose.

In 1808, the education methods in the school were restyled, with the help of Mr. Christian Curwen. Writing in 1809, he commented *"I view with more internal satisfaction the share I have had in the establishment of schools upon Dr. Bell and Mr Lancaster's plan, than anything else I have undertaken."* [03] Around 1789, the basics of this system of education were developed by Dr. Andrew Bell (1753-1832); whilst he was the superintendent of the *Madras Male Orphan Asylum* in India. After his return to this country in 1797, the educationalist widely published his method. It advocated a scheme of national education on *"general Christian principles"*, included technical schools and pioneered the use of pupil teachers. Lakes poet William Wordsworth wrote of the system in several of his letters and noted dramatic improvements in his own son's education (Thomas Wordsworth), when his schoolmaster had adopted Bell's system. Wordsworth felt the *"main spring"* of this form of tuition, was each pupil *"cultivated the habit of valuing knowledge for its own sake and for the good that may and ought to come out of it, the unmixed pure good"*.

Dr. Bell's methods also received valued support from many other prominent literary figures, including Samuel Taylor Coleridge and Robert Southey. Southey had an extravagant belief in him, and wrote Bell's biography. Around 1803, James Lancaster (1775-1838) a Quaker, applied Bell's methods and later amended the system for the better. His basically *"undenominational"* tuition, roused some fears and apprehension from the Tory party and Anglican Church. But the Whig party saw it as a guarantee of more religious liberty. This may explain why John Christian Curwen appeared so fervently in support of the

"I have read Dr. Bell's book upon education.....it is a most interesting work and entitles him to the fervent gratitude of all good men" **William Wordsworth** 1808.

[01] James Winder (1753-1803) was the son of John Winder, of Burnyeat Place, Dean. Educated at St. Bees school. Nominated schoolmaster at Workington on 24th August 1778. Died 23rd May 1803. ■
[02] Rev. Anthony Dalzell was the son of Thomas Dalzell. He is shown as perpetual curate of Clifton, in the Parson & White's 1829 *Directory*. ■
[03] John Christian Curwen refers here to schools in both Workington and at Douglas, Isle of Man. In 1809, there was thought to be around three hundred children on the Workington school roll. Two other school's on Bell's system, admitting pupils from 6 yrs old, were opened in Whitehaven around December 1813. ■

revised system for his Workington school.

Christian Curwen also united the school with his experimental farm at Schoose, believing that *"whilst it promotes my agricultural objects, it makes the system of education more complete. The wages so earned are paid in the presence of the whole school. Each boy receives what is due to him; and none are ever suffered to work, whose general conduct is not good."*

He employed *"those of my school, who were of a proper age"* to do several tasks. *As well as the annual October potato picking, children were asked to extirpate and pull up every weed from amongst the clover in each field, soon after the grain was cut."* Christian Curwen believed they were better fitted for this work than adults, *"Stooping is to them attended with no pain or difficulty - to grown persons it is very irksome".*

No child was allowed to work who misbehaved, by paying them for their efforts, he rewarded both their hard work and their good conduct. A not so obvious additional benefit, was each pupil could now make some contribution to their parents, sometimes very meagre income. If nothing else, the child *"might be taught to earn sufficient to pay for their learning".* Originally, when the school was first established it appears that the children's tuition was free, being funded principally by the Curwen family. However, Bishop Gastrell's *Notitia* of 1714-1725 shows parents had since been asked to contribute six old pence (2½p) per quarter for each child. In 1829, this had increased to 1d-1½d. per week for each scholar, with books being provided at the cost of the Curwen family.[01]

In 1813, John Christian Curwen moved the school to a room in Portland Square and demolished the old school-room. He then began to exploit the coal reserves under the school and in the adjoining area. Again the question of title to what was now commonly referred to as the Workington school lands, resulted in legal action. It later was found that *"the lands could not be recovered for the use of the school".* Furthermore, the title to the actual ground where the school stood had never formally been conveyed to the school trustees, and therefore remained the property of the Lord of the Manor.

By 1829, Parson & White recorded the school was now known as the *National School*. It then had around 250 pupils, still instructed on Dr. Bell's system. All expences of this large seminary were still being paid by the Curwens, Mr H. P. Gladders was the schoolmaster, assisted by Mrs. Ann Wear. By 1847, the school roll had risen to about 200 boys and nearly 100 girls. Mrs. Ann Wear was still teaching at the school, whilst Robert Thompson was the schoolmaster.

As well as the annual October potato picking, children were asked to "extirpate" and pull up every weed from amongst the clover in each field

[01] Samuel Jefferson in 1842, recorded that the fees for John Christian Curwen's *Lancastrian School* in the town were still this amount. Then there was said to be about 194 boys and 86 girls on the roll. ■

In December 1831, A new school was opened on Guard Street, then simply known as the *"Guards"*. The original building was not as substantial as some older readers will recall. (see sketch below) Originally, the school consisted on just the central block (shown dotted). Before 1900, it was extended in both directions, up to the corner of Bank Road and down towards Harrington Road. Sometime before 1923, a further block was also added on the Harrington Road corner. Whellan in 1860 described it as a *"good and substantial stone building, two stories high"*.

On the first floor was the Infants school, with an average attendance in 1860, of 70 pupils. It was perpetually endowed by Thomas Wilson (b.1760) who had also paid for the first building to be erected. [01] He established a trust fund of £500, the interest from which was payable half-yearly to the teacher; together with the interest of a further £100, for any necessary repairs to the building. The School of Industry also shared the premises. Whellan tells us it was limited to twenty pupils, and supported by the ladies of the town, having its object *"the inculcation of habits of industry in young females, so as to make them notable housekeepers and good Christians"*

Because of its founder the school is often referred to as *Wilson School*. Above its main entrance doors was a stone plaque with the following inscription. *"These Schools for the Education of the Children of the Poor in Religious and Useful Knowledge, were erected from the bounty of a kind Providence, by Thomas Wilson, 1831"*

[01] Thomas Wilson was born in London in 1760. The 1814 St. Michael's Vestry minutes lists his occupation as a *"wine merchant"*. By 1851, the town census shows he was retired and lived in Christian Street, along with his son John Wilson (b.1791), a Doctor. ∎

BELOW - a sketch of the front elevation of Guard Street School, first opened in December 1831. The central block (shown dotted) is the original school, the remainder are later additions. The stone plaque referred to in the text right, can be seen above the entrance doors, of this older block.

As the towns population had increased dramatically, In January 1859, two new *"Church of England Schools"* were proposed (often also referred to as the *Free Schools)*. The first to open (on 31 March 1860) was *St. Johns School*, on the east side of the upper section of John Street. Today, the site is occupied by St. John's Shopping Precinct. It's first pupils attended on 9 April 1860, when upwards of 100 pupils enrolled. The building was originally divided into two separate areas for boys and girls.

St. Michaels School on Cooke Lane (later Station Road), the other *Church of England School*, was opened quite soon after. Today, we can still see the original school building on the corner of Station Road and Falcon Place. It too was also once segregated for boys and girls. Then of course the Infants School building, a little further down towards the station, simply didn't exist.

In addition, many of the less prosperous townspeople once relied very much on the town's Sunday Schools to provide elementary education for their children. One of the earliest was established by the Wesleyan Methodist Church in 1810, and was dedicated to providing a basic *"secular"* education. The level of attendance at the Workington's Sunday Schools, is revealed in details of a procession through the town, to celebrate the marriage of Edward VII in March 1863. Then there was seven active Sunday Schools, with a total of 1052 pupils and 112 teachers. (see list to right) They all cheerfully marched together through the streets bearing flags, banners, flowers etc.

Numerous smaller private schools also existed throughout the town. Where teachers, many working in their own homes, taught the brighter pupils of the more weathly townspeople. Often the children also boarded with their tutor. Their advertisments in the local newspapers, suggest they all followed a more *"classical and mathematical"* form of education. As far back as 1790, Mrs M. Barker in the town was charging £14.14s.0d (£14.70) for *"boarders"* per quarter, and 3s for *"day scholars"*.

Workington Sunday Schools
(March 1863)

Number of pupils in each school, with the number of teachers in brackets.

Presbyterian Church	110	(15)
Prim. Methodists	130	(20)
Congregational	116	(12)
Wes. Methodists	160	(28)
Roman Catholics	114	(6)
St. John's Church	162	(18)
St. Michael's Church	260	(13)

ABOVE - Sketch of the datestone from the old St. Johns School. ∎

WORKINGTON'S LIBRARIES

JOHN Martin in his research of the town's libraries, identified that the *"earliest library of any importance, to which the public had some access"* was that attached to the nondenominational *Sunday School*. Around 1794, it was established by private subscription, and is thought to have met in the Assembly rooms, in Portland Square.[01] Despite meeting on a Sunday, they were not restricted to religious teachings. They also attempted to give some basic instruction to those unable to afford normal weekday school. In addition they catered for children, who by sheer necessity, had to work during the week, inorder to supplement their families meagre income.

Mr Martin also noted that the school, made up of several groups (perhaps segregated not just into boys or girls, nor by age, but also by their religion) built up a substantial library of some 970 *"distinct publications"*. Unfortunately, when it closed in 1806, the library was broken up. Later in 1817, the ladies of the Guard Street *School of Industry,* attempted to revise this Sunday School system, and another similar library was established.

In 1810, a News-room was opened in Portland Square. Here subscribers could visit and read a selection of both national and local newspapers. This venture was evidently successful for it was still in operation in 1860. Then the membership fee was 25 shillings (now £1.25) per annum.

By the middle of the nineteenth century, the industrial revolution had brought major changes and advancement in science and technology. Even those with little formal education, were now anxious to acquire new knowledge. Around 1847, the *Mechanics Institute* was established in the town. It then occupied much of the Savings Bank building in Pow Street.[02] On the ground floor was space for a library and reading room, a news room, and small museum. Whilst there was large lecture hall facilities, on the first floor. [03]

Whellan in 1860, tells us that the Mechanics Institute library then had 1700 volumes. Later, Sergeant C. Hall's 1883 town history paints a far less rosy picture. He felt the library was quite neglected by the Institutes commitee, commenting on it's *"empty book shelves"*. He also added that the Institute's *"objects are the diffusion of knowledge in literature and the arts, and sciences. This it accomplishes by means of two billiard tables, a chess board,a box of dominoes, a collection of spar and the Shipping Gazette".* It is now difficult to confirm if Hall's criticism was really justified or not.

[01] The Assembly rooms were located in the south east corner of Portland Square, facing north. (see page 125) ■

[02] The Workington Savings Bank was established in 1828. It was situated in a substantial building (erected in 1844) on the south side of Pow Street, set back from the pavement (almost opposite where the Marks and Spencer store now stands). Nikolaus Pevsner (in 1967) gave us the following description of the building *"three bays, stuccoed, with pediment all across, pairs of angle pilasters and a porch of four thin unfluted Ionic columns".* In 1859 the bank had 672 depositors and funds totalling over £22054. Then there were six trustees and around twenty-six directors. Accountant Joseph Tordiff Fell, the son of prominent shipbuilder Jonathan Fell, was for many years the secretary of the bank. He was also a churchwarden at St. Michael's Church, his elaborate and precise *"copperplate"* handwriting often appearing in the Vestry minutes. The bank was later to be absorbed into Trustees Savings Bank. ■

[03] By 1859, the Mechanics Institute had a membership of around 300. The annual subscription for ordinary members (including females) was then five shillings (25p), for honorary members ten shillings (50p) and for life membership £5. ■

The Wesleyan Methodist Church also established a *"lending library"*. Although little further is know of dates and the range or scope of the books stocked, access was however free of charge. It may not have commenced until the new South William Street Church was built in 1840. Some believe it's was started only when its School rooms were built in 1883. (see page 87-88)

In 1845, a *"Parochial"* (or parish) library was also set up in the Guard Street school building. There were also other subscription libraries established in the town from around 1830. The advantages of such a library were that for an annual fee, subscribers had access to numerous books at low cost. *"The Gentleman's Library"* was one such early subscription library. It was housed on Dickinson's premises in Wilson Street. The annual membership fee was twelve shillings (60p). John Martin noted another subscription library, which he calls a *"more philanthropic"* than others. It was ran by Bertha Gate, from her home in Christian Street. Although a annual membership fee was charged, Mrs. Gate is thought to have also allowed free access to the poorer reader.

As reading became increasingly commonplace, another type of library sprung up. It was the *"circulating library"*, generally ran as a commercial venture, being usually operated by a printer and bookseller. Now books could be hired for a period of time, without the need to pay a members subscription fee. In Nov 1777, one of the town's first such libraries was commenced by William Eckford. He was a bookseller and stationer, who had just opened a shop in Portland Square. Volumes from his selection of *"modern and entertaining books for ladies and gents"*, could be borrowed for 2d (1p) per book per week. Alternatively, readers could chose to pay Ten shillings (50p) per annum.

Despite the first *Public Libraries Act* of 1850, it was forty years later, before Workington got it's first free public library. This was not through the Local Board (later the Borough Council) neglecting their duties or responsibilities. The act had then, only allowed a town with a population of greater than 10000 people, to increase its rates to pay for a new public library. Workington's population was then only around 6200, and the provisions of the 1850 act could simply not be applied. In April 1890, when town eventually got a public library, it acquired the stock and shelving of the Mechanics Institute, and rented the same premises above the Savings Bank.

Despite the first *Public Libraries Act* of 1850, it was forty years later, before Workington got it's first free public library.

CHAPTER FIFTEEN

ROADS & EARLY RAILWAYS

BEFORE the arrival of the railways in the nineteenth cen tury, Workington lay in a remote corner of the country. Anyone travelling wanting to reach the town from any distance, had a long journey and needed to negotiate poor quality roads. Few were little more than pot-holed, muddy tracks, which became almost impassable in bad weather. Anyone trying to reach the town did so usually by ship, and virtually everything was brought in and out of the area, through the port.

Things did improve with the *General Turnpike Act* of 1773. This system granted franchises to local companies and individuals, for the maintenance of public roads; allowing them to receive tolls, from those who travelled on the roads. A group of local trustees oversaw the maintenance of the road and regulated the tolls. Two such turnpike roads ran into the town. One led from Cockermouth to Workington, entering the town through what was known as Stainburn Gate. The other road, very much longer, ran from Cockermouth to Maryport, via Northside road and Siddick. Travellers then entered the town across the bridge over the River Derwent at the foot of Calva Brow.

From 1840, despite improvements in road construction generally, with the work of engineers Thomas Telford and John Loudon McAdam. The turnpike road system was gradually becoming less profitable for it's operators. Now having to compete with the new railway being laid down.

The *Whitehaven Junction Railway Company* (WJR) built the first railway to run to Workington. Incorporated by an Act of Parliament on the 30th June 1844. It's track ran from Whitehaven; north through the town and then onto Maryport (connecting with the *Maryport & Carlisle Railway*); and following virtually the same route as today's west coast line. Eventually, a further junction was also made just north of Workington, with the *Cockermouth & Workington Railway*; and the line continued further south (from Whitehaven), with the addition of the *Whitehaven & Furness Junction Railway*.

The arrival of the railways in West Cumberland, heralded a period of rapid growth and well-being to Workington and it's port. Locally available coal and iron ore could now be easily transported to the town's blast furnaces or harbour for export. Finished products such as the much sort after Bessemer pig iron, could also be sent the length and breath

"I have no doubt that in a few years, Railways will be general throughout the length and breath of the land"
John Waite
Workington's Customs Officer
(Jan 1838)

of the country, over an ever increasing railway network. As more new railways opened nationwide, so the town's economy also benefited, for they too consumed massive quantities of iron and steel in their construction and coal to operate them.

Those who initially promoted this first line, and became directors of the new company, all had large interests in the area's mines and ironworks. Without their forethought and that of those who later also invested vast sums in other local railway companies, the town would never have realised it's periods of prosperity.

It was over eighteen months, before the first section of the WJR, running between Workington and Maryport, was officially opened on 19 January 1846, By the following May, the line was completed as far south as Harrington. Initially, in order to reduce construction costs the company laid down only a single track. But by 1860, encouraged by the erection of six new blast furnaces upon Oldside [01] and anticipating a rapid increase in iron-ore traffic, the railway company felt justified in doubling up the line. It is thought that the total cost of the additional track was around £45000, being first opened to traffic on 18 March 1861.

The town's first railway station was built very close to the site of today's station. (see plan overleaf) It was quiet a basic single storey timber building of just three rooms, with a small narrow platform to the east side of the line. (see sketch overleaf) On the opposite side of the tracks there was only a small simple timber open shelter (similar in appearance to today's bus shelter) to protect the waiting passengers from the elements. Thomas Bulmer said no one would have called it a *"fine specimen of railway architecture"*; and despite a rapid rise in the town's population and rail passenger traffic, the station remained unchanged for around forty years. By then it's facilities were totally inadequate and it was in a dreadful state of repair, being subjected to almost constant ridicule in the local press. It was finally replaced by the present yellow brick station buildings in 1886.

Interestingly in 1856, the fastest passenger train between Workington and Whitehaven, then of course drawn by steam, took 22 minutes. The fastest of today's diesel trains cover the same journey in about seventeen minutes, but others are much slower. There were then also six return weekday trains between Whitehaven and Carlisle, and two each Sunday. At present, there are fifteen weekday journeys and six Sunday services.

The *Cockermouth and Workington Railway* (C&WR) was incorporated by an Act of Parliament on the 21 July 1845, just over twelve months after the WJR. It's track ran from Cockermouth into the town where it joined the WJR line, just north of its bridge over the Derwent. [02]   Opened on

George Stephenson
(1781-1848)

This prominent civil engineer was appointed as consultant for the *Whitehaven Junction Railway* (WJR). Famous for building the world's first public railway, the *Stockton and Darlington Rwy.* (opened 1825). Also for winning contest to design best steam engine with his locomotive *Rocket* (1829). He undertook consultant work on the WJR and many other British and foreign railways, after retiring from active practice in 1840. Claimed to have also devised the miner' s safety lamp, before Sir Humphry Davy (1815). ■

[01] Previously there were only four blast furnaces at the Workington Haematite Ironworks site. By 1860 two more were under construction, to meet the rapid demand for Bessemer pig iron. Whilst another four additional furnaces were also being built at the new plant of the West Cumberland Haematite Ironworks. (see chapter twelve) ■
[02] See photograph of Workington Junction Railway's bridge over the Derwent on page 105. ■

210

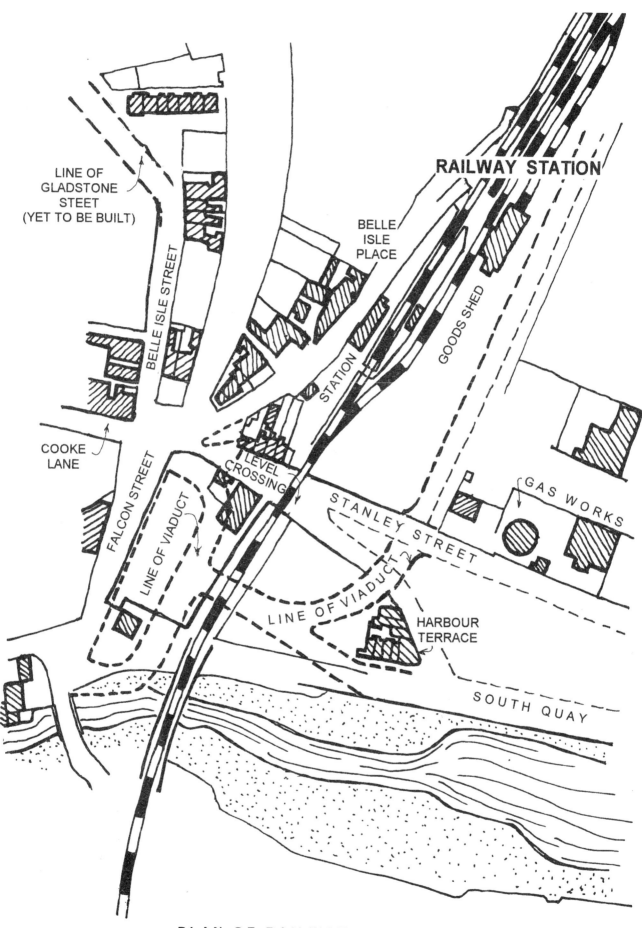

LINE OF GLADSTONE STEET (YET TO BE BUILT)

BELLE ISLE STREET

BELLE ISLE PLACE

RAILWAY STATION

GOODS SHED

COOKE LANE

FALCON STREET

LINE OF VIADUCT

STATION

LEVEL CROSSING

STANLEY STREET

GAS WORKS

LINE OF VIADUCT

HARBOUR TERRACE

SOUTH QUAY

PLAN OF RAILWAY STATION (c.1865)

211

28th April, 1847, it's total length was eight and half miles, following a picturesque route almost along the banks of the River Derwent.   After leaving Workington, along it's north bank; there were stations at Workington Bridge, Camerton, Broughton Cross, Brigham and Cockermouth, where the line terminated.[01]   In August 1846, another Act of Parliament was obtained to extend the railway further east, to Keswick. This was then extended eastward with the addition of the Cockermouth, Keswick & Penrith Railway.

Although during 1848, the C&WR obtained authority to run passenger trains to and from Workington station. The majority of it's early revenue came from transporting the coal produced from the collieries at Clifton.   In the mid 1850's it is recorded that around 120 wagons of coal were hauled daily, the short distance down to Workington.[02]   Like the WJR, only a single track had initially been laid.   As revenues rose a further Bill was submitted to Parliament in November 1862, to authorise the widening of the track.   In addition it was also necessary to replace some of the smaller bridges, with more permanent structures, as they were initially built principally of timber.

Both the WJR and the C&WR were amalgamated in the summer of 1866, and worked thereafter by the London North Western Railway Co.   The last goods trains ran on the C&WR line in June 1964, with the final passenger train in April 1966. Now with the track lifted and long ago removed, little remains to remind us of this railway.   There is still the odd embankment, cutting or piece of bridge structure, but much of the trackbed has disappeared under the A66 road to Cockermouth.

[01] In 1856, the passenger train journey time between Cockermouth and Workington was around 41 minutes. Then there was four return weekday trains and two each Sunday.■
[02] The bulk of this coal was then mined at the Lowther, Harry Gill, Crossbarrow and Clifton pits.   Each railway wagon contained approx. 55 cwt (2.8 tonnes). ■

BELOW - sketch of the town's first railway station, built very close to the site of today's station. (see plan left)   It was quiet a basic single storey timber building of just three rooms, with a small narrow platform to the east side of the line.   It was replaced with the present buildings in 1886. ■

CHAPTER SIXTEEN

RIVER DERWENT & THE CLOFFOLKS

WE can trace the source of the River Derwent almost to the heart of the Lake District. For it begins with rain falling upon the summit of Great Gable, over 2900 feet above the sea level. As it drains from the eastern slopes of one of England's highest mountains, towards the picturesque Styhead Tarn, so begins a journey of around 35 miles before it finally reaches the sea. Whilst it winds its way through Derwentwater and Bassenthwaite, past Cockermouth onwards towards the town, it is also fed by the rivers Cocker, Marron and numerous other smaller tributaries. The River Derwent eventually receives water from upwards of 210 square miles of surrounding West Cumbrian countryside.

In ancient times before the sea level dropped (see chapter one) it is likely that small boats could easily navigate several miles inland along the river to at least Camerton. This is clearly evident if we examine the levels of the existing broad Derwent floodplain, consisting principally of sedimentary material that the river itself has deposited.

The name *Derwent* is thought to have been derived from the Old British *"Derventio"*, a name formed from "derwá", meaning oak. Perhaps the earliest mention of the river is in the writing of eighth century religious historian, the Venerable Bede. When he mentions Saint Cuthbert's visit to the *"Deruventionis fluuii"*.

The use of water-power dates from ancient Greece and Rome, where wooden waterwheels were used for the milling of corn. For almost a thousand years, and perhaps even longer, the River Derwent has also acted as a natural source of power. During the Middle Ages, Workington must have possessed at least a couple of water driven mills, one of the earliest being that granted to the monks of St. Mary's York, by Ketel, around 1125. It's exact location is now unclear, but we believe that Workington Hall mill has existed since before 1250. First built soon after the Curwen's moved across the river from Burrow Walls. No doubt then, it was the manorial mill used principally for grinding corn. As it was when mentioned in 1329 after the death of Gilbert [ii] de Curwen, as *"a water mill for grinding corn worth 30s. yearly"*.

For many years until 1796, the mill had been let by

"Derwent having gathered his waters into one streame, entreth into the Ocean at Wirkinton, a place famous for the taking of Salmons"
Wiliam Camden's *Britannia*
(1586 - first published in 1610)

the Curwen family to William Patrickson. The existing mill building was rebuilt shortly afterwards, and then rented to Messrs. Beck and Gaff. It was then driven by at least two undershot timber waterwheels (each nearly 3.5 metres diameter). Positioned against its north wall, one wheel was externally fixed, whilst the other was contained within the mill itself. Both were fed from a mill race, which still winds its way from the Yearl, across Hall Park, the Clof-folks and into the South Gut at the harbour. Although unclear, a further smaller waterwheel may once also have existed, fixed against the main north wall of the mill, a few yards upstream. Several Victorian photographs clearly show that the mill eventually became quite derelict and dilapidated, many paddles missing from its main wheel.

Around 1907, it was eventually repaired and like many other now obsolete corn mills converted into a saw-mill. It's timber wheel being replaced with a new *"drum-like"* one of several cast iron segments, built by Neil & Turner's Engineering works in Church Street. It is said that the oak from the old timber water wheel was later re-used to panel out the small closet or turret room, off the Salon in Workington Hall. George Douglas the joiner to the Curwen estate, is thought to have carried out the work. Obviously, this cannot now be confirmed as no joinery work remains within today's ruined hall.

Today (1998), although the Hall mill has been converted into a dwelling by the Reeves family, it is still possible to see marks on the thick stonewalls, once inscribed by the turning wheels. The race which carried water through the north-west corner of the building, to power the internal wheel, has also been retained.

The 1863 OS town plan reveals several other businesses which took their power from the South Gut mill race. Although clearly it existed many centuries earlier as it is shown on the 1569 town plan. (see page 121) At the foot of Hall Brow was the *Derwent Paper Mills* (opened in Easter 1863) and ran by Messrs. Briggs.

Opposite the site of the paper mills was *Friars Well*, built into the bank, below Hall Brow. This small single storey building is said to be where the townspeople once drew their drinking water, and was built over a fresh water spring. This flat roofed brick structure, with stone quions can still be seen today. From a once elaborate iron spout, next to the only door into the building, water still constantly drips.

A little further downstream was the High Brewery, which obviously found it essential to have adequate supplies of water. It is likely that a water wheel must have once existed here, where it was located is unclear. Obviously

Although the Hall Mill has been converted into a dwelling, it is still possible to see marks on the thick stonewalls, once inscribed by the turning wheels.

some form of power would have then been required to grind the malt or for pumping purposes. Although as this business is thought to have been established in co-operation with John Christian Curwen, [01] perhaps in the early years, the malt may have been ground at the Hall Mill.

Certainly when the brewery was advertised for sale in 1839, it was then described as *"extensive and commodious"*, with every *"convenience for carrying on the Brewing and Malting Business upon an extensive scale"*. The Malting buildings had then only recently been rebuilt with upto date facilities, including a malt mill for grinding. It seems likely that some water power must now have been used, as there is no specific mention of a steam engine in the extensive sale particulars.

Vast amounts of water would have also then been drawn from the stream to quickly reduce the temperature of the boiling hot wort, ready for fermentation. On the site, in addition to the brewing and malting buildings, there was then also a large house, a cart house and stables for the horse drawn drays; and a cooper's shop for making the brewery's own wooden barrels and casks. Finally, there was even a cow house, not uncommon for a brewery as it was one way of recycling the waste husks from the wort, as cattle feed.

As the mill race continued along the southern edge of the Cloffolks, below Brow Top there was a Marble works. Here another waterwheel provided power to cut and polish the stone. Not far away was the Low or Old Brewery, at the east end of Griffin Street (also sometimes called Brewery Street). The 1863 OS plan suggests that the brewery building were situated on both side of the street, and linked together at high level, forming a bridge over the road below. Unfortunately, very few further details are known of the site. A brewery certainly existed here well before 1793, being then operated by Fosset & Co. Although its exact origins are unclear, some Curwen papers suggest it was first established here sometime soon after 1767, when Henry [v] Curwen leased the land known as *"Low Green"* to John Sibson of Maryport. Further down stream, on Bell Street was a Shaft Mill also driven by water power, again little is known of the actual building. By 1900, the section of the mill race from the Low Brewery westward towards the South Gut, had been filled in and the flow of water was allowed to run into the existing stream across the Cloffolks.

The Cloffolks area was then much larger than today, measuring around a mile long and 200 yards wide. The three sports stadiums of Lonsdale, Borough and Derwent Parks, together with the C&WJR's *"Navvies"* Bridge and

---

The Cloffolks was then very much larger than today, measuring around a mile long and 200 yards wide.

---

[01] This brewery was first established in 1792. Although it is thought to have been at least 1795, before production was actually commenced. Jollie's *Trade Directory* of 1811 mentions Wood & Co as then running the brewery. Whilst John Faulder Lowes later ran the business until its sale to John Iredale in 1839. It remained in this family, passing to his sons Thomas, Peter and John, until they created the *Workington Brewery Co Ltd.*, in 1891. ■

Northside road bridge had all yet to be built. It is today quite difficult to believe that then this open area of land stretched from the harbour almost to Hall Park, and from the south bank of the Derwent to Brow Top, was used as a simple meadow or common.

It is known to have once also been used as a race-course, one of the earliest recorded races there probably being ran in April 1687. Then at least one of the horses was known to have belonged to Henry [iii] Curwen, who acquired the legendary *Galloping Harry* title by virtue of his horse racing and breeding activities. Horse racing generally traces its origins to Saxon times, and by the Middle Ages, nobility and gentry often indulged themselves running races. From 1624, regular horse racing meetings, throughout the country, had become an essential part of the sporting calendar. Then they were said to have been ran for sport and pleasure rather than profit, gambling being of only minor importance. In 1777, Nicholson & Burn also recorded that *"Seagate or Sigget"* (Siddick) was once *"formerly a very famous horse course"*.

No history of the town would be complete without some reference to the famous Easter contests of the *Uppies & Downies*. Today (1998) we think of the annual mass ball game as a three day event, centred around Easter. But originally until at least 1878, there was only one game played annually, each Easter Tuesday. In earlier centuries, it is believed to have been just a contest between the colliers and sailors, who generally lived in the old Uppergate and Priestgate areas of the town. [01] Later the shipbuilders and ironworkers also joined in the game. If this is so, then the origins of the event must date from no earlier than perhaps 1700, as the town was then only really beginning to develop. Similar football games generally were certainly established elsewhere by the mid seventeenth century.

The rules are very basic, by virtually any means available, the Uppies must force the ball towards Workington Hall; whilst the Downies push it towards the Quayside. Once either side reaches it's goal or destination, they must hail the ball by throwing it up into the air three times. [02] The game traditionally commenced with the ball being thrown into an immense crowd, assembled in the centre of the Cloffolks. Special cheap trains were ran from Maryport, Cockermouth and Whitehaven to bring hundreds of spectators eager to watch the contest. It was usually started in the late afternoon, and often developed into a prolonged struggle lasting many hours. Traders then also had stalls along Brow Top and Derwent Street to cater for the crowds.

Workington's Easter Tuesday Football - *"an old custom peculiar to the place, and which has existed for time out of mind, and induces hundreds to come from a distance to witness".*
William Whellan (1860)

[01] The majority of the earlier newspaper reports of the event simply refer to the game being played between the colliers and sailors. The name Uppies & Downies only appears to have been generally used from the late 1870's. ■
[02] Newspaper reports of the event, suggest that the Uppies had once to hail the ball over the park wall (in 1863), whilst the Downies had to reach the capstan at the end of the quay (in 1857). ■

In 1860, Whellan gave us an excellent, almost timeless description of the foray when he wrote: *"Every exertion is made on both sides; they haul and pull one another like demented men, in many instances tearing each others clothes to pieces.....the town is almost in a state of siege as the lower class think whatever wrong they do on that day, the law cannot lay hold of them"*

Not everyone in the town was allowed to enjoy the annual *Uppies & Downies* game. It was customary for the Wesleyan Methodist Sunday School to arrange a *"tea and entertainment"*, each Easter Tuesday to coincide with the contest. This was to prevent scholars and students attending and to act as a *"counter attraction to the excitements and rowdyism" of the event"*.

Many legends surround the actual origins of what many have called *Workington Football*. Some suggest it was once played with a large pudding, others more gruesomely imply it was first played with a human head or skull. Although some accounts suggest the game here, started only around three centuries ago. Keith Wallace (who has studied the event more than anyone else) believes it was probably played, in Norman times. Drawing comparisions with other ancient mass football, still played today, in France.

From medieval times until the nineteenth century, the salmon fishing along our stretch of the Derwent has always been of prime importance both to the Lord of the manor and the Church. One providing a cheap source of food for the town's inhabitants. J.F. Curwen tells us that before 1200, Thomas [i] de Wyrkinton granted to the monks of Calder Abbey. *"20 salmon yearly at the feast of St. John Baptist and one net in the Derwent."*. Around 1250, his son Patric de Curwen also granted St. Bees Abbey the privilege of receiving *"14 salmon yearly to be obtained from the pool"* of his Workington mill, *"by the hand of"* his miller. Whilst in 1329 the fishing in the Derwent was said to be worth yearly 13s 4d (67p) to the Curwen family. This may seen quite a trivial sum by today's standards, but it was then equivalent to the annual rent one might have been expected to receive from around 40 acres of land.

Angus Winchester in his 1987 book *Landscape & Society in Medieval Cumbria*, tells us that on the lower reaches of the Derwent there was at least one fish weir (or fishgarth) at Workington in 1278, although it's exact location is unknown. [01] We can surmise it was likely to have been close to the present Yearl (found spelt *Hearl* in old documents). It is likely to have retained a head of water for the Workington Hall Mill. We know a mill certainly existed from before 1250 and should have had some form of pond

"Every exertion is made on both sides; they haul and pull one another like demented men, in many instances tearing each others clothes to pieces."
William Whellan 1860
(writing about Uppies & Downies)

[01] It is said that this fishgarth was illegal, in that it obstructed the passage of fish, being to narrow in mid stream for *"a sow and her five pigs"*. Clearly this was a form of measurement in medieval times. ■

or reservoir. Interestingly around 1794, when the new Dock Quay was being constructed upon Crossfitts to the south side of the harbour. The workmen are said to have discovered the remains of another ancient fish weir, close to its southern edge. As this was formerly Church or Glebe lands it may have been erected for the benefit of the Rector. Unfortunately, nothing very much is now known about the structure.

We know from court papers referring to a 1601 dispute of the fishing rights in the Derwent, that the late Sir Henry [v] Curwen may also have exercised *"his right to make weirs"*. Such were the once abundant and prolific stocks of salmon in the river that a few years later, William Camden in his 1610 *Britannia*, noted how the town was *"a place famous for the taking of salmon"*. By the 1680's the fishing rights were said by Thomas Denton to yield a rental of £300 per year to the Lords of the Manor, *"three hundred of those great fishes having frequently been taken at a draught"*.[01]

Stake net fishing was also once quite prominent around the river estuary, until the beginning of the nineteenth century. Despite being often *"detrimental to navigation"*, and restricting access into the harbour, it was 1863 before they were finally abolished. The Church seems to have benefited greatly from the letting of the fishing rights, around their Glebe lands, upon Crossfitts and Priestgate Marsh. We know from the records of St. Mary's Abbey, York (that prior to 1201) they were entitled to collect a *"tithe for fish"* at Workington.

Exactly when stake net fishing was first used in the estuary is unclear. As previously mentioned, Thomas [i] de Wyrkinton is said to have granted one net to Calder Abbey around 1200, but the type of net is not clearly defined. Angus Winchester suggests stake nets had been laid on the River Eden at Burgh by Sands, since as early as 1225. There are also few really reliable descriptions of the stake nets themselves. Often they differed from region to region and are sometimes also called *Raise* or *Trap Nets*.

Several plans (dating from around 1750) exist of the Derwent estuary. Many clearly show where stake nets were set, often in semicircles across the course of the river. Amongst these, Lord Lonsdale then had nets, almost 200 metres long fixed on the north bank. Unfortunately, there are few accurate records of catches etc.

Between 1792-9, John Christian Curwen is known to have let the *"sea coast fishery"* to Richard Graham, for around £250 per annum. A good indication that the fishing must have been substantial and lucrative to justify such a high sum. Graham's nets were placed not in semicircles, but stretched for over 400 metres almost along the low water mark, on

"......three hundred of those great fishes (salmon) having frequently been taken at a draught".
Thomas Denton (c.1688)

[01] A draught is believed here to refer to the contents of a net. ∎

By the middle of the nine-teenth century, the rapid increase in industry began to dramatically affect the fish stocks in the Der-went.

[01] The Salmon season at Working-ton, according to Richard Graham was August to October, and some-times in February.
Hutchinson records that in 1797, fresh salmon was sold in the town's market for around 4d (1½p) a pound, some-times a little as 2d. (less than 1p to-day). By 1814, it's price had risen to 1s 6d (7½p) Today in 1998, you would expect to pay an average of £2.30 per pound. ■

the south side of the estuary. He is likely to be the same Richard Graham, mentioned by Hutchinson in his 1797 *History of Cumberland*. He describes in detail another quite novel way of catching salmon.

"*The salmon hunter is armed with a spear of three points, barbed, having a shaft fifteen feet in length. When the fish is left by the tide, intercepted by shallows, or sand banks, near the mouth of the river, or at any inlets on the shore, where the water remains from one foot to four feet in depth, or when the passage is obstructed by nets, they show where they lie by the agitation of the pool: when my horse is going at a swift trot, or a moderate gallop, belly deep in water, I make ready my spear with both hands, and at the same time hold the bridle: when I overtake the salmon, I let go one hand, and with the other strike the spear, and seldom miss my stroke, but kill my fish: then with a turn of my hand I raise the salmon to the surface of the water, turn my horse's head the readiest way to shore, and so run the salmon on to dry land without dismounting. In the fishery I am establishing at Workington, in the proper season,* [01] *by different modes, I can kill one day with another, one hundred salmon a day; methods of my own invention I intend to put in practice, which never were practised before in any part of the world; I have tried them, and they answer, and when known, they may become a public good. I can take the fish up at sea in ten fathom water. A man, in no ordinary way of salmon hunting, well mounted, may kill forty or fifty in one day; ten salmon is not a despicable day's work for a man and a horse. My father was the first man, I ever heard of, who could kill a salmon on horseback.*"

By the middle of the nineteenth century, the rapid increase in industry began to dramatically affect the fish stocks in the Derwent. Sulphuric acid was then being discharged directly into river from the tinplate works at Barepot. Crushed coals and cinders were constantly being dumped along its banks from the collieries between Cockermouth and the town, whilst slag was deposited from the furnaces near its mouth. Other major pollution, including raw sewage and waste from the leather tanneries at Cockermouth contributed greatly to almost obliterate fish stocks.

In 1842, Samuel Jefferson believed the fishery was now worth only about a third of it's 1688 value. Whilst an 1860 report from the *Salmon Fisheries Commission*, stated how "*the early salmon, known as spring salmon had almost entirely disappeared*". Without such fish migrating annually upstream to spawn each late spring or early summer, eventually adult salmon stocks are bound to be depleted.

From earliest times poaching must have always been prevalent along the banks of the river. Particularly when the fish stocks were so much higher than today. Many of the earliest newspapers contain several accounts of men charged with *"taking fish with a click hook"* or *gaff* hook. Working generally in the dark they had little fear of being caught. In 1858, one bailiff wrote they avoided him because it was simply impossible to *"be eyeing the entire river at every moment"*. In Victorian times poachers were dubbed the *"lawless night prowlers"*, and when unlucky enough to be caught they were heavily fined. If they defaulted on their fines, often they were committed to Carlisle gaol for anything upto two months hard labour.

Perhaps the earliest mention of a bridge over the Derwent, exists in a grant by Thomas [i] de Wrykinton to Calder Abbey around 1197. J. F. Curwen tells us that he allowed the monks to fish using *"one net in the Derwent between the bridge and the sea"*. The exact location of this early bridge is unknown, but the geography of the estuary suggests it must have been quite close to the present Workington Bridge, at the bottom of Calva Brow. According to Thomas Denton, it was rebuilt by the *"County"* in 1650. A century later, George Pattinson (a County bridge inspector), recorded how it was now in a dangerous condition. Commenting that its *"west end requires much care, or else in the time of flood will be in great danger of falling"*.

It was 1763, before it was finally replaced again by one of three arches. A look at the Schoose Farm plan on page 200, tells us that this bridge originally crossed the Derwent well upstream of the present one. Whellan later wrote that it was *"so exceedingly narrow and dangerous"*, it became the scene of numerous accidents. An early nineteenth century view of the town in my possession (dated approx. 1825 - artist unknown) appears to indicate that the bridge approaches were then also quite steep, rising to the centre of the bridge.

By 1841, it too was replaced with the present bridge adjoining the Soapery. In its centre is a stone with the following inscription, *"Workington Bridge, built A.D. 1841; Thomas Milton, civil engineer; Thomas Nelson, builder"*. Soon after it was built it was depicted in a fine painting by a young Sam Brough, [01] the Carlisle landscape painter. The finely detailed view (dated 1842) shows the three central elliptical arches, it's stonework a bright yellow colour. Fixed along it's parapet were elaborate cast iron gas light fittings, the remains of which can still be seen today. This painting was once thought to have been commissioned by the Curwen family, as it also depicts Workington Hall, from the south east. They are certainly known to have once owned it, but it is far more likely that it was painted for the bridge builder Thomas Nelson also of Carlisle. We know from Stanley Gilpin's biography of Brough that

In Victorian times poachers were dubbed the *"lawless night prowlers"*, and when unlucky enough to be caught they were heavily fined.

[01] Sam Brough, born in 1822 at Carlisle, went on to become one of the country's best natural or realistic landscape artists. His delightful and mature Workington Bridge painting was produced when he was only around twenty years old. ∎

he encouraged and supported the very talented young local artist. A small print of the painting is on display at Workington's Helena Thompson Museum.

In ancient times prior to the building of any bridge, the only other way to cross the river (without a boat) was via a ford. Unfortunately only the location of one ford can now be clearly identified. It crossed the Derwent very close to where Borough Park (the football ground) now stands, being reached by a track across the Cloffolks, from the foot of William Street. It is shown on the 1863 OS plan and must have still then been in use. For when the *Cockermouth & Workington Railway* was built, a small bridge was constructed to take the new line over the ford road just before it joined Northside Road, almost opposite the large house called Derwent View.

Then the only other means of crossing the Derwent by foot was over the cantilevered wooden pathway added to the west side of the existing *Whitehaven Junction Railway* bridge. Opened in November 1860, it was principally for the use of local people employed at the two ironworks, then situated just north of the river at Oldside. At it's northern end was a small hut, where an attendant collected a halfpenny (½d) toll from each of those wishing to cross the river. William Lowther is thought to have contributed to the bridge and given permission for a footpath on his land. Later for obvious reasons it became known locally as *"Ha'penny Billy's Bridge"*. With many hundreds of townspeople then working on Oldside. It saved not just time, but also an additional 1½ mile walk, to cross by Workington Bridge. [01]

With the exception of the old *Cleator & Workington Junction Railway* Bridge (built c.1880) formerly referred to locally as *"Navvies Bridge"*, and now converted to little more than a footbridge over to Northside. The only other bridge now remaining across the Derwent is the road bridge, just west of Borough Park, generally referred to as *"New Bridge"*. This was not built until around 1899, when the Borough boundary was extended to include part of the Parish of Seaton, lying over the river.

With many hundreds of townspeople then working on Oldside. *"Ha'penny Billy's Bridge"* saved not just time, but also an additional 1½ mile walk, to cross the river by Workington Bridge.

[01] See photograph on page 105 of the Railway Bridge. Today, the boards of the wooden walkway have now been removed and we can no longer cross the river here. There remains handrailing and the graceful curved brackets, that once supported the pathway are still visible. ■

∻ CHAPTER SEVENTEEN ∻

LOCAL GOVERNMENT

IN 1840, a Local Act of Parliament appointed a group of prominent townspeople as trustees, *"for paving, cleansing, watching and otherwise improving the town of Workington".* It also gave them extensive powers to lay roads, light the streets with gas, build a gas works, regulate slaughter houses, lay sewers and water mains, name streets and number the houses, and much more. To fund this work they were allowed to levy rates on the businesses and householders.

Similar Local or Private *"Improvement"* Acts were then quite common, being promoted by many towns and cities up and down the country. Generally, their primary aim was to tackle poor and inadequate santitation, inorder to improve the general health and well being of the town.

In the preceeding years the regulation of the town had been quite ineffective and very haphazard. It's population had grown rapidly by almost fifty per cent in the last twenty or thirty years. Most of the town had polluted water supplies and no proper sewers. Around 1830, a report into the town poor condition concluded that *"there is very little comfort or opulence".* It was *"not in a flourishing condition"*, being *"ill-paved, not lighted, and presents a mass of small and indifferent houses".*[01] There was also an overall decline in the coal industry, the area's only principle employer. Made even worse following the disasterous flooding of the Chapel Bank pits in 1837.

The overall poor santiation of the town, had already resulted in several rampant outbreaks of cholera and other serious infectious diseases. One such epidemic began in July 1832 and was to last around six months. An indication of the anxious situation is clearly displayed in several surviving letters from the town's Custom's officer John Waite. One tells how in three weeks nearly fifty people had died, with the cholera *"increasing in violence everyday".* Another recounts how there were *"three cases in the house directly opposite.....three next door but one to the right of us.....and opposite a little further down three more cases, altogether in 40 yards, round about us upwards of 40 cases".*

Death from cholera could occur very quickly, often in just a few hours after the onset of symptoms. The mortality rate being as high as 50% in untreated cases. John Waite continued by saying *"people are flying from the town in great*

"....people are flying from the town in great number. I am affraid the Medical Gentlemen know very little of the disease as they appear quite at a loss how to proceed"
John Waite (6 August 1832)

[01] This report even proposed that boundaries should be amended so the town could be joined to the more prosperous Whitehaven. Conscious of the often bitter Lowther-Curwen rivalry, which must also have fuelled similar competition amongst the inhabitants of each these neighbouring towns. This suggestion alone may have been sufficient to spur the townspeople of Workington into action. The promotion of the 1840 Act, would ensure that they remained fiercely indpendant. ∎

number". Commenting that *"the Medical Gentlemen know very little of the disease as they appear quite at a loss how to proceed".* [01] Glancing at the burial registers for this time makes quite poignant and solemn reading.

When the *Improvement Act* received Royal Assent on 19 May 1840, Rev. Henry Curwen, William Lindow Dickinson, Ralph Clay, Michael Falcon, Thomas Falcon, Thomas Bowman, Joseph Tyrrell, Thomas Hamilton, George Irwin and Robertson Crosthwaite were initially appointed as the first trustees. New members could be elected, providing they earned more than £5 per annum, only licensed victuallers (or publicans) were specifically excluded from appointment. Other interesting duties, were to regulate the misbehaviour of carriage drivers, impound stray cattle, and take action against anyone polluting or *"conveying washings"* into the rivers and streets.

This group of trustees were the forerunner of the Local Board or Borough Council. They had basically the same duties and powers, as these later municipal authorities. In earlier times the local townspeople had assembled at Vestry meetings, inorder to debate, overseer and manage local affiars. They were then essentially a parochial body with power to levy a church rate upon the parish inhabitants, to cover the cost of any improvement works. [02] Other than the general upkeep of the church, their principle responsibilities were looking after the needs of the poor and the maintainance of the roads. They too could also appoint or elect constables and (what we call today) Trading Standards officers, then referred to as *"Weights and Measures"* inspectors.

The 1840 trustees also had similar powers, they too could *"appoint constables and assistant constables (a competent number of able-bodied men) for keeping the peace therein and executing all such warrants, precepts and orders as the justices direct....to prevent fires, murders, burglaries, felonies and other outrages, disorders and breaches of peace.....with powers to arrest all felons, malefactors, vagrants, beggars, disturbers of the peace, all disorderly and suspected persons, prostitutes and night-walkers".*

The appointment of constables was nothing particularly new. Thomas Denton (1688) wrote that in the 27th year of Elizabeth (1585), she appointed *"constables to keep ward on"* or protect the town. Then, their main duty was to bring offenders to justice and work closely with the Manor Court and the Justice of the Peace. In early days, the Manorial court (or Court Leet) was responsble for dealing with crimes and sorting out disputes and other problems. This was originally held within the Justices Hall, of Workington Hall. (see chapter nine) In 1829, Parson & White tell us that Henry [vi] Curwen then held such a court, twice a year.

[01] Pigot's Trade directory lists four doctors in the town in 1834. These were Jonathan Bowman (Market Place), Hamilton Hamilton (Curwen Street), John Stamper Dickinson and William Lindow Dickinson (both of Portland Square). William Lindow Dickinson is listed amongst the first town trustees appointed by the 1840 Act. ■

[02] The parish vestries which previously managed the town's affairs, did so in an easygoing friendly way, without any statutory origins. The minutes of the St. Michael's Vestry meetings still exist from February 1762. One of their achievments was the building and upkeep of Ellerbeck Poor or Workhouse (see page 127). After the 1840 act they continued to meet, but many of their previous duties were now undertaken by the new town trustees. ■

The County and Borough Police Act of 1856, now made the maintenance of police forces obligatory. William Whellan in his *History of Cumberland*, published in 1860 tells us that *"The constabulary for the counties of Cumberland and Westmorland was established at the January Quarter sessions of 1857. For Police purposes the two counties were united, and are under one chief constable, being the only counties in England that are so."*

Cumberland was then divided into six areas, with Workington being part of the Allerdale-above-Derwent district. In 1858, the town had one inspector and two constables, based at the police station in Nook Street. The superintendent of our district was based at Whitehaven. The annual cost of then maintaining a force in the Allerdale Above Derwent ward was around £1220, a quarter of which was to be met by the treasury.

In 1847 the town's trustees purchased the Gas Works, which had been established as a private company in 1840. It was situated on the west side of Harrington Road, [01] around where Charters Close now stands opposite the older parts of St. Joseph's School. Around 1861, inorder to provide an adequate supply to the lower end of the town a new gas works was built, on the south side of Stanley Street. [02] The siting of the new gas works, close to the railway station resulted in considerable savings in avoiding the cartage of coal. Both sites were thought to have operated up until around 1885, then the Harrington Road site was converted into a Slaughter House.

Gas was then traditionally produced by coal carbonisation, a method now superseded by natural gas. [03] It was then used not just for industry and household heating or cooking, but also for lighting the streets and homes. Electricity was not available to Workington's townspeople until 1925. Originally, gas was first produced from locally available coal, later it is thought the Local Board switched to using Newcastle coal. Apparently the volume of gas produced from local coal was around 8000 cubic feet per ton, the imported coal provided around 50% more.

It is also known a small gas works once also operated at Isabella Pit. John Waite on his 1835 town plan recorded how the light on the end of John Pier was *"lit"*, with gas piped from the nearby colliery. Perhaps methane gas may also have been pumped up from the mine workings and also utilised for lighting, we certainly know it was elsewhere.

In 1864, the trustees agreed to formally adopt the Local Government Act of 1858, and afterwards became known as the Workington Local Board.[04] The following year they agreed to purchase the *Workington Waterworks Company Limited*. This private company had built the town first wa-

[01] The town's first Gas Works on Harrington Road was built by James Malam of Hull. It eventually had one gas holder or gasometer, capable of holding 11500 cubic feet. and 13 retorts. The town then also had 122 public street lights. The site later became a slaughter house. ■

[02] The Stanley Street Gas Works built at a cost of £2050, initially also had just one gasometer with a capacity of 36000 cubic feet. Although it had been designed to produce a supply of gas for double the present town's population. This was quite a prudent move by the town's trustees for the population did rapidly increase from around 6400 in 1861 to over 14300 by 1881. ■

[03] It is recorded that the price charged for gas, in 1847 was expensive and *"quite prohibitive"*, being 7s 6d (37½p) per 1000 cubic feet. This was likely due to the need to recover the initial investment cost of works and later extending the plant. By 1883, gas in the town could now be bought at exactly half this old price.■

[04] The Workington Local Board was formerly dissolved and later become *Workington Borough Council*, after being granted a Charter of Incorporation (under the Municipal Acts) on 6 Sept 1888. ■

terworks between 1858-9, at a cost of around £8000. The money being raised by the issue of £5 shares. It's first directors, some of whom were also town trustees, included Rev. H. Curwen, Charles Lamport, William Lindow Dickinson, Charles Litt, Michael Falcon jnr., John Alison. For the first time a relatively clean, good water supply was available in every street or lane, where it had been so essentially needed. Previously water had been generally taken by hand from the Friars Well (see page 213) or the stream which ran across the Cloffolks. It is little wonder that the town's inhabitants had previously been striken by plaque and illness. For the notes on John Waite's 1835 plan, reveal the mill race through the town was then very polluted acting like an open sewer for refuse and waste.

The engineer responsible for designing the water scheme was Thomas Hawkesley. Two large steam engines (built by Hawthornes of Newcastle) raised the water from the River Derwent (nearly opposite Seaton Mill) upto a new reservoir, located on the crest of the hill behind the Old Hall at Stainburn. The reservoir was capable of holding sufficient water for two day's consumption, which after filtration was feed down to the town. Unfortunately, the engineers failed to anticipate the town's rapid rise in population. For within a decade or so the waterworks was running at full capacity. [01]

[01]　In 1878-9 this method of the town's water supply was replaced by a new main gravity feed directly from Crummock Water, 16 miles inland. This work was authorised under the *Cockermouth & Workington Water Act* (1878), where the construction costs were shared by the towns. The previous water supply had rapidly become totally unsatisfactory, both in quantity and quality. It is recorded that this lack of clean and pure water had contributed greatly to two severe Cholera epidemics. As mentioned in chapter sixteen, the River Derwent was then so extremely polluted, that the once very abundant salmon stocks had greatly declined. ■

CHAPTER EIGHTEEN

MARY QUEEN OF SCOTS

A S I sit down to write this chapter, I think it quite appropriate that today exactly four hundred and thirty years ago, Workington received probably it's most famous and historic visitor. Researching the life of Mary Stuart is not difficult, there's a mountain of material and books in almost every library. There's also nearly as many historical novels, some very good, but all are embroidered with elements of fiction woven between the true facts.

In assembling this account of Mary Queen of Scots visit to the town, I have added only basic additional biographical information. Obviously in a book of this type it would be inappropriate (if not impossible) to give the reader a full account of her colourful and eventful life. Afterall in 1873, Agnes Strickland compiled two volumes while more recently Lady Antonia Fraser's 1969 biography contained over seven hundred pages.

For much of the year prior to Mary's arrival, she had been cruelly imprisoned by the rebel Scottish Lords, on an island at Lochleven. But on 2 May 1568, after over ten months' in captivity, her friends effected a well-planned and brilliantly executed escape. Within days the Scottish Queen is said to have gathered together an impressive army of upto six thousand loyal men. In truth it may have been only half this number, and some records suggest they were prone to quarrel bitterly amongst themselves. Her intention was to march these forces upto Dunbarton, but they encountered the Earl of Moray, the Scottish regent's army near the small village of Langside.[01]

Here on 13 May, at the *Battle of Langside*, the Queen's forces suffered a heavy defeat. She is said to have watched the gloomy contest from a nearby hill. With the battle lost, guided by Lord Herries [02] the dejected Queen was whisked away to escape Moray's forces. Travelling south by horseback, over rough and wild country, they covered over sixty miles on the first day. Later Mary wrote how she had to endure sleeping outdoors upon the ground, with no bread only oatmeal and sour milk to eat. Later she also rested sometime at Lord Herries' own castle at Corrah, before finally reaching the castle at Terreglas, just north of Dumfries.

Here she carefully assessed her options, she could flee to France in the hope of rallying some support there. Or

[01] George Macdonald Fraser in his book *The Steel Bonnets* identifies the site of the Battle of Langside as being not far from Hampden Park (the football ground), Glasgow. ■
[02] The Lord Herries who accompanied Mary Queen of Scots was Sir John Maxwell (often called *Johnny*) - the 4th lord. He served several times as Warden of the Scottish West March. ■

attempt to defend her already very weak position in her native Scotland. Finally she could seek refuge in England and hope to pursue an alliance with her cousin Queen Elizabeth. Quite unexpectedly and apparently against the advice of some of her most trusted friends, she chose the latter option. Lord Herries wrote immediately to Sir Richard Lowther, asking for permission for Mary to come to England.

But the often stubborn twenty five year old Queen, didn't wait for the return of the messenger. Many historians, including Claude Nau [01] in his *History of Mary Stewart*, believed that as a disquise, she now had her head almost shaved to remove her beautiful long distinctive red hair. Leaving Terreglas Castle, and accompanied by Lord Herries and Fleming, she travelled the eighteen miles or so, south westwards to Dundrennan Abbey. Here she wrote to the English queen, telling how she was being *"forced out"* of her kingdom, and asking that she *"may be conducted to"* acquaint her of all her affairs, *"After God, she has now no hope save in Elizabeth"*.

On the afternoon of Sunday 16 May, the Queen of Scots stepped into a small fishing boat, moored a couple of miles south of Dundrennan, at the mouth of Abbey Burn (stream). Accompanied by around twenty loyal followers [02] they set sail across the Solway Firth, for the English coast. She was never again to return to her beloved Scottish kingdom. Some have suggested that their ultimate destination was infact France, but the existence of Mary's letters and other correspondence tends to allow us to easily discount this theory. It appears that this suggestion may merely stem from a legend implying that Mary had a *"sudden premonition"* of the ultimate fate awaiting her in England, and ordered the boatman to take her to France.

The eighteen mile (15.6 nautical mile) journey across the Solway is believed to have taken around four hours.[03] We know from a letter written, the next day by Richard Lowther, to Sir William Cecil, *"about 7 of the clock in the evening, the Queen of Scots arrived upon these Marches at Workington"*. Who exactly met Mary as she disembarked at Workington is the subject of some controversy. The majority of accounts seem to suggest she was received by Henry [i] Curwen and possibly his second wife, Janet. But in 1883, when the notes of Mary's secretary Claude Nau were first published, it clearly states that Henry and his wife were actually away in London at the time of her visit.

Nau continued by saying that upon their arrival at Workington, Lord Herries an intimate friend of the *"Laird"* Curwen sent a message upto the Hall, saying he *"had brought*

[01]   The Frenchman Claude Nau was Mary Queen of Scot's secretary between 1575-86. It is thought he wrote out much of the life history, from her actual dictation, hearsay or other earlier notes. What is believed to be his original manuscript, written in french is deposited in the British Library. John Flavel Curwen later revised his family history to include Nau's notes, commenting that it *"is so full of detail that he (Nau) must have had a considerable groundwork of reliable information to base it upon"*. ■

[02]   A letter dated 17 May 1568 exists from Richard Lowther to William Cecil (Secretary of State) confirming those who accompanied Mary Queen of Scots on her journey across the Solway, were Lord Herries and Flemyng (Fleming), Lord Cloyde (Claud) Hamilton and sixteen *"servitors"* or attendants. J. F. Curwen believed that the Lord Fleming was John, the fifth Lord. ■

[03]   No metrological records exist to tell us what the weather was really like on the 16 May 1568. So it is difficult to determine if *"four hours"* is a long journey time for such an apparently short distance. Anxious to follow in Mary Queen of Scots footsteps, We would love to make a comparable journey in a similar sailing boat, but it has not been possible yet.

We did however, discover a short account of a comparable journey also made under sail, from Whithorn to Harrington. It is contained in Joe Lovell's book on *Harrington Harbour*. Here he tells of currents off the coast around Wigtown Bay for around a mile or so offshore. Recounting how *"these caused very troubled waters and quite large waves to come at one from any direction"*, to delay a boats progress.

Lovell and his crew, made their 1981 crossing in a 6.5 metre long wooden sailing sloop in winds that averaged around force 4. It took them just under seven hours, to cover around twice the distance. If we take into account the greater efficiency of the modern boat, then Mary's *"four hour"* crossing does now seems quite feasible. Finally, what really convinced me to include these notes was the significance of the date of Lovell's crossing - 16 May 1981. ■

with him a young heiress whom he had carried off in the hope of her to marry Curwen's son" Nicholas. The answer which was returned stated that Henry was away, but the house was put at their disposal, by one of his *"principal servants"*. Obviously, Herries' invented story of bringing a bride for Nicholas was intended so Mary could retain her anonymity, until she was safely inside the Hall. It appears to have been successful, for Nau tells us she was only recognised by a Frenchman servant, employed by the Curwens.

Somehow Richard Lowther, the deputy warden of the English West March [01] had received intelligence or been formally made aware of the Queen's arrival. [02] For on the following day he arrived at the Hall, with a troop of *"well neigh"* four hundred horsemen. Lowther now conducted Mary to semi-captivity at Carlisle Castle, stopping on route overnight at Cockermouth Old Hall, the home of Henry Fletcher. These details were confirmed in Lowther's letter to Cecil (mentioned above) were he states *"Her Majesty hath this day made repair to the town of Cockermouth..........I do intend tomorrow to conduct the same to Carlisle, and there to lodge her in the Queen's Majesty's Castle with such entertainment as I well can or am able upon sudden, until such time as I may know the Queen's Majesty my Sovereign's pleasure in that behalf."*

Whilst at Workington Hall, she is said to have slept in the room, which once existed to the western end of the eighteenth century Dining Room. It is here she sat and wrote again to Elizabeth I. Her original letter, marked *"From Workington, the 17th of May 1568"* is presently deposited in the British Library. Written in french by her own hand, it tells again of her bitter struggle for the Scottish throne and pleads for Elizabeth *"to fetch"* her as soon as possible. Emphasising that she had *"nothing in the world but what I had on my person when I made my escape"* from the *Battle of Langside*. A full translation of Mary's letter is set out overleaf.

After being detained at Carlisle Castle, Mary was moved from prison to prison. She was to remain in captivity for around nineteen years, and never did get to plea her case before Elizabeth. In October 1568 after being implicated in a plot to murder the English Queen, she was sentenced to death and later beheaded on 7 February 1587.

John Flavel Curwen in his Curwen family history comments how *"historians have thrown a halo of romance over the visit of Mary to Workington"*. Numerous almost purely fictitious accounts exist, attempting to describe her stay in infinite detail. Unfortunately, nearly all these are based on just speculation for there is no accurate contemporary record of the visit, other than of course Nau's notes.

The following day, Robert Lowther arrived at Workington Hall, with a troop of *"well neigh"* four hundred horsemen, to escort Mary Queen of Scots to Carlisle Castle.

[01] Richard Lowther was then the deputy of the English West March. His superior Henry, Lord Scrope, would normally have carried out such an important task, but he was also said to be then away in London. ■
[02] A letter from Workington to Thomas Percy (Earl of Northumberland), was sent on the day after her arrival (Monday), informing him of Mary's arrival. But it was not received by him till the Tuesday, at about 1.00pm. It was signed by George Lampluge (Lamplugh), Rychard Symson and Henry Flycher (Fletcher). It is quite possible a similar note was also sent to Richard Lowther. The above letter also seems to confirm Henry [i] Curwen was away from Workington at the time as it states *"Mr. Curwen and his bedfeloe is at the Bathe".* ■

228

MADAM, MY GOOD SISTER,   From Workington, the 17th May 1568

I believe you are not ignorant, how long certain of my subjects, who from the least of my kingdom I have raised to be the first, have taken upon themselves to involve me in trouble, and to do what it appears they had in view from the first. You know how they purposed to seize me and the late King my husband, from which attempt it pleased God to protect us, and to permit us to expel them from the country, where, at your request, I again, afterwards, received them; though, on their return, they committed another crime, that of holding me a prisoner, and killing in my presence a servant of mine, I being at the time in a state of pregnancy. It again pleased God, that I should save myself from their hands; and, as above said, I not only pardoned them, but even received them into favour. They, however, not yet satisfied with so many acts of kindness, have, on the contrary, in spite of their promises, devised, favoured, subscribed to, and aided in a crime, for the purpose of charging it falsely upon me, as I hope fully to make you understand. They have under this pretence arrayed themselves against me, accusing me of being ill advised, and pretending a desire to see me delivered from bad counsels, in order to point out to me the things that required reformation. I, feeling myself innocent. and desirous to avoid the shedding of blood, placed myself in their hands, wishing to reform what was amiss. They immediately seized, and imprisoned me. When I upbraided them with a breach of promise, and requested to be informed why I was thus treated, they all absented themselves. I demand to be heard in Council, which was refused me. In short, they have kept me without any servants, except two women, a cook, and a surgeon; and they have threatened to kill me, if I did not sign an abdication to my Crown, which the fear of immediate death caused me to do, as I have since proved before the whole nobility, of which I hope to afford you evidence.

After this they again laid hold of me; and they have accused, and proceeded against me in Parliament, without saying why, and without hearing me; forbidding at the same time, every advocate to plead for me; and compelling tile rest to acquiesce in their unjust usurpation of my rights, they have robbed me of every thing I had in the world; never permitting me either to write, or to speak, in order that I might not contradict their false inventions.

At last, it pleased God to deliver me, when they thought of putting me to death that they might make more sure of their power, though I repeatedly offered to answer any thing they had to say to me, and to join them in the punishment of those who should be guilty of any crime. In short, it pleased God to deliver me, to the great content of all my subjects. except Moray, Morton the Humes, Glencarne, Mar, and Semple, to whom, after that my whole nobility was come from all parts, I sent to say, that notwithstanding their ingratitude and unjust cruelty employed against me, I was willing to invite them to return to their duty, and to offer them security of their lives and estates, and to hold a Parliament for the purpose of reforming every thing. I sent twice. They seized and imprisoned my messengers, and made proclamation declaring all those persons traitors who assisted me, and were guilty of this odious crime. I demanded that they should name one of them, and that I would give him up, and begged them at the same time to deliver to me such as should be named to them. They seized upon my officer, and my proclamation. I sent to demand a safe conduct for my Lord Boyd, in order to treat of an accommodation, not wishing, as far as I might be concerned, for any effusion of blood. They refused, saying that those who had not been true to their Regent, and, to my son, whom they denominate King, should leave me, and put themselves at their disposal: a thing at which the whole nobility was greatly offended.

Seeing therefore that they were only a few individuals, and that my nobility were more attached to me than ever, I was in hope that, in the course of time, and under your favour, they would gradually be reduced; and seeing that they said they would either retake me, or all die, I proceeded toward Dumbarton, passing at the distance of two miles from them: my nobility accompanying me, marching in order of battle between them and me: which they seeing, sallied forth, and came to cut off my way and take me. My people seeing this, and moved by that extreme malice of my enemies, with a view to check their progress, encountered them without order, so that, though they were twice their number, their sudden advance caused to them so great a disadvantage that God has permitted them to be discomfited, and several killed and taken; some of them were cruelly killed, when taken on their retreat. The pursuit was immediately interrupted, in order to take me on the way to Dumbarton; they stationed people in every direction, either to kill, or take me. But God, through his infinite goodness, his preserved me; and I escaped to my Lord Herris's, who as well as other gentlemen have come with me into your country, being assured that hearing of the cruelty of my enemies, and how they have treated me, you will, conformably to your kind disposition and the confidence I have in you, not only receive me for the safety of my life, but also aid. and assist me in my just quarrel; and I shall solicit other Princes to do the same. I entreat you to send to fetch me as soon as you possibly can, for I am in a pitiable condition not only for a Queen, but for a gentlewoman; for I have nothing in the world but what I had on my person when I made my escape, travelling sixty miles across the country the first day, and not having since ever ventured to proceed except in the night, as I hope to declare before you if it pleases you to have pity, as I trust you will, upon my extreme misfortune; of which I will forbear complaining, in order not to importune you, and to pray God that he may give to you a happy state of health and long life, and to me patience, and that consolation which I expect to receive from You, to whom I present my humble commendations. From Workington, the 17th of May.

Your most faithful and affectionate good sister and cousin, and escaped prisoner,

MARIE R

ABOVE -
A translation of the letter Mary Queen of Scots wrote from Workington, the original (in french) is in the British Museum.

Some portray the quayside at Workington, lined with numerous inquisitive townspeople anxiously awaiting her arrival. Even William Wordsworth in his sonnet *Mary Queen of Scots (landing at the mouth of the Derwent)*, refers to *"the throng"* of people gathered on the shore. [01]   The odd casual observer may well have witnessed her small fishing boat approaching, but few would have surely known who was aboard. How could anyone in the town have really had any prior knowledge of her arrival. [02] Claude Nau confirms Mary was only actually really identified when she eventually reached the hall. Furthermore the town's entire population was then little more than a few hundred.

William Wordsworth's Sonnet
Mary Queen of Scots (Landing at the mouth of the Derwent)

Dear to the Loves, and to the Graces vowed,
The Queen drew back the wimple that she wore;
And to the throng, that on the Cumbrian shore
Her landing hailed, how touchingly she bowed !
And like a Star (that, from a heavy cloud
Of pine-tree foliage poised in air, forth darts,
When a soft summer gale at evening parts
The gloom that did its loveliness enshroud)
She smiled; but Time, the old Saturnian seer,
Sighted on the wing as her foot pressed the strand,
With prelusive, to a long array
Of woes and degradations hand in hand -
Weeping captivity, and shuddering fear
Stilled by the ensanguined block of Fotheringay !

There is even a fine old engraving of *"Mary Queen of Scots Landing in England"*, from a painting by Robert Smirke. [03]   It depicts Mary stepping ashore at Workington harbour, onto a very well developed wharf and quayside. But in 1568, Workington simply didn't have a recognised harbour, goods were then just transferred on and off the shore or river bank. The 1569 town plan seems to clearly confirm this was so. All these accounts merely erode the already slender gap between myth and reality. How easily past authors have been misled, then quoted and copied time and time again over the years. So much so that many people today actually fervently believe this was how it actually happened.

Tradition tells us that as Mary Queen of Scots left Workington Hall, she is supposed to have presented Henry [i] Curwen, with a small Scotch agate drinking cup.[04] But as we now learn from Nau's notes, it was quite likely that he was away from home during Mary's visit, and never actually met her. I do not wish to totally discredit this quaint tradition, but it is quite likely this little cup (around

[01] William Wordsworth is thought to have composed his 14 line sonnet, around 1833. About this time he is known to have often been a visitor at Workington Hall. His son John was married to Henry Curwen's daughter Isabella, in October 1830. Whether or not his stays at the hall inspired the few lines is not known. The entire poem is reproduced left etc.■

[02] Mary was essentially a fugitive and afterall there was then no telephones, media etc. To travel between Dundrennan and Workington by land (around eighty miles) would have taken a messenger on horseback, at around seven hours. Imagine the scene today, we would have live uninterrupted television coverage of both her departure, voyage and arrival, beamed by satellite all over the world. Then of course we would see a large crowd on the harbourside.■

[03] Robert Smirke (1751-1845) was the famous portrait painter, born in Wigton. In 1804, he was elected the keeper of the Royal Academy. Who actually commissioned the above Mary Queen of Scots picture is not clear, but we do know he also painted a portrait of John Christian Curwen. The engraving is by J. Neagle, and measures approx 240 x 140mm. It bears the date 1820 and was published by *J. Stratford, Holborn Hill, London*. It was reproduced in J.F. Curwen's *History of the Ancient House of Curwen*. Where the family biographer sensibly describes it as *"fanciful".*■

[04] Agate is a mineral composed of layers of quartz sometimes of different colours. It can be carved, turned and polished to a high gloss, it is often used for many ornamental purposes. The small Curwen cup is in shades of cream and light brown.■

ABOVE - sketch of the "Mary Queen of Scots" clock (see text right) ■

[01] The "Luck of Workington" was for many years, formerly exhibited in a glazed display case in the Drawing Room of Workington Hall. From around 1975, it could be seen at Belle Isle, Windermere. ■

[02] The 1951 *Historical Exhibition* was organised by the *Cumberland News*. Held at Tullie House, between 2nd -15th August, it formed part of the Festival of Britain celebrations. There was several hundred exhibits, covering local history from Prehistoric to Modern times. ■

[03] Augsburg in Bavarian Germany, was then one of the most prominent sixteenth century cities. It was noted for its fine gold and silver products, particularly its clocks. As well as being one of the leading money markets and trading centres of Europe. ■

[04] Two clocks are actually mentioned in Collingwood's transcripts of the accounts and inventories of the Mines Royal at Keswick. The 1581 inventory includes *"a fair clock with his works and plumments all of metal and gilded wrought fair"*. Whilst 4/6 (22½p) was spent in repairing the clock of L.Stamler, who was employed by the company from 1566-75. Although it should be noted no positive link can be found to the Mary Queen of Scots clock. ■

two inches diameter, was brought from Dundrennan Abbey. Perhaps amongst the refreshments provided for her sea voyage. Such legends are often never written down until several generations later, obviously the true facts can become distorted or lost in time. The cup which was to become known as the *Luck of Workington*, was for many years proudly preserved at the Hall and later also displayed at Belle Isle. [01]

We are also often led to believe that an ancient travelling clock was also given to the family, by Mary Queen of Scots. However, J. F. Curwen in his family history does comment *"but of this there is not so much certainty"*. The clock for many years stood on the mantelpiece above the fireplace in the library at Workington Hall. It was once also exhibited along with the *Luck of Workington*, at the 1951 *Carlisle Historical Exhibition*.[02] On this occasion the catalogue entry was not quite as cautious in its description, it stated: *"TRAVELLING CLOCK - Ornamental clock of brass, 9ins. high. [225mm] Said to have been given to Sir Henry and Lady Curwen, of Workington Hall, by Mary Queen of Scots in 1568."*

A closer look at the clock's particularly elaborate and distinctive style, does suggest it as being German, a typical Augsberg [03] spring driven clock. This being so, it could certainly have been made during the sixteenth century. But there is no real further evidence to give us a positive link to Mary's visit to the Hall. Even her *"Workington"* letter to Queen Elizabeth, clearly states she had *"nothing in the world but what was on my person"*.

Interestingly in October 1568 (just five months after Mary's visit), Henry [i] Curwen agreed to lease some land on the Derwent estuary, to the *Company of Mines Royal*. This German based company was then mining copper at Keswick. We learn from the writings of William G. Collingwood that they were actually based in the city of Augsberg. His 1912 transcripts of their original company account books, (discovered in the City archives of Augsberg) also tell us that the Curwens traded regularly with them, up until at least 1576. They had also raised some capital by essentially pawning around 9300 kg of copper, with the Curwen's and others. Records also suggest that several officials of the Mines Royal also travelled back and forward to Augsberg on several occasions. Was the Augsberg clock actually acquired by the Curwen family, during the land negotiations or the subsequent trading. Perhaps being used as a bargaining tool, maybe simply given as a gift or even purchased from the Germans. [04]

I remember seeing the clock being displayed at

Belle Isle (Windermere), during a visit to the island on August bank holiday 1981. After a guided tour of the house, I certainly came away with the impression that this generation of the Curwen family now believed the clock to be a genuine gift from the Scottish Queen. But once again I now merely suspect four centuries of time, has transformed the tradition from fiction to fact, giving provenance to the legend.

Finally, there once hung a portrait of Mary Queen of Scots, on the main staircase at Workington Hall. This too is said to have been a gift of the Scottish Queen, or perhaps sent later after her visit. I tend to be of the opinion that it was likely to have been commissioned by the Curwen family themselves, to remind them (and visitors) of their royal guest. The style adopted by it's artist, certainly does not suggest it as sixteenth century. Whilst it's likeness to other known portraits of Mary is quite questionable. Despite this, an engraving (reproduced below) was made from the picture and appeared as the frontispiece to volume IV, of Agnes Strickland's 1853 account of *The Lives of the Scottish Queens.* [01]

ABOVE - the small agate cup, tradition calls the *Luck of Workington.* ■

[01] This engraving by J. C. Armytage, was first published in Agnes Strickland's 1853 work, and later used again in volume II of her *Life of Mary Queen of Scots*, published 1873. ■

GENERAL BIBLIOGRAPHY and GUIDE FOR FURTHER READING

GENERAL LOCAL HISTORY REFERENCE

CAMDEN, William BRITANNIA - A 1586 survey (Philémon Holland 1610)
CUMBERLAND NEWS HISTORICAL EXHIBITION Catalogue - August 1951 (Cumb News 1951)
The CUMBRIA PAPERS FROM BISHOP GASTRELL'S NOTITIA (C&WA&AS 1998)
CURWEN, John F. A HISTORY OF THE ANCIENT HOUSE OF CURWEN of Workington, Cumberland (Titus Wilson & Son, Kendal. 1928 2nd ed)
DAYSH, G.H.J. & WATSON E.M. CUMBERLAND - A survey of Industrial Facilities (1951)
DENTON, John An ACCOUNT OF CUMBERLAND (MS dated c1610)
DENTON, Thomas A Preambulation of CUMBERLAND & WESTMORLAND (MS dated c1687-88)
FERGUSON, R.S The DENTON MANUSCRIPTS (C&WA&AS 1894)
FLEMING, Daniel Description of County of Cumberland. (C&WA&AS 1889)
FRASER, George Macdonald, The STEEL BONNETS (Barrie & Jenkins 1971)
HALL, Sergent C. THE INDUCTIVE HISTORY OF WORKINGTON (West Cumb Times 1883)
HODGSON, Henry W. BIBLIOGRAPHY of the HISTORY and TOPGRAPHY of CUMBERLAND & WESTMORLAND (Carlisle Record Office 1968)
HUTCHINSON, William History of the County of CUMBERLAND (F. Jollie 1794-97)
JARS, Gabriel. Voyages Métallurgiques ou Rescherches et Observations - 1769 en Allenmagne (Regnault 1774)
JEFFERSON, Samuel. HISTORY & ANTIQUITIES OF ALLERDALE WARD, Above Derwent (1842)
LANCASTER J.Y. & WADDLESWORTH D.R. IRON & STEEL INDUSTRY OF WEST CUMB. (British Steel 1977)
LONSDALE, Henry WORTHIES OF CUMBERLAND (Routledge 1867)
MARSHALL, J.D. PORTRAIT OF CUMBRIA (Robert Hale 1981)
NICHOLSON, Joseph & BURN, Richard The History & Antiquities of WESTMORLAND & CUMBERLAND (1777)
OWEN, Hugh THE LOWTHER FAMILY (Phillimore 1990)
PEVSNER, Nikolaus. Buildings of England - CUMBERLAND & WESTMORLAND (Penguin 1967)
ROLLINSON, William A History of CUMBERLAND & WESTMORLAND (Phillimore 1978)
SANDFORD, Edmund ANTIQUITIES & FAMILIES OF CUMBERLAND (MS dated c1675)
SELINCOURT, Ernest de (ed). Letters of William & Dorothy WORDSWORTH (Oxford)
SMITH, D. Ian. CENSUS ENUMERATOR'S BOOKS -1861, 1881-91 (C&WA&AS 1994)
SUGDEN, Edward H. HISTORY OF ARLECDON & FRIZINGTON (Richard Byers 1997)
The UNICORN - Journal of WORKINGTON & DISTRICT LOCAL HISTORY SOCIETY (vols 1-5)
VICTORIAN HISTORY OF CUMBERLAND 2 vols (University of London 1901-5)
WHELLAN, William History & Topography of the counties of CUMBERLAND & WESTMORLAND (Whellan 1860)

NEWSPAPERS

CUMBERLAND PACQUET (or WARE'S WHITEHAVEN ADVERTISER) 1775 - 1860
WEST CUMBERLAND TIMES
MARYPORT LOCOMOTIVE

GENERAL LOCAL TRADE DIRECTORIES ETC

BULMER, T & Co. History, Topography and Directories of CUMBERLAND (1883 & 1901)
JOLLIE, F CUMBERLAND GUIDE & DIRECTORY (1811)
KELLY, DIRECTORIES OF CUMBERLAND & WESTMORLAND (1873, 1894, 1897, 1906, 1910, 1914, 1921)
MANNIX & WHELAN, History & Directory of CUMBERLAND (1847)
PORTER, Frank POSTAL DIRECTORY OF WHITEHAVEN, WORKINGTON & MARYPORT (1882)
PARSON, W & WHITE, W   History & Directory of CUMBERLAND & WESTMORLAND (1829)
PIGOT & CO,DIRECTORY OF CUMBERLAND (1834)
SLATER, Issac Royal National Commercial Directory of CUMBERLAND & WESTMORLAND (1869)

GENERAL HISTORY & REFERENCE

COLVIN, Howard Biographical Dictionary of BRITISH ARCHITECTS 1600-1840 (Murray 1978)
FLINN, Michael W. The HISTORY OF THE BRITISH COAL INDUSTRY -Vol 2 (Clarendon 1984)
HAWS, Duncan Lamport, Holt & Booth Lines (TCL 1998)
PALMER, Alan & Veronica The CHRONOLOGY OF BRITISH HISTORY (Century 1992)
PARKER, Geoffrey (ed) THE TIMES ATLAS OF WORLD HISTORY (Times Books 1993)
PARRINDER, Geoffrey Dictionary of NON-CHRISTIAN RELIGIONS (Hulton 1981)
Imperial Dictionary of UNIVERSAL BIOGRAPHY (William Mackenzie)

ADDITIONAL CHAPTER BIBLIOGRAPHY

CHAPTER ONE - INTRODUCTION

CAIRNS, William J. OLDSIDE RECLAMATION PROJECT (Workington Borough Council 1971)

CHAPTER TWO - ROMAN TIMES

ASHMORE, Brian. SENHOUSE ROMAN MUSEUM (Senhouse Museum Trust 1991)
BELLHOUSE, R.L.   ROMAN SITES ON THE CUMBERLAND COAST (C&WA&AS 1989)
BLAKE, Brian The SOLWAY FIRTH (Robert Hale 1955)
COLLINGWOOD, R.G. ROMAN ESKDALE (Whitehaven News)
COLLINGWOOD, R.G. & WRIGHT R.P   The ROMAN INSCRIPTIONS OF BRITAIN Vol.1 (Oxford 1965)
DIVINE, David The NORTH WEST FRONTIER OF ROME - A Military Study of Hadrians Wall
                              (Macdonald & Co, London 1969)
GRANT, Michael, The ROMAN EMPERORS - Biographical Guide (Weidenfeld & Nicholson 1985)
WILSON, R.J.A (ed) ROMAN MARYPORT and its setting (Senhouse Museum Trust 1997)

CHAPTERS THREE & FOUR - ANGLO SAXON & VIKING TIMES

BAILEY, Richard N. & CRAMP, Rosemary CORPUS OF ANGLO-SAXON STONE SCULPTURE in
                ENGLAND Vol 2 Cumberland, Westmorland & Lancs. (British Academy 1988)
BALDWIN, John R. and WHYTE, Ian (editors) SCANDINAVIANS IN CUMBRIA (S.S.N.S. 1985)
BLAIR, Peter Hunter, An Introduction to ANGLO-SAXON ENGLAND (CUP 1956)
BROWN, Peter The BOOK OF KELLS (Thames & Hudson 1980)
EKWALL, E. Concise OXFORD Dictionary of English Placenames (Oxford 1970)
HAYWOOD, J. The HISTORY ATLAS OF THE VIKINGS (Penguin 1995)
MAGNUSSON, Magnus VIKINGS (Bodley Head 1980)
PALSSON, H & EDWARDS, P EGIL'S SAGA (Penguin)
RICHARDS, Julian D. VIKING AGE ENGLAND (Batsford 1991)
ROOM, Adrian Dictionary of PLACENAMES IN BRITISH ISLES (Bloomsbury 1988)
STENTON, Sir Frank The Oxford HISTORY OF ENGLAND - Anglo Saxon England (Oxford 1971)

CHAPTER FIVE - THE CURWEN FAMILY (Lords of the Manor since Norman Times)

CURWEN, John Flavel A History of the Ancient HOUSE OF CURWEN (Titus Wilson 1928 rev ed)
FANTOSME, Jordan Chronicle of War between English and Scots 1173-4 (Surtees Soc.)
MAQUIRE W.A. (ed) The REVOLUTIONARY WAR IN IRELAND 1689-1750 (Blackstaff 1990)

CHAPTER SIX - CHRISTIANITY, CHURCHES & CHAPELS

BACKHOUSE, Janet The LINDISFARNE GOSPELS (Plaidon Press 1981)
BATTISCOMBE, C.F. The RELICS OF ST CUTHBERT (Durham Cathedral 1956)
BENN, Ivy. ST. MICHAELS CHURCH (Cumb Religious History Soc. Bulletin XIV)
BURGESS, John The ACHIEVEMENTS OF CUMBRIAN METHODISM (Cumb Religious H.S. 1982)
CUMBRIAN RELIGIOUS HISTORY SOCIETY Journals (published July 1980 - Oct 1994)
DIRSZAY, Patrica Church Furnishings - A NADFAS guide (Routledge & Kegan Paul 1978)
HOLE, Charles A Manual of ENGLISH CHURH HISTORY (Longman, Green & Co. 1910)
MILLAR, E.G. The LINDISFARNE GOSPELS (British Museum 1923)
MARTIN, John ST. JOHN'S CHURCH, Workington - Sesqui-Centenary Brochure (1973)
MARYPORT LOCOMOTIVE The WORKINGTON RIOTS OF 1814
OUR LADY & ST. MICHAEL, WORKINGTON - Centenary Brochure (1976)
RAWNSLEY, Rev H.D. ROUND THE LAKE COUNTRY (MacLose 1909)
THOMPSON, Rev. D.P. LADY GLENORCHY & HER CHURCHES (Crieff Research Unit 1967)
WOODS, David, HISTORY OF ST. JOHN'S CHURCH, WORKINGTON (1966)
BURTON, Janet E. (ed) ENGLISH EPISCOPAL ACTA - Diocese of York (British Academy 1988)

CHAPTER SEVEN - PORT, HARBOUR & SHIPPING

ALLERDALE District Council. THE MARSH, its housing, community and environment. (Report 1976)
Calender of STATE PAPERS (relating to Ireland) 1603-06 (Public Record Office/Longman 1872)
EDGE, Brian (ed) FIRST DICTIONARY OF PARANUMISMATICA (Edge 1991)
FERGUSON, R.S. The COLLIERY, HARBOUR, LIME & IRON TOKENS of West Cumberland (C&WA&AS 1898)
GIBBON, Ronald T. To The KING'S DECEIT - Smuggling in the Solway. (Friends of Whitehaven Museum 1983)
LOVELL, Joseph E. HARRINGTON HARBOUR (Lovell, 1982)
SIMMONS, Jack & BIDDLE, George. Oxford Companion to British Railway History (OUP 1997)
SMITH, R.A. (ed) Catalogue of MONTAGUE GUEST COLLECTION of Badges, Tokens & Passes (Brit.Museum 1930)

CHAPTER NINE - WORKINGTON HALL

ROMNEY, Rev. John. Memoirs of the life & works of GEORGE ROMNEY (1830)
HEAL, Sir Ambrose. The LONDON Furniture Makers from 1660-1840 (Batsford 1953)
NICHOLS, Sarah C. Furniture made by Gillows & Co. for WORKINGTON HALL (The Magazine Antiques 1985)

CHAPTER TEN - COAL INDUSTRY

DUNN, Mathias A Treatise on the WINNING & WORKING OF COLLIERIES (1852)
FLETCHER, H.A. The HESLOP ENGINE, a Chapter in the History of the Steam Engine (1879)
FLETCHER, Issac ARCHAEOLOGY OF THE CUMBERLAND COAL TRADE (C&WA&AS 1877)
GALLOWAY, Robert L. A History of COAL MINING in Great Britain (David & Charles 1969)
WOOD, Oliver WEST CUMBERLAND COAL (C&WA&AS 1988)

CHAPTER ELEVEN - SHIPBUILDING

RICHIE, L.A. (ed) The SHIPBUILDING INDUSTRY, Guide to Historical Records (Manchester University 1992)
Country Life Book of NAUTICAL TERMS UNDER SAIL (Country Life 1978)
SIMPER, Robert BRITAIN'S MARITIME HERITAGE (David & Charles 1982)

CHAPTER TWELVE - IRON & STEEL INDUSTRY

Barraclough, Kenneth G. Bessemer and Sheffield Steelmaking (Sheffield City Museums)
Bessemer, Henry HENRY BESSEMER F.R.S (Engineering 1905)

CHAPTER THIRTEEN - AGRICULTURE

CHANCE, Sir Frederick, SOME NOTABLE CUMBRIANS - John Christian Curwen (Thurnam 1931)
LONSDALE, Dr H. The WORTHIES OF CUMBERLAND (vol 1)
MITCHELL, Emily AGRICULTURE IN CUMBERLAND (W&DLHS - Unicorn journals vols 1 & 2)
ROBERTS, E.J. STORY OF OUR CATTLE - Young Farmers' Club Booklet No. 22 (Evans Bros nd)
WARNER, George Townsend. LANDMARKS IN INDUSTRIAL HISTORY (Longmans 1910)
WORKINGTON AGRICULTURAL SOCIETY Rules & President's Reports (1809-1812)

CHAPTER FOURTEEN - EDUCATION, SCHOOLS & LIBRARIES

MARTIN, John J. LIBRARIES IN WORKINGTON (Unicorn Journal - vol.4 1989)
ROBINSON, F.J.G. TRENDS IN EDUCATION IN NORTHERN ENGLAND during the Eighteenth Century.

CHAPTER SIXTEEN - RIVER DERWENT & THE CLOFFOLKS

GILPIN, Stanley. SAM BROUGH R.S.A. (1905)
WINCHESTER, Angus. Landscape & Society in MEDIEVAL CUMBRIA (Donald 1987)

CHAPTER SEVENTEEN - LOCAL GOVERNMENT

KEITH-LUCAS, B. ENGLISH LOCAL GOVERNMENT in 19th & 20th Centuries (Hist Assoc 1977)

CHAPTER EIGHTEEN - MARY QUEEN OF SCOTS

NAU, Claude. (Stevenson, Rev. Joseph. - ed) HISTORY OF MARY STEWART. (Paterson 1883)
STRICKLAND, Agnes. Lives of the Queens of Scotland (Blackwood 1853)
STRICKLAND, Agnes. Life of Mary Queen of Scots (Bell 1873)

ACKNOWLEDGEMENTS

As both author and publisher I wish to acknowledge and gratefully thank the following people and organisations who so freely (and often so enthusiastically) assisted my research. To compile and produce any book is a monumental task. I am indebted to you all, without your wide knowledge and sound advice this history may never have reached fruition. Your contribution has certainly greatly enhanced the final product. Finally, occassionally someone is mistakenly omitted where their contribution should have been acknowledged. If that is you, I apologise in advance.

Capt. Andrew Douglas (Editor - Sea Breezes Magazine). Duncan Haws (Author - Shipping). Margaret Evans, Claire Birtwisle & Rachael Mulhearn (Merseyside Maritime Museum). Roger C. Norris (Durham Cathedral Library). Simon Stephens (National Maritime Museum). Peter Barber (British Library - Map room). British Library (Reader Enquiries & Patent office). Andy Byers (TALULAR). Joyce Byers (former Chairman - Workington & District Local History Society). Chris Webb (Borthwick Institute of Historical Research, York). Tim Paddley (Tullie House Museum, Carlisle). Keith Lowe (British Museum - Prehistoric & Romano British Antiquities). Virgina Smithson and Claudia Freeman (British Museum - Medieval & Later Antiquities). Moira Birks, Lyndsay Jones & Liz Smith (Royal Commission for National Monuments). David Bowcock & Susan Dench (Carlisle Record Office). Peter Eyre, Catherine Clark, Anne Dick and other staff (Whitehaven Local Studies Library & Record Office). Bette Hopkins (Cumbria County Council - Sites & Mounuments). Andrew Johnson (Manx Museum). Paul Flynn and Philip Cracknell (Carlisle City Archaeological Unit). Adrian Lindsay Jobson (Public Record Office, Kew). Ross Trench-Jellicoe. Murdo MacDonald (Archivist - Argyll & Bute District Council). Stephen Sartin (Curator - Judges' Lodgings Museum, Lancaster). Chrissie Freeth (Bradford University Archaelogical Sciences). Jonathan Becker & Paula Jackson (Cumbrian Gazette). Leeds Metropolitan University. Trevor Jones & staff (Workington Public Library). Whitehaven Public Library. Hemel Hempstead Public Library (Local Studies). Lancaster University Library. Lancaster Public Library. Lancashire Record Office (Preston). Leeds City Library (Local studies). Manchester University Library. Newcastle University Library. Newcastle upon Tyne Central Library. Nottingham Library & Archives Service. Westminster Reference Library. Pat Haywood (King's Manor Library, University of York). Derek Woodruff (Allerdale Borough Council - Workington Hall). Senhouse Roman Museum, Maryport. Historic Scotland. Conservative Association (Central Office, London). Meriel Stokoe & Anne Simpson (Beacon Heritage Centre, Whitehaven). Kendal Museum. Neil Irving & Peter Fitzgerald (Science Museum, South Kensington, London.) Howard Coulter (Ministry of Agriculture etc - fisheries). Tea Council. Laing Stonemasonry, Carlisle. Ian Ferguson (Custodian, Helena Thompson Museum, Workington). Canon Terence H. M. Sampson (Rector - St. Michael's Church, Workington) Eric Martin (St. Michael's Church, Workington). Helen Wakely (Lambeth Palace Library). Royal Institute of British Architects Library, London. Caroline Picco (Cheshire Record Office, Chester). Anne Lambert and Geoff Cowton (Wordsworth Museum, Grasmere). Southend-on-Sea Central Library. York City Library. Patrick Mitchell (Liberial Democrat History Group, London). Steve White & other staff (Globe Lane Library, Carlisle). Father Anselm Cramer (Monastery Library, Ampleforth Abbey & College). Natalie Diane Byers (Moresby Primary School), Jeremy Rex-Parkes (Archivist - Christie's Auctioneers). Frank Skinner (American Embassy, Vienna). Alex Kidson (Walker Art Gallery, Liverpool). Rev. Andy Edwards & Alan Johnston (St. Bridget's Church, Moresby). Jackie Currie (Environment Agency). Jean-Charles Forgeret (Direction de L'archeologie, Ministère de Culture, Paris). Mr & Mrs Ward Thomas.

PHOTOGRAPHS ACKNOWLEDGMENTS

"The joys of life consist, in some instances, in its difficulties. To accomplish objects that require great exertion, gives stimulus to the mind, that calls forth all its energy. When judgement holds the balance equally between hope and fear, great are the efforts men are capable of making"

John Christian Curwen
16 Nov 1812